A Harem Boy's Saga
Book V – Metanoia

A Memoir by Young

This memoir is dedicated to those who witnessed and encountered preternatural entities during their life on earth. You are not alone.

"We always have angels and faeries by our sides."
Bernard Tristan Foong
(a.k.a. Young)

All rights reserved. No part of this book may be used or reproduced in any manner whatsoever including Internet usage, without the written permission of the author.

Author's Website: www.aharemboysaga.com
Author's email: young@aharemboysaga.com

The contents of this book constitute a work of NONFICTION. It documents the author's experiences and is not intended as an exposé. Names of actual places and people have been changed to protect their privacy.

No portion of this book may be transmitted or reproduced in any form, or by any means, without permission in writing from the author or publisher, unless for brief excerpts used for the purposes of review.

This book contains substantial sexually explicit material and language which may be considered offensive by some readers.

Prologue

"All the world's a stage,
And all the men and women merely players;
They have their exits and their entrances,
And one man in his time plays many parts,
His acts being seven ages. At first, the infant,
Mewling and puking in the nurse's arms.
Then, the whining schoolboy with his satchel
And shining morning face, creeping like snail
Unwillingly to school. And then the lover,
Sighing like furnace, with a woeful ballad
Made to his mistress' eyebrow. Then, a soldier,
Full of strange oaths, and bearded like the pard,
Jealous in honor, sudden, and quick in quarrel,
Seeking the bubble reputation
Even in the cannon's mouth. And then, the justice,
In fair round belly, with a good capon lined,
With eyes severe, and beard of formal cut,
Full of wise saws, and modern instances,
And so he plays his part. The sixth age shifts
Into the lean and slippered pantaloon,
With spectacles on nose and pouch on side,
His youthful hose, well saved, a world too wide
For his shrunk shank, and his big manly voice,
Turning again toward childish treble, pipes
And whistles in his sound. The last scene of all
That ends this strange eventful history,
Are second childishness and mere oblivion,
Sans teeth, sans eyes, sans taste, sans everything."

William Shakespeare

The world is a stage certainly rang true when I was under my fifth Arabian household patriarch, Tad Abdul Hafiz's auspice. Not only did my experiences in his ménage transform my worldview, but it also left me hyperventilating for the halcyon days when life was tender and oh so mellow.

This effervescent sportsman could turn south impetuously, rousing injudiciousness to those near and dear into relegated tailspins. Like a dog chasing its tail, this enthralling champion could charm any male and female to do his bidding. There were many a time when Andy and I almost lost our cool with one another or with the athlete. Thanks to our Enlightened Royal Oracle Society's mentorship, we kept our prudent sagacity. Maneuvering through Tad Abdul Hafiz's household, وكر الذئب *Aldhdhib Dann (Wolf Den)* with ease and grace before plummeting headlong into my sixth Arab household with unscathed audacity.

My seventh and final harem assignment proved to be more challenging than anticipated when I became a *Big-Brother (BB)* to a *Freshman*. Although I fulfilled my *BB's* duty with aplomb, it was not without trials and tribulations. My unwavering guide, mentor, lover and friend, Andy whose valiant stance proved invaluable. Advising and steering me towards the right direction in every step I took.

"And then the lover, sighing like furnace, with a woeful ballad made to his mistress' eyebrow," the Shakespearean monologue did hold true, in my instance, it would read as: *"And then the lover, sighing like furnace, with a 'consequential' ballad made to his 'master's' eyebrow,"* while Andy and I burrowed our way through the *Wolf Den*.

Although ex-Valet and my *"sixth age"* has yet to manifest, we had matured and hopefully grown wiser from our youthful woes.

Within the pages of *Metanoia*, reflective introspection plays a significant role. Although my topsy-turvy experiences at *Wolf Den* proved to be exhausting, yet from turmoil rose equanimity. Our time with Tad challenged **mine and Andy's** relationship to remain sang-froid rather than explosive. During those months, we were eager to conquer the world and blessed to emerge unscathed as our intimacy flourished by leaps and bounds. As Ms. Mary Hopkin sang so eloquently in her 1968 song: *Those were the days, we thought they'd never end...* But it did end in woebegone remorse and tearful goodbyes when in 1970 my Valet and I went our separate ways, never to reconnect again until forty-three years later.

Although we re-established communication in 2012, we have yet to meet. Ever since we laughed away the hours and dreamed of all the great things we **had done**, oh long ago. We now have dubieties and ambiguities to overcome. We are in stable relationships with another, is it worth our while to relive those halcyon years? I continue to ponder.

It seems decent for us to sing and dance forever and a day via long-distance communication. But when push comes to shove, my continual reservations bug me caution if we are to meet. After all, we'd lived the life we chose and fought the fight and never lost. For we were young and sure to have our way. Why then should I even contemplate to elicit the past in the present? What good will rekindling our lost love if not render another set of heartaches that will imperil our relationships with our current partners?

Had I lost my starry notions when the busy years went rushing by? Only happy to hear Andy's tales through our extensive correspondence?

Will I experience strange reflections if Andy did walk through the door? That familiar laughter I'd often seen on his face when he called my name? Oh, my beloved friend, we're older but are we wiser? For in my heart the dreams are still the same. Does it ring for you too, Andy?

These are questions I dare not comprehend if we do meet again.
Young.

Table of Contents

Prologue

PART ONE

Chapter One - The Perfect Storm
Chapter Two - Preternatural Vs Natural
Chapter Three - Beckoning You!
Chapter Four - By Divine Grace
Chapter Five - Antichthon "Counter-Earth"
Chapter Six - Relevant Connexions
Chapter Seven - The Power of Love
Chapter Eight - Mythical Beings
Chapter Nine - Secret Confessions
Chapter Ten - Fairy Sightings
Chapter Eleven - Where Angels Fear to Tread
Chapter Twelve - Lethal Temptations
Chapter Thirteen - Gender Schemata
Chapter Fourteen - For the Beauty of Earth
Chapter Fifteen – Faith
Chapter Sixteen - The Right Moment
Chapter Seventeen - Gender Fluidity

PART TWO

Chapter Eighteen - Release & Allow
Chapter Nineteen - Intimate Propositions
Chapter Twenty - Ménage à Trois
Chapter Twenty-One - Angelic Visions
Chapter Twenty-Two - Where Is The Love
Chapter Twenty-Three - The Down
Chapter Twenty-Four - Inspired by Admiration and Motivated by Envy

Chapter Twenty-Five - Beware of Wolves in Sheep's Clothing
Chapter Twenty-Six - Sleeping to the Top
Chapter Twenty-Seven - Abri Sûr
Chapter Twenty-Eight - In My Master's Chambers
Chapter Twenty-Nine - Stay In The Present
Chapter Thirty - By Hook Or By Crook
Chapter Thirty-One - One Night in Lucerne
Chapter Thirty-Two - Femme Fatale
Chapter Thirty-Three - Could It Be Magick
Chapter Thirty-Four - In The Kasbah
Chapter Thirty-Five - The Pursuit of Happiness
Chapter Thirty-Six - Sexual Starvation
Chapter Thirty-Seven – Mentorship
Chapter Thirty-Eight - A Dead Ringer Scuffle
Chapter Thirty-Nine - Being A Big-Brother

PART THREE

Chapter Forty - A Puppet On Strings
Chapter Forty-One - A House of Cards
Chapter Forty-Two - Tango Buenos Aires
Chapter Forty-Three - Pride and Prejudices
Chapter Forty-Four - The Tango Of Love
Chapter Forty-Five - A Peculiar Request
Chapter Forty-Six - The Game Of Kings
Chapter Forty-Seven – Feud
Chapter Forty-Eight - The Uniqueness of Being Human
Chapter Forty-Nine - Astute Resolutions
Chapter Fifty - The New Look
Chapter Fifty-One - Beauty Pageants
Chapter Fifty-Two – Infatuation
Chapter Fifty-Three - Terma Centaurs
Chapter Fifty-Five - Nip and Tuck
Chapter Fifty-Six – I Don't Know How To Love Him
Chapter Fifty-Seven - A Cut Above the Rest

PART FOUR

Chapter Fifty-Eight - What Is Love
Chapter Fifty-Nine – Friendship
Chapter Sixty - Helius' Despondency
Chapter Sixty-One – Catharsis
Chapter Sixty-Two - The Lightness of Being
Chapter Sixty-Three - Romance, Love & Sex
Chapter Sixty-Four - Bitten By The Love Bug
Chapter Sixty-Five - In The Gardens Of Osbourne House
Chapter Sixty-Six - Put On The Ritz
Chapter Sixty-Seven - The Power of Love
Chapter Sixty-Eight - What's Love Got To Do With It
Chapter Sixty-Nine - Serendipitous Reminiscence
Chapter Seventy - Splintered Emotions
Chapter Seventy-One - There Are No Gay People In The Arab World
Chapter Seventy-Two - Double Standards
Chapter Seventy-Three - The Anatomy of Unconditional Love
Chapter Seventy-Four - The Wedding
The Final Chapter – Emptiness

Epilogue

Author's Bio
Acknowledgments

PART ONE

Mexico – Acapulco
England – Grasmere, Bassenthwaite Lake, Keswick, Penrith
Tunisia – Hammamet, Sadi-Bou-Said, Tunis

The Perfect Storm (Chapter One)

"The storm is a good opportunity for the pine and the cypress to show their strength and their stability."

Ho Chi Minh

October 1968
Acapulco, Mexico

I was tossed about in the tiny confines of *Murashshahaan* (*Running Mate*), Sheik Fahrib's eleven meters' sailboat. A month before the races the doctor had transported this top of the line vessel from its mooring facility in Musandam Dibba Al Hisn, the Sultanate of Oman to Acapulco; in readiness for the 1968 Summer Olympics yachting competition. Tad (his team-mate) and he had been out daily to acclimatize to the sailing conditions in this Mexican playground of the rich and famous.

A week preceding the competition, my Valet and I left from Daltonbury Hall to join them. With our *Assalamu Alaikum* service behind us, Andy and I needed the repose, to revivify our love and friendship. Our summer vacation was spent traveling around the tranquil English countryside, soaking up the beauty of the Lake District and getting reacquainted with one another. We needed to necessitate our physical and mental bond before departing to *Aldhdhib Dann* وكر الذئب (*Wolf Den*) and *Manarat Lilddaw'* منارة الضوء (*Beacon of Light*); Tad Abdul Hafiz's London and Riyadh residences. The both of us had a hunch that our services at our fifth household would not be as smooth sailing as compared to our previous assignments.

Much like Count Mario, Tad was a playboy at heart. His irrational and spur of the moment decisions often send those close to him into dramatic tailspins of immense proportions. It was under this circumstance I now found myself at the mercy of howling winds, roaring waves and pounding rain. Thrown repeatedly from the hull to the rear of this racing vessel. The vicious waves and torrential downpour lapped at my person. Not only did I puke up the gastronomical contents I had consumed not so long ago, but I also had to hold on for dear life in the unfortunate event I would be swept into the ocean. Seasickness had overtaken my person, and no help was available since every strong hand was working furiously to keep *Murashshahaan* afloat.

Hard-pressed at the helm, the sheik steered his vessel away from colliding rocks while Tad and Andy held firm on either side of the riggings to steady the dinghy; in the unfortunate event that the mast should collapse under the onslaught of the ferocious winds. Within this treacherous weather condition, I was left to fend for myself.

Not knowing how long this perilous dilemma would last, I rocked, slid and vomited while keeping myself from slipping into the abyss of this bottomless ocean.

Suddenly, a hand reached for my collar to pull me away from the slippery taffrail. I was dragged into the boat's cabin that was now filled with ankle-deep water. As if I had gone bonkers the sportsman glared at me transfixed.

"What in the world were you doing on deck. You were repeatedly told to stay below. This is not a time to tamper with the forces of nature. You could have been swept into the ocean and drown!" he chastised sternly.

"You, Fahrib and Andy are above deck...," I muttered meekly.

He scowled at my defiance. *"We are experienced seamen and you, boy, is not,"* he admonished. *"The last thing we want on our hands is your dead body floating in the water."*

"*Andy isn't an experienced sailor,*" I negated truculently.

He raised his hand to land me a slap for being an insolent brat. Before his hand could touch my cheeks, the boat's violent oscillations hurled us in opposite directions. I crushed against the bulkhead while the athlete pulverized onto a dividing panel.

Before he left me to my own expedient, his grimace had sent chills across my trembling body. When we finally came ashore, search teams were already scouring the vicinity for distressed boats adrift at sea.

The *Running Mate* was indeed one resilient lady whose damage was next to none. Thanks to our two experienced yachtsmen, we were relatively unharmed. Besides some minor bruises and concussions, the four of us were up and running after a good night's sleep.

I did not relate to my Valet what transpired in the cabin. After all, I conceded I was in the wrong and shouldn't have put myself and crew in harm's way, causing further perturbation if I should indeed fall into the turbulent waves. That would have been an unforgivable disaster.

Hotel Casablanca, Acapulco

The seafarer and I did not speak until late morning the following day. My lover and I were already consuming a hearty brunch at Acapulco's Hotel Casablanca, the then top of the line stomping ground for Hollywood stars and wealthy millionaires. The likes of Elizabeth Taylor, Frank Sinatra, Elvis Presley, Eddie Fisher, and Brigitte Bardot were regulars at this popular establishment. This was also one of several official hotels international yachtsmen from forty-one nations stayed during the months leading up to the 1968 Summer Olympics.

My gaydar immediately gravitated to two attractive blondes as they were guided to their table by a good-looking waiter. Like mine, my chaperone's eyes followed their every move.

"I know what you are fantasizing," Andy imparted.

"What?" I answered nonchalantly.

"You are musing over those two like me," came his reply.

"And which two is that?" I feigned ignorance.

We laughed. My lover gave me ludic slaps as we carried on playfully like a couple of dogs in heat.

A couple of tables away, the blondes ogled at us. Their tanned faces grinned impishly, speculating if our licentiousness were directed at them. We exchanged roguish smiles before they joined us at our table.

"I'm Ronnie, and this is my sailing companion, Iian," the sinewy cutie introduced. Awestruck by the man's ruggedness, I stared at him arrestingly when Andy hawked, to bring me back to reality. I extended my hand to shake theirs as we exchanged pleasantries.

Just then Tad appeared and was surprised to see us chatting animatedly with his competitors. The Arab asserted when he came over to join us. *"I'm glad to see the both of you so lively after yesterday's shake-up."* His declaration was apparently directed at the blondes.

"What shake-up?" Andy queried.

Iian exclaimed before Ronnie could respond. *"That darn mast broke when we were out at sea. Our boat is being rectified as we speak."*

"Sorry to hear that," the Arab sniggered as if he welcomed the news, despite the look of concern he gave to his yachting opponents.

"'Supercal' will be back to her competing self in a day or two. She'll be ready for action in a few," Ronnie pronounced proudly.

"Excellent! We look forward to the challenge," the athlete declared with an air of superiority.

"We too," came their reply as they excused themselves to leave.

Ronnie gave my chaperone and I a wink before disappearing from the restaurant.

The Boys

As soon as the blondes were out of earshot, Tad announced. *"Who do they think they are? Getting special treatment…"*

Andy chimed, *"What kind of special treatment?"*

Our host vociferated. *"First off, their boat is docked away from the rest of the competing vessels.*

"Secondly, the Olympic yachting committee allowed Supercal's sail to be flat and vertical, while all the participants' sails are bowed."

He paused for breath from vexation. He resumed, *"A British pilot specifically flew out in yesterday's thunderstorm to check their safety, while the rest of us had to rely on our impetus to make it to safety. In my book, they should be banned from competing. These cheaters should be eliminated from participation."*

Andy quickly changed the topic before the Arab could continue lambasting the blonds.

"Which country are they representing?" My guardian asked when we already knew they were from the United Kingdom.

"I believe one is Scottish and the other, English. They are representing Great Britain."

I asked, *"Did you know them before our meeting a few moments ago?"*

"I was aware of Ronnie but had not met them until now.

"Ronnie is an intensely private individual and had kept his own counsel and the media at arm's length. If I'm not mistaken, his first sailing victory was racing at the British School's Championships before joining the navy.

"His current team-mate was an ex-competitor during their School's Championship days. Their height and build gave them an added advantage in the upcoming races.

"Not to mention his unfailing determination to win and talent..." he trailed off as if reluctant to bestow his competitor further credit.

I remarked, *"You and Sheik Fahrib are similarly built and were ex-classmates. Does it provide added leverage for the both of you too?"*

Tad did not answer my appraisal. He remained silent before Andy commented, *"In my opinion, I think he sees the press as an unwanted distraction from him winning."*

I chirped before either man had a chance to speak. *"Iian mentioned they were school chums."*

"Well, in that case, they deserve each other," the Arab sneered.

My lover and I exchanged impish glances every now and then, privately acknowledging that we knew more than our host. Tad continued his lambastes against the blondes until we bid him leave after a delicious brunch.

One thing we did not mention to the athlete; we had exchanged room numbers with the boys before his arrival at our table.

Preternatural Vs Natural (Chapter Two)

> *"The fairy poet takes a sheet*
> *Of moonbeam, silver white;*
> *Her ink is dew from daisies sweet,*
> *Her pen a point of light."*
>
> Joyce Kilmer

Mid-June 1968
Grasmere - Westmorland, England

Auntie Mary welcomed Andy and me with open arms, conferring *faire la bise* on our cheeks. She uttered excitedly, *"Bonjour, vous deux. Comment êtes-vous?"*

Andy responded similarly as if the two were of French descent. *"Aunty Mary, you are as beautiful as ever,"* my chaperone complimented before he introduced her to me.

Aunty Mary's older brother, Herr Finckenstein was Andy's father. In her younger years, to the chagrin of their conservative father, Herr Finckenstein Senior, Mary had eloped to France with a Frenchman. In her heyday, the vivacious Mary and her free-spirited lover were entranced by the Parisian bohemian lifestyle and were a part of the cafe society. Unfortunately, her lover's eyes strayed to another and left the woman to care for herself. Mary's mother urged her daughter to return to the fold, but she refused to be housed under the same roof as her orthodox father and brother, Finckenstein Junior. With a tough decision to be independent, she vowed to possess her own destiny.

Through her freewheeling connections, her career as an illustrator and writer flourished in France. She managed to carve a stable income to support herself and bought a comfortable home in rural England. It was in the English Lake District that my faerie inculcations were tangilized by my lover's beloved Aunty Mary.

Her illustrations, writings, surroundings, and our dialogues were of subliminal proof of otherworldly existences, to an otherwise monochromatic reality; since the woman was a staunch believer of the supernal. The charming *Fay Haven* provided her the solitude to create.

Akin to the famous English nursery rhyme:

Mary, Mary, quite contrary,
How does your garden grow?
With silver bells, and cockle shells,
And pretty maids all in a row.

Fay Haven, Auntie Mary's charming abode was as contradictory as her person. At the drop of a hat, the artist's charm and congeniality could be overshadowed by an outburst of melancholic apprehension. Like her beautiful edifices of blossoming roses, hollyhocks, foxgloves, primroses, pansies, and sweet peas; weedy dandelions, bluebells, clovers, and forget-me-nots were also competing for survival within this burgeoning horticultural sanctuary. Her graphic art and novels depict enchanted fairies and magical sprites in epic battles with heinous ogres and odious goblins. True to form, Mary's real and imaginary mind had chartered a course for her subliminal creativity, and she prospered within the corporeal and the metaphysical world; even if she insisted that these contradictions were only bridges between the celestial and the sublunary.

My lover and I were blessed to have had the opportunity to spend some quality time with this extraordinary woman before she departed for her month-long vacation in Europe. My conversations with this erudite lady proved to be didactic encounters that eventually spearheaded my own artistry in the years that followed.

When it came to rancorous discussions of Herr Finckenstein Senior, Andy's father, and the illustrator's older brother, she and her nephew had a lot in common; since both were black sheep of the Finckenstein's clan. When their conversations turned to family matters, *I* would discretely evaporate into a different corner of the cottage or garden to give them latitude to converse in private.

Catching Up

Mary commented at High Tea on the day of our arrival, *"How have you been Andy? The last time I saw you, was the summer of 1965 when you returned from the Middle East."*

"Couldn't be happier. I'm having a blast," my chaperone responded excitedly.

"Now that you have found the love of your life, you should be ecstatic!" our hostess chimed merrily.

My chaperone and I exchanged secret glances and wondered how his aunty had knowledge of our intimate relationship.

The artist resumed, *"When your beloved mother, Maria told me you were visiting with a young companion, I was keen to know more of the boy."* She turned my direction before she resumed, *"Now tell me about you, Young?"*

My lover replied on my behalf. *"Young's family is from Malaya. He's my charge at school."*

"My dear Andy, you don't have to be canny with me. I know your preference. When you visited me in Paris at thirteen, your fascination with my male friends was irreproachable. I knew you were gay then," the sophisticate remarked cheerfully. *"It's too bad your persnickety father*

cannot see eye to eye with the nature of 'true love.' My father and brother are from a similar mold. I'm glad I followed my heart and broke away from them. Otherwise, I would have turned into a grumpy spinster.

"My advice to you dear nephew is to heed your inner voice and do what is best for you," she counseled.

It took a moment for Andy to gather his thoughts before he replied, *"You are my favorite auntie. You can read my mind before I know my thoughts."*

"My darling, you know I love you very much," the artist trilled adoringly.

"Now that I have the privilege to meet the 'fairy' prince, I want to know more about Young." She directed her gaze at me.

I was caught off guard by her exuberance, and I was afraid to say the wrong thing; so I turned the attention back to her.

"*I love your art. You are a keen faery observer,*" I quipped nervously.

She and my guardian burst into merriment.

"*I like you already. You have such a witty sense of humor,*" the woman expressed. "My dear, I am not just a keen faerie observer, I am also a mediator between the preternatural and the natural world."

Faerie Realms

Although my response to the artist's inquiry was meant to be a compliment rather than an incipit, my chaperone gandered at me as if I'd just unlocked the doorway to another realm.

Since I did not understand the word preternatural; Mary explained, *"Preternatural or praeternatural is that which appears outside or beside our natural world; where the mundane and the miraculous is suspended."*

Her comment perked my interest. I peered at her intently.

"It is the space where the sprites dwell," she added.

I questioned inquisitively, *"Have you visited this space? What is it like?"*

The artist grinned before she answered, *"It's impossible to describe these domains unless you see them yourself. You may have the opportunity to visit their kingdoms when you're at 'The Lakes.'"*

I stared at her fixedly. *"How do I get to visit the fairy kingdoms?"*

"By invitation," she declared. *"Magical portals will open if or when you get invited into their realms."*

I queried inquisitively, *"How do I get myself invited?"*

"By striving to experience life through the eyes of a child. 'For the kingdom of God belongs to such as these. Truly I tell you, if anyone does not receive the kingdom of God like a little child, he will never enter it,'" Mary quoted from the Gospel of Luke: verses 16 & 17.

My Valet, who had remained silent, japed, *"This 'child' likes to invite himself everywhere. He's a handful."*

The woman countered musingly, *"Ahh! If that's the case, perhaps, this 'fairy' prince will be one of the lucky few who will receive invitations to the spritely realms."*

The female exhorted, *"Be mindfully conscientious if you accept the fairies invitations to their kingdoms. That sprightly world is also blotched with inky enchantments, extreme ugliness, stony superficiality, forbidding malice, and agonizing tragedy. It is far richer than the make-believe fairy-tales you read in children's books."*

My lover interposed, *"I'm sure my facile auntie will also inform you that faeries are wildly attracted to all manner of creativities, and share deep affiliations with poets, artists, writers, sculptors, weavers, and musicians. Aren't these the faery traits you told me when I was a lad?"*

Mary announced lightheartedly, *"My dear nephew, you forgot to mention 'lovers.' All arts are indebted to this invisible, capricious, sensible, delicate, incomprehensible and powerful force which we humans term as 'inspiration' or 'Muse.' It is irresistible in its present."*

I inquired blithely, *"Do I fulfill the requirements you mentioned? If I do, I must do my utmost to secure an invitation to their kingdoms."*

Our spritely conversation did not terminate until well-passed supper when I excused myself to bed; to allow my lover and his aunty latitude to catch up on lost time.

October 1968
Acapulco, Mexico

Prince P, Count Mario and a certain Mrs. Andrea Swarovski (a wealthy widow from the famous Swarovski family) flew to Acapulco to join our party to witness the 1968 Summer Olympics. The dispirited Mrs. Swarovski had accompanied the Italian Count to this playground of the rich and famous in the hope that she will again find romance after her late husband's demise. There was no lack of tall, tan and handsome men in Acapulco for this widow to preoccupy herself during the Olympic season.

The wealthy, the elite, the beautiful and the not so gorgeous had flocked to this vicinity to see, and be seen, and to get and to beget. Without exception to the rule, this wealthy Swarovski heiress had admirers and competitors who vied for her attention and to challenge her stance.

It came as no surprise to Andy and me that Mrs. Swarovski had her eyes on my Master, Tad. She, like many others, was smitten by the well-built, and suavely put together champion; even though she had no clue that this perfect specimen swung both ways. One thing she did know was that Andy and I were under the auspice of the Arab and we were stationed in his residences.

The morning after their arrival I found Mrs. Swarovski sunbathing by the hotel swimming pool. Since she was immersed in a book about mermaids and sirens, I did not want to bother her and went in search of an empty pool lounger.

"Young, come and sit by me," she called.

"I do not wish to disrupt your reading, ma'am," I answered politely.

"No worries. It is a book I picked up to keep me company during my travels. Besides, I'll like to have a chat with you. Where is your chaperone?" the widow enquired.

"He is out rowing. It is one of his passions. I prefer to swim in waters where my feet touch the ground," I replied genially.

Within the pages of her open book, I noticed an illustration of a group of sirens.

"I know the artist," I exclaimed. *"This illustration is done by an enlightened woman I met a few months ago."*

"Who is she?" the lady queried.

I answered without hesitation, *"She is Andy's, Auntie Mary. She is a prolific illustrator, and novelist in praeternatural subjects."*

"What is praeternatural?" she questioned.

I explained to her like Mary did to me. Before I could finish my explanation, she'd already changed the topic.

"Tell me about Tad?" she inquired.

Caught off guard by her question, and unsure if I should divulge confidential information about my Master, I expressed noncommittally, *"Tad is a kind, generous and a benevolent man."*

She pressed, *"I know that. But what is the athlete really like?"*

Since it was not my place to disclose Tad's personal information or our intimate liaisons to a stranger, I commented facetiously, *"You should get to know him better and discover for yourself, rather than to listen to my titter-tatter."*

Since I was more intrigued by Mrs. Swarovski's book than prattling about my Master, I let our conversation hang.

Beckoning You! (Chapter Three)

"I think every little gay boy is fascinated by mer-people, especially that of brawny Poseidon and strapping Triton. Or imagining themselves to be The Little Mermaid."
                                                Andy A. Finckenstein

Mid-June 1968
Fay Haven - Westmorland, England

"There are two reputed fairy sites near Bassenthwaite Lake, just off the main road by its banks is Castle How Fort. The other is Elva Hill. This impressive fairy hill hides the secret gateway into the otherworld. It only opens to those innocents of spirit and pure of heart," Auntie Mary remarked.

Andy gave a smug smile before he asked, *"Why is the mount called Elva Hill?"*

"This is the site of Glanoventa (Walls Castle) where King Eveling, king of the faeries lives with his daughter, Modron. This is also the home of the elves, hence the name Elva Hill," his aunt replied earnestly.

"On the southern hill slopes is a perfect Neolithic stone circle where fairies craft 'elf arrows.' That was before the witches took over to cast their magical charms."

I questioned, *"Do faeries still craft 'elf arrows' at this site?"*

"Unfortunately, they retreated into obscurity after they were driven away by the witches. Young, when the both of you visit Bassenthwaite Lake, you'll find The Dodd, it is a heavily wooded fell that rise above the southern end.

At dusk, discarnate voices and shadowy figures lurk amongst trees during the summer and winter solstices.

"*Spiritualist, such as myself believe that during the Dark Ages, condemned witches return to haunt this vicinity,*" she exhorted. "*Bassenthwaite Lake is a 'thin place' and a beautiful area to visit and to enjoy a day out in the country.*"

"What's a 'thin place,'" I queried.

The spiritualist answered, "*It's a spot in the landscape where the enchanted veil perforates through to the other dimension and is easily penetrated for those seeking magic and mystery.*"

October 1968
Hotel Casablanca - Acapulco, Mexico

Count Mario appeared when Mrs. Swarovski handed me her book. "*Here, you can have it since you're so captivated by its contents. I've other reading materials to keep me occupied; besides this handsome man,*" she commented as she gazed at her friend, the attractive photographer.

Mario said jestingly. "*You, 'Ms. Merry Widow' has a way of making me feel delectable.*"

"Aren't you?" she chimed jocosely.

It was evident that she once had the hots for the Italian until she discovered his homosexual preference. Since their interest laid in luxury consumerism and the accumulation of attractive males; they became platonic pals.

Changing the topic, the Count teased, "'Countess' (a nickname he gave his pal), who do you have eyes on now?"

She glanced at me to indicate that I was not to reveal the nature of our prior conversation.

Instead, the widow reverted Mario's question back at him, *"And who do you have your eyes on, Count?"*

The duo burst into merriment before the playboy negated, *"Shall I ask this young man? I'm sure Young will tell me all your naughty little secrets, 'Countess.'"*

They continued playfully, each trying to outdo the other.

I excused myself, to a quiet corner to delve into my newly acquired book.

Before I left, Mario asked amusingly, *"Is this woman inculcating you with spry lore?"*

"I'm intrigued by mer-people, and Mrs. Swarovski kindly loaned me her book," I stated.

The Italian quipped, *"Did you hear the wailing sirens when you were at sea with Tad and Fahrib?"*

Although I knew his banter was a wisecrack, I blurted, *"Indeed, I did, sir."*

"You did?" he exclaimed at my repartee.

"Tell us what you heard," he expressed divertingly.

I was caught off guard, and unsure if I should continue or leave.

The photographer pressed, *"Come on, boy, Tell us."*

Reliving the Storm

I had told no one, not even my chaperone of my sighting, yet a compulsion washed over me to reveal what I had witnessed; since Mario and I had been in situations where difficult topics were openly discussed. I was confident that the couple will not ridicule my unprecedented disclosure.

I began, *"I suffered severe seasickness when I was in the Murashshahaan on the evening of the thunderstorm. Amidst howling winds and roaring waves, I puked above deck. That was when I heard a series of faint whistling noises whisked through my ears.*

"I am certain the whistling voices did not come from the sheik, Master Tad, Curt, and Andy who hollered at one another to stabilize the boat; but from the depth of the ocean..."

Andrea queried before I could continue, *"Were the whistling voices melodic?"*

"It was doleful as if someone was wailing or pining for a lost love. It was otherworldly," I declared.

Mario encouraged me to continue.

"I didn't pay much attention as I was in physical disarray but when I leaned over the boat's ledge to puke, the voices grew stronger. I thought they were distress calls from other dinghies, but the wailing sound persisted. I've never heard such soulful voices until then. The music transformed into a mournful chant.

"When a series of lightning flashed and illuminated the turbulent waters, I noticed a shoal of bright objects circled the Murashshahaan as violent waves crushed the sides of the rocking boat. Tad came to my rescue. He pulled me to safety. Otherwise, I would have fallen into the ocean," I related distressingly.

"Did you see the Piscean shoal again?" Mrs. Swarovski questioned.

"What's a Piscean shoal?"

Andrea explained, *"It's a group of amphibious creatures that thrive on land and water. Piscean is a derivative from the Latin word* Pisces, meaning fishes.*"*

"After Tad hauled me into the cabin, I never saw the Piscean shoal again," I replied.

Since I had no intention to bad mouth my patriarch to anyone, especially to his friends and acquaintances; I omitted to inform them of the athlete's displeasure with me below deck.

"Why didn't you tell me your encounter with the sirens earlier? Is that the reason you're intrigued by the book I was reading?" the widow promulgated excitedly.

Surprised by her exhilaration, I muttered sheepishly, *"I'm piqued by Auntie Mary's mer-people and siren illustrations. I want to be sure what I saw resembled the mer-creatures in her drawings."*

"Who is Auntie Mary?" the Count enquired.

"Andy's aunty. We stayed at her home, Fay Haven a few months back. She's a superb illustrator and novelist on praeternatural topics, and she taught me a lot about mythical beings," I declared.

"Oh me! Oh my! You do get around, boy," Mario teased.

Mãe das Águas

Mrs. Swarovski expressed, *"Joking aside, ancient Tupi and Guarani mythology have it that 'Mother of the water bodies' or 'Water Queen,' Mãe das Águas, also known as Iara and her shoal of water nymphs, sirens or mermaids were spotted in this part of the world. They are beautiful women with green hair, copper-colored skins and brown eyes with a body resembling glistening dolphins, manatees or fishes.*

"They sit on rocks and lacustrine places combing their hair or dozing under the sun when the waters are calm. They also sing sweet lullabies to lure men into their duplicitous web. Under their spells, men will abandon their sanities to live with them underwater forever. Though they cater to her lover's needs; which isn't necessarily bad, they're also implausibly vindictive if they discover their lover's infidelities.

"It's known that their aggravations will churn up storms and destroy everything around them. Little room is left for escape, especially for men at sea when they hear their bewitching songs. They view the male species as betrayers of their love.

"It's documented that they beckon men to follow their whistling tunes and doleful chants. When tempestuous lightning strikes, those bewitched are drowned. Their spites are anguish cries for lovers lost and injured pride of their tortured souls."

The Italian quipped, *"Aren't most women like that?"*

Andrea gave a hearty laugh. *"Indeed, we are. Don't you ever cross us, or you'll suffer our wrath."*

With her sharply manicured nails, the widow pinched the playboy's nose before she inquired playfully, *"Now, tell me about Tad."*

"I'm sure Young can tell you more than I," the photographer parried.

I did not know how to respond, so I stood silent. As if by divine intervention Sheik Fahrib appeared at our side.

"Oh! Here you are. Taddy (the sheik's nickname for Tad) wants to see you. You'll find him in his suite," the doctor called to me before he joined the Count and the 'Countess.'

I excused myself.

Come Here You!

Although the Enlightened Royal Oracle Society (E.R.O.S.) rules that recruits are to have their respective Valets/'Big-Brothers' present when summoned by their patriarchs or their guests; I took matters into my own hands and went unaccompanied to see my Master. Since my chaperone was out rowing, and I'd spent time alone with Tad, I decided to venture into the athlete's boudoir alone.

I knocked on the door, and my Master hollered for me to enter.

"Shall I wait in the lounge?" I chirped.

"Come into the shower and join me," he instructed.

I stripped down to my briefs and entered the steamy stall.

Sprays of cascading aqua careened down the Arab's Herculean back and streamed down his firm buttocks before they glided down his muscly legs. He drew me into a passionate embrace, and my excitement sprang to attention. I melted into his musculature when he pried my lips open to receive his yearning tongue. Our throbbing mightiness slithered in anticipation as the water roused us to throb against one another. The athlete encased our carnality into a cocoon of heated passion as if I would evaporate into the steaminess that veiled our enclosure. He, unwilling to relinquish our probing kisses, reached to twinge my perkiness and spawned my libido to propitious intensity.

As much as I cavort my 'Master's' commanding presence, I had also promised my Valet that I would reserve myself for him, and to both yachtsmen whom Tad had warned us to avoid. Since I did not expect my 'Master's' lascivious summon that afternoon, Andy and I had arranged a secret rendezvous with Ronnie and Iian. I had assured my guardian that I would be chaste for the day; in expectation of an unbridled tryst that evening.

I would have capitulated to this rousing intimacy with gusto if I had not pledged chastity to my beloved. As inflamed as I was to surrender myself to my Master's fervor, I had to assess ways of pleasing the athlete without sacrificing my fealty.

As I knelt in supplication to the sportsman's drumming masculinity, my nimble fingers reached to squeeze his hairy chest and spurred his pounding velocity to heady intoxication. He drove into my oral hollow to euphoric groans of spasming ecstasy while I gleaned his rosiness with cherished insobriety.

Afraid I would relinquish his cherished offerings; his fiery cogency exacerbated to brutish urgency as his forceful hands clenched my cranium to receive his gushing potencies. I encircled my tongue to suckle his prized possession until he reluctantly withdrew his luscious trophy; only to share his tasty treasure in sweet kisses. Without having to renounce my rectitude, I guzzled the champion's remains with glee.

"You haven't cum, boy?" my Master commented before I departed his love chamber.

"As long as you are satisfied sir, so am I," I announced appreciatively.

On that note, I disappeared down the corridor with my integrity intact as I had promised my beloved.

By Divine Grace (Chapter Four)

"One creates oneself."

Grace Jones

1968
Hotel Casablanca, Acapulco, Mexico

As I headed towards my suite, Señor Victor Angel Triqueros, my ex-*Assalamu Alaikum* professor was exiting his chamber, located on the same floor as Andy and mine. Under Dr. Fahrib's auspice, he was the acting tutor to a couple of new E.R.O.S. recruits stationed at the sheik's household. Although Victor was no longer my official tutor, our ex-student/teacher relationship continued to flourish.

The Señor enquired, *"Young, where are you hurrying to?"*

"I've to dress and be ready for a dinner engagement," I replied.

"Are you and your chaperone joining our entourage for supper?" he enquired.

I blurted in haste. *"We are meeting Ronnie and Iian…"*

"The Sheik and Tad's yachting competitors?"

"Err… Yes," I stammered.

"Be careful boy, you may get burnt if you play with fire," he advised before disappearing into the elevator.

La Cabana

The duo was already waiting at the open-air seafood restaurant when my chaperone and I arrived in our summer fineries.

"Oh, me oh my! The both of you look like you'd just stepped out from the pages of Esquire," Iian quipped when we shook hands.

"We weren't sure to dress casual or formal? So, we went midway," my Valet quipped.

"We'll have to peel them away as the night wears on, wouldn't we," Ronnie teased and gave us wicked winks.

The captain was upon us before we could continue.

"Welcome to the 'famous diamond necklace,' where the beautiful Señorita Taylor married her beloved Mike Todd." He paused before he resumed, "And Elvis Presley had 'Fun In Acapulco.' This is also where the sassy Ms. Zsa Zsa Gabor jumped naked into the swimming pool, while Señoritas Gina Lollobrigida, Brigitte Bardot, **Rita Hayworth, Hedy Lamarr, Lana Turner,** and Ava Gardner made headlines at **La Caleta**," the captain bloviated while handing us the menu.

"Besides silver screen divas, La Cabana also entertains famous bullfighters and international songstresses."

"Need I add Olympic champions to our list of distinguished guests?" It was evident that the maître d' knew who our companions were.

I questioned curiously, "What's the 'famous diamond necklace'?"

The man pointed to the brightly lit bay before he replied, *"You see the sparkling lights? It forms a perfect U, like a diamond necklace. We refer to Acapulco as the 'famous diamond necklace.'"*

"And what's La Caleta?" I asked.

"The place where you'll find topless and naked sunbathers soaking up more than just the sun. It's the 'hottest' and 'sexist' beach this side of the cove."

He burst out in laughter and waved his hands to the sides of his face pretending to fan off the heat.

"Since Errol Flynn's arrival in the forties, this sleepy fishing village had transformed into a tropical paradise where Hollywood comes to play and...," he paused before he added jestingly, *"...Sinatra's escape from the mob."*

"Now. Gentlemen, **would** *you like to start with 'coco locos'?"*

"What's 'coco locos'?" I queried.

Iian quipped, *"It's a 'cock-tale' served in a green coconut."*

Ronnie laughed at his friend's tongue-in-cheek remark.

Our flippant chitter-chatter progressed throughout our delicious meal. By the time dinner was over, the captain had recommended we head over to Tequila a Go Gó; the 'In' place to party.

"Tell Teddy Stauffer, 'Mr. Acapulco,' the nightlife impresario I sent you. He'll make sure you boys will have a good time," the captain grinned cheekily.

Tequila a Go Gó

The discotheque was already in full swing with a queue that stretched beyond our periphery. When the doorman and bouncer spotted the champions, they waved us through without checking our I.D.s; much to the roisterers' chagrin.

When we were guided to the cordoned VIP section of the club, it was apparent that my Valet and I were in the company of famous yachtsmen.

Within this smoke-filled establishment, the star-studded cast that occupied the stage and dance floor certainly made up for the lack of space. Stoned revelers with arms swinging, hips swaying and feet tapping, they gyrated to the latest disco beat.

The two DJs in their respective booth competed fiercely in the art of record spinning while performers and Go-Go dancers enraptured the audience's attention to heights of narcissistic ecstasy.

As if I would deliquesce by these uninhibited carousals my gallant lover wrapped his arms around me.

Iian grimaced over the loud music. *"Are you afraid Young would be escorted out of the premise?"*

"The lad is in safe hands, except ours," Ronnie sniggered.

Just then a Junoesque woman clad in thigh high patent leather boots appeared from behind a velvet curtain. She was naked except for a skimpy patent leather G-string that exposed her shapely buttocks. Draped on her bonny neck was a giant boa constrictor which coiled artfully around her voluptuous bosom. The excited crowd retracted and created a path for her grand entrance. Her geometric coiffure accentuated her angular features, and her sultry voice matrixed by **the song made famous by** Édith Piaf would soon propel this Jamaican singer/model to international stardom. She was none other than the Grace Jones.

The moment I saw the elegantly composed diva I was bewitched by her hypnotic performance. The Brobdingnagian serpent was but a fashion accessory to her resonating vocals and charismatic stature. A decade later this supermodel goddess and songstress became a blatant provocation to both the fashion and music world.

That evening at Tequila a Go Gó my companions and I were smitten by the 'Grace' bug as was the corybantic audience who went hysterical over her performance.

I noticed three familiar figures at the bar when I was whirling on the dance floor to Ms. Jones' rendition of *La Vie en rose.*

For a fleeting second, Tad's eyes met mine. I was startled by this unexpected fortitude and turned away rapidly. I did not know how to react. I rustled loudly into my Valet's ear to whom I just saw.

Fortunately, the throng made it impossible for Tad to jostle his way towards our direction.

"It's too late now to retreat. Play cool!" Andy counseled.

The 'Countess,' the Count and the athlete were next to us as soon as Grace disappeared backstage after her act.

Mario announced, *"What an incredible performance! I'm going backstage to meet this amazing woman."*

"You must feature her in Vogue Italia. She's magnificent!" Mrs. Swarovski endorsed while my Master glared at me forbiddingly as if I'd committed an atrocity. I dared not look him in the eye.

The charismatic Arab greeted his opponents cordially when he introduced the Count and the 'Countess' to Ronnie and Iian.

My chaperone and I knew we would be summoned by Tad upon our return to the hotel. But within this playpen of the rich and famous, we played along to my Master's tune.

Besides being bowled over by the 'Grace' bug, Mario was as enamored with Ronnie and Iian like Andy and me. Before the evening was up, the Count had arranged a photo shoot with the British yachtsmen; much to the chagrin of his pal, Tad.

Andy and I were left in the company of Tad and Andrea when the photographer, Ronnie, and Iian disappeared backstage to congratulate Ms. Jones.

My Master vociferated to me privately, *"You're not of age to be in a discotheque. Leave now, before I have the bouncers escort you out. And meet me in my suite when I return to the hotel...."*

Before he could continue, the coquettish Mrs. Swarovski had draped herself onto the athlete's shoulders. She coaxed him to the dance floor and later for an after party nightcap at her boudoir. I was glad that the widow extricated me from my Master's wrath, if only temporarily.

To my chagrin, my chaperone and I never got to see Ms. Jones' second act. She had appeared as a ferocious tigress while crooning the song, *Nightclubbing* and ripped the pants off from several male admirers along the way. That evening, her intercellular presentation was an advent to the post-disco Eighties where matrixical sounds veered towards a contemporary musical delivery. This divine 'Grace' was a decade before her time.

At the time I did not realize that Ms. Jones' style would impact my future design philosophy. The diva's collaboration with the late fashion illustrator, Antonio Lopez, solidified her as an international fashion icon. This rare bird of paradise had unconsciously substantiated my style philosophy that of Less is More.

Andy and I did not have a chance to bid the British yachtsmen farewell from our hurried departure. But from Mario's beaming comportment the following morning I was sure that he had substituted my lover and me in their boudoir that night.

Third Week of June 1968
Bassenthwaite Lake, English Lake District

Aunty Mary had packed her nephew and me a picnic basket for our day's sojourn. She had much to complete before her upcoming vacation and declined our invitation to join us at **Bassenthwaite Lake**.

Mary had professed during one of our conversations, *"The lake, waters, meres, tarns, and mountains this side of England have become my landscape, my real world."*

It was one of those lazy, hazy magical afternoons that Auntie Mary had described in one of her novels when Andy and I laid our picnic blanket around a plat of wildflowers by the lake.

Our conversation drifted to my chaperone's aunty.

I opined, *"Mary is a cultivated lady."*

"She is, and I love her dearly, but at times she gets carried away by her faery lore," my lover remarked.

"Do you not believe what she says?"

"That's debatable. My aunt claims she encountered sprites and had entered their domains. I find that difficult to accept." Andy asserted.

"Why is it difficult to believe? I've encountered angels, and they had given me good advice," I expressed.

"Having angelic dreams are quite different than entering otherworldly realms when lucid?"

I countered, *"What's the difference whether one is in the physical reality or in a phantasmal state? The reverential message and experience are the same."*

My guardian negated, *"Although the message and experience are similar, my logical mind has difficulty inscribing the ethereal as tangible. I need evidential validation that her spritely experiences are real."*

"Are you disputing my angelic experiences that Monsieur Dubois (my ex-private tutor) had verified in his Zentology studies as phony?" I catechized. *"Are my dreams less substantial than actuality?"*

Unable to conjure up a proper response, Andy explicated, *"That's why I'm studying engineering than fashion designing."*

"What has studying engineering or learning to be a fashion designer to do with my questions?" I pressed.

He kissed my forehead before he declared, *"I, my boy, am a left-brainer and you, my darling, are a cut above the rest."*

My Valet was obviously evading my questions. *"I'm going to recce the vicinity,"* he chirped.

"By divine grace, I hope the path will be revealed to you and me," he iterated and walked away.

Antichthon "Counter-Earth" (Chapter Five)

"Nothing comes sailing by itself."
                                        Alexander Dale Oen

October 1968
Club de Yates, Acapulco Bay, Mexico

The 1968 Olympic Sailing program consisted of five sailing classes (disciplines). There were seven races in each category. Sailing was organized in the triangular Olympic courses off the Acapulco Bay.

The *Murashshahaan* and *Supercal* were competing in the two sailors dinghy, the 'Flying Dutchman' category. As spectators gathered to witness the start of race one, the majority were unaware that the starting line was excessively biased and absurdly short, due to the insufficient organizational slate of the race officer. This resulted in a disastrous mêlée where several boats rafted together; *Supercal* being one of them. Those rafted sailed in the hind after the start signal was flagged. Despite the hiccup, Ronnie and Iian crossed the finish line with flying colors, only to be disqualified for foul play.

Although this mishap surged a false sense of victory to the competitors; especially my 'Master,' who was elated by his opponents' adversity. Fahrib, his sailing partner, advised not to rejoice too soon. Yet, the athlete could not contain his elation and treated our entourage to a private fiesta. Even-though the sheik, my Valet, Professor Curt, Señor Triqueros, and I shared similar sentiments, the rest of our group went along with Tad, especially Mrs. Swarovski who was now the athlete's unauthenticated lover. After Andy and my departure from Tequila a Go Gó, those two had spent a night of fiery passion together.

I waited for my 'Master's' summons after my discotheque's debacle, but none came. Now that the 'merry widow' had occupied his leisure slate, Andy and I were glad to evade Tad's wrath. I had become second fiddle, only to be called upon when he needed de minimis sexual gratifications. At the very least, I was temporarily extricated from the Arab's eccentric erraticism.

On the other hand, I had become Andrea's resonator. A role I played to perfection. Even at that young age, I knew the importance of communication, taught me at the Bahriji. This vital part of my E.R.O.S. educational programme was an artistic sonata in and of itself, a movement that consisted of three sections: the exposition, development, and recapitulation, usually followed by a coda.

The Exposition

I would often bump into Mrs. Swarovski by the hotel pool, sunbathing and reading; when I swam after my morning tutorials. My swimming regiment was part of my new tutor's coaching curriculum. Professor Curt Eberhardt philosophized that a dose of daily aquatic exercise would improve the pliancy of mind, body, and spirit.

Like my Valet, my teacher's handsome physique often stole the pool loungers' eyes. Although most gandered from behind their reading materials, the audacious few struck up conversations with the jock after our natation exercises. Their goal was to garner a private audience with the hunk, be it in or out of their chambers.

During these intrepid moments, **Madame** Swarovski would beckon me over for small talk. Often our conversations drifted to her and Tad's pridian encounters. Her delineations would shift from the casual to the intimate. My role was to remain quiet, even when her blabbers turn to counsel solicitations. Usually, her postulations were self-analytical rather than advisory. I was there to lend a sympathetic ear. In short, I had taken on the role as her therapist even-though I didn't realize it at the time.

The Development

That morning, our chatter turned to the book she had given me.

"Have you finished reading the novel I gave you?" the widow asked.

"It's fascinating, ma'am. Aunt Mary's merpeople illustrations bore strong resemblances to what I saw during the thunderstorm," I remarked. *"Although the creatures I witnessed were shimmering and iridescent, unlike the black and white prints in the book, the written descriptions were similar."*

Just when the widow was about to comment, my teacher was by us, dripping wet from his laps. I handed him a towel when the 'Countess' quipped, *"Do the mermen resemble your tutor?"*

"What mermen?" Herr Eberhardt questioned.

Not knowing how to respond, I stared into space.

"Didn't Young tell you, he saw sirens on the night of the thunderstorm?" Andrea announced.

My educator stared at me for an answer.

I replied hastily, *"I didn't want to alarm anyone until I'm positive about what I saw."*

"Tell me what you saw and see if I can shed some light?" Curt declared.

The Recapitulation

Left with little choice, I reiterated my thunderstorm experience. I omitted to tell the professor about Tad's cogent reaction below deck.

Eberhardt pondered before he began, *"Following Columbus's expedition to the Americas, there were sideshows in Europe that advertised 'recently discovered' mermaids from the new world. These creatures turned out to be deceased sirenian...."*

"What is a sirenian?" I questioned before he could continue.

"You like to jump the gun, don't you?" my teacher voiced. *"A short time ago, the skeleton of a 'mermaid,' as it was called, was brought to Portsmouth. It had been shot on the island of Mombasa. When submitted to the members of the Philosophical Society; it proved to be a Dugong."*

Again, my curiosity overshadowed my prudence.

I interjected, *"What's a Dugong?"*

"You're such an inquisitive fella." The jock tweaked my nose sportively before he resumed, *"A Dugong is approximately six feet long. It has lower dorsal vertebrae, with broad caudal extremity. Thereby creating the likeness of a powerful fish. To untrained eyes, especially during a heavy thunderstorm and/or under tumultuous waves, its forelegs; from the scapula to the extremities of the phalanges can easily be misconstrued as a female arm."*

My professor gave me a sad look and added, *"Sorry lad, to shatter your phantasies of witnessing sirens in action."*

The Coda

I questioned again, *"Are Dugongs typical of this region?"*

Curt shook his head and answered smilingly, *"These sea mammals thrive in the Arabian Peninsula and in your neck of the world."*

"My neck of the world? You mean Malaya?"

The man nodded. *"Especially in Palau and Abu Dhabi. Within the three thousand years old Tambun cave; drawings of 'Ladies of the Sea' (the Malay translation of Dugongs) were discovered in 1959.*

"Per Malayan and Palauan lore, dugongs were once beautiful women before their transformation into gentle grazers. Illustrated wood carvings of dugongs who assisted fishermen lost at sea were found in that region."

"Can dugongs shapeshift back to humans?" I inquired.

The jock burst out in laughter. *"Maybe, you should consult the sheik, the prince or your 'Master.' They may be able to give you a definitive answer,"* he teased.

"I thought you know everything about dugongs. I've never heard of them until now," I quipped.

My teacher chortled heartily, *"Don't take everything I say as the end all and be all. I'm only quoting from reputable travel magazines, periodicals, and journals.*

"My advice to you, young man, is to go with your gut feeling."

My fascination with merpeople and sirens continued to bug me after our conversation shifted to other topics. I knew I had to get to the bottom to what I saw in the ocean.

Third Week of June 1968
Bassenthwaite Lake, English Lake District

As I laid by the grassy banks of Bassenthwaite Lake, wild butterflies and buzzing insects whizzed by without a care in the world. I gazed nonchalantly at the changing cloudscape; enthralled by its transformational shapes from human portraitures to animal caricatures, before changing to angel depictions.

Perched on a reed by the water's edge was an iridescent dragonfly. Upon closer observation, a tiny object was in conversation with the insect. Fascinated by the scenario, I moved closer to the plant. What I saw was beyond comprehension. A minuscule entity whose physique resembled a robust child with sophisticated features and ears that resembled a giant tilted leaf spoke an obscure language to the insect, which appears to understand his directive.

He noticed my presence and jumped rapidly onto the Odonata, ready for flight. He behaved as if he would be apprehended under my watchful eyes, yet he was curious about my proximity to his propinquity. We stared at one another motionless.

I broke the silence. *"Don't be afraid. I mean you no harm,"* I whispered.

As if he had become invisible, he sat unmoved.

"Are you a fairy?" I asked.

Alarmed by my question, he tapped the dragonfly's hind to fly. Even though the Odonata's wings were flapping, they remained static as they continued to ponder my oddity.

When he finally spoke, I was clueless about his mutteration, yet I understood him via telepathy.

"I think he's the one. Maybe he's the one?" he murmured to his companion, who nodded in agreement.

"Who's what one?" I questioned.

Though my query was unanswered, he beckoned me to follow. Before I could question further, they were airborne. The dragonfly flew slowly so I could catch up. When they lost sight of me, they would buzz around to await my reappearance. We faded into the woods.

As we journeyed further into the forest, my inquisitiveness absconded my prudence. Neither my guardian nor my safety was of concern. Soon, the landscape morphed from normalcy to phenomenal.

I had gradually diminished from five feet eleven inches to six inches in height. I was now three inches taller than the entity I followed.

Finally, we arrived in a lea, filled with wild blossoms. Colorful snapdragons, hollyhocks, lupines, and cornflowers surrounded our path. My preliminary sentiment was that of entering the land of *Oz,* yet unlike its garish Hollywood cousin, this place exudes sophistication. I was also enraptured by the diminutive denizens that dwell amidst the resplendence flora and fauna. Curious by my presence, they peeked from pint-sized windows. Some greeted me by bowing their heads while others gave me princely curtseys. I had assumed their nakedness was the reason for their shyness, but upon later acquaintance, I realized that their bashful modesty was unrelated to their nudity. As nature intended, they were at ease unclothed.

Throughout our sojourn, I was unaware that the sky had become a reflection of the ground since I remain focused on my guides. Within this Lilliputian universe, everything was infinitely smaller; even though the dimensions above were that of the human world. My surroundings had also shrunk, which rendered me oblivious to the parallel universe I now inhabit.

A great variety of arthropods lived alongside these tiny inhabitants. They flew on the backs of winged insects, birds, butterflies, dragonflies, damselflies, and honey bees wherever they travel.

The elfin on the dragonfly settled on a green blade by the edge of a circular pond before he jumped onto the foliage and announced in the language I did not understand but did via telepathy.

"Welcome to the Kingdom of Ferrisabatwa." He greeted me with a bow.

Mid 2014
An Unexpected Message

A notification appeared on my computer screen during my penning of *A Harem Boy's Saga – III – Debauchery*. This Facebook message arrived from a person named David whom I had never met nor was introduced to.

Since I started writing my autobiography in 2011; friends and fans had congratulated my candidness and courage in the documentation of my tendentious teenage experiences. Yet, none had ventured forth to profess similar harem experiences like mine. David was the first, and I am confident will not be the last to share his seraglio adventures with me.

David's Message

Hello Young, I finished reading *A Harem Boy's Saga; Initiation* and *Unbridled* within a week. Your schooling experiences described in *Initiation* is like mine. Although I was educated in Sweden, I was one of three students selected to enter a secret fraternity. After my initiation ceremony, I was whisked to an oasis school outside of Riyadh for further education.

Like you, I was schooled in carnal knowledge before I was allocated to several Middle Eastern households. My harem experiences differed slightly; I and the other heterosexual recruits were summoned by the household females and not by the men. Our allurements were clandestine and hush-hush affairs. Unlike you, we did not travel extensively with our household patriarchs and his male entourage. When we did go with the paterfamilias, the womenfolk were a part of their cortège. Like you, we had Big-Brothers, private tutors, and mentors to accompany and to assist us throughout our terms of service.

I had kept my anomalous adventures to myself over the years. I hope we can become friends and share our experiences openly. That said, I want to congratulate you on the candidness of your erotic descriptions which you documented so eloquently in your writing.

You can reach me via Facebook or email me. I hope to be better acquainted with you.

Best wishes,
David

Relevant Connexions (Chapter Six)

"Strange encounters are cerebral adventures. They are moving experiences with heedful messages to note."
                                                        Victor Angel Triqueros

October 1968
La Quebrada, Acapulco, Mexico

The competing participants were busy nailing down their concluding act the week leading up to the Olympic finals. Sheik Fahrib and Tad were immersed in daily preparations for their forthcoming challenge that *Murashshahaan* was up to its tasks.

After our night out with the boys, I scarcely encountered Ronnie and Iian except in passing. They were preoccupied with *Supercal* and worked tirelessly on their dinghy in readiness for the clincher. Although they were disqualified in the first race, the duo labored arduously after that and won the subsequent races with their patience, persistence, and perseverance. The blondes snatched the gold in the denouement and rendered their competitors; especially the sheik and my 'Master,' who were sore losers to an otherwise friendly match.

Time was on our hands before and after each tournament. We, the cheerleaders notably my sports enthusiast professor suggested we visit La Quebrada; to watch the daredevil stunts performed by famous high divers.

Although cliff diving at La Quebrada had been around for many years, the La Quebrada Cliff Divers was formed in 1934 by a famous diver named Raoul Garcia. He and the late Teddy Stauffer ("Mr. Acapulco"), who was credited with turning Acapulco into a world-class resort together with their band of like-minded compatriots propelled the cliff diving boys into sports stars.

The 1963 Elvis Presley movie - *Fun in Acapulco* and the *ABC's Wide World of Sports* catapulted cliffs and divers to international stardom, making cliff diving an advent of extreme sports. To this day foreign high divers consider La Quebrada a must venture to dive venue. It was little wonder that Herr Curt Eberhardt advocated our entourage to witness this adventurous sport.

Our entourage arrived half an hour before performance time, while the sinewy divers were in concerted predive preparations for their thirty-five meters head-on collision with the ocean below.

The depth of the water within the gulch varied between six to sixteen feet, with an average of twelve feet in depth, depending on the size of the waves. Therefore, the timing was crucial for these daredevils. During the evening performances, the divers held fiery torches to illuminate their descent.

Just as the glowing sun was about to dissipate into the horizon, several teenage divers knelt in silent prayers before the shrine of the Virgin of Guadalupe. Their prayer rituals were for a safe and harmless dive before their allotted three-second free-fall into the abyss. Each performer coincided their jump with an incoming wave so they would not risk cracking their skulls on the rocky ocean floor.

I caught sight of a handsome teenage diver who was no more than a few years older than me. He was in deep contemplation when I went over to him. He opened his eyes from his trance-like prayer.

"*Why do you pray before the performance?*" I queried.

He extended his hand to shake mine.

"*I'm Jesús and you?*" he asked.

"*Young,*" I replied.

"*I've to visualize my dive, so I wouldn't be injured. My job is dangerous,*" the lad remarked.

"*Why do you do it when it's so perilous?*"

He responded with a wan smile and said, "*I've to help support my parents. This is a job I can earn a decent living and am good at.*"

"*Surely, there are safer jobs to make a living. Aren't you afraid to plunge to your death?*" I enquired.

He declared solemnly, "*When I was a little boy, I was afraid of the ocean. It was my father and brothers who encouraged me to carry on the family tradition. So, I started jumping from a little rock, and little by little I came to enjoy the free fall. The adrenaline rush makes me jump from higher and higher grounds. I feel at one with God and free from responsibilities when I fall.*"

My curiosity got the better of me.

"*Can you sustain in this profession when you grow older?*" I questioned.

He shook his head and shrugged his shoulders.

"*My father's eyesight is getting worse with each dive. He'll likely go blind from plunging into the water, and maybe one day he'll crash into the rocks like the pelicans,*" he sighed emphatically and made the sign of a cross with his hand.

"*Gracias a la Virgen de Guadalupe, ningún zambullidor ha sido asesinado hasta ahora (Thanks to the Virgin of Guadalupe, no diver has been killed thus far),*" he muttered in Spanish.

I was about to resume questioning when Mario and Señor Triqueros came to join us. Victor was curious with my inquisitiveness while Mario, the philanderer, was hoping to score with the attractive Mexican.

My ex-tutor enquired, "*What were the both of you discussing?*"

"*I asked Jesús about cliff diving,*" I chirped.

The Count remarked, *"I read in the news that high divers often face injuries such as back and neck impairments, detached retinas, ruptured eardrums, and broken forearms."*

The diver mumbled under his breath, not realizing that the Italian and the Spaniard spoke Spanish fluently. *"Virgen de Guadalupe, por favor, aleja a esta gente ignorante de mí (Virgin of Guadalupe, please get these ignorant people away from me)."*

Triqueros apologized on behalf of Mario, *"Lo siento mucho, no pretendemos unnerve usted, especialmente cuando estás a punto de realizar su salto (I'm so sorry, we don't mean to unnerve you, especially when you're about to perform your jump)."*

The Count changed the topic rapidly.

He expressed, *"Johnny Weissmuller made the jump from this cliff in the 1948 movie, 'Tarzan and the Mermaids'."*

The Mexican negated, *"Mr. Weissmuller did not make the jump. My father, Raul, stood in as his stunt double."*

The photographer exclaimed, *"Is your father still alive? I like to meet him. Rumor has it that Johnny's stunt double died during the immortalized 'Tarzan's' leap."*

This declaration prompted Jesús to respond enthusiastically, *"Of course, Señor. My father is very much alive. I'll be delighted to take you to him."*

"Shall we meet later so we can talk further?" Mario inveigled flirtatiously.

Before the diver could provide a definitive answer, he was called to the line for his performance. Like the philanderer, I also vied to have a fling with this young specimen; but more importantly, I hope he could shed some light on my sirens sighting.

My chance arrived that evening after the daredevil performance when the Count solicited my presence to join him and Jesús for a late-night supper.

Third Week of June 1968
The Kingdom of Ferrisabatwa

"*The Kingdom of Ferrisabatwa!*" I exclaimed telepathically. *"Where in the world is this place?"*

The little man chuckled before he replied, *"Our kingdom is between third heaven and fifth earth."*

"*What?*" I cried. *"Where in heavens is third heaven and fifth earth?"*

"The Kingdom of Ferrisabatwa," came his extrasensory answer.

"You're not answering my question," I vociferated vexedly.

He brushed my question aside.

"I'm Plucole, a ferrish from the Land of Ferrisabatwa. At your service prince human," he introduced himself and bowed.

I was astounded by his address.

"I am no prince human but a human adolescent," I remarked.

The elfin read my thoughts before he delivered, *"I'm the official keeper of our kingdom's library. I recognize a prince human when I encounter one."*

He scrutinized my expression before he resumed, *"I've summoned the castle guards to escort you to the Regent."*

Before I could riposte, a procession of red ants came in our direction. An army of brawny bite-size soldiers sat atop these deadly creatures. Their sun-drenched complexion resembled Zulu warriors. Their protection was nothing more than an array of small shell shields, and an assortment of sharpened sea-glass bow and arrows and spears. The battalion positioned themselves in battle formation under their chieftain's command.

Plucole communicated with their leader in the language I did not understand. The ferrishyn finally sensorized me after he spoke for some length, *"Nkosi Sfiso is an abatwaian from the Land of Ferrisabatwa, and we will take you to the Regent."*

With me behind Plucole, we marched away atop an ant.

"Do not under any circumstance deem these warriors small or tiny, especially their manhood. They are stature sensitive and will injure you if you mock their size," he cautioned telepathically.

After we circled the pond three times, an image of a magnificent castle coruscated in the water without a visible citadel on land. I was flummoxed when our infantry strutted into the pond. As we swaggered deeper into the water, it reverted to dry land. The lake had turned upside down. Now, the castle in the pond loomed before me.

I was dumbstruck as we proceeded into the fortified walls. Anthill mounds surrounded the bastions. These Abatwaian cantonments were placed strategically to protect the citadel's denizens and its royal inhabitants.

"Who are the flora and fauna dwellers from the world we left?" I besieged the ferrish.

General Sfiso's cognitive response threw me off guard. *"Those haughty, ne'er-do-well pixs who scrounge for a living and prank us regularly,"* he admonished.

Before he could continue, Plucole countered, *"Don't be so hard on them, they have their use."*

"Those scoundrels are excellent at eavesdropping. Other than that, they're an irresponsible lot," the Nkosi huffed.

Before either entity could resume, the sound of a marching band rounded the castle entrance where a large oak portal stood. With trumpets blaring, cornets blasting, trombones screeching, saxophones squawking, clarinets hooting, piccolos croaking, and drums booming; this horrifying music could drive their enemies away. Yet, this weird sound was the Ferrisabatwaians welcome salutation to me, the prince human.

I covered my ears from the sonos horribilis, which the denizens interpreted as an affectionate gesture from their guest. As soon as the dreadfulness concluded, Plucole headed to the portal. Single-handedly he pulled open the ginormous oak door before inviting me into the lifeless sanctum. Up till that juncture, I had no clue that this modest ferrish possessed such herculean prowess. The boisterous onlookers cheered when he guided me into the royal palace.

Mid 2014
My response to David's Message

David,

Thank you for connecting. You're the first to substantiate my Middle Eastern harem experiences. I'm grateful for your candidness. If you have no objections, I would like to include our correspondences in *A Harem Boy's Saga – V – Metanoia*.

If you are uncomfortable publishing your actual name, a pseudonym will work splendidly. As I had clarified in my writings; *A Harem Boy Saga* memoir series is not an exposé but cognitive accounts of my real education that I wish to illuminate the larger world.

Not only did my sui generis tutelage shape my worldview, but it had also pathed the way to my life choices. Hopefully, we can travel down memory lane and share our enlightened experiences with this topsy-turvy universe. This planet that often devaluates the classics for the neoteric.

Since you've read *Initiation* and *Unbridled*, you're aware that I've reconnected with my ex-Valet, Andy. He has kindly agreed to lend his perspective to future volumes in the series. If you have no objections to his input, I'll be happy to introduce the both of you. I'm sure he'll be delighted to be acquainted with your good self.

I look forward to our collaboration. Meanwhile, be well, stay healthy and best wishes to you and your kin.

Regards,
Young

Euphemistic Behests (Chapter Seven)

"All classic fairy stories have always been scary and dark."

Helena Bonham Carter

October 1968
Pie de la Cuesta, Acapulco, Mexico

After the teenager's dramatic cliff diving performance, Jesús guided Mario, Victor, Curt, Andy and I to the sleepy village of Pie de la Cuesta; the home of Raoul, Maria Garcia and their three sons, Miguel, José, and Jesús.

Since Mario wanted to meet Jesús' father, he invited the clan to dine at a local eatery. This provided me the opportunity to conduct my sirens hypothesis.

While the Count, Victor, Curt, and Andy chatted with the older Gracias; I asked Jesús, *"How long have you been a professional diver?"*

"It's been three years since my first performance," the teenager replied.

I questioned nonchalantly, *"Have you seen any mermaids or sirens in these waters?"*

"I've encountered Sirenos," he responded.

"What are Sirenos?"

"They are mermen that guide fishermen to safety when there's a thunderstorm," Jesús declared indisputably.

I queried bewilderingly, *"What do they look like?"*

He gave my chaperones, and the photographer sly glances before he replied mischievously, *"They look like them from the hips up. Below they are big and long."*

"Do they have hairy chests, like Andy and the Count? How big and long are their tails?" I probed mischievously.

The boy gave a rascally grin. He was obviously besotted by the Caucasians.

He stressed desirously, *"Their tails are sexy, plump, and long."*

"Where and what happened when you saw the mermen?" I prodded.

He sniggered at my inquisitiveness before he whispered, *"I'll tell you if you promise not to tell my family."*

I nodded and made the sign of a cross as a confidentiality pledge.

"Do as I tell you. After the meal excuse yourself to the inodoro (toilet). I'll meet you at the back of the restaurant and show you what transpired," Jesús muttered.

I nodded, just when the scrumptious food arrived at our table.

Sirenos

I waited at the restaurant's rear when the lad arrived. Without uttering a word, the teenage diver beckoned me to follow.

I asked, *"Are they still chatting in the restaurant?"*

He did not answer. Instead, he waved for me to keep pace. We arrived at a nearby lagoon before he pointed at a nearby cliff.

"This is the place where my father made the 'Tarzan' jump," he announced.

I looked at the precipice and wondered what he was getting at. Against the night sky, an outline of a reclining silhouette revealed itself. Before I could question, the teenager motioned for me to follow. He beckoned me to hurry. As we climbed the narrow pathway, I lost sight of the Mexican. Left with little choice, I proceeded towards the peak on my own.

What I saw was beyond trepidation. Two figures were in the throes of passion. Upon more precise observation, the hairy-chested man was none other than the Count. He jabbed his prying tongue into my guide's oral fissure as he ripped Jesús' shirt away from his sinewy physique. I stood transfixed at this unanticipated scenario, yet their erotic foreplay aroused my libido. The immediate thought that ran through my mind was, *"Where are the Mermen I was guided here to witness?"*

An unexpected pair of hands clenched my waist. Without having to turn around, I felt my lover's masculinity coursed through my person. His hardness gyrated against my derriere as his fingers caressed and tweaked my nipples to jubilations.

I turned to receive his probing tongue and mirrored the image that played out a few feet away. From the corner of my eyes, another couple had joined the duo. They were my current and ex-professors; Herr Eberhardt and Señor Triqueros.

My preemptive *Sirenos* encounter evaporated into thin air by this unexpected development. Bewildered, bewitched, and enraptured by my Valet's tantalizing amorosity I granted my lover's access to the deepest recesses of my unbridled longing.

I rotated my buttocks to seduce my chaperone's drumming hardness to salacious indulgence as my jeans swirled around my ankles.

"This boy must be punished for disappearing into the wilderness without my permission," he whispered in my ear before he slapped my tilted buttocks.

Not only did my subservience emboldened Andy's enthusiasm it also triggered the Count and his accomplices to echo my lover's exertions.

The machismo Italian whacked the diver's naked derrière with his leather belt as the lad sucked my teachers' palpitating stiffnesses.

The Count's carnality thrust his conquest to euphoric submissions. In the opposite direction, the boy surrendered to Curt and Victor's oral impalements. The lubricious teenager implored his masters to inflict further retributions on and within his willing receptacles.

Andy, enkindled by the sadomasochistic foursome, plowed into me with desperate ferocity. I squealed in agony at the sudden onslaught. The discomfort soon gave way to euphoric pleasures. My lover's dexterous pounding and my animalistic groans catapulted us to orgasmic gratifications.

With a final slap on my shapely mounds, he released his manliness into my repository and filled my compliance to overflowing capacity.

I floundered my propensities onto his handsomeness before I unleashed his sliding deposits back into his oral cavity. Our tongues interlocked in succulent exchanges as we sealed our fiery passion with sprightly affection.

The philanderer and the educators plowed into their collaborator as his compliance sufficed their dominance with vivacity. Mario tugged forcefully at the diver's hair as he rode the juvenile towards his climatic liberation.

While Jesús' tormentors lashed at his bootylicious stern, jets of molten libations poured forth from Curt's chalice of love. Victor intercepted the abundance into the lad's mouth before he shared the sportsman's sacred potencies with his conspirator and the teenager. The quartet shared their unbridled deliverances with sensual kisses.

Within the confines of his illicit recipient, Mario's hydrous outpour streamed into the lad's palpitating enclosure. He poured into the lad's furthest recess and sent Jesús over the edge of no return. Only after the teenager milked the remnants from his companions' euphoric transcendence did the men loosen their grip

We made our way to Coyuca Lagoon to frolick under the glowing moon in this secluded paradise.

"*Didn't we have fun with a couple of Sirenos tonight? Are you happy with your 'Mermen' encounters?*" These were Jesús' parting words as we waved goodbye to each other.

Third Week of June 1968
Palais Ferrisabatwa Royale

My eyes adjusted to the darkened halls as soon as we entered the Royal Palace. Plucole read my thoughts.

"*You are an inquisitive human, you're forever curious to what is about to happen,*" he relayed.

"*I can't help myself, I'm that way since birth,*" I telepathed.

He counseled, "*Be respectful to The Regent. Otherwise....*" He stopped midstream.

We arrived at a set of humongous doors before the unassuming ferrish heaved them open without effort.

Out of the darkness, a battalion of abatwaian soldiers atop an army of black ants appeared. As if they had been waiting for Plucole to open the floodgate, they trooped across the corridor. As speedily as they had arisen, the infantry with waving flags and drumming drums disappeared down the gallery.

Groups of whiffling objects careened around the large chamber we just entered. At first glance, they resembled fireflies, but upon closer inspection, they were gossamer-winged changelings. These creatures resemble little children, yet their musculatures was that of well-endowed adults. They clustered around an enormous object.

My curiosity got the better of me. I sensorized Plucole, "*Who are these creatures?*"

He glared at me as if I had put my foot in my mouth.

"They are not, and I repeat, NOT CREATURES but are of noble descent," he counseled.

"Are they fairies?" I questioned.

He gave me a nod of approval before he responded, *"We address the males as fayçon and the females as fairelle. Our Regent had bestowed each imperial sibling with an august title."*

Fairies had gathered around an ornate two-poster bed that was partially veiled by a diaphanous canopy. I could not decipher the nature of their assemblage. In the language I did not understand, Plucole vociferated a series of sing-song phrases.

The cortège parted from the bed, only to reveal a voluptuously naked abatwaian female. Her legs were spread open for the attending assembly to lap at her dexterous womb. Her contorted expression and euphotic noises disclosed an erotic tale of sexual ecstasy.

Like a queen bee whose sole duty was for reproduction, this Regent was an embodiment of a fertility goddess. Her endless supply of fulvic acid, a purgation that was vital to the kingdom's survival; was delved into by an endless cycle of fluttering fairies. In the process of being fed by her life-giving nutrients, Her Highness was also pleasured by their suckling exertions.

I enquired of **Plucole**, *"Why are the fairies weaning and grazing in and around the Regent's vagina?"*

The ferrish enlightened me. *"Fulvic boosters keep the fairies young. It slows their aging metabolism and improves their digestive system. It also protects their brain deterioration."*

I riposted, *"You mean; like bees to honey?"*

"Yes. To put it simplistically. Something to that effect," he remarked.

Plucole let out a shrilling cry. The fairies stopped dead in their tracks. For the first time since our arrival, the Abatwaian female opened her dreamy eyes.

The Librarian announced in a foreign tongue, *"Your Highness Dame Régence?"* He paused before he added, *"I present a prince human for your inspection."*

I bowed In convivial acknowledgment. All eyes turned my direction. The fairies opened a path for my approach when Her Highness beckoned me. The winged creatures assessed my physique with one another as I stood before the female abatwaian.

After the Regent had looked me over, she waved her ebony hands to shush away the entourage and left Plucole as our intermediary.

No sooner did the ferrish closed the massive doors, *"你是一位良好的王子的人类标本 (You are a fine prince human specimen),"* Dame Régence commented.

Taken aback that she spoke in my mother-tongue, I conceded, *"*感谢您, 殿下 *Dame Régence (Thank you, Your Highness Dame Régence)."*

"You are indeed a polite prince human." She adjured, *"I have a personal request for you."*

I replied courteously, *"*是的, 殿下, 我怎样的服务? *(Yes, Your Highness, how can I be of service?)"*

"Tell your earthling compatriots not to tamper with our kind. We will retaliate if they continue to destroy our habitations," she behested.

Since I did not understand her demands, I remained silent. She glared at me for a response before she vociferated, *"Return to your world and tell your kind to be respectful. If they mess with us, there'll be consequences!"*

She shook me violently.

"I'll summon you again," she concluded.

Mid 2014
David's Message to Me

Thank you for your speedy response. I'm honored to share my harem experiences with you and Andy. I hope our discussions will be beneficial to your readers. I am delighted to connect with like-minded individuals of similar backgrounds and experiences.

I will forward a questionnaire to the both of you. Hopefully, this will scintillate our discussions.

I forwarded a copy of this email to Mr. Finckenstein. I'm a man of action – a go-getter, so to speak. LOL!

On this note, I bid you well and take care of your handsome self.

Sincerely,
David

Mythical Beings (Chapter Eight)

"Dreams are often most profound when they seem the craziest."

Sigmund Freud

October 1968
Hotel Casablanca - Acapulco, Mexico

After *Supercal's* win in all six races, the sheik did his best to persuade his pal, Tad to move on; yet, he kicked up a storm, accusing the Olympic organizers of favoritism towards the British team. Although Dr. Fahrib was despondent with the outcome, he proved to be a winner in accepting *Murashshahaan's* loss.

Mrs. Swarovski, the 'merry widow' did her best to comfort the athlete but to no avail. Mario managed to drag the disgruntled Tad aboard the *Ship*, that flew our entourage to the ancient port of Hammamet, Tunisia, for our cruise around the Atlantic and the Mediterranean, before we ended in Tangier, Morocco; while the Count left for Milan for a photography assignment.

The morning before our Acapulco departure I met **Andrea at the hotel swimming pool**. After her regular titter tatter, she said hesitantly, *"I know it's none of my business, but I'm curious...."* She paused.

I stared at her wondering what she was about to disclose.

She resumed hesitantly, *"Is Tad into men?"*

Caught off guard by her question, my mind ruminated to how I should respond without revealing my Master's private life.

I replied, *"You should consult him directly. He can answer your query himself."*

She commented with uncertainty. *"I think your patriarch swings both ways. Don't you?"*

I did not answer.

She resumed, *"Are you one of his lovers?"*

I did not expect such a direct question, so I fumbled for an appropriate reply when Andy showed.

Saved by my Valet, I chirped, *"Here is my lover."*

I gripped a befuddled Andy, who was clueless about my statement.

"Señor Victor wants to see you," my chaperone conveyed.

This provided me with an excuse to leave **Mrs.** Swarovski in Andy's company, thereby leaving her question unanswered.

By the time, I bid *au revoir* to the merry widow; she had invited my chaperone and me to Paris, for the unveiling of the Swarovski Haute Couture fashion presentation.

Conversation with **Señor Victor Angel Triqueros**

My ex-tutor was having tea in the hotel lounge when he delved straight to the point.

"Curt told me you saw mermaids and sirens in these waters. Is that true?"

I nodded.

"Tell me what transpired," he pressed.

I related my sightings to the Señor.

"Young, although many don't believe the existence of water nymphs, I beg to differ.

"In my experience, mermaids and sirens sightings are often indications of temptations, deceptions, distractions and destructions in one's path. Sirens are lost souls that lure the ingenuous into disasters.

"*Be heedful of your emotions young man, it may lead to disappointments if you're not vigilant,*" Triqueros advised.

Victor stared at me unflinchingly before he resumed, "*Did you hear their songs?*"

"*I didn't hear singing but heard faint doleful whistling noises, as if someone was wailing or pining for lost love. It sounded otherworldly,*" I declared.

"*Siren songs are omens of trapped feelings, fatal passions, and self-destruction - the emotional side of your identity.*

"*Are you having mixed feelings about someone?*" the erudite scholar queried.

I nodded and kept quiet.

"*Who?*" the Señor questioned.

He waited for my promulgation with concern. I did not answer.

"*Young, I'd forewarned you about falling for those we serve. Have you forgotten my cautionary advice?*" he asserted.

I was afraid to look him in the eye, so I lowered my head.

"*Does your Valet know this?*"

I shook my head.

"*Why didn't you discuss your poignancy with your chaperone? He's here to guide you through your turmoil.*"

"*I'm afraid he'll be angry with me,*" I answered sheepishly.

Triqueros held my hands and counseled, "*You may not understand your siren encounters are connected to your dark inner seductive and sensual forces.*

"*Having any kind of relationship with these water minds often end in separation, sadness, despair and in the worst case - death.*"

He paused before he resumed, "*Are you having problems with Andy?*"

"No," I assured.

The professor continued, *"Is your lover falling for another?"*

"Not that I know of."

"Are you unhappy with the E.R.O.S. programme? Or are you undergoing erotic frustrations?" Victor pressed.

Under my ex-tutor's intensive scrutiny, I had little choice but to confide my masochistic concupiscence to him.

As soon as I finished relating my unusual experience, Victor cautioned. *"Young, you are playing a dangerous game. The outcome will not be pretty and is treacherous.*

"I strongly advise you to have a heart-to-heart talk with your Valet, the sooner, the better.

"You, boy, never fail to surprise and amaze me with your erotic innuendos." These were the professor's parting words before we bid each other farewell.

The Señor departed with his *Assalamu Alaikum* household students to Sharjah, while Tad, Sheik Fahrib, Prince P, Herr Eberhardt, Andy and I headed towards the northern peninsula of Cap Bon; where Tad's luxury yacht, *Sindbad* awaited our arrival.

Third Week of June 1968
Bassenthwaite Lake, English Lake District

My beloved woke me from my vivid praeternatural dream. I rubbed the drowsiness from my eyes.

"Was someone hammering you violently? You were kicking and rolling around in your sleep. Did you have a nightmare?

"We should head back to Fay Haven for dinner. It's getting late. Auntie Mary leaves for France tomorrow

afternoon. I promised to be back early to assist her with dinner preparations. Let's go," he stipulated.

Conversation with Aunty Mary

I had a chance to talk with the artist while Andy was busy setting the dinner table.

"How was your outing?" Mary inquired.

I uttered, *"I've something to ask you, Auntie Mary."*

"What is on your mind, young man?"

I lowered my voice and said beguilingly, *"I believe I entered a sprite kingdom at Bassenthwaite Lake."*

Without looking away from her chore, she commented, *"Did you really. Tell me everything."*

"I didn't tell Andy about my spritely encounter. He may think me nutty," I muttered abashedly.

She said smilingly, *"I'm sure he'll not think you silly. Since he was a child, I'd told him fairy stories. I'm sure he'll understand your experience."*

I did not repeat my lover's praeternatural skepticism since I had no desire to quell the spiritualist's esteem.

I commented, *"Andy is a man of science, and sprite encounters are not scientifically proven. He has a hard time comprehending their existence."*

"Don't be silly. Andy is an open-minded adult. He'll respect your experience. After all, you're his cherished beau, and he loves you very much."

"Shall we discuss your encounters over dinner?" the female remarked enthusiastically.

Dinner Deliberation

Andy expressed over dinner, *"Aunty Mary, I'm sad you're going to France tomorrow. I enjoy catching up with you. I hope we can see each other more often."*

"My darlings, you're welcome at Fay Haven anytime. Are you sure you want to be with an old lady like me? The both of you have busy lives," Mary responded jokingly.

"You're always welcome at my humble abode if you want to see more of fay kingdoms," she added before she directed her gaze at me. *"Our 'fairy' prince here, has something to enlighten us."*

Andy glanced at me surreptitiously. I stalled since I did not know how to begin.

I finally blurted, *"I had an unusual dream at Bassenthwaite Lake."* I peeked at my Valet for his reaction. He stared at me expediently.

"A ferrish invited me to a place named Ferrisabatwa," I announced.

"You met a Ferrish? This is exciting!" Mary exclaimed.

The duo looked at me intently as I related my Ferrisabatwaian experience.

As soon as I finished, the illustrator commented, *"Young, Ferrishyn (the plural of Ferrish), originates from the Isle of Man. They are known by various names such as Sleih Beggy (Little Folk), Mooinger Veggy (Small Ones), Guillyn Veggey (Lil' Fellas or Little Boys) and Sithichean (Peaceful Ones). They're a part of the Trooping faery clan.*

"Like your description, they are approximately three inches in height. Although, some can grow to a foot tall. They have dark wavy hair and dark complexions.

"They are also horse thieves and are often blamed for the kidnapping of human babies and replace them with Leanamh Tacharan, a baby-like fairy."

I chirped, *"That must be the reason Plucole was suspicious of me when we met. He thought I'm after him for stealing horses and babies."*

Mary resumed, *"That could be the reason. I'm not surprised you walked through water to get to their lodgings because that's where they like to live. They can't bear the artificial light, silver, horseshoes, salt, hearth fire ashes, and yellow flowers, except Brooms."*

"Why are they not repelled by Brooms?" I questioned.

"Broom blossoms have magical properties. These flowers are used in purification and protection spells against poltergeists," the illustrator explained.

Before she could continue, I interjected, *"What are poltergeists?"*

"Poltergeists are supernatural beings that manifest itself by making loud rapping noises to create disorder," Andy interposed.

"Excellent, nephew," Mary praised. *"Throw Broom in the air to raise the winds. Burn Broom and bury the ashes to calm the winds. The penetrating smell of broom can tame wild horses and dogs."*

I asked scrupulously, *"What does Broom smell like? Is this the flower that Ferrishyn use to steal horses with?"*

Mary explained, *"Broom smells nothing like one would expect of a flower. It has a top-note of lime, hay and dry tobacco, followed by a dense woody, nutty and heady old leaves with an under-note of fermented fruits."*

"Are Ferrishyn malevolent?" my lover asked.

"I wouldn't describe them as malicious. Ferrishyn is artfully sly, clever and mischievous and they know how to play the parties to their advantage," the lady advised. *"Evidently Plucole recognizes Young as beneficial to his kingdom's cause. That's the reason, he invited you to their realm.

"It is also possible that he and the Regent want Young to convey to humankind the dangers of worldwide deforestation."

I exclaimed, *"How can I be of use to their cause when I know nothing about ecological issues?"*

The spiritualist contemplated before she spoke, *"At this juncture, I wouldn't worry about your role. Let's wait to see if you're summoned again. For now, my boy, enjoy your vacation with your handsome beau.*

"I'll introduce you to my friend, Professor Frederick Thomason tomorrow morning. He's a botanist and a fairy expert. You can ask him for guidance if you reencounter praeternatural beings. He lives in the village of Keswick, not far from Bassenthwaite Lake."

"Thank you, Aunt Mary. I would definitely like to meet him." I welcomed the news exuberantly. Incredulous Andy was not pleased to be dragged in for a visit.

My chaperone remarked indifferently, *"Can you tell me about Abatwaians?"*

Aware of my lover's skepticism of fairy existence, the novelist answered carefully, *"Frederick is erudite in both science and the mystical. My darling nephew, you'll find his viewpoint perspicacious and insightful. Hear him with an open mind. I'm sure you'll gain much to what he has to say."*

My guardian scrutinized his aunt before he replied, *"Auntie, you know I will listen to his explanation if it bears heuristic provenance."*

"Superb! Now, back to your question: Astride his stead, he sits majestically; chest puffed, shoulders back and head held proudly. He is of the Abatwa and will look down on you even though his stead is an ant, and his height is matched with that of a fat pea. Some would group him within the faery realm, but Abatwaians are proud little warriors. I will caution to ever call an Abatwa small," our sprite expert pronounced.

My lover chuckled at his auntie's delivery. She resumed, *"Abatwaians are of the Zulu tribe, with the exception that they are tiny, and ride on ants. They also like to camouflage under tall blades of grass. It is widely believed that when the Zulu nature spirit Vash'Nok wept, and his tears touched the ground; they erupted into Abatwaians."*

Andy could not contain himself. He burst out in laughter. His auntie silenced his outburst before she continued, *"Abatwaians live in underground tunnels deep in the soil. Their subterranean homes are lavishly decorated with seed mosaics and paintings to echo their haughty nature. They are nomadic and do not inhabit these homes forever."*

I chirped spiritedly, *"That explains why there were so many anthills around Ferrisabatwa. I bet hidden passageway must be aplenty in and around the fortress."*

Mary nodded in agreement. She added, *"Hunting is Abatwaians primary food source. An entire tribe can fit atop a horse with each astride behind another - from the horse's neck to its tail. This is their hunting mode of transportation. The tribe will devour every morsel of their kill before they proceed to the next. In between hunts, they forage seeds to satisfy their hunger.*

"They use tiny spears and poison arrows to hunt and for self-defense. If their ant mounds are disturbed or destroyed, they will use their weapons against the enemy. Although their weaponries can kill small game, it is inadequate to kill humans. If a person is inflicted, the victim can get boils in the areas where he or she has been struck. There are cases, where it can be fatal.

"Although Abatwaians are generally peaceful and relatively shy, they are easily offended; especially when you consider them tiny. One has to be careful when crossing paths with Abatwaians."

I injected, *"That's the warning Plucole gave me when I encountered General Nkosi Sfiso and his army."*

"Plucole is correct. My advice to you, Young, is to stroke their plump egos and tell them that their stature is ginormous, and they are visible from long distances.

"Not everyone has the privilege to meet an Abatwa or a tribe of Abatwaians. They predominantly manifest to magicians, pregnant women, and young children. They will reveal themselves to humans on special occasions, and to share intimate knowledge of their land with the chosen individual. Like they did with Young," our fairy expert appraised.

Andy questioned, *"Why do they reveal themselves to pregnant women?"*

"To grant her knowledge of her fetus gender," the artist propagated and added, *"My darlings, Abatwaians are small, brave and proud warriors. Like most mythical beings, Abatwaians are reality-based. When the Nguni tribe migrated from Central Africa to what is now the region of Kwa-Zulu Natal in South Africa, they became a part of the Zulu clan.*

"After they encountered the indigenous short San people who relied on venomous bows and arrows to catch game; they were reminded of the Batwa tribe in Central Africa. These little warriors are dilation of the Batwa tribe."

"How did they come to ride on ants?" my lover enquired.

"That, I'm not certain. What is irrefutable is; when you come across an anthill, you may want to think twice about disrupting its inhabitants, lest you find Abatwaian weapons flying your direction." Aunty Mary ended our discussion with this cautionary advice before she gave us goodnight kisses on our cheeks.

Secret Confessions (Chapter Nine)

"Grow stronger with the pain, don't let it destroy you."
                                                  Andy Finckenstein

End October 1968
Hammamet, Tunisia

*S*indbad was a top-of-the-line luxury yacht with elegant accouterments to match. While Prince P and Sheik Fahrib occupied the Master suite, my Valet and I shared a queen, leaving my Master in the third cabin. The intrepid sporting enthusiast, Professor Eberhardt, volunteered to sleep on the couch above deck. *"To be close to nature,"* he said.

As soon as we had deposited our luggage in our respective chambers, Tad suggested we venture to the Sheraton Hammamet for a scrumptious all-you-can-eat buffet. We welcomed his suggestion wholeheartedly as our stomachs rumbled incessantly.

Hammamet at a glance reminded me of the Grecian island of Santorini with its cobalt roofs atop whitewashed houses. As our speedboat moored among a sea of fishing boats, vendors were already gathered to harass us with their fragrant mementos. Whiffs of sweet-smelling jasmines whiffed up my nostrils.

P commented, *"The indescribable scent of jasmine draws me into the city, whenever I am in the port of Hammamet."*

Before the prince could finish, a teenage boy with a basket of floral blooms handed His Highness a finger size blossom that was fashioned into the shape of a graceful umbrella.

The sheik, beguiled by such a charming gesture, remarked endearingly, *"As Sir Sacheverell Sitwell so rightly stated: 'Morocco - the warrior, Algeria - the man, Tunisia - the woman.' Hammamet is indeed an embodiment of feminine graces within our Arab culture. For any man who has the scent of jasmine imbue upon his hand, this place is his lifelong summer."*

Flashes of my encounter with Professor Ludwig Abid Safar flooded my mind. Not only did I fall head over heels with the handsome German Arab, but it also prompted my participation in the fun-filled parades of the Sahara Festival of Douz. Dr. Fahrib's poetic indication caused goosebumps on my skin as I mused over Professor Safar's wellbeing.

My chaperone saw my wistfulness and wrapped his arms around my shoulders.

"Are you alright, Young?" he queried.

I nodded nostalgically.

It was then that I knew I had to confide my secret to Andy as Señor Triqueros had suggested. But, for now, it must wait.

Confessions

Whether it was the abundance of jasmine fragrance that calmed the perturbed athlete or being away from ruthless Acapulco; the happy-go-lucky Tad had returned with a vengeance. Over dinner, the athlete chatted animatedly about our future cruise and hike to the two Arab aristocrats. While my tutor mapped out our journey, Andy and I excused ourselves to explore the grounds of the Sheraton Hammamet.

As my Valet and I admired the disappearing sun, a desire washed over me to confide my masochistic concupiscence to my lover.

I muttered, *"Andy, I have something to tell you."*

My lover did not answer nor did he look me in the eyes. Instead, he gazed pensively at the fading horizon.

I had difficulty putting thoughts into words before I finally said, *"You must think me strange."*

"Why would I think you strange?" my chaperone questioned.

"Because..., because I'm a masochist," I voiced.

Andy burst out in laughter. *"Do you know what the word means?"*

I nodded sheepishly.

"Tell me what it means?" he remarked.

"Uhh..., it means a willingness to subject oneself to trying, and unpleasant experiences," I answered shakily.

"In that case, tell me your trying, and unpleasant experiences." He observed my expression in the fading light.

"I didn't know how to react to Tad's furious displeasure when he accused us of befriending Ronnie and Iian. In a fit of rage, he threw me onto the bed, pulled my pants off and whacked my backside. Though I pleaded for him to stop, my appeals stirred him to spank me harder. When I tried to escape his blows, he tied me to the bedpost. The more I resist, the more aroused he became. He accused me of betraying my loyalty and slapped my derriere until it was red and raw," I disclosed.

Andy vociferated, *"Why didn't you call out to me? I was waiting for you outside his chamber."*

"Because..., because he had gagged me with a kerchief and..., and I secretly relish the pain he inflicted on my buttocks. Not only did his capriciousness intensify my desire to be punished, but it also foisted covetousness I never felt before.

"The more supercilious he was, the more aroused I became. When I thought he would strike my derrier with another blow, my erection would throb precipitously. His

hardness bobbed uncontrollably as he held onto my waist and glided his dripping viscousness against my butt cheeks. I was intoxicated by his Spartan vigor as his swirling tongue jabbed into my willing mouth. He muttered obscenities into my ears and demanded I obey his every desire."

Aroused by my narration, my lover reached into his pants to adjust his erection. *"Tell me more,"* he urged.

"When I refused to accept the blame for befriending his rivals, he walloped my buttocks harder. When I thought another blow would land on my backside, he would caress the smacked area, and stirred my libido to ecstasy.

"My stiffness drummed defiantly to his tortuous probe as he stroked my bulbous propensity to jubilation. Not only did his harrowing provocations heighten my lubricious craving, but my helplessness also served to amplify his copulatory wantonness.

"He wanted to please and be pleasured simultaneously. My tilted derriere seduced his immenseness to invade my core. Although I felt venerated and despised, it also produced an erotic sentiment that was foreign to me...."

Transfixed by my narrative, Andy could no longer stave off his desire. He planted a slithery kiss on my mouth before he unleashed our stiffness to the night.

My guardian's sudden exertion tossed me into disarray. I surrendered to my lover's virility like I did with my Master. Similar to the athlete, my chaperone was captivated by my acquiescence.

Andy subjugated me on my knees as I worshipped his bulbousness with unbridled devotion. When I came up for air, he beseeched me to resume my erotolalia.

"I supplicated to my Master's authority like a slave, as his sternness drove into my cavern. I surrendered to his mental and physical dominance. Waves of erotic

fulfillment swept over my person," I avowed before my guardian jammed his organ into my oral orifice again.

He clenched my hair and jabbed his phallus into my throat before he pulled my head away for another round of seamy elucidation.

I confessed, *"Tad continued to thwack my already reddened buttocks as I squealed for clemency. He basked in my affliction as much as I extol his dominance. Unable to evade his lasciviousness, he unleashed his potencies into my twitching hallow. His unfettered deliverance soared with intemperate enthusiasm...."*

My lover could no longer withhold his liberation. His spritely release blasted onto my face and coated my gaping mouth with a cornucopia of livid wantonness. I lapped up the dripping remains with gratuitous fervor as it was too potent to be wasted.

As we returned to rejoin our buoyant entourage, my chaperone declared, *"I too have a confession to tell you."*

The Third week of June 2014
David's Message to Me (Part One)

Hi Young,

I hope this email finds you well. First and foremost, I respect the pseudonym you selected for the clandestine organization – The Enlightened Royal Oracle Society (E.R.O.S.) for your memoir series, and you had altered the names of the people involved.

For our discussions, I will name my coeducational boarding school - *Valkyrian Templers Abbey (V.T.A.)*. Like you, I do not wish to be held accountable by my school moniker.

Initiation Ceremony

Unlike your E.R.O.S. initiation ceremony at a nondenominational chapel; my induction ritual was conducted in my school's Guides & Scouts Hall.

This candlelit auditorium held twelve witnesses. They were our school's headmaster, two female teachers, three male professors, together with six V.T.A. members.

Klara, Arthur and me were the new recruits. Big-Brother Jacob, Lucas, and Big-Sister Sofia, our respective chaperones accompanied us.

It was Professor Agnes who officiated the ceremonial rites. Unlike your baptism inception; my ritual was rooted in the fiery element. Klara, Arthur and I recited verses from *Nils Holgerssons underbara resa genom Sverige (The Wonderful Adventures of Nils)* by the Swedish Nobel Prize Literature recipient, Selma Ottilia Lovisa Lagerlöf. We proceeded through a ring of fire after our recitations. We were then anointed with scented oils by Professor Agnes.

I'll never forget this high point of my adolescent life. Like *Nils* in *Holgerssons underbara resa genom Sverige*, my initiation ceremony altered the way I viewed the world.

My questions for you and Andy:

How were your relationships with your Big-Brothers/Valets?

Did you ever consider breaking ties with E.R.O.S. during your years in harem service?

What credible excuses did you provide to your household patriarch to liberate yourself from not wanting an intimate relationship with a household member/members?

How did you grapple with unyielding household patriarchs/matriarchs who insisted on sexual correlations when you were reluctant to comply?

How did you cope with household members who developed strong ties or connections with you or vice-versa?

I look forward to Andy and your comments.

Best wishes,
David

Fairy Sightings (Chapter Ten)

"Immerse yourself in nature."
Elena Notara

Last Week of June 1968
Keswick, Cumberland, North West England

Upon our arrival in Keswick town, Andy and I rented a couple of bicycles to explore the scenic areas. We stumbled upon **Keswick's local lake, Derwentwater,** a short distance from the city's enchanted gardens of Hope Park. To the west of **Derwentwater** rose the fells of Cat Bells while the spectacular Friar's Crag jutted into the lake to the east. At its southern foot, the enchanted Borrowdale Valley laid in quiet splendor. It is of little wonder that John Ruskin, the Victorian art patron, watercolorist, botanist, social thinker, and philanthropist described this area as one of the four most beautiful spots in Europe.

To this day, Friar's Crag is said to be the departure point for monks on pilgrimage to St Herbert's Island where the saint was believed to have lived.

In the infamous Beatrix Potter fictional tale: The Old Brown from Squirrel Nutkin, had also sailed to this island. In Ms. Potter's fairy story, this isle was referred to as Owl Island. Positioned on the opposite side of Derwentwater was the famous Lingholm Woods where Beatrix's drew many of her woodland and nature sketches.

The largest of the four islands of Derwentwater is Derwent Isle and is only assessable to the mainland by boat. Visitors could see the boathouse across the water from the boat landings.

A certain Joseph Pocklington built a majestic mansion on this remote island in 1770. To this day, firework displays, and fake naval battles continue to be staged by the lakeshores around the islands during festive occasions.

Lord's Island is another remote isle off St Herbert Island and was once the home to the earls of Derwentwater. The smallest of the four but by no means least is Rampsholme Island.

While I bicycled around the lake, to take in the picturesque landscape; Andy, the rowing enthusiast, was elated to get into a rowboat to explore the islets. Before he left the wooden pier, my Valet pronounced jestingly *"Don't you disappear to fairyland. I expect to see you here upon my return."*

An amatory enchantment washed over me as I watched my lover paddle away. From a distance, Andy's strapping physique resembled a demigod in his prime. I was thankful for this earthly Apollo who loved and guided me unconditionally. Smitten by gratitude, I was filled with joyful tears when I noticed a school of bright objects surround his vessel. I wiped away my tears to focus intently.

Like I had witnessed in my dream, these glowing entities resembled the Ferrisabatwaian fairies. These Fayçons and Fairelles were rocking my lover's boat violently. Andy continued to row as if oblivious to what was happening. As if sudden turbulence had taken hold, his boat swayed uncontrollably. This eddying upheaval threw him into a state of confusion even though he did his utmost to steady the vessel but to no avail. I stood dumbfounded and wondered what the fairies were up to.

A loud splash occurred before I could alert my guardian. He and the overturned boat were hurled into the lake simultaneously. I stood petrified as my beloved disappeared below the lough. I had expected him to bob up for air, but he was nowhere in sight.

His head rose above the water just as I was about to shout for help. He gulped a mouthful of air and vanished below the water.

An elderly man and his dog stood enthralled by the scenario. The dog barked incessantly. Seeing the terror on my face, the man in the trench coat and hunting cap declared, *"He'll be fine, boy. He is okay."*

I shrieked in alarm, *"He's drowning, and he is not fine. I need to get help!"*

"Calm down lad. He'll be alright," he said assuasively.

Just as I was about to run off to seek aid, the man pointed at the capsized location. Andy's head had reemerged above the water. With herculean strength, he and the fairies had rectified the vessel to its original condition.

My guardian was soaking wet when he got into the vessel. He took off his clothes to scoop the residuum out of the boat. He signaled to me that he was okay before he rowed away. He paddled forcefully while the fairies pushed his boat towards Derwent Isle.

I stared in disbelieve when the trenchcoated man tapped my shoulder and beckoned me to follow. I did as was told. He gave me a thorough inspection as we sat on a nearby bench.

"You look exactly the way Mary described you," he commented.

Astonished by his proclamation, I voiced, *"Who are you?"*

"Can't you guess?" he chortled.

"Are you, Professor Frederick Thomason? How did you know we are at Derwentwater?" I vociferated.

He gave me a Cheshire Cat's grin and answered, *"I can know a great many things before they happen."*

I blurted, *"Are you a clairvoyant?"*

The scholar found my exuberance prepossessing. He smiled. *"I'm by no means a psychic like Sherlock."* He patted his German Shepherd who sat quietly beside him.

"Sherlock takes credit for guiding me to you and your guardian," he spoke to the dog.

"How did he know we were at the pier?" I queried.

"Sherlock detects many things that we, humans are incapable. The dog's ears can hear a pin drop, its olfactory perceptions are seldom inaccurate, and Sherlock's discerning vision is beyond human stigmatism," he venerated while his companion laid unperturbed by his master's compliments.

"But..., how did Sherlock know where we are?" I pressed.

The botanist stated, *"Sherlock asseverated we go for a walk and my companion led me here."* He paused before he added, *"That was when I saw Andy's boat overturn and you in a panic."*

"Did you see the fairies rocking the vessel?" I voiced.

He nodded but did not respond.

"Why didn't you try to help Andy?" I questioned.

"The fairies were playing a prank on your beloved. They mean no harm," the man sallied.

"They were teaching him a censorious lesson of their existence. Didn't they hoist him back into the vessel after that?" Frederick remarked. *"Those façon and fairelle are a mischievous lot."*

"Do you see praeternatural entities like me?" I inquired.

Again, he kept silent. When he finally spoke, he expressed, *"Mary told me that you are a 'fairy' prince. I understand why."*

This time around, it was I who went mute.

He resumed, *"You're a stylish lad. No wonder Mary calls you a 'fairy' prince. You fit the mode."*

"What mode?" I chirped before I added, *"Andy calls me a 'snazzinalian.'"*

He burst into hilarity before he announced, *"He's correct, boy. You glow like a 'fairy' prince in your mannerisms and **voguish** clothes."*

"Don't you laugh. I'm going to fashion school when I graduate from Daltonbury Hall. Fashion is a serious field of study, and many great designers are men," I responded earnestly.

"I'm not sniggering at your chosen career. I'm laughing at myself for not recognizing talent when confronted with one," **Thomason** verified. *"Please accept my apology. Now, shall we discuss spritely topics?"*

I gave an appreciative nod.

End of October 1968
Calypso Club, Hammamet, Tunisia

The moment we set foot in Hammamet, Tad's carefree party boy self-returned with a vengeance. He was the first to propose a visit to the newly opened *Club Calypso.* This nightspot was the talk-of-the-town, where wealthy vacationers, together with a handful of locals could gain unhindered entry. This was the place to see and be seen. Besides attracting the rich and famous; good-looks, an attractive appearance, and well-connected statures were other criterions for admission.

Like Acapulco's *Tequila a Go Gó,* this fancy discotheque promoted foreign and local musicians. That evening's guest performer was none other than the British pop singer, Cliff Richard, the then runner-up to the 1968 Eurovision Song Contest. That year, *Congratulations* was spun around the world, and *Calypso* played host to this suave looking artist.

When my Master gave the green light for me to join our entourage to dance the night away, I jumped at the opportunity. Revelers the world over had flocked to *Calypso* to see the good-looking Cliff.

Without fail, our royal entourage was ushered to the VIP section of the house. Immediately, Tad, headed to the table next to ours; to kiss the hand of an elegant female who possessed a certain *je ne se quois* which was uniquely hers. She wore a quirky veiled hat that tilted at a calculated angle and concealed an eye while observing everything with the other. A cornucopia of shocking pink silk blossoms sat exquisitely on her feline shoulders of her fitted black ensemble. She resembled a famous fashion designer I had seen in the pages of international fashion magazines.

When my Master introduced her to our group, I was dumbstruck. She was none other than Ms. Elsa Schiaparelli; the one and only who had collaborated with prominent Surrealist artists, such as Salvador Dali and Jean Cocteau. Never had I imagine I would come face to face with this living fashion legend in a Tunisian dance club.

She extended her gloved hand for me to kiss before she uttered in French, *"Venez vous asseoir avec moi, beau garçon (Come, sit with me handsome lad)."*

I stammered in broken French when her male companion made room for me next to her, *"I..., je suis honoré de vous rencontrer, Madame (I..., I'm honored to meet you, Madam)."*

She answered approvingly, *"Jeune homme, vous êtes très élégant (Young man, you are very stylish)."*

Since my French was tested to its limits, I looked to my Valet for help. Madam iterated in English before Andy could respond on my behalf, *"You're well put together, young man. Are you from England?"*

I was taken aback that she spoke in English. *"I..., err..., you are very kind Madame,"* I blurted stupidly.

Amused by my awestricken demeanor, she took my hand and stroked it a couple of times before she announced, complimentarily, *"You have beautiful hands, like an artist."*

I was a nervous wreck. I look to my chaperone for assistance. Andy, the perfect gentleman, extended his hand to mine.

"Madame, allez-vous l'obligeance de nous excuser. J'aime la danse avec mon compagnon (Madam, will you be so kind as to excuse us. I like to dance with my companion)," he announced politely.

Before I departed to the dance floor with my guardian, I mumbled to the Grande dame, *"Je vous remercie, Madame. C'était un plaisir de parler avec vous (Thank you, ma'am. It was a pleasure to speak with you)."*

On that note, my lover whisked me away and left our entourage in the company of Madame Elsa Schiaparelli.

The Third Week of June 2014
Andy's Email Message to Me

Young,

I received an email from a person named David. Do you know him? He said he had been in communication with you, and you have agreed to discuss and share our E.R.O.S. and Arab Household experiences.

I wanted to be sure that this stranger is a reliable gentleman and not a scammer who is out to discredit our positive harem experiences.

Keep me in the loop before I respond to him.

Hope all is well with you and Walter.

Your loving Andy,
XOXOXO

Where Angels Fear to Tread (Chapter Eleven)

> *"There are thorns everywhere,*
> *But along the path of vice,*
> *Roses bloom above them."*
>
> Marquis De Sade

End of October 1968
Aboard *Sindbad*

Tad did not return with Curt, Andy or me to the yacht. Instead, the prince, the sheik and he remained at *Calypso* until the wee hours of the morning; before they retired to Hotel Sindbad Hammamet. Earlier that evening, they had dispatched aids to reserve several luxury suites at this brand new five-star hotel in preparation for their sojourn in the city.

Since I had tutorials with Professor Eberhardt the following morning, we left the discotheque before the stroke of midnight. When my chaperone and I were alone in our cabin, we had a heart to heart chat. I could hardly believe my ears when my Valet made an extraordinary confession.

Andy sat half-naked on the bed and waited for me to emerge from the bathroom.

"*I thought about your confession at the beach,*" he began.

I looked at him puzzlingly and wondered what he was getting at.

He continued, "*Young, you do know I love you very much.*"

His query was more a statement than a question.

"I know, and I love you very much too," I replied.

"But not as much as I love and adore you...," he trailed off as if he was withholding some private information.

He patted the side of the bed for me to sit. I did as told. He held my hand to his.

"You know I will not hurt you under any circumstance. Yet, I yearn to possess you," my lover confessed.

"I'm already yours," I stated.

"You're not comprehending my proclamation?" he declared.

I shook my head since I did not understand my guardian's implication.

"Do you trust me?" he propagated and kissed me affectionately.

I nodded and wondered where our conversation was heading. Before I had time to ponder his question, he pushed me onto the bed and tied my wrists to the bedpost and pried my mouth open to receive his swirling tongue.

Tantalized by my submissiveness, he ripped away my covering to reveal my bobbing hardness while his masculinity palpitated visibly behind his towel. He tore his towel apart to show me his supremacy. He blindfolded me before I had a chance to muse over his prized possession.

My heart pounded in befuddlement as I mulled over my Valet's sudden exhilaration. This unfettered perplexity served only to heighten my lubricious carnality. My considerate lover who had never imposed dominance over my person had transformed into a brute. Unexpected slaps thwacked my soft bottom as blows of potent punishment rained down my backside.

I writhed and squealed in resistance to his erotic onslaught. Yet I coveted his torturous perpetration. My avoidance served only to ignite his haughty desires. He pushed my face onto the bed and spat into my twitching hollow as cogent wallops rained down my reddened tush. Although I welcomed his masterful advances, I clammed up my quivering orifice. He commanded me to yield. When I disobeyed a series of bellowing smacks would rain down my buttocks. Inflamed by my defiance, he pried apart my warmth with his swirling tongue and invaded my sacredness with aplomb. Waves of irrepressible wantonness suffused my desire for his bulbousness.

He plunged into my core with unbridled lasciviousness. His rousing spanks together with my frenzied shrieks whipped our libidinous provocations to jolting coitus maximus. My unyielding defiance torched my captor's aggressiveness to sweltering passion as his plummeting strokes plowed into my inner sanctum with debaucherous devotion. Unable to shun our galvanizing sadomasochism my lover planted raunchy kisses on my mouth as I heartened his lusciousness into my holy of holies. Andy had unwittingly become my cognitive slave while I, his corporeal doyen. Empowered by our recalcitrance, we furrowed our way towards an ambiguous gratification. We forged ahead where angels fear to tread.

My defenselessness had hypnotized my captor. He probed my core with gustatory depravity. Under his mighty onslaught, I could no longer withhold my seed. Gushes of explosive spills catapulted onto the queen while his molten ecstasies blasted into my yearning hollow. Streams of his potencies contoured around my twitching cavern to provide succulence for his unceasing invasion.

We were drenched with fervid amorousness when he fired another round of avid cogency into my already overloaded chamber. Yet, I welcomed his deposit with debaucherous tenacity and greeted his dominance with relish. Neither of us desired this ribaldrous game to end.

We sealed our liaison dangereuses with kisses of raunchy ardencies. We were already drugged by these exhilarating yet perilous mavericks of bondage, discipline, dominance, submission, and sadomasochism.

End of June 2014
My Response to Andy's Private Message

    Andy,

I appreciate your concerns regarding David. I too had apprehensions before I googled his profile. He is an esteemed New York interior decorator and restaurateur. My appraisal is, he is genuine.

    I c/c you a copy of my response to David. I hope you will participate in our discussion.

    Love,
    Young
    XOXOXO

My Message to David and Andy

    Hi, guys,

    Thank you for your E.R.O.S. initiation ceremonial description. During my service at the various Arab households, there were also a couple of Enlightened Royal Oracle Society recruits who went through different inception rituals.

    At my sixth household, a female recruit, Abbie told of her rites performed in the sky. She, her peer and the initiator were flown above the clouds on their school's jet. Her ceremonial ritual was conducted with the initiator and her two naked inductees, parachuting from the plane in an intimate circle while reciting short verses by an erudite scholar from their country of origin.

    Joshua, a recruit from my seventh household related his evocation rite being performed within the earth. With their heads exposed above ground, the rest of their naked bodies laid buried in the land. The instigator put a handful of soil atop their heads, while they recited sonnets from a revered philosopher.

To me, it was evident that our initiation ceremonies were rooted in the five classical elements: earth, fire, water, air, and aether.

My ex-E.R.O.S. tutor, Professor Curt Eberhardt once explained to me the meaning of aether and the other elements, and I quote:

"Ancient cultures in Egypt, Babylonia, Japan, Tibet, and India have similar elemental lists. In local languages 'air' is referred to as 'wind' and the fifth element as 'void.'

The Chinese Wu Xing system lists Wood (木 mù), Fire (火 huǒ), Earth (土 tǔ), Metal (金 jīn), and Water (水 shuǐ); though these are described as energies or transitions than as types of material."

Eberhardt explained, *"In classical thought as proposed by Empedocles; the four elements: earth, water, air, and fire occur frequently. It was Aristotle who added the fifth element – aether (referred to as akasha in India). In Europe, it is known as quintessence.*

"The concept of the five elements also formed an analysis for both Hinduism and Buddhism. In the esoteric context, Hinduism - the four states-of-matter is one of the distinct forms that matter takes shape, with a fifth element that is beyond the material world.

"Similarly, the four great elements in Buddhism, to which two others are also added, are not viewed as substances, but are deemed categories of sensory experiences."

I am intrigued by the denotations of these five elements since the Enlightened Royal Oracle Society employed them in our initiation rites. I did some fieldwork, and these are my discoveries.

In Hinduism

The *pancha mahabhuta* – the "five great elements" of Hinduism established in Vedas, especially Ayurveda, are *bhūmi* (earth), *ap* or *jala* (water), marut, vayu or pavan (air or wind), *tejas* or *agni* (fire), and vyom or shunya (space or zero) or *akash* (aether or void).

These ascertainments suggest that all creation, including the human body, is composed of these five essential elements. Upon death, the chassis dissolves into these five natural components, thereby balancing the cycle of creation.

These five elements are also associated with the five senses. They act as the sensations aggregation.

Earth, the primary element is created from the four and is perceived by all the five senses – sound, touch, sight, taste, and smell.

Although the higher element Water, has no odor, it can be heard, felt, seen and savored.

Fire is heard, felt and seen.

Air is heard and felt.

In regard to *Akasha* (aether), this element is beyond the smell, taste, sight, and touch; and is only accessible through sound.

In Buddhism

Buddha's precepts regarding the four elements are the base of observational sensations rather than philosophy. These four properties are cohesion (water), solidity or inertia (earth), expansion or vibration (air) and heat or energy (fire). He also propagated that mind and matter are composed of eight types of *kalapas*. The four elements are the primaries, with color, smell, taste, and nutriment, being secondary derivatives to the principals.

In China

The Chinese postulate a slightly different series of elements - Fire, Earth, Metal (literal meaning - gold), Water and Wood. These represent different energy fields that continually interact with each other. Unlike the Western elemental concept.

Although the Chinese word *xing* means "changing states of being," "permutations" or "metamorphoses of being," these energies are frequently translated as an *element*, even-though sinologists cannot concord on a single translation. The Chinese *elements* are ever changing and moving. One translation of *wu xing* is accorded as "the five changes."

Wu Xing is an ancient mnemonic device for systems with five stages. The preferred translations are "movements," "phases" or "steps" to that of *elements*.

In the bagua, metal is associated with the divination figure 兌 *Duì* (☱, the lake or marsh: 澤/泽 *zé*) and with 乾 *Qián* (☰, the sky or heavens: 天 *tiān*). Wood is associated with 巽 *Xùn* (☴, the wind: 風/风 *fēng*) and with 震 *Zhèn* (☳, the arousing/thunder: 雷 *léi*).

Given the durability of meteoric iron, metal became associated with aether; that is often conflated with Stoic *pneuma*. Since both terms referred to air; the former being higher, brighter, more fiery or celestial and the latter being warmer, thereby vital or biogenetic.

In Taoism, *qi* functions similarly to *pneuma* - a prime matter (a fundamental principle of energetic transformation) that are both biological and inanimate phenomena.

In Chinese philosophy, the universe consists of heaven and earth; together with the five dominant planets associated with and named after the elements: Jupiter 木星 = Wood (木), Mars 火星 = Fire (火), Saturn 土星 = Earth (土), Venus 金星 = Metal (金), and Mercury 水星 = Water (水).

The Moon represents Yin (陰), and the Sun (太陽) is equivalent to Yang (陽). Yin, Yang, and the five elements are associated with themes in the I Ching - the oldest of Chinese classical texts that describe an ancient system of cosmology and philosophy.

The five elements also play an important part in Chinese astrology and Chinese geomancy. They are known as *Shui*.

The doctrine of five phases describes two cycles of balance, a generating or creation (生, shēng) cycle and an overcoming or destruction (克/剋, kè) succession of interactions between the phases.

(生, Shēng) - Generating/Creation Cycle

> Wood feeds fire;
> Fire creates earth (ash);
> Earth bears metal;
> Metal collects water;
> Water nourishes wood.

(克/剋, kè) – Overcoming/Destruction Succession

> Wood parts earth;
> Earth absorbs water;

> Water quenches fire;
> Fire melts metal;
> Metal chops wood.

Characteristics of the Five Elements

Wood = Benevolence
Wood represents the person's fate - lowliness, nobleness, extractive, luxuriant, brilliant, blooming and flourishing.

Fire = Propriety
Fire establishes the person's attributes, such as strength, consistency, power, influence, bravery, and intensity.

Metal = Righteousness
Metal constitutes a person's lifespan like longevity, termination, dangers, difficulties, and obstructions.

Water = Wisdom
Water symbolizes the person's talent such as aptitude, brightness, agility, and sound of mind.

Earth = Fidelity/Honesty
Earth enunciate a person's status – that of prosperity, poverty, birth, and growth of all things.

I comprehend the rationale behind our initiation rituals through the representations of these elements. The objectives to our E.R.O.S. elemental initiation ceremonies served as our mission statement and for us to remember that we were the embodiment of the elements - earth, water, air, fire and last but not least, aether.

David, I will attend to your other questions in my future correspondence. For now, I bid you guys au revoir.

My friends, be well, stay healthy, wealthy and wise.

Regards,
Young ☺

Lethal Temptations (Chapter Twelve)

"In the realm of human relationships, nothing is as potent as fatal attractions."
                                                    Bernard Tristan Foong

Last Week of June 1968
By **Derwentwater**, Keswick, North West England

As we sat by a lakeside bench, Professor Frederick Thomason began, *"Tell me, Young, about your fairy encounters."*

The botanist listened assiduously as I repeated my fairy dream.

After I finished my iteration, he spoke.

"It's unusual for Ferrisabatwaians to introduce you to their sovereign at the first encounter. That is, if...," he paused for thoughts. *"If, they adjudge you to be of equal esteem,"* the professor imparted.

"The thing I find puzzling is that Plucole and Dame Régence called me, prince human. I'm human but certainly not a prince," I expressed.

Frederick resumed, *"Some time ago, I had the opportunity to visit Ferrisabatwa. Unlike you, I was shown the cantonments instead of the castle."*

"You mean the anthills surrounding the bastions?" I questioned.

"Yes. Cooliure, my ferrish guide didn't take me to the Regent. Instead, she introduced me to Commandant M'sizi; whom I may add wasn't the pleasantest of men. He grilled me as if I was a criminal before he commanded a sergeant to demonstrate their Calvary's defensive drill...."

He chortled before he continued, *"M'sizi thought me a spy because he attested to the punishment they would inflict on deceivers if I weren't genuine."*

"In my encounter with General Nkosi Sfiso, he wasn't personable either. Although he didn't grill me, he was cautious of my proclamations. Maybe, they are assigned as chieftains because they are sourpusses," I quipped.

Sherlock rose to probe his master's sudden guffaw.

"Was Sherlock with you at the fairy realm?" I queried.

He nodded. *"We go everywhere together. She never leaves my side."*

"Sherlock, is a she?" I exclaimed.

He broke into hilarity.

"The last I checked, Sherlock is a she. Let's take a walk," the man suggested.

"We have bicycles. Shall we ride instead of walk?" I proposed.

"It is safe to leave the bikes here. No one will steal them," the professor remarked.

"How can you be sure?"

"Trust me, boy. I know the townsfolk like the back of my hand. No one will pilfer your rentals," he jested.

Fairy Codes

Frederick commented as we proceeded down a path, *"Young, you may or may not realize that fairies hold certain values in high esteem. These attributes comprise a Fairy Code in their dealings with other fairies. Even the naughtiest fairies abide by these rules; though not necessarily when interacting with humans."*

"What is a Fairy Code?" I questioned.

"Me oh my, you are an inquisitive fellow, aren't you" he teased.

"They are playfulness, cheerfulness, tidiness, politeness, friendliness, being hardworking, generosity, honesty, the ability to keep secrets, kindness, and last but not least, humorousness."

I twittered, *"These are similar traits taught in my school."*

The fairy scholar responded lightheartedly, *"The fairies who pranked Andy, are Asrais. These delicate entities dissolve in water if captured or exposed to sunlight for lengthy periods."*

"I thought they were Fayçons and Fairelles?" I expressed.

"Fayçons and Fairelles are land fairies. Their wings will disintegrate if they touch the water.

"Although both groups belong to similar lineage, Asrais are water nymphs. They live and thrive around natural waterscapes unlike their distant cousins who are land sylphs," counseled the fairy expert.

"What do Asrais thrive on?" I enquired.

The man answered mischievously, *"Their main sustenance is mermen's semen. Much like the Fayçons and Fairelles who sup on their Regent's vulvic secretions."*

"So, mer-people do exist?" I exclaimed.

He nodded.

"Have you seen them? Do they look like Aunty Mary's illustrations?"

"Mary's sketches are pretty accurate," he answered before he added, *"There are high levels of protein in spermatozoa. This nutrient generates robust growth and revitalizing longevity for the Asrais. Their secondary food source is plankton."*

Will O' the Wisp

Surrounded by ancient oaks, mature elders and seasoned hawthorns, our entrenched discussion turned judicious as we tracked further into the woods.

Sherlock had wandered ahead sniffing at shrubberies and anything that was of interest. When she barked incessantly, we ran in her direction. Some distance away, while the botanist attended to his yelping companion, I noticed a ball of floating flame.

When the professor saw the fiery sphere, he indicated for us to be silent. Sherlock instantly ceased to woof.

Frederick whispered, *"It's a Will O' the Wisp."*

"A what?" I asked puzzlingly before I declared, *"It's a florid fairy ring with their leader pirouetting in the middle."*

The fairy maven marveled, *"They are 'Celebrating Ellyllons' with their Queen."*

"What is 'Celebrating Ellyllo...?" Before I could finish my question, Sherlock cavorted towards the flame.

The diaphanous circle rose in the air and disappeared into the forest. We ran to keep stride as the ebullient Sherlock chased after the object.

Finally, the radiance perched itself above a gigantic Elder. Beneath us were toadstools of radiant browns and effervescent reds.

The surrounding trees weighed down by white elder blossoms, flowering hawthorns, budding floral ashes and monoecious clusters of dangling catkins, provided a dreamlike backdrop I had not witnessed until then.

I was transfixed by the magnificence when the barking dog and her master snapped me back to reality.

The orb had transformed into a numinous spheroid.

Both humans and animal were at a loss.

End of October 1968
Aboard *Sindbad*

Andy laid asleep when I was awakened by the swaying *Sindbad*. I crept noiselessly above deck. I needed time to cogitate, to marvel at the tranquil ocean-scape and to listen to the twittering bird songs of the breaking morn.

Above deck, I did not anticipate soft groaning noises from my teacher's sofa bed. Curt did not detect my presence. I stood in silent observation as he massaged his tumescent with voracity. Captivated by his virility, my libido grew in sync to his jerking gesticulations. The sportsman's eroticism had tantalized my hardness to attention. I peered intently at this unanticipated development while my heart palpitated rapaciously.

Even though we secretly desired one another our student/teacher relationship had been chaste. My Valet and patriarchs had implicated that Herr Eberhardt fancied the opposite sex, but he had behaved differently on occasions; like his three-way liaison with Jesús, and Count Mario. My inner voice carped that this man was more complicated than what he led us to believe.

Many males and females had solicited my professor's attention, but none had succeeded in winning his affection. My educator was devoted to his métier and a private man of few words. He was an enigma to behold. Many had scrutinized his sexuality and seduced his integrity, but none had triumphed. It was within this illicit lacuna I spied his privacy as we lecherously sought physical gratifications. Our immodest reveries were adrift in lust.

Flurries of unbridled concupiscence overshadowed my propriety. I was incarcerated by Curt's machismo as I masturbated. Our gaze met in approbation. He beckoned me to him.

My fantasy was now a reality, yet I was flummoxed and baffled by its repercussions. Although in the past, I had made love with educators and mentors but never had I met a man like Professor Eberhardt – a teacher who rarely displayed capriciousness or volatility, let alone pruriency.

Lethal Seduction

Enticed by the clutches of his illicitness I fell under his spell. Like an arthropod caught in a spider's web, we tumbled down a path that would eventually alter the course of our teacher/student dynamics.

I was lost in his masculinity when his hypnotizing emeralds pierced the depth of my soul. He held me to his hairy chest. My jouissance throbbed in anticipation.

Eberhardt's tenderness was a welcome change after a night of profligacy with dominant Andy. Curt had emboldened the pliancy I lacked with my chaperone. At times, Curt was the alpha and me, the omega. When I mounted the sportsman with rousing intensity, our alternation had precipitated my lubricity to exuberance. Similarly, his protuberant adoration of my tenderness also rendered me helpless.

Our unhurried coitus unfurled our twirling tongues to explored every crevice of our yearning hollows. My teacher's twitching receptacle greeted my bulbous onslaught with elation as I glided effortlessly into his loving sanctuary. He received my unbridled invasion with rapturous moans.

Amidst ribaldrous groans of incognizance, he sucked my jabbing tongue as I deposited my abundance into his quivering recess. He lapped away my effervescent remains as we sealed our precarious endearments with an abiding kiss.

He flipped me around immediately and penetrated my shuddering cleft to claim his prize. No longer able to withhold his efficaciousness, he sprayed into my pulsating vault. He stayed buried within my gasping furrow until his heaving subsided. Only then did he retreat to feed me his remains, I so desirously covet.

His strong musculature swaddled me in sweet amorosity before he bid me *Guten Morgen* and plunged into the Gulf of Hammamet for his quotidian laps.

Gender Schemata (Chapter Thirteen)

"A gender-neutral society would be one where the word 'gender' does not exist: where everyone can be themselves."

Gloria Steinem

Early July 2014
Andy's Email to David, CC to Me

Dear David,

I'm glad to be introduced. Young told me a little about you and asked if I would join the group discussion. You are aware that I was Young's Valet for four years during our E.R.O.S. years and I am protective of this ex-charge of mine. He means a lot to me, and I continue to watch over him from afar. Nothing will I permit to dishonor his noble character. I hope you too will merit our unimpeachable integrity as we will do with you.

That said, I have given Young permission to utilize portions of our email correspondences for *A Harem Boy's Saga; a memoir by Young* - his memoir publications. It is in my understanding that you will also agree to this proviso. The contents we discuss will not be propagated elsewhere, except within the pages of Young's autobiography.

If you are in accordance to our proposition, we can proceed.

Yours sincerely,
Andy

David's Response to Andy, CC to Me

Hello Andy and Young,

I am aware of the confidentiality of our discussion and am compliant to your adjuration. I am an ex-Enlightened Royal Oracle Society member and rectitude is part of my edification. I am no exception to the rule. Our discussions are classified information unless we agree to release our confidential materials.

I have no objection to Young using selected segments for *A Harem Boy's Saga; a memoir by Young* publications. My contributions are not for personal gains but for greater appreciation of our real education.

Andy, I understand your consternation. When we become better acquainted, you and Young will find we have much in common. I, like most E.R.O.S. members, avow a gentleman's agreement in high regards.

Until our next correspondence, I bid you gentlemen au revoir.

      Yours faithfully,
      David

End October 1968
Morning Tutorial with Professor Eberhardt

By the time, my teacher finished his morning exercises, we were ready to commence my morning tutorials. Andy prepared breakfast at the nearby kitchenette.

The professor began, *"Our lesson this morning is sex roles, sex-role stereotypes, and sex-role socialization."*

He paused to sip his coffee before he resumed, *"There are sets of attributes, attitudes, personality traits, abilities, interests, and behaviors that are defined as appropriate for both sexes.*

"Besides males and females' anatomies being different, they also behave and express their feelings dissimilarly; even-though, specific behavioral differences are determined biologically.

"The reason males are considered more aggressive than females are attested to the male testosterone. That said, there are also many nonanatomic differences that are grounded in sex roles; be they learned or ingrained in the individual. In other words, people are taught to be masculine or feminine."

Before the professor could continue, I queried, "Why are we taught to be masculine or feminine rather than allow nature to perform its task?"

Curt declared, "You see, Young, roles are sets of behavioral norms that define a race or culture in each social spectrum.

"For example, people in a particular occupation are subjected to sets of expectations concerning the work performed and the style it is accomplished.

"While one might anticipate a mechanic's soiled appearance to be the norm, such occurrence for a dentist would be considered unsanitary and unprofessional. Similarly, specific roles apply to other occupations like teachers, firefighters or family relationships such as mothers, sons, fathers, daughters and so on. Sex roles propagate to all people and to one's life.

"Therefore, it is important to understand how each of us learns his or her sex role and the significance it pertains to our daily life."

I remarked, "You haven't answered my question, sir."

"I'll get to that, young man. Allow me to continue," my tutor replied.

"The concept of sex-roles are sets of shared expectations a community characterize suitable for individuals, based on their gender. These shared roles *imply that the majority sanctions the expected behaviors as appropriate for men and women. As a society, we expect males and females to play their assumed positions.*

"Although, there is no direct correlation between biological sex and various social aspects of sex roles; some psychologists advocate the term sex be applied to identify biological maleness and/or femaleness as opposed to gender role."

I enquired again, *"What's the difference between sex and gender role?"*

"Gender role denotes basic notions of masculinity and femininity. Much of what we consider masculine and feminine is taught or affixed due to socialization experiences. Therefore, it is not a biological necessity but a cultural expectation that is passed from generation to generation," my teacher explained.

Sex-role Stereotypes

"When individuals employ these sets of behavioral rules as criteria, sex-role beliefs transform to sex-role stereotypes. In traditional western society, women are regarded as delicate and more compassionate than men. Thereby, feminine stereotypes include domesticity, gentility, prettiness, emotionality, dependence, meekness, passivity and so on.

"By contrast, men are construed to be competitive and less emotional than their counterpart. Masculine stereotypes are ascribed to unemotional, strength, independence, actively aggressive, ruggedness, etc.

"These implicit or explicit expectations are taught at an early age. It is common to see family and friends revel energetically with male infants than with female babies," the professor elucidated.

My Valet had remained silent until now.

"Sex-roles are changing as we speak. Aren't we are living in the age of gender fluidity?" Andy expressed over a mouthful of breakfast cereal.

Eberhardt concurred, *"You are correct, Andy. It is recently that women abated their traditional role and forged into masculine mantles, especially in career choices."*

"It is not just in career options but across the spectrum; from sexual freedom to women's rights," my chaperone countered.

"That is true. Yet common beliefs regarding the way the sexes should behave, continue to exist across societies. Even though, variations prevail between cultures that do not correspond to the stereotypes within the industrialized nations. Therefore, sex roles are cultural constructions and not biologically determined.

"Stereotyping is a cognitive process. The act of forming general impressions allows us to categorize the information we experience. That said, the excessive use of masculine and feminine labels foster restrictions on individual attitudes and behaviors. Sex-appropriate behaviors do determine the kind of experiences we are exposed to throughout our life," the professor counseled.

Sex-role Socialization

Curt continued, *"From infancy to maturity, we receive simple, yet strong impressions of our role in society. As I mentioned earlier, male and female infants are handled differently. Family members continue to cultivate masculine and feminine traits by encouraging young adults to behave and develop interests they consider appropriate by the child's sex, and discouraging activities deemed inappropriate.*

"Often, parents reward and praise a daughter's interest in sewing and housekeeping while discouraging a son who shows similar interest.

"When a child is of school age, his or her peers provide additional information about what is considered acceptable or unacceptable within his or her sex role."

I chirped animatedly, *"Like my dad wanting to butch-me-up in what he considers as masculine activities, while my mum did the opposite."*

My guardian gave a hearty laugh.

"My darling boy, you are one unique specimen whom I love and cherish dearly even-though you are a cute and sassy 'fairy,'" he quipped.

Herr Eberhardt gave me a wary glance as if a pang of remorse had washed over his person. I felt a strange premonition that our sexual encounter was more than a moment of passion, but an emotional entrenchment he had cleverly camouflaged during our student/teacher relationship. Until that juncture, I never suspected his feelings for me was romantic other than a dutiful response to a student. This transmogrification was a sign to our teacher/student dynamics.

Although Andy seemed unaware of Curt and my erotic convergence, his endearment had ignited my tutor's concealed ardor for me to the surface.

I was propelled back to the present when my professor's dignified demeanor resumed as rapidly as it had dissolved.

Curt stated, *"This past year, sex-role development is now an area of extensive research. The initial step consists of a child acquiring his or her gender identity and label himself or herself accurately. He or she can also categorize others appropriately as male or female.*

"Most children understand they will remain the same sex throughout adulthood by age four. This is referred to as gender stability. A child's ability to recognize

that someone remains male or female - despite a change of clothing or altered hair length demonstrates the development of true gender constancy.

"Sex roles have become increasingly flexible. Although, 'masculinity' and 'femininity' had long been at opposite ends of the same continuum - meaning a person could be one or the other but not both. It is within these last years that psychologists conceive masculinity and femininity as two separate dimensions. Thereby, a person can simultaneously be compassionate and independent, and gentle and assertive. Many no longer regard fearfulness or tenderness as unmanly emotions, neither is a woman unfeminine when she is confident. Nowadays, men and women hold jobs that were once considered inappropriate for their specified gender."

I questioned, *"Sir can you explain the term, gender fluidity?"*

"That will be our next lesson."

My teacher ruffled my hair and called it a day.

Last Week of June 1968
Within the Arboretum

Frederick and I stared in bewilderment at the mysterious spheroid as it grew in size. Suddenly, it burst into rays of fluorescent sparkles that fell like brightly colored raindrops atop the effervescent toadstools. Both dog and humans were agape at this mystifying sight.

The fairy queen had grown to human size throughout the evolution. Her auburn hair floated weightlessly behind her gossamer wings. Like a pirouetting ballerina on points, she descended lightly to the ground. She was toeless like the cascading Ellyllons whose feet ended in points. Both the queen and her subjects' naked bodies glowed in translucency.

Surrounded by 'Celebrating Ellyllons,' the professor, Sherlock and I stood spellbound. The queen extended a pointy hand to us. Frederick was the first to proffer his middle finger to the queen's squiggly tip. A gesture I learned as a greeting of peace and goodwill. I followed suit. Sherlock lifted her paw to the sovereign. The royal rubbed the canine's nose instead of tapping her claw. This kindled the animal's eyes to pivot to the center like a cockeyed dog. The 'Celebrating Ellyllons' broke out in mirth and thought it the funniest thing they had seen.

We communicated via telepathy since we did not understand the queen's language.

ElderOakAsHawthorn

"Welcome to the Queendom of ElderOakAsHawthorn," she addressed.

As soon as she finished her pronouncement, three Ellyllon horn blowers tooted their Gjallarhorns loudly. Their instruments sounded euphonious rather than blaring reverberations.

"I am Queen Mab," she telepathized. *"We are honored to have a prince human among us."* She turned in my direction.

I stared at her agape wondering how I had acquired the prince human title in fairydom. Before I had a chance to inquire, the sovereign whipped out an iridescent wand from her diaphanous ensemble. She circled the curved rod in the air and created a cloud of glistening dust in midair. The fairy dust rose towards the blossoming arboretum. We gazed fixated at the enchantment.

The 'Celebrating Ellyllons' had also grown in stature. Although their head and facial features were as pointy as their hands and feet, they were shorter than their queen. The party resembled jovial teenagers in readiness to commence a celebration.

No sooner had the fairy dust settled on the blooms, the 'Celebrating Ellyllons' formed an assortment of ring circles. They reminded me of Dionysian festivities depicted in paintings by Grand Masters of yore, and I wondered if the ancients did witness such bacchanalian jollifications. Before I could ponder further, I was tossed back to the moment by the queen.

"We have much to discuss." She beckoned us into a gigantic oak.

We followed her lead.

For the Beauty of Earth (Chapter Fourteen)

"The land of literature is a fairy land to those who view it at a distance, but, like all other landscapes, the charm fades on a nearer approach, and the thorns and briars become visible."
                                                                Washington Irving

Early July 2014
Andy's Reply to David's Message – CC to Me

Hi David, Thank you for your candid response. Like Young, I want to add my take to the use of water in our E.R.O.S. initiation ritual.

Water, like Wind, Earth and Fire are one of the four essential Elements that represent the substance of the world. Many races and tribes throughout Caelereth share this belief. Plants, animals or sentient life forms depend on this element to survive.

It is said, that water is the depth of a philosopher's soul and an inspiration for artists. There is an ancient Santharian proverb that said, and I quote, *"He who acquires everything from the Water Goddess will elude everything to her."*

Water is the mother of all liquid matters. The Santharian Goddess of the Sea and Water, *Baveras* did not only create aqua but the blood and milk of everything liquor. Water, the *"primal liquid"* is the purest. It transmutes into a variety of shapes and forms, yet it retains its elemental properties.

Spiritual Water

Water epitomizes *"open"* emotions of diversity and acceptance of the new. It is the creative inspiration to new ideas, hopes, and desires that are constantly changing within the contemplative self.

Flowing water is its strength as it continuously rearranges to pave for the unknown. On the other hand, stagnant water putrefy and symbolizes demise. Hence, water is used for cleansing, renewal, rejuvenation and for the survival of the fittest.

The E.R.O.S. recruits from Daltonbury Hall were submerged in fresh water to remind us of our flexible will-power, wisdom, and are at ease with our sexuality. This is my explication to Young and my Enlightened Royal Oracle Society inception rituals.

Illuminate me to the use of fire in your initiation rite.

Regards,
Andy

End October 1968
Sadi-Bou-Said, Tunisia

When my professor, Valet and I rejoined our Arabian entourage, Count Mario was chatting animatedly with a handsome couple. The Italian photographer and Penny, a gorgeous female model who had returned from Milan after a three-day fashion shoot to join our entourage. Although they were Tad's guests, they lodged in Sheik Fahrib's luxury yacht, السهم الثاقب (*Piercing Arrow*), docked next to *Sindbad*.

At *Calypso,* Tad had befriended a German named Siegfried and Kalf, his Tunisian boyfriend. After a night of unbridled revelry, he invited the duo to join our entourage at a charming gourmet restaurant; nestled above the hills of the mythical village, Sadi-Bou-Said.

This charming hamlet, steep in history and spirituality was and still is the cross point for many artists and writers. Within this ancient settlement, colors appear in synchrony as if the ocean blues had washed over its decorative doors. Intricately crafted *moucharabiehs* (Arabic for a projecting oriel window enclosed with carved latticework and stained glass) counterbalanced the whitewashed walls to perfection. Fragrant jasmines and orange blossoms, together with shades of pine, palm and bougainvillea provided a utopian magnetism to this languid community. Throughout the day, the mutable play of light and shadow against an ever-changing sky and oceanscape, inspired my creativity to blossom unceasingly. Lost in artistic introspection, I was snapped back to reality by my Valet and teacher. We had arrived at the restaurant.

Our ten-person entourage sat on the terrace overlooking the Mediterranean. Delicious Tunisian cuisines were served up to us. Apart from Kalf who was two years older than me, I was the youngest. We gobbled mouthfuls of delicacies as if we had not eaten for days.

Siegfried

Our dinner conversation turned to our new acquaintances.

"Siegfried, which part of Germany are you from?" my teacher enquired.

"I was born in Leipzig. Currently, I work as an interior decorator in West Berlin. I shop for North African antiquities for my emporium and clients," the German responded. *"And you, sir?"*

Curt gave a mischievous grin before he answered, *"I'm from Münster. I live and work around the world."*

"What line of work are you in, sir?" the decorator looked at my tutor curiously.

Eberhardt elucidated proudly, *"I'm a private tutor to privileged students. I travel when and wherever my services are required."*

My Valet informed, *"Professor Eberhardt is Young's educator."*

"How wonderful to travel the world and earn a good living as a private educator," Siegfried remarked with envy.

My teacher quipped, *"You are not doing too poorly yourself. You work on your passion and with a delightful companion to boot."*

He turned to the Tunisian before he resumed, *"What's your profession, Kalf?"*

"Kalf assists me in my business," the German answered on his boyfriend's behalf.

I blurted without thinking, *"Monkey business?"*

My professor and chaperone stared at me in disbelief that I would utter such an unruly remark in polite company.

Kalf burst into laughter while his boyfriend glared at him. The rest of the group turned our direction and wondered why the Tunisian was in a giggling fit.

My gallant Valet came to my rescue once again.

"This mischievous lad is playfully silly," Andy appeased.

His remark did the trick.

Tad seized the opportunity to announce, *"Shall we sail to Tunis after brunch? Kalf said he knows the city well and will be our guide."*

"Of course, I'll be happy to show you my hometown," the Tunisian uttered delightfully.

Louise Emma Augusta Dahl-Wolfe

Mario expressed, *"I've heard a lot about Tunis. Penny had done a few shots in that city for American Vogue."*

"I fell in love with that vibrant city when I modeled for Emma," Penny championed.

The Count injected, *"I was Louise Emma Augusta Dahl-Wolfe's apprentice in the early days as a photographer. I collaborated with her on several shoots, and she has an excellent eye."*

"It was she who introduced me to Carmel Snow, the editor of Harper's Bazaar and Diana Vreeland. In the early sixties, they gave me my modeling break when I posed for the magazine," the model stated.

I was all ears at the mention of Who's Who in the fashion arena and hung onto every word of the conversation.

The photographer praised, *"I love Louise's 'environmental' fashion photography. Her play of natural light in outdoor locations are incredible. You know, she preferred portraitures to fashion photography and was accredited for discovering the teenage Lauren Bacall whom she photographed for Bazaar's cover."*

Prince P opined, *"Mario, your photographs are equally captivating. You learned from the best."*

The sheik turned his attention to me and said, *"In turn, this lad here is mentored by another great artist, you."*

"Count, before we ramble on about fashion, I have a favor to ask of you," Tad entreated.

"Yes?" the photographer expressed.

The athlete gave his pal a naughty grin before he implored, *"Will you and your apprentice take some enticing photos of these beautiful people?"* He indicated to his guests around the table.

The photographer answered wickedly, *"I plan to do just that."*

He glanced flirtatiously at the handsome Tunisian who pretend to look away coyly.

"When the lighting is right, and the circumstance is correct, my camera and equipment will be at the ready. And so, will my apprentice," the Count declared mischievously.

Except for my professor, our group chuckled indecorously. I peered at Andy for his reaction. Even though he appeared in oblivion, my presage told me differently.

Last Week of June 1968
Within the Querceta (Oaks)

The moment Frederick, Sherlock and I stepped through the towering oak, we were faced with a querceta. These stupendous trees were mirror images of one another. It was impossible to decipher the layout of this labyrinth if lost.

We trailed behind the sovereign and her horn blowing trio. She did not communicate with us until we reached the edge of the maze.

Not able to see beyond the horizon from our vantage point above a steep cliff, Queen Mab pointed the tip of her squiggly hand towards the expansive forest-scape. Pockets of flat land where ancient trees once occupied lay barren. Vast areas were burned to the ground while others were being bulldozed. The professor and I stared at the devastations.

"I want to show you the destruction humans had inflicted upon Gaia. For eons, we had shared this realm in harmony. Now, consumed by personal gains, earthlings are destroying our Mother's habitat," the sovereign telepathized to Frederick and me.

She resumed, *"To counter this cataclysmic occurrence, Fairydom's crowned heads had unanimously agreed that we must solicit assistance from empathetic humans on this issue."*

I sensorized, *"What is expected of me? I'm a teenager who knows nothing about deforestation."*

Her Majesty countered, *"Quite the contrary. Young man, you are capable of convincing the rich and powerful to stop raping Mother Earth for their gains."*

I remained silent. Although Professor Thomason was clueless that I moved within the Arabian elite and influential coterie, I understood the queen's request.

The botanist communicated, *"Your Majesty, In a week I will be in an international forum with members of the Botanical Society of the British Isles, and our international allies. I will definitely bring their attention to this catastrophic problem and will find solutions to terminate this adversity."*

My heart reached out to the whimpering Sherlock, who was obviously saddened by the disastrous sight. I patted her head to calm her agony.

Had not the Gjallarhorn sounds beckoned us back to the moment, we would still be in anguish over the rape of Gaia.

On our way back from whence we came, the queen and I had a chance to interact privately.

"I now understand the reason Your Majesty, and Dame Régence refers to me as prince human," I sensorized.

She grinned but did not respond.

I resumed, *"Do the fairy monarchs have knowledge of my Arabian connections?"*

She remained silent.

I continued, *"Though I cannot make promises, I will do my best to consult my 'Masters' and patriarchs about this pressing issue. They indeed can end this detrimental problem."*

She looked at me solemnly.

"I know you have the capability to help. If you reach out to your Masters, your patriarchs will listen because you possess the power of persuasion," the queen conveyed.

I bowed to Her Majesty.

"We will be following your progress, but for now, I bid you and your companions farewell and a safe return to Derwentwater."

She circled her wand several times and voila, we were back at the bench by Derwentwater, where Andy and my bicycles leaned untouched against a gigantic oak.

Faith (Chapter Fifteen)

"Faith is taking the first step even when you don't see the whole staircase."

Martin Luther King, Jr.

Last Week of June 1968
By **Derwentwater**, Keswick, North West England

The botanist and I sat bewildered. We wondered if our recent experience were figments of our sprightly imaginations or warranted reality. Sparkling fairy dust that flew off Sherlock's furry coat provided the answer. She resembled a fluttering snow globe as the sparkles fell around her.

Frederick patted his companion lovingly for the dog's response to our bafflement.

The professor pronounced, *"Wow! What an adventure."* He glanced at me before he resumed, *"Thanks to you, prince human, we got a chance to visit Fairydom."*

I, dumbfounded by the recent event, did not respond to his pronouncement.

He continued, *"Aren't the Seelie Court playful?"*

"What's the Seelie Court?" I queried.

"Haven't you heard of the Seelie Court?" the fairy expert simpered.

I shook my head in ignorance.

"The Seelie Court, also known as The Shining Throne, The Golden Ones or The Summer Court, seeks to help humans and to warn those who offend them. They return the favor when humans honor their kindness. They also avenge injustices foisted upon their kind," he explained.

"I thought the faeries we encountered were Celebrating Ellyllons," I chirped.

"Celebrating Ellyllons is part of the Seelie Court. Although they are known to play pranks on humans, they are not malicious. Due to their lightheartedness and merrymaking attributes, their disheartenments are quick to dissipate."

"Is that why they had a Dionysian revelry?" I twittered.

"That's correct," Frederick expounded.

"If the Seelie Court is benevolent, is there also a malevolent court?" I questioned.

"Definitely! The malignant fairies are known as the Unseelie Court. Unlike the jubilant faeries, these dark entities will inflict harm and assault humans at will whether injuries had or had not been inflicted.

"That said, Unseelies have been known to be affectionate to humans, especially to those who grace them with respect. They'll treat them like pets. Bogies, Bogles, Boggarts, Abbey Lubbers and Buttery Spirits are part of this group," Thomason explained.

"I didn't know there are so many different types of faeries," I remarked.

Before the fairy expert could respond, I noticed my lover rowing ashore. We went to greet him at the pier.

Over Tea

Andy was astonished when I introduced the professor.

"How did the two of you...," he asked puzzlingly.

The botanist voiced before my Valet could complete his sentence, "Earlier, we saw you wrestle with your boat, and you fell into the water."

"Rarely do I have problems when I am in a boat, but the undercurrent is havoc in these waters," he surmised.

Frederick glanced at me not to comment. He did not wish to let on the Asrais' prank until the correct moment arose.

The professor announced, *"A cup of tea will do us good."*

We followed Sherlock and the faery expert to *Greenlawn*, their humble abode.

"Thank you, professor, for the invitation," my Valet expressed, as Frederick placed a pot of brewing Kangra and a plate of delicious cookies before us.

"The pleasure is all mine, Andy. Sherlock and I were expecting you."

Our host added, *"She has a way of detecting your presence."* He patted his companion. *"This lady has been with me since I moved to* Keswick. *One day she pawed on my door, and she never left. I thought she had wandered away from home, but nobody claimed her."*

"She's such a good companion," I opined.

The dog pricks up her ears.

Sherlock growled when Andy reached to pat her.

"Sherlock, stop snarling, be respectful to our guest," her owner reprimanded as if he knew the reason to the German Shepherd's unsettling behavior.

The botanist enquired, *"Andy, do you believe in fairies and preternatural entities?"*

My guardian replied, *"Even though I'm open to their actuality, I'm a skeptic unless their existence is scientifically proven."*

"Andy, many things are empirical and cannot be scientifically proven," the professor remarked cautiously. *"Faith is an excellent example. The dictionary defines Faith as having the confidence or trust in a person or*

thing; or the observance of an obligation from loyalty, and fidelity to a promise or engagement."

Frederick continued, *"James W. Fowler, the American theologian proposed a series of faith-development or spiritual development stages throughout the human life-span."*

"What are the stages?" my Valet asked.

"Fowler's theory relates closely to that of Piaget, Erikson, and Kohlberg in regards to aspects of human psychological developments. Fowler defines faith as an activity of trusting, committing, and relating to the world based on a set of assumptions of how a person relates to others and the world around him or her."

"What are you getting at, sir?" Andy interjected before the professor could continue.

Thomason resumed, *"Andy, I'm not trying to dissuade you from your belief system. I am merely providing you with another perspective to the power of faith."*

"Please carry on," I opined.

Stages of Faith

The botanist resumed, *"A child goes through a stage of confusion and impressionability through stories and rituals during his/her pre-school period.* **Psychologists call it** Intuitive-Projective.

"The child is **provided adequate information that conforms with social norms** *when he/she goes through the School-going phase. This duration is termed as Mythic-Literal.*

"Throughout his/her adolescence, Synthetic-Conventional comes into play. Whereby the acquired faith is concreted in the child's **belief system.** *It is during this* **phase when he/she** *forewent his/her personification and*

replaced it with individuals or groups **authority** *that represent his/her beliefs."*

"Are these theories methodically proven?" my chaperone questioned.

"Although no hard-and-fast rule requires faith pursuing individuals to go through all six stages. There is a high probability for individuals to be anchored in a particular stage throughout his/her life; especially between stages two to five," **Thomason explicated.**

"What are the rest of the stages, professor?" I queried.

The scholar resumed, *"Very often, young adults analyze their critically adopted and accepted faith to other belief systems. At this Individuative-Reflective stage, the strengthening or disillusionment of their taken faith are frequently based on individual needs, experiences and paradoxes.*

"During mid-life Conjunctive faith sets in. This happens when the individual realizes his/her logical limitations when faced with life's paradoxes and **transcendence. This is when the individual** *accepts the 'mystery of life.' Oft-times, he/she will return to the sacred stories and symbols of their pre-acquired or re-adopted faith."*

Thomason paused to observe Andy's expression before he continued, *"The final stage of an individual's 'enlightenment' phase is when the individual transcends from all existing belief systems, to live the universal principles of compassion, love, and uplifting services to others with self-confidence. This is termed as Universalizing faith."*

"Can everyone attain Universalizing faith?" my guardian inquired.

"This summit of faith is seldom attainable, except for superlative sages. The individual has to be void of all ingrained or preconceived notions, and be in Oneness with

the universe," the savant counseled. *"Boys, many mysteries are beyond methodical understanding and faith is often more potent than science. The preternatural realm is one such heuristic mystery. It is faith in the knowledge that supernatural beings exist. It is through faith, the believer will enter the secret realms of the veiled."*

Early November 1968
Parc du Belvédère (Belvédère Park), Tunis, Tunisia

Penny, the beautiful teenage American model, was a free-spirited bohemian. She was discovered by Bruce Cooper, Wilhelmina's husband from the newly formed New York Wilhelmina Models. After a couple of modeling assignments in the Big Apple, this stunning beauty was dispatched to Milan by her agency to gain international exposure. Entranced by her nonconformist and independent attitude, Count Mario enticed her to join us for our North African segment of his photographic project – *Sacred Sex in Sacred Places*. She agreed.

It didn't take long for my friendship with the five feet eleven inches' powerhouse to solidify. Penny's intrepid sprightliness and my audacious inquisitiveness bonded our affinity to perfection. Ours was a kind of brother and sister relationship. I was curious to learn of her origins; from a destitute orphan to a sought-after model, while clueless about her parent's existence. She, on the other hand, was eager to learn about my upbringing without the company of a sister but surrounded by female relatives. We became the best of friends.

Tad suggested we rest our tired feet at the opulent Casino du Belvédère after a busy morning perusing the souks of Tunis. This proposed location was situated within the tranquil Parc du Belvédère.

While we waited for our Arab contingent to while away the afternoon at the betting tables, those who did not gamble sipped and nibbled Turkish and French delights at the veranda café.

When Siegfried, Andy, and Kalf were in conversation at one end of the table, I enquired of Penny, *"Doesn't your boyfriend mind you being away for such a long time?"*

The female burst out in laughter.

"What makes you think I have a boyfriend?" she queried.

My teacher commented, *"Surely, there must be a lot of handsome beaus after a pretty girl like you."*

Forlornness brushed over the model. She was silent. When she finally spoke, dejection fell over her otherwise chirpy demeanor.

"It's not easy for me to have a relationship with a boy."

"Are you a lesbian?" I blurted.

She broke into mirth. *"I wish it were that simple,"* she replied.

My professor inquired, *"What is it then?"*

A hint of reluctance overshadowed her desire to reveal her disquietude.

I declared, *"We're good at keeping secrets."*

She broke into hilarity again. *"The truth is, neither my doctor nor I know how to treat my problem."*

This partial disclosure kindled me to prob. *"Are you not well?"*

She answered, *"Let's take a walk. I need some fresh air."*

Penny's Avowal

Within the English-style garden, designed by Joseph Lafacade, the then chief gardener of the city of Paris; Penny, Curt and I meandered. The female remained silent throughout the stroll.

When we sat under the shade of a large tree, the model muttered, *"My doctor uses the word 'Intersex' to describe my condition."*

"Is it the same as hermaphrodites?" my teacher enquired.

"Not quite," she answered.

We looked to her for further clarification.

She resumed after a brief silence, *"I..., I don't have a vaginal opening."*

I blurted thoughtlessly, *"How do you pee?"*

She suppressed a laugh when Professor Eberhardt stared at me abhorrently. I went silent.

"My doctor says my clitoris is abnormally large, but she can't provide a conclusive rationale to this phenomenon."

Eberhardt probed, *"What kind of treatment is your doctor prescribing you?"*

"She advises me to go for surgery, but I don't feel the need to," Penny said disenchantingly.

"Have you consulted other physicians?" Curt enquired.

A thought flashed through my mind. *"Perhaps Dr. Sheik Fahrib can help? He's a learned physician who is knowledgeable in women's issues,"* I chirped.

"Now you are talking, lad. That is indeed a viable suggestion. It's a good idea to get another opinion," the sports trainer seconded.

Penny looked away. She was lost in thoughts. There was sadness in her voice when she finally spoke, *"Do you think the sheik will examine my condition?"*

"There's no harm in asking. Fahrib is a compassionate and solicitous physician. I can ask him privately and see what he says. That is if you agree," I entreated.

"What an excellent idea. After all, you are the doctor's confidant. He'll listen to you," my tutor advocated.

"Have faith, Penny. I am sure Dr. Fahrib will consult with you," I assured the despondent female.

The Right Moment (Chapter Sixteen)

"Life was always a matter of waiting for the right moment to act."
                                                        Paulo Coelho

Early November 1968
Al-Zaytuna Mosque, Tunis, Tunisia

Tunisia, Algeria, and Morocco's architectural beauty, together with its liberal Islamic stances sparked Mario's creativity to continue his *"Sacred Sex in Sacred Places"* photo shoot. Like the Orientalist painters before him, he was charmed by the invariant customs and traditions that were and still are entrenched within these cities' confines.

Through Sheik Fahrib, Prince P, Tad, and their numerous affluent Middle Eastern contacts, the Count and Aziz secured privacy to work their artistic magic, that would otherwise be prohibited in these sanctified houses of worship. Even though the French legions had left North Africa many moons ago, their influences continue to imbue these Arabian communities to this day.

The Italian, never one to forgo an opportunity, packed his photographic equipment and models to the first historical monument in this vibrant metropolis; the capital's oldest Islamic house of worship, the Ez-Zitouna, also known as the Mosque of Olive. This massive building covers five thousand meters, approximately, one point two acres of land with nine separate entrances, and a hundred and sixty columns transported from the ancient city of Carthage. This monumental structure also hosts one of the first and greatest Islamic university. Many Muslim scholars, from Ibn 'Arafa (one of the greatest erudite

Islamic scholars), Iman Maziri (the notable traditionalist and jurist), to the infamous Tunisian poet, About-Qacem Echebbi, had passed through this old establishment.

As is the case, money can buy many a forbidden fruit. By making a significant donation to this preeminent musjid, Mario, and his princely associates were able to consummate their erotic photography passion.

Aziz, together with Señor Triqueros, and his three attractive E.R.O.S. students - Emily, Joshua, and Leon, from the *Assalamu Alaikum* household were hastily dispatched to Tunis to partake in this on-going provocative undertaking.

Counsel with Prince P and Sheik Fahrib

U nder the directorial supervisions of the two photographers; Penny, Emily, and Professor Curt's ménage à trois performance was a sight to behold. The opportunity to speak with my ex-household patriarchs; Prince P and Sheik Fahrib arrived when they observed the shoot from the fringe.

"*Your Eminences, may I speak with you?*" I muttered.

"*Of course, my boy, I'll always have time to speak with you. I'm sure P will find time for you too,*" the doctor expressed.

"*Can we talk in private?*" I asked.

"*Let's go to the inner sanctum,*" Fahrib replied.

We proceeded into a veiled antechamber.

As soon as we sat cross-legged on the carpet, the sheik enquired, "*What do you require, Young?*"

I related my conversation with Penny and Curt to the Arabs.

Before I had a chance to ask the doctor to examine the female model, Fahrib declared, "*Intersex is a general* term used for a variety of conditions in which a person is born with reproductive or sexual anatomy that doesn't fit the typical definitions of female or male."

"I believe that's the case with Penny," I uttered.

The doctor resumed, "Exteriorly, Penny appears to be female, but she may possess atypical male anatomy interiorly.

"I had a premonition that she wasn't altogether comfortable in her skin when I watched her interaction with Curt and Emily. I plan to ask her to see me after the shoot for an examination."

Fahrib continued, "A person may be born with mosaic genetics, where some of her cells have XX chromosomes, and some of them have XY; or a boy may have a notably small penis or a scrotum that is divided like a labia.

"In the medical field, we speak of intersex as a condition that doesn't show at birth. In many cases, a person isn't found to possess intersex anatomy until she or he reaches puberty, or they find themselves to be infertile. Some may never know they possess dual anatomy."

The prince questioned, "What sexual anatomy variations are classified as intersex?"

The sheik answered thoughtfully, "P, different physicians will provide different answers to your question because...."

He paused before he resumed, "Intersex isn't a discreet or natural category."

P questioned, "What do you mean?"

"Intersex is a socially constructed category that reflects different biological variation. To better explain this phenomenon, I liken the sex spectrum to the color spectrum.

"Nature has different wavelengths that translate into colors we view as red, blue, orange, or yellow. But the decision to distinguish, for example between orange and *red-orange is made when we're asking for a paint color. Sometimes social necessity leads us to make color distinctions that otherwise would seem incorrect or irrational. For instance, when we refer to people as 'black' or 'white,' when they're not especially black or white.*

"*Similarly, nature presents us with a spectrum of sex anatomies. Breasts, penises, clitorises, scrotums, labia, gonads vary in size, shape, and morphology. So are 'sex' chromosomes. Our culture often simplifies the sex categories into male, female, and intersex, to maintain orderly social interactions,*" the doctor explained.

"*If nature doesn't decide where the 'male' or 'female' categories end, or the 'intersex' category begins; is it humans who decide?*" I evinced.

"*You are a smart boy,*" His Eminence patted my back.

"*In our medical profession, doctors have a variety of opinions to what constitutes intersex. Some believe intersex applies to an individual with 'ambiguous genitalia'; even if his or her interior is of one sex and the exterior another.*

"*There are others which pertain that the individual's brain must be exposed to an unusual mix of prenatal hormones to count as intersex; even if he/she is born with atypical genitalia. Unless the person's brain experienced atypical development, he/she is not intersex.*

"*Last and but not least, some physicians exhort that intersex is individuals both with ovarian and testicular tissues,*" he elucidated.

P remarked, "*If there are so many different opinions, how then can the individual know if he or she is intersex?*"

The doctor grimaced. "*Rather than playing a semantic game that never ends, we at World Intersex Society for Humanity (WISH) take a pragmatic approach to the question of who counts as intersex. We work to build a world free of shame, secrecy, and unwanted genital surgeries for anyone born with non-standard sexual anatomy."*

He stated, *"Some forms of intersex signal underlying metabolic concerns - like a person who thinks she or he might be intersex. He/she should seek a diagnosis to find out if he/she needs professional healthcare."*

"That is why Professor Eberhardt and I asked Penny to consult Your Eminence," I chirped.

"That's a wise suggestion," the solicitous Fahrib announced.

I seized the moment to inquire, *"There's another topic I like to get your advice, sir."*

"We'll discuss your other topic this evening in private," the patriarch articulated before we rejoined our entourage.

Last Week of June 1968
Sharrow Bay, Lake Ullswater, Penrith, Lake District

Andy and I accepted Professor Thomason's dinner invitation at the elegant Lakeside Restaurant in *Sharrow Bay*. My lover and I were smitten by this charming boutique hotel and decided to spend a couple of nights in this tranquil sanctuary. Many a visitor had described this stunning location by the shores of Ullswater, as experiencing the *'Gentle Art of Sharrow,'* and we were no exception to the rule.

The three of us stood admiring the beauty of the setting sun at the restaurant's veranda before the maître d'hôtel showed us our table.

Frederick propagated, *"This mansion was built by the bachelor Anthony Parkin in 1840 before Sharrow Bay became a hotel. Many visitors, including the noted illustrator, Llewellyn Jewitt had professed Shallow Bay as* the most glorious and loveliest spot on the banks of this lake. He went on to announce that the pure taste of Mr. Anthony Parkin's home had surrounded it with every accessory that can render it attractive and filled it with a wealth of Art worthy of such a shrine. He also proclaimed that from this vantage, Ullswater is seen to wondrous advantage where its everchanging beauties can be thoroughly enjoyed."

I opined, *"This is certainly an enchanted spot."*

Both Thomason and Andy nodded in agreement before my lover expressed, *"This place is definitely worthy of angels and fairies."*

The faery expert and I were taken aback by the preternatural skeptic's remark.

My chaperone added, *"Did you tell the professor your angelic encounters?"*

Caught off guard by my Valet's unexpected remark. I did not respond.

Thomason broke the silence.

"Really! Why didn't you mention your angel encounters to me?" he questioned.

"The correct moment hadn't presented itself until now," I replied.

"Do share your experiences with me," our host encouraged.

Just as I was about to respond, the maître d' guided us to our table.

Angels

As soon as we were seated, the botanist inquired, *"I can't wait to hear your seraphic experiences. Do illuminate me."*

Although I had related my preternatural erotic encounters to Andy, I had not spoken about my experiences with anyone else.

Professor Thomason listened attentively until I finished before he declared, *"It's incredible that you are so attuned to the preternatural world. Although I'm no angel expert, I know a retired Oxford scholar, Professor Olivier P. Augustin who can enlighten you on your celestial rendezvous. He lives in Cornwall. Pay him a visit if and when you are in his neighborhood. I'll be happy to introduce you."*

"Thank you, I will love to meet Professor Augustin," I replied exuberantly.

"All I know of these divine messengers are from religious texts. Angels are well documented in Judaism and were heavily influenced by Zoroastrianism. Per Zoroastrian mythology, it describes a cosmic clash between Ahura Mazda and Ahriman – the forces of good and evil with their armies of angels and demons. Like Ahura Mazda, Yahweh from the Old Testament also has an army of angels battling Satan's evil forces, who, may I add resembles Ahriman."

I chirped, *"My teachers had mentioned these entities in past tutorials."*

"Then you are familiar with these religions," he commented before he continued, *"Superseding the Zoroastrian view, Judaism divided the universe into three parts: earth, heaven, and hell. Earth became the home of humans. Heaven is where God and his angels reside, and Hell is the shadowy domain of Satan and his cronies.*

"In both religions, angels link heaven with earth, by revealing God's laws and commandments to humans. As you know, their servitude is to carry out God's plan. These benevolent beings reward those who do good and punish the malevolent. They also assist earthlings to understand God's will, and to return righteous souls to the heavenly kingdom upon their passing."

Andy opined, *"The Christian concept of a three-part universe also correlate to Judaic and Zoroastrian paragons, including angels as God's messengers. They comfort sufferers and impart personal prayers to God."*

"What are the functions of a guardian angel?" I questioned.

My chaperone joked, *"To safeguard 'fairies' like you."*

The faery expert gave a suppressed chortle before he commented, *"Angels in the Islamic faith perform similar tasks as their Judaic and Christian compatriots. Per Islamic lore, they were created from fire, and can purport human or animal forms."*

I quipped, *"Like a shapeshifter?"*

The men laughed at my declaration.

"They can also be visible or invisible to the naked eye," Frederick expressed before our waiter arrived to take our orders.

Gender Fluidity (Chapter Seventeen)

> *"You can be a man or a woman*
> *I will love you the same.*
> *If you are a cis or a trans,*
> *Or a mix of the two;*
> *You are a beautiful person*
> *Just by being you."*
>
> Curt Eberhardt

The Second Week of July 2014
David's Response to Andy and Me

Thanks, Andy, for the Water analysis. Olivier, one of my ex-tutors explained Fire this way. He said, and I quote: *"Fire is a masculine element, its aspects are change, passion, creativity, motivation, willpower, drive, and sensuality. It represents physical and spiritual sexuality. Fire is used in spells, rituals and candle magic for healing, purification, breaking bad habits, destroying illnesses and dis-ease and sex. It is also the element of authority and leadership."*

He went on to clarify the properties of Fire:
Heat
Making things fruitful
Celestial light, and
Life-giving.
The Infernal Fire is its opposite:
Parching heat
Consuming all things, making everything barren in its wake, and
Darkness.

My ex-Valet, Jack, added that Fire is associated with happiness, love, passion, leadership, spirituality, insight, dynamism, aggression, intuition, reason, and expressiveness.

My Fire initiation ritual is a reminder to E.R.O.S./V.T.A. initiates of their forth-coming experiences in love, compassion, fun, joy, and pleasure. And most importantly, to share joy and laughter without thought of reward.

The Fire of Etherus

I believe that my Enlightened Royal Oracle Society/Valkyrian Templers Abbey initiation rite derived from *The Fire of Etherus* - that signifies love and compassion. In ancient lore, followers of Etherus lived a simple life. Acolytes of this order had sufficient food to eat, and wine to satisfy their craving. Clerics use the Ethelian weed to transcend their telluric existence to a sexually charged consciousness where they experience erotic encounters with a variety of partners.

These Etherus precepts are more than lustful transcendence. The flame of Lust and Love must be ministered, rekindled and refreshed for its fiery passion for aggrandizing and envelope change. They desire to transform lust from affection to compassion.

It is also within this unbridled spiritual fire that hatred and anger dissipates. Thus, morphing these negative energies to love and happiness. It is the Fire element that motivates a person's survival instincts. It is the driving force for his/her rectitude, dreams, and beliefs; thereby, transforming his/her commitments to achievements.

Fire knows no fear, doubt, shame or mercy. It scorches everything that stands in its way from accomplishing its goal. These are the reasons our

E.R.O.S./V.T.A. initiates had to pass through a ring of fire; to disarm our fears, doubts, shame, and to replace our negativities with joy, love, compassion, leadership, spirituality, insightfulness, dynamism, aggression, intuition, resourcefulness, and last but by no means least, expressiveness.

Gentlemen, I look forward to your thoughts and insights regarding your respective relationships with your various Big-Brothers and Valets.

Best wishes to the both of you.
David

Early in November 1968
Aboard Sindbad, Off the Coast of Tunisia

My private moment with my ex-patriarchs did not materialize, until the following evening at a Hammam in the medina quarter of Tunis.

When we finished our provocative photoshoot, the first light of dawn had slipped through the intricate latticework inside the Mosque of Olives. As the muezzin's call to Allah's devotees echoed through the tall minarets to summon the faithful to their morning prayers; our entourage disappeared unnoticed via a series of secret passageways and corridors.

We slept till the early afternoon before Emily, Joshua, Leon, together with Señor Victor Angel Triqueros joined Curt and me for a group lesson aboard *Sindbad*.

Eberhardt began, *"Sex roles, sex-role stereotypes, and sex-role socialization were the topics of my last tutorial with Young. I promise him that I will discuss gender fluidity in this session."*

He looked to Triqueros for a response.

"Curt, that is an interesting topic. Please start the discussion," the Señor responded obligingly.

My teacher gave me an adoring glance before he resumed, "Do any of you know the meaning of gender fluidity?"

None of us answered.

He continued, *"For some individuals, gender is not just being male or female. Their identification can change from day to day or from hour to hour. When gender expression shifts between masculine and feminine, gender fluidity are often displayed in the person's style of dress; the way he or she expresses and delineate themselves."*

"Other terms to describe gender fluidity are Genderqueer (GQ) or non-binary gender," Victor injected.

Eberhardt resumed, *"Gender fluidity conveys a broader, more flexible range of gender expression, with interests and behaviors that change from day-to-day. In some cases, from moment-to-moment. Folks that are gender fluid are not confined by restrictive boundaries of masculine or feminine stereotypes. Their gender identity extends beyond a person's behavior and interests. In other words, some days a person may feel they are more female than male while on others, the reverse holds true. There is the possibility that neither term describes them accurately."*

The Señor voiced, *"Think of the varieties of hues and shades in a color spectrum."*

He paused before he resumed, *"Visualize the most feminine expression you have seen or the most masculine you've come across. Now, put yourself somewhere between the feminine and masculine range, then you'll understand what we are getting at."*

"Does that mean, gender fluidity is the identification of what feels right for the person at a specific time/day or situation?" Emily queried.

Our professor answered, *"Emily, you are partially correct, but not entirely. Genderqueer is a catch-all category for gender identities that are not exclusively masculine or feminine. These identities are outside of the gender binary and cisnormativity.*

"Genderqueers can be classified as one or more of the following:

Having an overlap of, or indefinite lines between gender identity.

Having two or more genders; such as bigender, trigender or pangender.

Having no gender, like agender, nongendered, genderless, genderfree or neutrois.

Moving between genders or having a fluctuating gender identity (genderfluid).

Or being third gender or other-gendered; a category that includes those who do not place a name to their gender."

Victor edified, *"A person who is genderfluid prefers to remain flexible about their gender identity, rather than committing to a single gender. They may fluctuate between genders or express multiple genders at the same time.*

"On the contrary, an agender person ('a–' meaning "without"), also called genderless, genderfree, non-gendered, or ungendered, is someone who identifies as having no gender or being without gender identity. Although this category includes a broad range of identities that do not conform to traditional gender norms, people who identify with any of these stances may not necessarily self-identify as transgender."

I questioned, *"What are cisnormativity and transgender?"*

"I'll get to that," Curt announced. *"Cisgender (often abbreviated to simply cis) is a term for people whose gender identity matches the sex that they were assigned at birth. Cisgender may also be defined as those*

who have *'a gender identity or perform a gender role society considers appropriate for one's sex'; which is the opposite of transgender.*

"This brings me to transgender. *This term applies to those who have a gender identity, or gender expression that differs from their assigned sex. Transgender folks are sometimes called transsexual - if they desire medical assistance to transition from one sex to another."*

Professor Triqueros clarified, *"Transgender is also an umbrella term that includes those whose gender identity is the opposite of their assigned sex – such as transmen and trans-women. It may also include individuals who are not exclusively masculine or feminine - people who are genderqueer, e.g., bigender, pangender, genderfluid, or agender. There are many definitions of transgender; like folks who belong to a third gender, or conceptualize transgender people as a third gender. At times the term transgender can also include cross-dressers, regardless of their gender identity."*

Victor added, *"Being transgender is independent of sexual orientation. Transgender individuals may identify as heterosexual, homosexual, bisexual, asexual, and the list goes on. He or she may consider conventional sexual orientation labels inadequate or inapplicable. The term transgender can also be distinguished from intersex - a term that describes people born with physical sex characteristics 'that do not fit a typical binary notion of male or female bodies.'"*

Eberhardt gave me a quick glance, to keep my mouth shut about Penny's gender condition.

I took the hint and stayed silent.

Curt clarified, *"An individual who feels genuinely authentic, accept his or her identity, and is comfortable within his/her external appearance is known as transgender congruence.*

"Although, many transgender folks experience gender dysphoria and some may seek medical treatments such as hormone replacement therapy, sex reassignment surgery, or psychotherapy; not all transgenders desire these treatments. These treatments are expensive and are out of reach to many, nor can their medical condition undergo such intensive surgeries."

"How do I address a genderqueer person?" Joshua asked.

"That's a good question," Victor blazoned.

Our German professor advised, *"Some genderqueer folks prefer to use gender-neutral pronouns such as one, ze, sie, hir, co, ey, or singularly 'they,' 'their,' and 'them.' There are those who prefer the traditional gender-specific pronouns – 'her' or 'him.' While others prefer to be addressed as he and she. There are also those who like to use their name without pronouns. Titles such as 'Mx,' is an appropriate address instead of Mr., Ms., or Miss."*

Leon interposed. *"These terms sound awfully complicated. I can't remember them."*

"Don't worry boy, you'll familiarize with the idioms as time goes by."

These were the Señor's final words before our lesson came to a close. Triqueros pinched Leon, his clandestine lover lightly on the cheeks, as we readied ourselves to join our patriarchs at a Hammam in old Tunis.

Last Week of June 1968
Sharrow Bay, Lake Ullswater, Penrith, Lake District

On the final night of our stay at *Sharrow Bay*, I was awakened by a shimmering glow outside the French windows in the room I shared with Andy. I crept out of bed to the veranda without waking my lover. I gazed at the serene moonlit lake. An unanticipated radiance encircled my head. I could not delineate its glowing silhouette. The bright object fluttered back and forth around a flowering bush to look for an entrance in to our chamber. Bedazzled, I remained unmoved.

Through an open window, it darted towards my sleeping chaperone. An array of glistening fairy dust fell over my dormant lover. Instantly an irrepressible radiance befell him as if he was in an ebullient dream. He did not stir. Before I had time to adjust my vision, the sky-dancer was atop my head. It scattered golden dust upon my person.

Exuberance enveloped me as if blessed by a divine entity. Romanticism tingled my body. The dancing light disappeared as speedily as it had appeared. Suddenly I registered this animated object. I had seen it in *An A-Z Fairies Encyclopedia,* the **illustrated** book that Professor **Frederick** Thomason had gifted me after our meal at the Lakeside Restaurant. This sky-dancer was an *Asparas*.

I was transfixed by the serenity that conceals the mysteries of the other realm when a pair of sturdy hands reached around my waist. My lover's intoxicating breath caressed the sides of my tender neck. Excitement coursed through my person. A heightened warmness had nuzzled every fiber of my person and propelled me into an eroticism that was lustfully loving. By divine intervention and without mortal interference I was overpowered by my Valet's lubricious intensity.

His adoring fingers tweaked my perkiness to sturdy attention as I gyrated my yearning derriere against his hardened masculinity. Within this patio of idyllic delight, we craved to unite our blazing fervor.

Was it the winsome moonscape that had bewitched our youthful vitalities or did the *Asparas'* enchantments pixilated our emotions? This I will never know. What I do remember was our erotic intensities grew in potency as our sprightly essence merged in concatenation.

Andy glided his throbbing stiffness into my pulsating cleft and sent my frenzied soul to unbridled jubilations. Our mind, body, and spirit coalesced into an otherworldly existence, a weightless immersion of mystical transcendence. From above, I witnessed our copulation. A surreal, out-of-body experience that Andy and I had encountered during our time in India.

This subliminal providence catapulted our concupiscence to unconstrained lasciviousness. Like the drunken revelry of the *Celebrating Ellyllons*, our **lovemaking** impelled me off my feet. His fiery passion pierced my irrepressible hollow and hurled me to nirvanic ecstasy. Our covetousness ignited every filament of our buoyancies as he torpedoed into my chamber of love. Every crevasse of our longing orifices spurred us into a palpitating unit of wanton indulgence.

He drove into me with unencumbered deliverance as I laid against his bosom of amorousness. I welcomed his rapturous onslaught before I exploded onto our gliding torsos. His divinity poured into my twitching recess with aplomb and enshrouded my core to overcapacity. From my leaking portal, I scooped to share his bulbous remains.

This Valet, chaperone, Big-Brother, guardian, and lover never fails to intoxicate me. He was and still is my soulmate. In which my ex-professor, Victor Angel **Triqueros** chronicled so artfully as *Sahasrāra*; the blossoming of a 'thousand-petaled.' The White Lotus that encircled Andy and my sacred union within our *Garden of Supernal Love*.

PART TWO

Algeria – Algiers
Morocco – Casablanca, Marrakech, Atlas Mountains
England – Cotswolds, Thornbury, Cornwall, London,
Daltonbury Hall
Switzerland – Lucerne
United Arab Emirates – Dubai

Release & Allow (Chapter Eighteen)

"I don't put the truth in a cage. I try to find a way to release it."

William Hurt

Early in November 1968
Kasbah, Medina of Tunis, Tunisia

Kalf, the young Tunisian knew all the secret places where the underground gay local community hung out. He guided us to an inconspicuous colonial-style mansion that could have been a private residence. Located within the old al-Ḥimāya al-Fransīya fī Tūnis (French protectorate of Tunisia), this walled manor house once belonged to a wealthy French family, before it fell into disarray after the country gained its independence. Away from the prying eyes of the Islamic government, an independently wealthy European merchant transformed this dilapidated property into a secret Hammam; where he and his like-minded compatriots could have erotic rendezvous with the gay locals. Similar to the arcane bathhouse in Mecca where Najib and Ismile took us, this establishment housed an indoor swimming pool next to a communal hot tub. Wonted accouterments and services were also readily available. This includes the procurement of *Tellaks* (bathing attendants) for "private services."

After an intensive scrub-down by the burly masseurs, an opportunity to speak with my Arabian patriarchs arrived as we sat by the pool. Our conversation soon turned to *Genies*, the spirits of the Hammam.

"Did you know that Jinn are shapeshifters and they like to dwell in wet places?" Tad expressed.

The prince and the sheik gave their playfellow a wicked grin before P remarked, "I know you're one such Genii who knows no boundaries."

Tad chortled at his friend's declaration.

Fahrib added, "Like you, genies are wickedly naughty. Males and females love their unscrupulousness."

The trio burst out in laughter at their zingers.

The sheik resumed, "Do you know that Genii is the Latin word for Genius, the spirits that watch over every man. Genius is responsible for forming a man's character and actions."

"I'm not doing too badly in that aspect?" the athlete quipped.

The prince sallied, "You are doing pretty well in cuckoldries."

"I can do whatever I please I'm not married like the both of you," Tad expressed before he turned in my direction.

He asked, "What do you think, Young?"

"Your prowess is in excellent condition, sir," I quipped complimentarily.

"Tad, you do have a way with fairy boys," the prince jested.

"Sir, do you believe in fairies?" I asked.

"I believe in adorable 'fairies' like you," Fahrib opined amusingly.

"When Andy and I were in the English Lake District, I encountered real fairies. They have a message for my three munificent hosts," I announced.

"Tell us what the fairies said," P inquired entertainingly.

I related my spritely experiences to my Arabian patriarchs. By the time I finish, they had beseeched me with a series of questions to authenticate my faery encounters.

Even though Andy was not a staunch preternatural believer, he substantiated my proclamations. He also verified our conversations with both the fairy experts - Aunt Mary and Professor Frederick Thomason.

Siegfried who was born in the land of fairy legends also related his empirical anecdotes to our group. His input was a welcome verification to my preternatural sightings.

Señor Triqueros reasoned, *"Although Young's fairy pronouncements may sound outlandish, many parallel realms co-exist with our world and deforestation is indeed a major problem. It has resulted in ecological, environmental damages, biodiversity losses, and aridity are just a few dilemmas our planet is facing. Deforestation is a serious issue nations must address. Otherwise, humans and animals will suffer the apocalyptic effects of this ongoing adversity."*

I was surprised that our bathhouse discussion did leave a subliminal mark in my patriarchs subconscious. A few months later, the athlete and the sheik confided to me that they had pulled their investments from a significant Madagascan development venture. A project that involved the cutting down acreages of virgin forest. Although, neither Masters mentioned their withdrawals were due to my fairy communiqué; I had a premonition that my message from Queen Mab was of vital importance. I had fulfilled my promise to relay her missive to the Arab sovereigns.

Early in July 1968
Cirencester, Cotswolds, England

The six and half hour train ride from Penrith to Cirencester was nothing short of scenic. As the tranquil English country-scape flew by the carriage windows, I couldn't help but reminisce about my recent fay encounters. I had written down my thoughts and experiences in a journal since I first set foot in the United Kingdom, and my faerie encounters were no exception to the rule.

My Valet and I were on our way to visit Albert, our dear friend who was expelled from Daltonbury Hall after his excessive drug abuse and misconduct at our last Arabian household. He was also barred from the Enlightened Royal Oracle Society. His fall from grace was nothing short of painful for E.R.O.S., Daltonbury and the boy's family. Andy had carted Albert back to the *Assalamu Alaikum* household before he was dispatched posthaste to the "Rabbit-Hole" (Daltonbury Hall's private clinic) for interim treatment. Doctor Hunton (Rabbit-Hole's resident physician) consigned the lad to a professional rehabilitation center hitherto given leave to return to his parent's Cotswolds estate to convalesce.

Andy, Albert's responsible Big-Brother and ex-lover suggested we pay the teenager a visit to check on his progress. My chaperone had telephoned ahead to inform his ex of our stay. His family had kindly sent their chauffeured Bentley to collect us from Cirencester train station to Mr. and Mrs. Levenport's ancestral home. Sissinghurst Court was a well-kept Victorian profligacy with its glorious Oriental gardens, and Maharaja style palace was our lodging during our time at Sissinghurst Court. Albert, the Levenport's eldest boy, would eventually inherit this sprawling country mansion.

Upon my return to London after the Cotswolds, I was to join my mother and her entourage for a two-week European tour before I headed back to Daltonbury Hall to commence my new school year. In the final week of July 1968, Andy and I reconvened at school before we were dispatched to our next Arabian household.

Sissinghurst Court

Our luggage was placed in separate rooms by the Sissinghurst Court footman. My high ceiling chamber was decorated in the grandest of style. Royal blue velvet drapes edged with gold trailed the sides of its massive French windows that open onto a semicircular balcony. Fragrant roses entwined the ancient balustrades as if Romeo would climb its vines to woo his beloved Juliet. A vast canopied bed welcomed me to a good night's rest. Andy occupied an adjacent room down the corridor that was as scrumptiously furnished as mine.

Mrs. Genevieve Levenport, a regal woman in her early forties, greeted us at the entrance as soon as we embarked the Bentley. Dressed in a floaty silk caftan with a turbaned headdress, she guided us to the garden where we found our school chum lounging in the warm sun. He was delighted to see us, especially my Valet.

His affection for his ex-lover had not waned. He had hung on the hope that Andy would ride in like a chivalrous knight to sweep him off his feet again; even if he was aware that Andy and I had resumed our romantic liaison.

My time at E.R.O.S. had taught me not to interrupt my lover from doing what he desires. It is by granting him the freedom, he will return to me on his own accord, and our bond would thus become more resilient.

The Tour

When Genevieve offered to show me her munificent estate after tea, I accepted her invitation without hesitation, to give Andy time to catch up with his ex. Our hostess breathed a sigh of relief as soon as we were out of earshot from the duo.

"Thank you for coming to visit Albert. He misses the both of you," the lady of the manor declared.

"We miss him too. He is recuperating well," I remarked.

Mrs. Levenport looked disheartened. "It has been an uphill battle, especially for the poor boy, but he is recovering well. I'm grateful that he is substance free."

She paused and gave another sigh.

"I hope Daltonbury will reinstate my son. We vowed to Dean Higgins that our boy will not recidivate his drug use if he is readmitted."

She was in tears. My heart reached out to her.

"Andy and I will put in a good word to our headmaster to have Albert reinstated," I comforted.

"That would be wonderful. The both of you know my son better than me. He misses your friendship. Albert looks up to the both of you. His forlornness evaporated as soon as he heard Andy and you were visiting," the hostess commented.

"Albert is our cherished friend, and we are delighted to spend time with him," I answered encouragingly; even when the lad had not been pleasant to me in our last household.

My erudite Professor Triqueros precepts had not fallen on deaf ears. He had fortified me to forgo my past grievances and to forge a productive life. The moment I released my resentments, relief flooded my person, and my lightness of spirit returned with a vengeance.

I assured my hostess, "Andy and I will do our utmost to assist Albert. He's a good person. I'm glad to be his friend."

She held my hands to hers before she uttered, "I'm happy to hear you say that. It means a lot to my family. Our home is always open to the both of you."

I thanked her before we rejoined my Valet and his ex.

Third Week of July 2014
My Response to David's Message, Cc to Andy

Hi David,

My jealousy rose its ugly head when my roommate, John slept with my ex-big-brother. Nikee was my first love. When I espied their lovemaking, I felt as if my world had crumbled, yet I was bewitched by their eroticism.

Jealousy is painful to control. It remains an unconquerable emotion for me to this day. Luckily, under my mentors' guidance, I can decrypt this abhorrent sentiment.

These were Nikee's words on jealousy:

"Jealousy is an emotion that refers to the thoughts and feelings of insecurity, fear, concern, and anxiety over an anticipated loss of status, something or someone of great personal value; particularly a human connection. This emotion consists of anger, resentment, inadequacy, helplessness, and disgust."

He went on to clarify that jealousy is a human relationship experience; a culture-specific phenomenon and can be cynical or reactive. It is a reinforcement of a series of intense emotions, constructed as a universal human experience.

He also specified that there are different models of underlying jealousy processes, such as cultural beliefs and values. Both are important factors that trigger jealousy, and its socially acceptable expressions of this sentiment. Suspicion is also based on the religious views of a person's faith.

My ex-Big-Brother was quick to point out that sexual jealousy is prompted when a person's significant other displays sexual interest in another person. The feeling of resentment is as powerful if one partner suspects the other of infidelity. The fear that their partner - the one who is unfaithful may lie about their actions to protect their partner.

Many believe that sexual jealousy is a biological imperative. A part of the human and animal mechanism to ensure access to the best reproductive partners in heterosexual relationships. Male jealousy is often influenced by their female partner's menstrual cycle phase. Males display more mate-retention tactics around and before ovulation. Furthermore, men employ mate-retention tactics if their partner shows interest in other men, during the pre-ovulation phase.

My ex-professor, Alain Dubois also explicated that emotional jealousy is more responsive in females than in males. Women are more violent than men when experiencing similar sentiments.

There are distinct emotional responses to gender differences in romantic relationships. Alain cited that paternal uncertainty increases in males over sexual infidelity. Women are likely to be upset by signs of resource withdraw (i.e., another female) than by sexual infidelity.

He counseled that jealousy is a life stage or experience a person encounters to the diverse responses to infidelity. When both sexes are equally angry, the blame is often directed at the fornicator; even when women are more hurt by emotional infidelity than her counterpart. Anger surfaces when both parties involved are responsible for their unruly behavior when sexual behavior and actions are controllable. Hurt feelings are activated by relationship deviation.

Jealousy had remained a temporary emotion for me. I am grateful to be taught the stratagem to subdue this green-eyed monster before it rears its ugly head once again.

This is one reason, my relationships with my ex-Big-Brothers/Valets/mentors (be they sexual or otherwise) had remained graciously respectful and reverential.

I look forward to hearing about your relationships with your ex-chaperones/Valets and counselors.

Best wishes!
Young

Intimate Propositions (Chapter Nineteen)

"One of the things you learn in rehab is that you're responsible for your own actions."
Albert James Levenport

Early in November 1968
Hotel Saint George, Algiers, Algeria

The moment the bell boys deposited our luggage in the historic Hotel Saint George, Tad announced his impending departure to Argentina. The athlete's agent/manager, Horacio had sent word that he was needed at the *Campeonato Argentino Abierto de Polo (Argentine Polo Open Championship)* conference in Buenos Aires. The athlete's original plan was to return to England after our Maghribian vacation before heading to South America for the scheduled tournament in December.

Professor Eberhardt, my Master's personal trainer accompanied the athlete to Argentina. I was left in the care of Señor Triqueros. Since Andy and I were under Sheik Fahrib and Prince P's patronage, we continued our sojourn to Algeria and Morocco before following the Count to Paris and Asia to assist him in his *Sacred Sex in Sacred Places* photography and *Carousel* discotheque projects.

Hotel Saint George, built on the site of a former Arab-Ottoman palace opened for business in 1889. This opulent Moorish architectural jewel overlooks the Bay of Algeria. Luxuriant Arden surrounded its extensive grounds that housed a vast variety of Mediterranean herbaceous vegetation and birds. Celebrity lodgers, the likes of Edith Piaf, Simone de Beauvoir, General Dwight

D. Eisenhower, General Mark W. Clark, and Sir Winston Churchill had enjoyed this peaceful milieu.

The famous French essayist, novelist, and dramatist, Henri de Montherlant once said of this renowned establishment: *"I'm glad to experience Heaven on earth."*

This lodging, named after the English Patron Saint George was the preferred address for many English bourgeoisie at the turn of the twentieth century. Although the name has changed to El-Djazair, this guest house remains an affluent venue in the Algerian capital and continues to be a benchmark for all national and international personalities to savor and to relive the splendor of a bygone era.

In My Master's Suite

It was within this Corinthian splendor that Tad summoned me to his chamber before his departure to Buenos Aires.

As soon as I entered the room, the athlete announced, *"Young, I need your help."*

"How can I be of assistance?" I inquired.

He asserted, *"I want you to seduce Siegfried during dinner."*

I looked at the man, puzzled by his request.

"Why?" I asked.

"Because the German is in our way," he declared before he implored, *"Mario and I want to have a ménage à trois with Kalf. We've been flirting with the lad since we met. It is difficult to woo the boy when his boyfriend is unwilling to share his swag. I want to have a rendezvous with him before I leave for Argentina. Will you help us? You'll be rewarded handsomely."*

I did not know how to respond by such a request.

He continued, *"Even though Siegfried desires to bed you, and Kalf with Mario and me; the two aren't open about their covetousness for other men. They are jealous lovers."*

"Sir, aren't you playing a dangerous game? Those two were already proprietorial at our Al-Zaytuna Mosque erotic shoot. When we left the mosque, they were at each other's throats," I expressed.

"If they don't find out we are playing them, we'll be in for a home run," my Master answered mischievously.

"Will you help us make it a win-win situation for everyone involved?"

I paused before I replied, *"I'll have to run it by Andy."*

"I have a better idea. Get your chaperone involved in a ménage à trois with Siegfried. The both of you can show the German that an open-relationship is more pleasurable than monogamy," the athlete chirped excitedly. *"We must put my plan to action. We've no time to lose."*

"What if the plan backfires?" I opined with uncertainty.

"If you guys follow my instructions it wouldn't backfire," he assured.

By the time, I left my Master's chamber, he had planted his plan into my ear. Yet, I wavered to his deviousness.

Conversation with My Valet

Andy was waiting outside the Arab's chamber when I led him into the tranquil garden, I related my Master's proposal to my Valet.

"What do you think of Tad's plan?" I asked.

"First and foremost, before we consider his scheme, we must ask ourselves. Do we fancy Siegfried?" Andy questioned.

I nodded.

"I'll have a fling with the German if the opportunity arises. I do like to have a fling with him. He is not someone I will consider for a serious relationship. I don't have the affinity with him like I do with you," I answered ardently.

"Do you fancy him?" I asked.

My chaperone broke out in laughter. *"I knew that was coming. I'm game if the rendezvous involves you. Young, whatever makes you happy will also bring me joy."*

"You are the most generous person I know."

I kissed my lover affectionately before I recited Elizabeth Barrett Browning's poem:

"How do I love thee? Let me count the ways.
I love thee to the depth and breadth and height
My soul can reach, when feeling out of sight
For the end of being and ideal grace.
I love thee to the level of every day.'
The quietest need, by sun and candle-light.
I love thee freely, as men strive for right;
I love thee purely, as they turn from praise. I love thee with the passion put to use
In my old griefs, and with my childhood's faith.
I love thee with a love I seemed to lose
With my lost saints. I love thee with the breath,
Smiles, tears, of all my life; and, if God choose,
I shall but love thee better after death."

Tears trickled down Andy's cheeks when I finished my delivery. A sight I seldom witnessed from my chivalrous guardian. As we melted into each other's arms, our manhood stood to attention.

"Before we forge ahead we better wait until I share you with another," he muttered wickedly.

I quipped, *"Thank you for loving me unconditionally even when you want me all to yourself."*

We broke into hilarity as we empathized with one another in a way that was uniquely ours.

Early in July 1968
Sissinghurst Court, Cotswolds, England

Although Albert's father, Anthony Levenport was away on business, we were joined by Miss Lilian Levenport, Albert's younger sister. This bright and fluttery female was then preparing for boarding school in Switzerland. The siblings were inseparable when growing up, but since her brother's adversity, contriteness had overshadowed their once gregarious relationship. Even though her parents had exculpated their eldest, Lillian continued to blame her sibling for tainting her family's good name.

Like many wealthy adolescent, egocentricity centered around her self-absorption and she feared mockery from her friends and peers. The gossipmongers in her close-knit community made no effort to curb their wagging tongues and news of her brother's misdemeanor spread like wildfire. It caused more harm than good.

That evening, over dinner, the girl lashed out at Albert and accused him of embarrassing her. When Mrs. Levenport rebuked her daughter's nasty assault, she reproached her mother for siding with Albert. Lillian locked herself in her room and refused dinner.

"Thanks to you, dear brother, I'll never have friends again! I hate you! I hate you! I hate you!" she bellowed through shut doors.

Genevieve was shocked and distressed by her daughter's incongruousness. Through no fault of her own, the poor woman apologized to my Valet and me. Our hearts reached out to her.

I escorted Albert into the expansive garden for a breath of fresh air, while my gallant lover stayed to console the distraught lady of the manor.

Apologies

The Oriental garden was a welcome divergence to the stifling atmosphere within the mansion. Tears of regret welled up in my friend's eyes as we strolled in silence. I handed him my handkerchief.

"Thank you for coming to see me," the boy muttered sobbingly.

"You are my friend. I'm delighted to see you," I comforted.

"I'm humbled by your rectitude and integrity to forgive me; after what I did to you at our last household," he cried.

"It's our imperfections that make us perfect," I heartened. Even when it was difficult to say those encouraging words.

"Since my expulsion from E.R.O.S. and Daltonbury Hall, it has been an uphill climb. I'm grateful for Andy and your support even if I am aware that the worse is not over."

I emboldened my peer, "Time will evaporate our transgressions, and they will be distant memories."

"I'm sorry for snatching Andy away from you and for my spitefulness," the boy muttered regretfully.

"My friend, our roads are forged with victories and pitfalls. It is better to focus on our successes than the pits and the falls. I'm glad you are recuperating speedily," I fortified.

He held my hand to his.

"I miss our time together. I'm envious of the love you share with Andy," he confessed. "I'm sorry jealousy got the better of me."

Without saying a word, I kissed him on the lips. He did not move away. Although he was as handsome as when we parted, his once puerile attitude had morphed into amiability, and his recklessness had matured into a youthful refinement that was beguiling.

Like blossoming blooms, we sealed our friendship with an ardent kiss. Our lips stayed locked for what seemed like an eternity.

When we finally unfettered our bond, I whispered, *"Will you join Andy and me tonight?"*

He nodded anxiously as we headed back to the house.

Last Week of July 2014
David's Reply to My Email, Cc to Andy

Hi Young,

Although I was seldom jealous of my Valets and chaperones, there were times when I was envious of their authority. During my E.R.O.S./V.T.A. training, I embraced their puissance and was eager to emulate their jurisdiction when I became a Big-Brother.

When my worldliness broadened, I begrudged their twenty-four-seven supervisions. I wanted to be my own man until I faltered and ran to my chaperones for help. Like the majority of teenagers, I was full of myself and possessed little patience. There were times when my Valets had to bail me from ruckus situations I had gotten entangled.

Oh oh! My wife is yelling at me to be ready. I forgot I had a scheduled appointment to attend to. I will share contretemps with the two of you in my next correspondence.

Chat soon.
David

Ménage à Trois (Chapter Twenty)

> "Siegfried exclaimed, "A three-way? You're kidding, right?"
> "Oou! A ménage à trois! Don't knock it 'til you've tried it," I replied."
>
> Young
> (A Harem Boy's Saga – V – Metanoia; a memoir by Young)

Early November 1968
Restaurant Le Saint George, Algiers, Algeria

Our entourage dined at Restaurant Le Saint George, the hotel's French/Algerian bistro, the evening before Tad's departure to Buenos Aires. I was sandwiched between Siegfried and Andy at the circular table while Kalf sat between Tad and Mario. The rests of our party surrounded us on either side.

I put my Master's plan into action as dinner progressed. I stroked my foot against Siegfried's ankle.

The German gave me a dispassionate glance and a wicked smile. He did not move his foot away but focused his attention on the chitter-chatter around the table. Embolden by his insouciance, I continued to slide my foot against his calf. He remains poised.

My astute Valet who was aware of the footsies below, slipped his hand in mine to galvanize my impudence. Before long, my toes had made its way into Siegfried's trouser leg. Although aroused by my unbridled provocations, he stayed unfazed. Just when I was doubtful if my seduction was active, the German took my hand and placed it on his crotch.

I titillated the bulge behind his pants. Before I had time to consider my next move, both Siegfried and Andy's hands were on my groin. Even though the German was befuddled, he remained aloof.

This hidden eroticism aroused us enormously. Across the table, Tad and Mario winked at me mischievously; a sign that my Master's plan was progressing effectively.

By the time we finished dinner, Andy had already slipped a note to invite Siegfried to our chamber for digestifs. Although Siegfried made no mention of our offer, his impish grin told us that he had accepted our provocation.

The German had already fabricated an excuse to his boyfriend so he could disappear without suspicion. This he did with enthusiasm and guilt. It was only after our exhilarant lovemaking that his remorse took hold, and triggered Siegfried and Kalf's passion to an end. Although the Tunisian was equally guilty of infidelity, he showered the blame on the German. In truth, both parties had harbored undisclosed fornications from one another in the past. Their hidden conundrums would soon bleed to the surface after a massive blowout. Several days after their respective three-way tryst, the duo separated in anguish discontentment.

Ménage à Trois

At the appointed hour, skittery Siegfried arrived at our suite. He relaxed instantly after he gulped down the Cognac Andy had fixed him.

I remarked, *"I'm glad you are able to get away."*
He kept silent.

I planted a kiss on his forehead. He did not move away. Instead, he kissed me passionately as if eager to cut to the chase. I dawdled to calm his nerves, yet he wasted no time to explore my oral fissure. It was evident that this man's sexual experiences were that of the "wham-bam-thank-you-man" variety. A sexual vocabulary that Andy and I found unfulfilling and unsated in our erotic encounters.

For Tad to accomplish his conquest that was happening simultaneously in the Count's boudoir down the hall, Andy and I had to prolong our foreplay and intercourse for this *ménage à trois* to play out successfully.

Siegfried did not take long to embrace my rhythmic groove. His pressing kisses soon morphed into an abiding French osculation. The digestif and Andy's participation soothed the man's nervousness.

I undid the German's dress shirt to reveal a chest of alluring curls while Andy freed the man's drumming hardness from his constrictive pants. Like a bumblebee attracted to an inviting stigma, I buried my face against his masculinity and nibbled at his protruding nipples to harden pruriencies.

I worked my lips down his firm belly to savor every inch of his heaving torso while Andy sucked the man's throbbing length. Together, we twirled our gliding tongues around Siegfried's glistening bulbousness to relish his expanse within our oral fissures. In preparation for his impending onslaught, my lover jabbed his curling tongue into the man's anal cavern while the German nursed my throbbing stiffness with glee. He luxuriated at my swell when I straddled his hairy chest. Andy and I plowed into the man without reservations.

My chaperone tied the ecstatic Siegfried to the wrought iron headboard. To gratify our palpitating manhoods, we took turns to splice into his orifices. Not only did our raunchiness trigger the German's jubilation, but his supplications also stirred us to buoyant exultations.

Andy was the first to shoot his ebullience into the man's quivering sanctuary and prompted the submissive to blast his blossoming swells onto my stirring palm. I wasted no time to ply his deposits onto my lover's pulsating shaft and guided Andy into my yearning hollow. My lover's stroking hardness and caressing hand precipitated my blissfulness to gush onto his palm. My deposits, the three of us shared.

I had a presage that my Master's plan had proceeded accordingly by the time I wrapped my arms around my lover in a peaceful slumber.

First Week of August 2014
Continuation of David's Message to Andy and Me

Hi Young,

Forgive my rapid sign off in my previous email. I was about to relate an experience I had with my Big-Brother/Valet, Steven during our Art of Sensuality lesson at the *Bahriji*.

I had mentioned my enviousness of my Big-Brothers. They seem to effortlessly attract the attention of swooning males and females into their boudoirs. I desperately wanted to imitate their self-assurance and pragmatism.

I remember the training I had with Maria, a beautiful *Bahriji* student. It did not take long for my Big-Brother to arouse her excitement. He motioned for me to join in a *ménage à trois*. I was already oozing with excitement from observing Steven's sensual tongue pry open her hot lips.

He caressed her young breasts as if he was nibbling at a couple of ripening cherries atop a rich cake. The female melted into his arms as my BB twitched and tweaked her perkiness to attention before he guided my mouth to wean on her nipples. I suckled her succulence like a newborn for nourishment while she squirmed in ecstasy. When Steven jabbed into her breach, I bit her knobs like a teething infant. Our actions prompted her vagina to flow exuberantly.

Aroused by their stimulus, I throbbed unceasingly. My BB guided the girl's mouth to my youthfulness. She basked on my virility while Steven's fingers probed her sanctuary. He kissed me passionately and guided my hand to stroke his protuberance. These sensual variants heightened my libidinousness to a premature release. Thanks to my tutor's acumen, he gripped my swell to halt my sudden release and enabled me to resume our foreplay without premature ejaculation.

When his exploring fingers invaded my anus, I was in erotic euphoria. It was a sensation I had never felt before until then. I was hooked on this enticing stimulation. I imitated my Big-Brother's actions and coaxed him to deliverance.

The sight of their eroticism hurled me over the edge. I blasted my seed onto Steven's palm as he catapulted his load on mine. His fingers continued to nuzzle Maria's pulsating clitoris to rapturousness. Her wetness coated our instructor's hand.

Before our sensuality lesson ended, we shared our deposits in a tender three-way kiss.

I never forgot this effervescent experience.

Guys, I look forward to reading Andy and your narratives. ☺

Best wishes!
David

Early in July 1968
Sissinghurst Court, Cotswolds, England

I crept quietly into Andy's chamber in the stillness of the night. A golden head of hair was already bobbing up and down my Valet's groin in the dimly lit boudoir. I knew Albert had beaten me to my lover's bed as I looked on in awe. My chaperone beckoned and pulled me to him. Soon, our adoring touch morphed to a desirous French kiss. He stared at me beguilingly as his hands stroked my affection to attention. I was intoxicated by his aggressive masculinity. Albert, enraptured by our oral fervency continued to pleasure his ex.

As if his sexual craving had not been gratified since his expulsion, the lad devoured our phalluses in a single gulp before he caressed our heaviness with avidity. The warmth of his oral stimulation teased our salaciousness to a frenzy.

We jabbed our tongues into his anal fissure as he knelt in supplication. He welcomed our invasions into his pleasure dome before he straddled Andy's stiffness. When I guided my manhood into his twitching hind, the teenager was already jouncing in delight at our BB's impaling length. We glided In synchronicity into Albert's tautness as he moaned and groaned in ecstasy. We were again united physically like we had welcomed Albert into our midst, the first time.

His hollow craved our bulbousness as we rocked our fulfillments into his affinity. His ribaldrous jubilance spurred Andy and me towards our release. We exploded into his tightness and coated the lad with our dripping rhapsodies.

Unable to withhold his deliverance, Albert thundered his libation over and above our lover's chest. We enshrined our spritely afterglows in contentment as we shared his residuum among us. Wrapped around each other, we fell into a peaceful slumber until the sparrows' morning songs beckoned us back to our respective chambers in silence.

Angelic Visions (Chapter Twenty-One)

"Philosophy will clip an angel's wings."
John Keats

Early July 1968
Thornbury Castle, Thornbury, South Gloucestershire, England

Our two days at Sissinghurst Court flew by quickly. Albert, Andy and I sat outdoors enjoying an afternoon tea at the Thornbury Castle restaurant. This eatery was operated by one of United Kingdom's top restaurateur; Kenneth Bell, and his culinary staff that included food critic Nigel Slater and master chef Simon Gault. Mrs. Levenport had recommended this locale and insisted we spend some quality time at this historic venue.

Andy enquired of Albert, *"There's a lot to be said about country living. It helped your speedy recovery."*

Our friend replied sheepishly, *"It's been a struggle. Thanks to my guardian angel, I made some extraordinary progress."*

I chirped, *"I didn't know you believe in angels? I thought comic books is what you care about."*

My Valet gave me an unappealing glance to admonish my inappropriate comment.

"Tell us your angel encounters," my chaperone queried. *"How did that come about?"*

Albert began, *"It started a night when I was in withdrawal at rehab. My cocaine craving was so intense, I wanted to escape to look for a peddler. No escape route was available except to break the window in my room. I was about to wreak the glass when I noticed a transparent* glow outside. I couldn't tell if the imagery was a fragment of my imagination or for real. The light glided through the window and transformed into a winged entity. I was dumbstruck.

"The being wrapped his wings around my person while my inner demons incited me to break the window and escape...."

Before Albert could continue, I interjected, *"How did you know the entity is male?"*

The boy resumed, *"The scent gave him away. It smelled like a mixture of fresh eucalyptus, musk, frankincense, and myrrh. As if I was divinely possessed, a surge of positive energy coursed through my body when I was embedded within his translucent musculature. Never had I encountered such an experience before."*

"What happened to your inner demons?" I asked curiously.

"They dissipated when the angel embraced me," Albert answered assuredly.

"What transpired after that?" Andy queried.

"The angel held me in bed, and I fell into a peaceful slumber. He was gone when I awoke the next morning, but his scent lingered. After his visitation, I grew stronger and more resilient to future relapses," the lad responded guardedly.

A compulsion swept over me to declare, *"Shall we pay a visit to Dr. Olivier Augustin in Cornwall?"*

"Who?" the duo exclaimed concurrently.

"He is the angelology professor, whom Dr. Frederick Thomason recommended we visit in Marazion, Cornwall," I stated.

"Young, are you insane? Cornwall is a three-and-half-hour drive from here," my guardian blurted.

Albert championed, *"What a superb idea. It'll be a nice outing for us. Michael, my family's chauffeur can drive us in one of our cars."*

We looked to Andy for his approval, which he gave reluctantly.

Second Week of November 1968
Ketchaoua Mosque, Algiers, Algeria

The inevitable happened in this Moorish-Byzantine house of worship. Our entourage obtained permission from the Ketchaoua Mosque's Iman, for our erotic photo shoot, the morning before we sailed to Morocco. Once again, we were hard at work before worshipers and visitors descended at this historical mosque.

Was it coincidence or Count Mario's purposeful orchestration, I would never know. I was teamed with Siegfried for an intimate coupling photo session. When we met in passing after our three-way rendezvous, the German had been cordial. Siegfried had already downed several glasses of hard liquor to calm his nerves by the time we stripped bare. Whether he drank to mask his guilt or to calm his nerves, his phallus was already at attention before we laid hands on one another.

As soon as we began our provocative pose, his tongue was eager to pry open my mouth to receive him. I went with the flow. The photographer clicked away to obtain the best angle when Siegfried pinned me against an ornate pillar. Excited to witness our lubricious proclivity, Mario handed my Valet a cord to tie my hands above my head as the German's pearly fangs sank into my tender neck. Like a vampire and his victim in heat, we moaned and groaned in ecstasy as our hardness massaged against one another.

Kalf watched with fury at our throes of passion. His indignation grew as Siegfried's unbridled foreplay continued to titillate me. Like a hungry infant, the German clenched my buttocks to suck my bouncing propensity deep into his yearning mouth. His oral play elevated my vulnerability to amplified proportions. As his probing fingers explored my holy sanctum, lecherous arrows of fiery passion pierced through my irrepressible weakness. For a moment, I envisioned myself as Saint Sebastian; a saint, an angel, and a martyr, all rolled into one.

The Tunisian, no longer able to bear the sight of our fervid copulation stormed out of the premise. In the hope to un-fluster the teenager's boiling emotions, **Señor Triqueros** and Andy followed the lad.

Neither photographer nor Siegfried made any effort to curtail the shoot. Instead, Mario coaxed us to greater arousal by encouraging the German to burrow his tongue into my derriere. I arched my hind to welcome him into my fold before I offered my succulence to his palpitating stiffness. He plowed into me with avidity.

The knowledge that Kalf was in a state of trepidation augmented my licentiousness. It also intensified my self-gratification. Was I obtuse to the feelings of others or was this perverseness innate in all humans? This is a question I had no answer to this day. The thing I was profoundly aware of was the emotional intensity I felt when the German fired his mastery into my hankering cloven. What I didn't know then, was, he had plied me as his scapegoat for his fatal relationship. I was "the other man" - the one to blame. The German and the Tunisian don't ask, never tell policy had jeopardized their relationship that was too late to salvage.

Before Siegfried released me, he whispered, *"You're a beautiful angel."* I did not respond. I was glad, he did not say, he was in love with me.

The Pandemonium

As I packed away the Count's photography equipment after the shoot, a livid Kalf stormed into the prayer hall. He splattered a string of raging obscenities at both Siegfried and me before he kicked his boyfriend in the groin. The German howled in pain. The angry Tunisian headed in my direction before I could escape. My Valet was at the ready to block the madman from causing further injuries. Thanks to my beloved, I did not suffer any physical injuries, except for a series of verbal vulgarities that splattered like wildfire around the sacred hall. Siegfried swore the denouement of their relationship as he cupped his groin in agony. Kalf's unruly insolence had us in shock.

To our surprise, the Count caught hold of the screaming Tunisian and planted a passionate kiss on the foul-mouthed lad. We watched in disbelief as the machismo photographer transformed the indignant Kalf into an obedient serf. Like a sacrificial lamb, he melted into the Italian's arms and was ready to be possessed.

Seigfried broke the silence and hollered at his lover for being a wretched whore and **pathological** liar this side of the Maghreb before he stormed out of the mosque in a huff.

In truth, both parties were to blame. Rather than with honesty, their partnership was built on lustful possessiveness and distrust, and could never withstand the tornado that had just swept through the prayer hall. I was glad that we, E.R.O.S. recruits were taught to abide by our society's honorable code - *The truth will set you free.*

After that tumultuous spectacle, the unamused and disapproving Ketchaoua clerics could not wait to shepherd us out of that historic structure. We were long gone before any devotees arrive at the venue where our flagitiousness had taken place a few hours earlier. By the time the call to prayer was broadcasted through the minarets speakers, our entourage was already aboard the الثاقب السهم (*Piercing Arrow*) and *Sindbad* to Morocco.

Our tongues wagged over the Count and Kalf's carnal covetousness. For one, my Master, Tad, would not be a happy camper if he found out that the apple-of-his-eye had fallen head-over-heels with his bosom buddy. Our entourage speculated that their outrageous ménage à trois was doomed for failure since the trio were as promiscuous as one another. On the contrary, some of us surmised that it may work wonderfully because they could bask in their bacchanalian revelries.

While Andy and I were safe on the *Sindbad*, the Tunisian was on board the *Piercing Arrow*. As for Siegfried, he had disappeared post haste and left us to ponder his whereabouts. That was the last I saw of the German.

Second Week of August 2014
Andy's Message to David and Me

D avid,

The relationships I had with my five charges were vastly different from yours. Although at times I wish Young hadn't put his foot in his mouth, he was an angel. By and large, this ex-charge of mine was the best and most acquiescent Little-Brother under my care. We have our quirks and idiosyncrasies, and it is our imperfections that make us perfect.

Besides Young, Albert (another charge of mine) proclaims to have divine visions. Though I'm not a firm believer in the preternatural, I do believe in a higher power. Messages from the uncharted are not to be dismissed but decoded by the receiver.

Some people receive their communiqué through visions while others hear weird sounds. Even if the messenger or messengers are beyond my sagacious comprehension, I acknowledge all forms of higher emanations with an open heart and mind.

The years I was with Young, we spoke to several psychics, mystics, and clairvoyants. They unanimously informed me that my charge is from the angelic realm and I respect their dictums. Although Young can see angels and other mythical entities, I had never witnessed any paranormality. But I empathize with his preternatural sightings.

I like to hear Young's take on this topic since he had had visions.

I look forward to your comments, David.

Yours,
Andy

Where Is The Love? (Chapter Twenty-Two)

"Love is the only force capable of transforming an enemy into a friend."

Martin Luther King, Jr.

Second Week of November 1968
Sailing to Casablanca aboard *Sindbad*, Morocco

My Valet had a word with me as I watched the waves rolled by.

"*What is going on between you and Professor Eberhardt?*" my chaperone enquired.

I answered ignorantly, "*What do you mean?*"

"*I mean what I said. What's going on between the two of you? There is more to your student/teacher relationship, isn't there? I noticed his special farewell embrace with you. He seems reluctant to leave you,*" Andy questioned.

I remained silent.

He resumed, "*I can tell you are hiding a secret. You know I'll find out sooner or later. You better fess up, boy,*"

"*Will you be angry with me if I tell you what transpired?*" I replied culpably.

"*It depends on what you're going to tell me,*" he expressed.

I snuggled into his arms and looked him in the eyes before I uttered, "*I love you very much....*" I trailed off since I was unsure how to paraphrase my delivery.

"*That I know. And...,*" my lover pressed.

I continued, "*And..., I'm also in love with my erudite educator.*"

Andy murmured impassively, *"Tell me everything from the beginning."*

My lover listened attentively. After a long silence, he spoke. *"Young, our relationship is built on integrity. Even though it came as no surprise, I respect you for telling me the truth. As you are aware, I am open to loving the people you love. There is no reason why the three of us cannot have a triplet affinity...."*

I interjected, *"Like we had with Oscar?"*

He nodded before he resumed, *"Is Curt open to such an arrangement?"*

"I don't know. We can ask my teacher when we see him in a few weeks," I responded heedfully.

"Are you open to another trois affaire de coeur?" he inquired.

"I'm happy to give it another try," I chirped before I added, *"That is if you are okay with such an arrangement."*

He opined, *"Although I like to have you for myself, I am open to the prospect of sharing our love with another if Curt is in accordance. I trust Eberhardt is an ethical man and will love you unconditionally like I do."*

"Let's put forth this idea to him and see what he says," I finalized.

Possessed by Love

The morning we arrived in Casablanca, Señor Triqueros gathered his students for our regular tutorials aboard *Sindbad*.

"I've invited a guest speaker to give us some insights on Maghrebian culture and romance," he announced.

We looked around to see who the mystery rhetorician was. There was none other except our cerebral professor.

He continued, *"Not only is our knowledgeable guest familiar with the Maghreb; he was also a fellow classmate of mine at the University of Paris-Sorbonne. This Belgian sociology educator is currently teaching at the newly opened Lycée Lyautey in Casablanca.*

"He has agreed to enlighten the four of you on the topic of 'Sexuality and Romance in Morocco.' Join me to welcome Professor Boch Van-Damme." Victor waved to a speedboat that had pulled up next to the *Sindbad*.

A suave looking man in his early thirties stepped aboard our yacht.

We applauded his entrance.

We shook hands before the Belgian positioned himself next to Triqueros.

The man began, *"We, in the Western Hemisphere, seldom hear about romantic love in the other parts of the world especially in non-Western cultures. This misconception has led many to believe that romantic love is a western invention."*

He paused before he resumed, *"Today's lesson we are going to explore this rhetorical question from the Maghrebian Arab Muslim cultural standpoint. Let's start with the Arab poetic tradition that had influenced European notions of courtly love. After that, we can examine the ideas of Muslim authors and scholars and their Islamic positions and influences about sexuality, love, and relationships.*

He added, *"Finally, we will search for evidence of these ideas in contemporary Maghrebian youth about their experiences of love; especially when marriages are often arranged by their parents as opposed to those desired by the couple and approved by their parents.*

"It is a fact that when young women are strongly attracted to potential suitors, her female pragmatism often precedes romanticism. While her counterpart, the male, is more likely to be 'possessed' or 'blinded' by romantic love."

Triqueros injected, *"In our modern society, most people 'fall-in-love' before selecting a long-term partner, spouse or spouses. Although in most of the world's cultural history, this has not been the primary criterion for marriage. Marriage was and still is an alliance between families."*

"Yet, the idea of romantic love is becoming an essential factor; not just in the Maghrebian Arab Muslim culture but across the globe. In the western part of the Arab world; Islam is pro-love and tolerant of sexuality when sanctioned by marriage," Professor Van-Damme stated before he went on to correlate.

"A Tunisian Iman once proclaimed, 'Unity is attained by the affirmation of Eros. God himself is a being in love with his own creatures. From the thing to the Supreme Being, love exists as a guarantee of unity.' He then went on to declare that sexual pleasure in marriage is both a privilege and a duty. On conjugal bliss, he described this emotion as a foretaste of paradise and a proof of God's love.

"On the other hand, Islamic accounts of love and sexuality often conclude that this divine model is seldom attained by humans. The rhetoric of love and erotic passion sanctioned by Islam has often led to the unleashing of excessive libidinal force, and to the subjugation of women as the objects of male lust."

Victor chimed, *"Doesn't this subjugation turn the woman into a plaything, a doll? Does it not limit love to the ludic and reduces the wife to a woman-object; whose sole function is for the satisfaction of her husband's sexual pleasure?"*

Van-Damme nodded smilingly. He resumed, *"This act does indeed reduce conjugal affection to mere pleasure. Whereas, desire is only an element to a larger equation. One often valorized the mother by stressing the child-bearing role of women.*

"A contemporary Arab scholar once contends that the privileged and circumscribed role of the child-rearing Arab Muslim mother have created a cult of the mother being the modal personality styles in 'Arab-Muslim' societies."

Triqueros questioned, *"What are the consequences of this personality structure?"*

Boch replied, *"They include the different responsibility for control of one's passions. The male is permitted freer rein, and in instances of fornication, the female is usually the one to blame. Since a mother-child bond holds the strongest tie in their society; women are idealized nurturers and sex-objects.*

"You see, the mother-centered Arabian household challenges the male child within a world of women. A female world which he will eventually renounce. This early immersion within a society of mothers, aunts, and sisters have erotic implications. For example, the boy is taken to the hammam (public baths) by his mother. This and other experiences of physical intimacy with women leave a legacy of charged images that are evoked in the context of adult sexual activity; thus fabricating the 'Arab woman as the queen of the unconscious. More than she is the queen of the home or of the night'.

"It is this ambivalent and primal femaleness which Arab scholars believe that the adult male faces in the Aisha Qandisha jinniya - the North African jinn-like being who possesses men and makes them her sexual slaves. Behind the idealized image of the pious and pure mother/sister is an antithetical fantasy of a fallen woman who is lustful, seductive, and dangerous."

Emily commented, *"Can you expand further on the Aisha Qandisha jinniya myth?"*

Señor Triqueros remarked, *"Please allow Professor Van-Damme to continue. I'll tell you more about the jinniya in another tutorial."*

The Belgian recommenced, *"Many Arab men are obsessed by the anti-wife, whom they seek in every possible form. From dancers, film stars, singers, prostitutes, to tourists and neighbors. The list goes on. This ludic and the severe disassociation continue and become a stumbling block to the sexual emancipation of men and of women within the Arab world.*

"North African contemporary societies are experiencing a sexual and religious crisis as women move beyond their traditionally assigned roles; while the men resist this change.

"Nowadays, Arab females strive to renounce the illusory kingdom of their mothers and aspire to a more affirmative and positive mantle, rather than mythopoeic. She is determined to affirm her ability to give: like 'I give love. Therefore I am love.' Yet there is an ambiguity in the concept of female liberation as if the partners could be dissociated from the question. If Arab men are not already severed by his own masculinity, he could then free himself."

Before Van-Damme could progress, our teacher conveyed, *"Boch, can you enlighten us on the gender differences in contemporary Moroccan society, and the relation of these disparities to Muslim history and its modern political and economic conditions?"*

The Belgian scholar answered earnestly, *"The Moroccan sociologist Fatima wrote several famous works on this topic. She argues that gender politics are rooted in Islam, and it reveals the political issues facing North African society today.*

"She alleges that the conservative wave against women within the Muslim world is a defense mechanism against profound changes in the roles of the sexes and in the hypersensitive topic of sexual identity. She points to an accurate interpretation of this male conservatism, that often resort to women turning to magic and superstitious rituals. It's an anxiety-reducing mechanism within the world of shifting, volatile sexual identity.

"She also asserts that in contrast to Muslim praise of legitimate sexual pleasure; conjugal intimacy threatens the believer's single-minded devotion to God. Hence the 'loving couple' is dangerous to religious society, while many Muslim clerics assert that the true basis of Islam is unity through love – be it attainable or not. Fatima concludes that 'the entire Muslim social structure is an attack on, and defense against, the disruptive power of female sexuality.' Her argument comes from the concept of fitna (chaos, temptation, trial, enchantment or distress, that is often applied to fornication). This, she contends is the embodiment of a woman's erotic potential for society to maintain its equilibrium. She went on to claim that from the time of the Prophet Mohammad; males have felt the need to veil and seclude women. And to circumscribe sexual activities with rule and regulations to shield men from women's seductive potential. Therefore, she ascribes that female sexuality is the force that drives erotic relationships in heterosexual encounters, and it fits well with the role of romance and magic. She also implies that the male is simultaneously anxious about his physical yearnings, and the loss of autonomy. By casting the woman as the agent of unrestrainable lust, he projects his fears and desires onto the female."

The arrival of the prince and the sheik punctuated our lesson. We were ferried to an eighteenth-century fortified bastion, north of Casablanca's city center; for a scrumptious savoir-faire, that only the *Marocain en français* knew how to prepare.

Third Week of August 2014
My Reply to Andy and David

Hi guys,

Sorry for my delayed response. The past week I've been swamped with work. First and foremost, I like to thank Andy for singing my praises. I'm humbled by his love and for holding me on a pedestal. I'm by no means an angel. Like all humans, I have foibles and idiosyncrasies even though my ex-lover/Valet chose to see me otherwise. ☺

Without further ado, I'll tend to the question at hand. My relationships with my ex-Valets and BBs had always been earnest and profound. I am grateful for their loving guidance and altruism, especially from Andy. I admire his inner strength and extraordinary gallantry. He was always at the ready to soothe the belligerent patches I had gotten into.

As the both of you are aware, our Arabian patriarchs, matriarchs, and their household members were not the easiest to please. The ego tends to incite excessive rapaciousness with wealth and power. I managed to outmaneuver these volatile minefields with ease and grace with the counsel of my Valets, BBs, and teachers. Without their skillful supervisions, I would have gotten myself into a ruckus. There were instances when the adolescent *moi*, acted defiantly. But when all was said and done, I scampered for their assistance. Their valuable advice helped me to cope with chaotic situations. I am grateful and thankful to my mentors for their unconditional love and unfading devotion.

David, I will address the subject of angelology in my next email. I wish you guys the very best.

Regards,
Young

The Down (Chapter Twenty-Three)

"Feathers appear when angels are near."
                                        Bernard Tristan Foong

Early in July 1968
Marazion, Cornwall, United Kingdom

Since our arrival at Sissinghurst Court, Mrs. Levenport was happy to see her son's radiance return. She was more than delighted to loan her family's chauffeur and car for our three-day sojourn to Cornwall. We agreed to deliver Albert back to the Cotswolds before Andy, and I left for London after our trip. I met Uncle James, my mother and her accompanying entourage for a two weeks' vacation in Europe; while my Valet stayed in London to spend time with his mother and siblings.

Little was I aware that my mum had gotten wind of my affair with my Big-Brother/Valet and chaperone. The real reason for her European tour was to whisk me away to obtain the truth about Andy and my relationship from *moi*. In the event I did not fess up, the accompanying aunties and cousins were drill sergeants to assist her to get the score.

But for the moment, Andy, Albert and I were absorbed in each other's company, and to enjoy the scenic drive from the Cotswolds to Cornwall. A crystal blue sky greeted our arrival at Cornwall's coastal town of Marazion. Half a mile offshore was the infamous *Karrek Loos yn Koos* (Cornish); better known as Saint Michael's Mount. This small National Trust tidal island was made passable to Marazion between mid-tide and low water via a causeway of granite setts. Passenger boats carry visitors between the two destinations during high tide.

The civil parish of Marazion was and still is lined with art galleries and curio shops. This enchanting community is where fantasy becomes a reality. When we finally arrived at *The White Unicorn*, a charming restaurant overlooking the water reverie washed over me.

The Angelologist

Andy had called ahead to Dr. Augustin before our arrival, and the angel expert had agreed to meet us at *The White Unicorn* upon our arrival. He was eager to hear Albert and my angelic encounters. When we stepped through the eatery, a suave looking gentleman welcomed us. He had on a pale blue suit, cream colored shirt with a matching polka dot bowtie, striped socks and a pair of tan colored loafers completed his ensemble.

He extended his hand to ours when he took off his Panama hat. I was enthralled by his youthfulness, and graceful mannerisms, not to mention his rich alto voice which reminded me of an operatic maestro. Dr. Olivier Augustin would be Sergei Diaghilev clone if the impresario were still alive. This retired professor also possessed a certain *je ne se quoi*, that Gustav von Aschenbach in the 1912 novella - Death in Venice would be proud of.

During my teenage life, I had encountered many debonair, but none had left such an astounding impression as this sophisticated angelologist opposite me at *The White Unicorn*.

He declared, *"You guys come highly recommended by my longtime friend, Professor Frederick Thomason. He told me about your fairy encounters."*

"It is Young who had the fairy encounters with Dr. Thomason." My Valet looked at me to comment.

No words came out. I was tongue tight in the presence of this illustrious gentleman. As if I had committed a crime, I nodded sheepishly.

Dr. Augustin stared at me intently and gave me a kindly smile.

"Don't be bashful, young man. I'm here to shed light on your preternatural experiences, not to intimidate you. Tell me about your angelic encounters?" he expressed.

"Albert can go first," I chirped.

While my friend explained his angelic contretemps, I was spurred into an out-of-body transcendence. As if I have extrasensory perception I saw through the angelologist guise. Concealed by his aging exterior was a pair of folded wings tugged snugly against his muscular back. Hidden behind his spectacled eyes were bright beams that saw through a person's identity. Golden effervescence encircled his receding hairline. His wrinkled face was not of a transitory man but a glowing immortal.

Although I was aghast by what I saw, I maintained equipoise. When Oliver turned his attention on me, his **obsecrated look** silenced my extemporaneousness. I knew instantly, I was face to face with divinity. **This man was a seraphic messenger. His mission was to illuminate and guide those who have had supernatural experiences and assist them in finding meaning in their celestial engagements.**

Angels

When Albert finished his angel narration, the professor spoke. *"My dear boy, angels are spirit entities and can assume different guises. Often, they take on a familiar form when they appear to an individual. Their task is not to frighten the person. Your heavenly vision is only* *comprehensible to you, and you alone can decipher the meaning of the angel's manifestation.*

"In the Jewish, Christian and Islamic traditions, angels are unseen apparitions that carry out God or Allah's bidding in care of 'His' flock. These numinous messengers assume different physical forms. Most humans are unaware they'd encountered angels."

I queried, *"How often do angels appear as humans?"*

"More often than you realize. In the biblical text: Hebrews 13:2, it states: 'Do not forget to entertain strangers, for by so doing some people have entertained angels without knowing it.' This passage clearly states that at any time it is possible *to encounter angels without the person/persons being conscious of their preternatural nature,"* Dr. Augustin explicated.

I glanced at the man meaningfully.

He added, *"You see, Young when an angel or angels appear, they often materialize in a configuration that is characteristic of those living in that area."*

He glinted at me surreptitiously before he resumed, *"I'll cite you some examples: in biblical times, Abraham's angels dressed and looked like the people of his day. On the other hand, an Andean missionary saw an angel that was akin to an Ecuadoran. And so, did a Mexican family who encountered two angels that resembled their skin color. While white Americans chanced upon Caucasian looking angels, Haitians met angels who were of dark skin tones. An angel's ministry is to be inconspicuous and be able to blend into the community they serve."*

I chimed spiritedly, *"The angels I saw were masculine and had strapping wings."*

"That's because you prefer your own gender. For you to grasp the angels' messages, they took on strong silhouettes, so you can better discern their directives," he responded knavishly.

"There are exceptions. The Good Samaritan-type of angels can appear as a person of another race or culture. 'God' is good at breaking down walls of prejudice. There are also empyrean warriors who are tall and sturdy. Like the angels, Joan of Arc grappled with. In their traditional forms, angels appear as beautiful entities to bolster a person's faith."

He paused before he resumed, "In Exodus 3:2, the Bible declared: 'The angel of the Lord appeared to Moses as flames in the burning bush.' Another verse from Psalm 104:4 conferred: 'Angels are a flaming fire.' Many subjects in my angelology sessions report that they saw angel or angels as bright lights, that start as a glow and eventually turn to sparkling brilliance - like a configuration of a person bathed in light. Yet, there are those who could describe the angel/angels they met in detail; from their features to their habiliments."

Albert questioned, "Is this how the sight of an angel's halo originated?"

Olivier broke out in mirth before he iterated, "Many observers told they beheld a pure white light that was brighter than any whiteness they had ever seen. And there are others who describe the iridescence as a pinkish glow, or opalescent mother-of-pearl, or a chatoyant blue, or of prismatic rainbow hues.

"The one feature that all angel visionaries agreed upon is the depth of love and compassion in the angels' eyes. They disclose that their seraphic experiences had left them with an enigmatic peace; a serenity they'd been searching for, for most of their life."

Augustin looked at me searchingly, "Young, now is your turn to reveal your beatified experiences. Your beloved revealed a little of your paradisiacal phantasm over the phone, but I want to hear your testimonial."

I blurted deucedly, "Sir, you're an angel. Aren't you?"

Disbelief crossed my companions faces. Neither Albert nor my Valet knew how to respond to my precipitous promulgation. It was the angelologist who evanesced my proclamation.

The man laughed heartily before he propagated, *"My dear fella, everyone is an angel in our peculiar ways. I'd spent most of my life immersed in angelology and have yet to derive a conclusion to their existence. Stories abound of angel sightings and experiences, but I have yet no empirical proof of their subsistence."*

"You don't need validation when you are an angel," I hallowed.

The man burst into another round of hilarity. *"Young, it's sweet of you to think of me as an angel. I pray you wouldn't witness my wrath when I'm enraged by wrongful deeds inflicted on the meek and helpless."*

"That is because you're a warrior angel; like Archangel Michael," I announced.

"Thank you for the compliment. You, young man, better not be present to witness my dudgeon when my fury takes flight," he quipped.

Angelology

Andy jumped in to curtail my averments.

"Dr. Augustin, please enlighten us about angelology," he requested.

"What is angelology?" Albert questioned.

"My dear boys, there are many viewpoints about angels. Some believe angels are human beings who have died while others believe that angels are dispassionate sources of power. There are also those who deny their existence. I hope my angelology seminars will rectify these false beliefs. The rudiments of angelology are the study of angels and their relationship to humanity, and their service

to God/Higher Power/Allah's purposes on earth. In this context, I use the term God or Allah to mean a greater power."

Andy asked, *"What does the Bible say about angels?"*

"First, I must clarify that humans do not become angels after they die. Although angels take on human form temporarily to fulfill a mission they are not human beings. The Almighty created angels like 'He' created humanity. These supernal entities are of a different order from homo sapiens," Olivier elucidated.

Albert inquired, *"Are angels assigned a gender?"*

"Neither the Bible nor the Quran sanction the gender of angels. Whenever gender is 'assigned' to an angel in the sacred books, it is implied as male. The names given to angels are Michael **(Mika'eel in the Quran)** *and Gabriel (Jibreel in Islam). These are epithets that are generally considered masculine monikers,"* the professor explained.

"Does everyone have a guardian angel?" I raised.

"There is no doubt that good angels help protect believers, reveal information, guide people, and minister to God/Allah's flocks. The unanswerable question is whether each person or believer has an angel allotted to him or her.

"My question to you, Young, is you've yet to tell me your angelic encounters," Augustin pressed.

I brushed his query aside and questioned, *"Are seraphim and cherubim, angels?"*

"Cherubim or cherubs are angelic beings involved in the worship and praise of the All-Powerful. In addition to singing God/Allah's blessings, they also serve as a visible reminder of the majesty and glory of 'His' abiding presence with 'His' people. The only biblical text that specifically mentions Seraphim is in Isaiah chapter 6. They are referred to as the 'fiery, burning ones.'

"Angelology gives us God's perspective on angels. Angels are intimate beings who worship and obey The Almighty. Often, 'He' sends angels to arbitrate the course of humanity and assists us to recognize the strife between God's messengers and the dark forces; like Satan or Maalik and his demons - the guardians of Hell as stated in the Quran. Once we comprehend that angels are created entities; angel worship or supplication pilfers the All Almighty's the glory that is 'His.'

"The key fact in angelology is found in the Bible - Hebrews 1:14. The text affirmed: 'Are not all angels ministering spirits sent to serve those who will inherit salvation?'" the angelologist declared before we departed *The White Unicorn*.

A pirouetting feather floated onto my palm when we were leaving the premise. I inserted the down into my trouser pocket without giving it a thought.

Inspired by Admiration and Motivated by Envy (Chapter Twenty-Four)

"Admiration looks through a telescope; envy, through a microscope."
Dr. Bosh Van-Damme

Second Week of November 1968
At Brasserie La Bavaroise, Casablanca, Morocco

Mario, being Mario, knew all the latest in places to go. This well-informed fashion and portrait photographer got wind of Brasserie La Bavaroise, a newly open French brewery. Not only was this refined Bavarian establishment artfully decorated, but it also boasts the most exquisite French/Moroccan gastronomic steak dishes outside of Paris.

Our guest of honor was none other than the Roman Catholic Belgian scholar, Dr. Boch Van-Damme. The professor's Moroccan girlfriend, Mariam Saadoune, his former student and a graduate of the Paris-Sorbonne in Music and Musicology, joined our party of twelve. This educated Muslim libertarian was progressive before her time and caused much anxiety in her orthodox family. Tall and talented, she was assigned by a Paris modeling agency to walk the fashion runways.

Mario wasted no time to solicit her participation in his *Sacred Sex in Sacred Places* photography project. Although her lover was apprehensive about her involvement, this young lass was eager to experience life. She did not get this far by abiding by convention. While her Orthodox peers were and still are forbidden from having sex before marriage, Mariam or Maria (her preferred pseudonym) was already fornicating with her Caucasian professor. For those in the know, Boch and her platonic façade was a cover-up to their sex before marriage relationship.

Like many women before her, she had slept her way to the top. An acceptable vocation to climb the ladder of success. Unlike, her fellow Maghrebian compatriot Kalf, who was her opposite in every way; this lass rose without shame or self-doubt but with credence and gaiety.

Although Kalf apologized to me after his unscrupulous outburst, it was done with civility and not from sincerity. His jealousy, insecurity, and immaturity eventually led to his untimely demise. A year and a half after our farewell in Marrakesh, he committed suicide. It was the Count who broke the news to Andy and me at Bryanna's wedding in Zürich. The photographer and Kalf's *affaire de coeur* lasted for two months before the Italian went on to greener pastures. With a new beau in tow, the Tunisian was history. Yet, during their brief involvement, the manipulative Kalf had unfurled a rift between Tad and his bosom pal, Mario. A fracture that took my Valet and me much blandishment to mend their once inextricable bromance before reparation was reinstalled.

For now, our party dined delightfully on the brasserie's specialty - grass-fed جبال الأطلس, Jebal al-Atlas steak served with pomme frites, and delicious French-style sauces, together with buckets full of الداخلة El Da<u>k</u>la oysters. And by no means least, an array of decadent Moroccan desserts.

Table Conversation

The conversation soon swiveled to the unexpected. Señor Triqueros remark sparked a lengthy colloquy among the adults.

"Boch, I'm envious of your accomplishments," Victor expressed facetiously.

"Vic, you are not doing badly," the Belgian parried.

"But you have a gorgeous girlfriend to boot," my teacher remarked.

The men laughed.

Van-Damme queried, "Is this a case of admiration and envy, my friend?"

Before the Señor could respond, Boch resumed, "Admiration is a noble sentiment. Like I admire you for admiring others. In this instance, I detect a taste of humility in your admiration. There are two paths to admiration and envy."

The Prince chimed, "What are the paths?"

The Belgian replied, "We usually associate envy as inherently bad – a 'feeling of mortification and ill-will occasioned by the contemplation of superior advantages possessed by another.' An envious person deprives others of their advantages, which to him or her is as desirable as it would be to secure the same benefits for him or herself. If this passion is to run riot, it becomes fatal to all excellence; even to those who exercise exceptional skill."

"Is that so? Or can something that is frustrating and painful lead to positive or to better ends than its more admired counterpart?" the sheik remarked. He was alluding to his clandestine relationship with the prince. The Arab's rib went unnoticed to our new acquaintances, but to us in the know, we smiled at his insinuation.

The scholar continued, "I must admit, not all envy is created equal. While some flavors leave nothing but a bad aftertaste, others may inspire us to reach new heights of achievement."

He paused before he added, "Typically, envy arises from a combination of two factors. The first is relevance. This envied advantage must be meaningful to us personally.

For example - a ballerina's grace is unlikely to cause envy in a lawyer, who once had professional dance aspirations of her own. The second characteristic is a similarity. The envied person must be comparable to us."

He glanced at **Triqueros before he resumed,** *"Victor, even though we're both educators, it is unlikely I will envy you. This is Aristotle's description of envy: 'Potter against Potter.' When we admire someone, we do so from a distance, but when we are envious of someone, we picture ourselves in their place."*

"Admiration and envy are opposites. Admiration inspires, while envy drags one down," the Count commented.

Van-Damme answered adversely, *"This duality may not adequately capture these emotional complexities. When I examined this concept in cultures across the world, I found that the word Envy is not as clear-cut as comprehend by English speakers. In English, envy means jealousy. But in other languages, bitterness takes on a dual semblance. In Polish, it is zazdrość and zawiść. In Thai, it is ìt-chia and rít-yaa. In Dutch, there's benijden - from the root beniden. It means to be unable to bear something and to begrudge. It also translates as benign and malicious envy.*

"Malicious envy is a feeling of frustration. This experience often led to motivations to hurt another. In the hope that the person being envied would fail in his/her endeavors.

"Regarding benign envy, the situation is more inspiring; when the envier tries harder to attain more for him or herself."

Penny opined, *"Admiration sounds a lot like benign envy."*

"The difference is: while admiration feels like happy self-surrendering, envy is unhappy self-assertion. Admiration is a pleasant feeling because we think of the

people we admire as being unlike ourselves. Whereas with people we benignly envy, they are like us. This realization hits close to home; hence it hurts," Boch clarified before he expounded, *"There is a stark contrast between benign and malicious envy. The two spur the envier to act in different ways. With malicious envy, the envier constantly complains about the person they envy; as opposed to the good envier, who strive to work harder to better him or herself. Benign envy is a driving change for the better, even when it is an unpleasant emotion."*

Mariam who had remained silent, opined, *"I believe enviers are more likely to experience an increase in their ability to pay attention to and to commit details to memory regarding the target of their envy. They spent the time to research their target's personal details."*

"When I was a student at the Sorbonne, I did a survey on the differences between benign envy and admiration. In a study, I handed two fake reading-comprehension exercises to my fellow students. Both tasks were biographies of fictitious scientists. Half of the written papers suggest that self-improvement is possible - if one works hard and he/she can succeed, despite obstacles. The other exegesis cogitated that success comes from luck – one is either born with it or isn't.

"Students who were primed by the first exercise felt benign envy toward the scientists. Their comment was: 'I could do that, too, if I tried.' Those who were primed by the second exercise felt admiration. Their opinions were: 'I shouldn't even try. I'll just admire the scientists from afar'. The students who felt benign envy pledged to study harder than they had in prior semesters, while those who felt admiration didn't."

Victor commented, *"In one of my research, I found that students who felt benign envy; not malicious envy or admiration, performed better on a test of creativity. They could provide, on average, 11.4 correct answers, as compared to 9.8 when they felt admiration; and 8.5 when they felt malicious envy."*

Peter, Joshua's Valet, declared, *"I'm sure no one will deny that the feeling of envy is unpleasant, or that enviousness can lead down a path they wish they hadn't taken. Envy is corrosive and destructive...."*

The Belgian interjected before the Big-Brother could finish, *"The right kind of envy do serve an important personal and social function. It spurs competition and improvement."*

"For your information, the research paper I mentioned was titled: 'Inspired by Admiration and Motivated by Envy,'" Triqueros declared before trays of scrumptious Moroccan desserts arrived at our table. Little did I suspect that Kalf bore malignant envy that was already ravaging his core.

Last Week of August 2014
Andy's Message to David, c/c to Me

Hi David,

You mentioned the envy you felt towards your Big-Brothers/Valets. I like to add my perspicacity to this emotion.

Often, envy is a secretly held emotion. If a person (I'll name this person X) is envious of someone (let's call him/her Y), it is unlikely that X will admit his/her enviousness to anyone; with the exception to another, who might also be envious of Y, and will share with X in denigrating Y.

The reasons in which X might be envious usually involve a social comparison or competition between X and Y. Such a match and contrast are a part of the yardstick by which X measure him or herself. In short, it is X's self-evaluation. When X sees him/herself as coming up short, envy is elicited. Hence, this experience is typically considered a conflicting emotion.

To neutralize X's envy, he/she must diminish the source, and/or elevate him or herself. Jealousy has a way of making X work hard, and it appears he/she will continue to measure his/her self-worth against Y.

One may ask: *"What is the purpose of envy?"*

In my vocabulary, envy is an emotion that enables our species survival. It is related to competition and the social comparisons between the self and others; a kind of self-evaluation.

First, let us consider the thoughts and feelings this emotion creates. It is to desire what someone else has, that you don't have. This accord the envied advantage and/or power.

Secondly, the self-assessments and predicaments that this emotion evokes create enmity toward the envied and anguish within the self. One might either defer this negativity to the envied or militate to eliminate him or her. Or, to ascertain to possess the coveted desired quality.

Envy is the unhappy feeling of the self as compared to the successes, possessions, and/or talents of another. It is an inferiority complex of the self. Instead of improving and attaining victories, the envier craves what the envied person has and wish that he/she would lose that quality or possession for the circumstance to appear fair.

Envy appears in a variety of manifestations. For example, it is possible to mistake attraction for another as envy. In this instance, the envious competitive hostility is amiss because the envier expects to obtain the envied attributes by association. Thereby, the envier can "fall in love" with the coveted to procure his/her qualities and possessions - such as wealth, status, power, connections, or intelligence; instead of loving the coveted for who he or she is. Disappointment often follows this fate of idealization.

Envy can also originate from one's parents. If the envier's parents struggled financially and longed for affluence; he/she might envy those who have this quality. On the other hand, parents might idealize a higher education that to them was impossible to obtain; in which case their children might envy those with intellectual superiorities.

The envier idealizes what is unobtainable for him or her. They imagine the envied qualities or possessions could bring them happiness and fulfillment. It's a fantasy of having what the envier lacks. Often the 'lack' is admiration for the envied attributes and/or possessions.

An exceptional way for an envier to define him or herself are his/her ideals, ambitions, and the things valued. The envier's ideal self derives from social comparisons, and self-worth and is continuously measured to his/her models. When a person's pride measures up, he or she feel enlivened. Shame and depression set in when it doesn't. A significant degree of a person's morale is one's comparison of his/her ideal self. It is often easier to project that ideal onto another in the form of envy.

When a person matures, the values against which him/herself has measured, changes, as they learn to evaluate their potentialities and limitations. If a person can live up to his/her realistic ideals, their self-esteem will not be threatened.

If the person's ideals are exaggerated and unattainable, his/her successes will be short-lived, as it will never feel like it is good enough. The dream for the impossible will continue to haunt, whereby envy will take root. The way to protect one's dignity from experiencing disappointment and jealousy is to embrace one's realistic *ne plus ultra*.

I too had envious thoughts, like most. Thus far, I've managed to trounce this unappealing emotion by giving myself a reality check.

Well, guys, I've spoken, and I await your feedback. ☺

Yours sincerely,
Andy

Beware of Wolves in Sheep's Clothing
(Chapter Twenty-Five)

"Outside the open window, the morning air is all awash with angels."
Richard Wilbur
(Love Calls Us to the Wings of This World)

Second Week of July 1968
Saint Michael's Mount, Mount's Bay, Cornwall

During our walk towards St Michael's Mount, Andy and Albert were busy taking snapshots of one another. I had a chance to speak with Dr. Augustin.

Olivier remarked cheerily, *"Young man, you are very perspicacious."*

I did not respond. I pulled out the feather in my trouser pocket and held it to the professor. He burst into jollity and jested, *"Me Oh My! You saw through me, you little devil."*

We laughed before he resumed solemnly, *"This mount is steep in history. Between 400 BC to 400 AD, it was a major export center for tin and copper to Europe. In classical literature, the island of Ictis is thought to be located here."*

Olivier pointed to the church on a rocky peak and said, *"You see over there. That church is dedicated to St. Michael the Archangel before a Celtic monastery was established on that site. It was Edward the Confessor who built the chapel before he handed the abbey to the Benedictine Mont-St-Michel in France.*

"The present-day church was consecrated by the Bishop of Exeter in 1144. During the Middle Ages, it was a

major pilgrimage destination; thanks to the legendary sightings of St. Michael, the archangel.

"Disguised as pilgrims, Henry de la Pomeray, and his coterie, seized the Abbey in 1193. In fear that Richard the Lionheart would return from the Crusades to appropriate the island, he built a castle to fend off the invaders."

I interjected, *"You must be whom I believe you are, to know the history of the Mount in such detail."*

He burst out in laughter and ruffled my hair before he resumed, *"In the fourth and fifth centuries the appearance of St. Michael the Archangel at this locus was one of many reported across southern Britain and northern France. Tales of this heavenly warrior slaying dragons abound. Some theorize that the archangel's victories over dragons are expressions of the struggle between the then-new Christian faith and native paganism in this part of England."*

I queried, *"What has the slaying of dragons to do with native paganism? I thought Angels belong to the Judeo-Christian and Islamic faith?"*

"You see Young. Angels are also significant entities in Buddhism, Hinduism, Celtic, Norse mythology, and in many Shamanistic legends; even though they are not referred to as angels. Similarly, not everyone denotes a prayer as a mantra or a spell of protection as a prayer. There is a profusion of labels to what is fundamentally the same thing.

"The Buddhist refer to angels as devas or celestial beings. Some Buddhist sects use the label dharmapāla or Dharma protectors. Whereas devas in Tibetan Buddhism are sometimes considered as emanations of bodhisattvas or enlightened beings. On the other hand, other Buddhist paths have specific devas – usually derived from pre-Buddhist cultural religions and unrelated to the prevailing Buddhist philosophy. These paths incorporated local and

regional pre-Buddhist mythology into their order," **Olivier explained before** he declares, *"There are numerous types of spiritual beings in Hinduism who perform tasks that are similar to angels. A good example is the minor gods or devas whom Buddhists refer to as the 'shining ones.' These beatified beings inhabit a higher astral plane. Hindu gods, devas, gurus, ancestors, and planets, such as Sani (Saturn) also play a protective role for humans."*

"How can one keep track of all the names bestowed on these sanctified Beings?" I expressed.

"That is not all, Young. Asuras is another component of Hinduism. These demonic spirits are fallen devas who inhabit the lower astral plane; the mental plane of existence – like fallen angels in the Judeo-Christian and Islamic faiths. If an Asura does a good deed, it reincarnates into a deva, thereby reprieved from the lower plane.

"There is more; in Hinduism, Apsaras and Lipikas are heavenly nymphs. They preside over sacrifices and regulates karma as compared to devas and asuras who can either inspire or hinder aspirants from their spiritual journey," Dr. Augustin expounded exponentially.

"In early Norse mythology, Valkyries were evil spirits of slaughter. Like vultures, these dark angels of death soared over the battlefields. They govern a warrior's fate in the name of Odin. They ferry the battles' heroes to Valhalla, Odin's celestial home for his ghostly honorary army.

"Later mythos romanticized the Valkyries as Odin's Shield-Maidens. An everlasting feast and mead were served to the heroes by these golden-haired and snowy arms virgins in Valhalla's great hall. As described in the Volsung Saga and Nibelungenlied, these lovely swan-maidens or splendidly mounted Amazonians soared over the battlefields. One such fallen Valkyrie was the beautiful heroine Brynhild."

I looked blankly at the angelologist before I exclaimed, *"This is bafflingly complicated!"*

He chuckled and added, *"As an angelologist, this is what I analysis and evaluate before presenting my findings to scholarly institutions and universities that specialize in angelology studies."*

I commented, *"I'm correct. You are an angel to comprehend, document and present these kinds of complicated angelology aggregations."*

Amused by my comment, the professor supplemented, *"In Celtic mythology, Faeries are helpers of humanity. They too have many correlations to their deeds as Angels. There are also some lesser Goddesses who play a functional role. Such as the goddess Sirona.*

"The concepts of angels and demons are found in Pagan Metaphysics, and in non-Pagan religions. These theories and beliefs collide and overlap with others that were set in stone; where details and structures cannot be crossed."

Before the angelologist could resume, we had arrived at the Mount's castle.

Exploring The Mount

Surrounded by blue waters and perched atop a rocky hill, the Mount's Abbey was a spectacular setting. It was easy to fantasize the myths and legends told of this sacred site; especially that of the dragon-slaying Saint Michael.

An impetus stirred me to query, *"Angels were well documented in ancient times, but they seem to have disappeared until their recent resurgences. Why is there an increase in Angelic sightings and encounters nowadays?"*

Augustin did not answer but paused to observe my Valet and Albert's lively exchanges.

He admonished, *"Young man, a word of caution. Beware of a wolf in sheep's clothing within your midst."*

"What?" I exclaimed.

"You heard me," he stated.

I was awed by the volume of books it contained as soon as we entered the castle's library. Not only was this Bibliotheca impressive, but it was also framed by a couple of red velvet chairs in front of a large fireplace. In the middle of the room was an exquisite 19th-century gaming table, explicitly built for chess, drafts and card games. While Andy and Albert gravitated towards the table for a set of chess, the angelologist and I continued our conversation by the fireplace.

Olivier resumed, *"Angels left the Earth only to return."*

"Why?" I questioned.

"Have you heard of the lost city of **Atlantis?**" he enquired.

I nodded.

"During the height of the Atlantean civil war before its ruination, angels were very much a part of that great civilization. The annihilation created a substantial karmic shift in the Universal energies. Our planet's universal connection was segregated from the cosmos. Earth's isolation was a Divine punishment.

"After the fall of Atlantis, some Atlantean survivors proliferated across the globe in what we entitled as the 12 Tribes of Abraham (the first children of God). Earth's quarantine cast our wisdom and knowledge back several hundred years, thereby diminishing the guidance from the Angel Kingdom. Angelologist termed this as 'The Veil of Forgetfulness.' Without the leadership and direct interaction with the seraphic kingdom, humans often floundered abysmally. The old ways of spiritual communication, belief, and healing were virtually lost. Through the process of redemption, new political and

religious powers strived to impose their influences on Earth.

"These past centuries the quarantine walls have shrunk from the egotistical ventures and the karma gained after the Atlantean destruction; that resulted in the Earth's redemption. With the shrinking of the Veil, angels can once again incarnate, interact, provide guidance, and knowledge to humans," Olivier explicated.

"Why do earthlings require guidance and knowledge at this juncture?" I queried.

"Young, consider it this way. The Divine force is like a major Nuclear power plant, and you are a beautifully constructed crystal chandelier. If you were to plug directly into the core of the power plant, you'd likely be overwhelmed with energy, and might explode in the process. For those who haven't yet learned to build their substation to handle the massive energy flow from the power plant, and to filter its energy into their filaments; angels are there to assist. It's my aphorism that some people have learned through many lifetimes their spiritual lessons on how to connect directly to the divine force without being overwhelmed. These enlightened folks are few and far between as it takes commitment and responsibility between the individual's soul to adhere to the divine forces. Thus, angels are available to be intermediaries between humans and the divine," the professor elucidated.

The angelologist continued to press me to reveal my angel experiences, yet I shied away when this question arose. I was afraid to confide my deleterious dreams to this extraordinary man whom I reckoned to be an angel. I wanted to brush away those disturbing nightmares and its dreadful consequences if they became a reality. Though I desired the erudite professor's opinion, I wanted our discussion to be private, in the absence of Andy and Albert.

I was glad to obligate when the angelologist agreed to consult with me confidentially at *Safe Haven*.

The Beginning of September 2014
My Response to Andy and David (Part One)

Andy, do you remember the time we spent with Dr. Olivier Augustin in Cornwall? You had pressed me to tell you what transpired at the private meeting I had with the angelologist. Although I conveyed my angel visions to the professor at the various Parisian basilicas and Monsieur Alain Dubois imputation that I'm a member of The Angelic Society - The Fog; I omitted to tell you my premonitory dreams, where my guardian angel, Azaziel evinced the disastrous aftermath of our separation.

Since we are on the topic of angelology, I can relate the pernicious events I saw on Azaziel's visit. After our sojourn to Sissinghurst Court, I had several disconcerting dreams. In one of my dreams; I was looking for you and stumbled into a dimly lit cave. Much like the bathroom in ARGOS, the leather bar in Amsterdam, the cavern reeked of stale acid and rancid urine. A luminescent light appeared before me when I was about to ralph. The brightness transmuted into the shape of a prodigious winged angel before it diminished to a shimmering glow. I recognized the sinewy silhouette to be my guardian angel, Azaziel. He extended his hand to mine. As soon as we touched, the glowing delineation transfigured into you, Andy.

You counseled, *"Do not venture into the cave."*

I did not heed your advice and pressed on. You tried to hold me back.

"Venture not into dens of perilous wolves in sheep's clothing for innocence lost is a hefty price to pay," you cautioned.

I ran ahead and pulled you with me. As we progressed into the enclosure, I heard distorted groans and moans through the walls of the cliffs. Bleary eyes and hissing sounds followed our footsteps into this eerie territory. The angel extended his wings to shield the parlous hands that reached to grab me.

My guardian angel warned, *"Hopelessness and wretchedness lie within these turpitudinous precipices. Do not fall prey to their intemperance for it will annihilate the chastity of your soul."*

I refused to listen but ran toward the ossuary's core. Azaziel's outstretched wings fortified my progress as he sped behind. What I saw were deadly serpents coiled around doomed souls to siphon their purity before they were cast to eternal purgatory. It was a horrific sight to behold, yet I pressed forward until my guardian angel heaved me away to safety.

To this day, Azaziel's words continue to echo in my mind. He had repeatedly said, *"Beware of wolves in sheep's clothing for innocence lost is a hefty price to pay."*

Sleeping to the Top (Chapter Twenty-Six)

"She's the kind of girl who climbed the ladder of success wrong by wrong."

Mae West

Second Week of November 1968
Le Royal Mansour Méridien, Casablanca, Morocco

This majestic five-star masterpiece opened in 1952 in the Old Medina of Casablanca and was patronized by Moroccan Royalty and Nobility. During our two-day stay before our entourage proceeded to Marrakech, we rested our tired feet in this social domain.

Penny and Mariam gave a splendid lesbian performance at the *Sacred Sex in Sacred Places* photography shoot in the old Eglise Sacré-Coeur de Casablanca. This former Art Deco style cathedral was transformed into a cultural center after Morocco's independence. This venue became the home of artistic happenings and contemporary exhibitions.

Although Prince P and the American model, Anastasie was dating at the time, their busy schedules left them with little time to be together. This bisexual prince and his clandestine lover, Sheik Fahrib were enamored by Ms. Saadoune's performance. While Fahrib's veneration for the musicologist was of platonic amity, P's adoration was of sexual lasciviousness.

For Mariam, she saw this opportunity as an advancement towards the ladder of success. She wasted no time to seduce the already smitten prince while double handling the sheik with their correlation for music. No sooner had her scheme oscillated to her advantage, she discarded her Belgian boyfriend, Boch. Meanwhile, she played the farouche maiden in a sultry guise to perfection as she slithered towards her goals with punctilious precision.

It didn't take long for the erudite educator, Señor Victor Angel Triqueros to pierce her veil of duplicity, even when her comportment appeared innocently unimpeachable. After my daily tutorial, Victor broached the topic to Andy and me.

The Señor enquired, *"What do you make of Mariam?"*

"She knows how to butter up to our hosts," my Valet commented.

"So, Andy, you envisage what is in my mind? I feel sorry for Boch. He should have seen it coming," my teacher remarked.

"Seen what coming?" I questioned curiously.

The men laughed at my naïveté before Victor expressed, *"Young, have you wondered why certain things are considered wrong and others right?"*

"Err?" I stretched my head in puzzlement.

He resumed, *"Boy, though you are bright, you still have a lot to learn about the ways of the world."*

His statement perked my attention.

"Do enlighten me, sir?" I pressed.

He declared, *"I believe that sleeping one's way to the top is an acceptable advancement stratagem."*

I did not notice our French Moroccan model friend sneak up behind us.

"There are many I know who diminish a person's career success by attributing it to sexual favors he or she bestows upon their superiors," an unexpected voice chimed behind my back.

I turned, and there he was.

"Driss! I didn't know you're in Casablanca? When did you arrive?" I exclaimed excitedly.

The male model greeted Andy and me with pecks on both cheeks before Andy introduced him to my professor.

"*How did you know we're here?*" I questioned.

"*I smelled your intoxicating scent and followed,*" he joked.

"*I thought we were to meet in Marrakech?*" my chaperone queried.

"*I couldn't wait to see you guys, so I came here instead. Do continue, don't let me interrupt your conversation,*" Driss twittered enthusiastically.

"*I would like to learn more about sleeping one's way to the top,*" the model quipped before he added, "*Why is utilizing sex to achieve one's goals a less legitimate means than strong negotiations or kissing-up skills?*"

Victor expressed, "*I have no qualms with anyone sleeping their way to the top if he or she can perform their allotted tasks on hand with aplomb.*"

"*That depends on your definition of 'performing the allotted tasks on hand with aplomb,'*" the handsome model sallied.

I looked at the sardonic men bafflingly, before my chaperone opined, "*Most people have some traits or skills they credit to their career successes; such as intelligence, the gift of the gab, charisma, working hard or working smart. These are perfectly acceptable strategies.*

"*I think the reason sex is unacceptable is nothing more than a value judgment because an influential person or a group of people deemed it inappropriate. And for eons, many have happily played along with this perception.*"

The French Moroccan model commented, "*A female friend of mine once postulated that the characteristics of the powerful are thought to be better than the characteristics of the powerless. Whereby logic has nothing to do with it. She cited an example and posed this* question, 'If magically, men could menstruate, and women could not? What would happen?'"

We waited with bated breath for Driss to continue.

"*The answer is clear – menstruation would become an enviable, boast-worthy, masculine event. Men would brag about how long and how much. Boys would mark the onset of menses with religious ritual and stag parties,*" the model proclaimed humorously.

"*My aunt promulgated that men would boast that 'my cup runneth over' when menstruating. The reason men construe menstruation as a defect, an inconvenience or a curse is valued judgments. If it had gone the opposite direction, it would be considered a divine revelation. Like some ancient cultures acknowledge menstruation to be living proof of women's distinction and superiority. After all, it is this blood that shows a woman's ability to incubate life,*" Victor professed.

"*I have a friend who had built a stellar career out of befriending his superiors. This skill got him promoted with mind-boggling regularity. It has nothing to do with what he does or how well he does it. He's aware that people do nice things for people they like and so he works hard at being liked by the right people,*" my Valet asserted.

"*There are also many who have made themselves a packet by unofficially being the person whose job it is to make the superior look good. Their job titles rarely betray their personal job description, and they quietly do the job while the bigwig takes the public glory. Often ambition and career success are achieved through things that don't go on their curriculum vitae,*" Triqueros imbued.

The handsome model delineated, "*Perhaps the objection is a moral issue; along the lines of sex being a pure expression of heartfelt love. As is often the case, the objector has never engaged in premarital sex or had sex for any reason other than for the purpose of procreation and the expression of genuine love for his or her partner.*"

"Driss, have you applied this noteworthy skill to your advantage?" Andy inquired jokingly.

We laughed at my guardian's imputation since the four of us were following the path of our discussion.

Before any of us could comment, my Valet appended *"In that case why are the pots calling the kettle black?"*

His comment roused further amusement.

The Señor remarked zanily, *"I rarely meet men who are explicitly against prostitution. Using sex to get ahead in one's ambition and career is akin to prostitution. Many people spend hours working a vocation they dislike which they often find morally reprehensible; like selling a product, they do not believe in, to people who don't need it, in exchange for dineros. Their legs may be firmly closed, but their body and mind are regularly doing something that feels wrong. Yet they do it for the money. Which would you like to be, the pot or the kettle?"*

"You have a point, professor," Andy commented.

"Since it is impossible to prove or disprove, the only problem with this tactic is it can easily tarnish reputations. It riles me that this is often used as a weapon against women. Seldom are men accused of sleeping their way to the top. If they did, they'd probably reframe it as an acceptable strategy," Driss inferred.

I had kept silent throughout their exchanges.

"Women have a different relationship with sex. Perhaps male subordinates are better off showering them with compliments, chocolates, cosmetics, and fabulous clothing. They'd probably term it the 4Cs of aspiration advancement," I remarked.

The men burst into another round of hilarity.

"Only you, my darling has the insight to the 4Cs," my chaperone parried.

"Why are we discussing Mariam's motives rather than accepting the way she is? Kalf would be a more

interesting topic in this sleeping to the top discussion. Don't you agree?" I commented.

"Sleeping to the top has been adjudged negatively because the general populace deemed it so, but we don't have to play along with this implication. We can easily reframe this employed stratagem, and not diminish our achievements," my tutor finalized.

Before our party went our separate ways, Victor and Driss had bonded. The French Moroccan was invited aboard the *Sindbad* to provide his perspicacity on the mythological jinniya, Aisha Qandisha to Triqueros' students.

Andy and I were glad to reconnect with our buddy, in and out of bed.

Abri Sûr (Chapter Twenty-Seven)

"When you free your mind, body, and spirit from earthly constraints, the impossible becomes possible."
                                                             Dr. Olivier Augustin

Second Week of July 1968
Abri Sûr (Safe Haven), Cornwall, England

As if I had stepped into a sacred vortex of seraphic aegis, the moment our sedan entered *Abri Sûr's* driveway a sanguine élan enveloped my person. To the naked eye, this six-bedroom manor on the grounds of a beautiful estate and filled with priceless antiquities was the home of Professor Olivier Augustin. But, for those in the know, this was a beatified refuge for those seeking reverential equanimity and not just an earthly abode of the angelologist and his altruistic assistant, Emanuel Parris.

Not only was Emanuel Parris good looking, but he was also compassionate. This young man suffered a devastating bicycle accident. He was hit by a speeding vehicle that plummeted into a nearby couloir, killing both the driver and his wife. The doctors attested that Emanuel would never walk again.

An angel visited Parris in the height of his despondency and challenged him to amble off his wheelchair. He improved by leaps and bounds since his angelic encounter. The young man vowed that he would help accident victims back to resplendence.

At Oxford, Emanuel befriended Dr. Augustin. The angelologist invited Parris to lodge at *Safe Haven* for as long as he wants. Three years had passed since the Parris' accident, and the lad had become a permanent fixture at the estate. Not only did he become the professor's assistant, but he also aided the hapless back to normalcy.

After a delicious home-cooked meal, the five of us retired to the drawing room. Our conversation soon gravitated to the topic of angels.

Angels in Islam

I was fascinated by the sheer volume of books in the professor's study, especially those that dealt in angel mythologies and legends.

I enquired, *"Professor, I've come across many illustrations of Western angels, but I seldom see Islamic angel iconography. Is there a reason for this?"*

Olivier replied earnestly, *"Young, angels are often hidden from our perception of Islamic doctrine. These preternatural beings are neither divine nor semi-divine. They are a group of Allah's created entities who will eventually die.*

"Like Biblical angels, Islamic angels do not deliver personal prayers to Allah nor are they objects of worship. Their mission is to carry out the Creator's commands."

"Are there fallen angels in the Islamic worldview?" Albert questioned.

"There are no good and evil angels in Islam and Satan is not a fallen angel, but a jinn created by Allah. Angels are created from light. Hence, their graphic and symbolic depictions in Islamic art are rare. In Muslim scriptures these heavenly beings are beautifully winged entities," the angelologist explained.

Emanuel expressed, *"There are a variety of angel hierarchies and orders, depending on their size, status, and merit."*

The professor resumed, *"As documented in the Quran, the Prophet Mohammad saw angel Jibreel (Gabriel} in his original form, together with other attending angels of Allah's throne. These throne carrying angels beseeched the Creator to forgive humans of their sins."*

I asked, *"Do angels eat, drink or get bored with worshipping Allah?"*

The men chuckled before Parris quoted Quran 12:20, *"'They celebrate His praises night and day, nor do they ever slacken.' And the answer to your other question, Young, angels do not eat or drink."*

"How many angels are there?" Albert inquired inquisitively.

Andy quipped amusingly, *"God only knows."*

We burst out in laughter.

Augustin expedited solemnly, *"Muslims proclaim that above the Kaaba (the black cube in Mecca) is the Angels sacred heavenly sanctuary - the 'Much-Frequented House.' Daily, seventy thousand angels come and go from this domain, only to be followed by different angelic assemblage."*

"Like the Changing of the Guards outside Buckingham Palace?" I sallied.

The men laughed at my comparison before I resumed, *"Are the names of Muslim angels, similar to angels in the Judeo-Christian faith?"*

"There is no easy answer to your question, Young. Although, Muslims believe in specific angels mentioned in the Bible; like Jibreel (Gabriel) and Mika'eel (Michael). There are others such as Israfeel and Malik (the Guardian of Hell) who are not listed in the Bible.

"You must understand that angels possess great powers bestowed to them by God. They take on different shapes and forms. During the conception of Jesus, Allah sent Jibreel to Mary in the guise of a man; as documented

in the Quran 19:17: '...Then We sent her Our angel, and he appeared before her as a man in all respects.'

"Angels also visited Abraham in human form. Similarly, angels also manifested as good-looking men to deliver Lot from danger. Angel Jibreel often visited the Prophet Muhammad as his disciples, and as handsome desert Bedouins," Olivier declared.

Parris supplemented, *"Jibreel is Allah's heavenly messenger to humanity. The Quran 2:97 states: 'Whoever is an enemy to Jibreel - for he brings down the (revelation) to your heart by Allah's will....'"*

"What are the tasks of the Muslim angels?" my Valet inquired.

"There are many. Some angels execute Allah's law in the physical world. For example, Mika'eel is responsible for directing rain to wherever the Creator wishes for it to fall. Other angels assist Mika'eel to direct the winds and clouds in the direction they are to blow," the professor answered.

He paused before he recommenced, *"At the onset of Judgement Day, Israfeel is accorded the task to sound the judgment horn. The Angel of Death and his assistants are granted the mission to guide souls out of the bodies of the deceased, as affirmed in Quran 32:11: 'The Angel of Death, put in charge of you, will (duly) take your souls; then shall you return to your Lord.' There are also guardian angels whose duties are to protect the believers throughout their mortal life."*

Emanuel augmented, *"Some angels are responsible for recording an individual's deeds - be they good or bad. These preternatural beings are known as the 'honorable scribes.'*

"Then there are Munkar, and Nakeer, Their job is to test the deceased in the grave. And among them are the keepers of Paradise and the nineteen 'guards' of Hell led by Malik.

"Atop that, some angels are assigned to breathe life into the souls of fetuses. These angels indenture the newborn's provisions, life-span, and actions. They also determine the individual's fate."

The angelologist indicated, *"There are roamer angels who travel the globe to spread the word of Allah, so the Creator is exulted.*

"Angels are The Almighty's grandiose creation, and they vary in numbers, roles, and abilities. In reality, God and or Allah; whichever you prefer to call the Creator has no need for these entities. The knowledge and belief in angels add to the awe a believer feels towards God/Allah. Therefore, the magnificence of 'His' creation is proof of the Almighty's magnificence."

I said sarcastically, *"Doesn't it make The Almighty an arrogant being?"*

"That's one way of viewing The Father," Dr. Augustin noted before he whispered in my ear, *"I'll illuminate you further during your stay in Safe Haven."*

The Beginning of September 2014
Continuation of My Response to Andy and David (Part Two)

David here is more room for thoughts. An awkward encounter presented itself on the final evening of Andy, Albert and my stay at *Safe Haven*. We were allocated individual rooms at *Abri Sûr*.

I woke in the middle of the night to use the bathroom. Upon my return, I noticed the translucent silhouette of a man at the foot of my bed. I rubbed my eyes to be sure I wasn't experiencing a phantasmagoria. I got back into bed since there was nothing but darkness. Just as I was about to cascade into slumber, the hazy delineation reappeared. The opalescence resembled the angel guise I perceived of Dr. Augustin at *The White Unicorn*. From the photographs I have seen in *Safe Haven,* this entity was a young Olivier. He beckoned me to him.

Suddenly, a pair of opaline wings enveloped my naked person. Galvanizing energy coursed through my physique and jolted me to a magnified spiritual awareness. His feathery touch aroused every fiber of my being a thousandfold. I surrendered to his embrace as our lips met in a passionate kiss. I returned the fervor with frenzied ferocity when his delirious tongue probed my yearning mouth. We merged into a cocoon of prurient amorousness. Our gyrating hardness did little to conceal our libidinousness but capitulated our desire to seal our union in humming concessions. I melted into this striking specimen as he cradled me like a newborn. Our tongues swirled, lapped and sucked at each other's tenderness.

He lifted my legs to receive his stiffness into my core. Bolts of indescribable approbation galvanized my mortality and catapulted me to seventh heaven. Buried in his beatified bosom, he glided his rigidity into my expedient appetency. Euphoria paved our peregrination as his denseness stroked my inviting crevice.

Unannounced, his undulating wings elevated us out of the French window. Through the twinkling night sky, we flew. Southern winds guided us above aromatic pastures and babbling streams while his gliding massiveness furrowed into my orifice with winsome pleasure. Lighter than air and freer than birds, we soared until our desires overshadowed our exuberance.

Our elation served to deliver our synchronized liberation beneath the fulsome moon. We sealed our divine carnality in jubilant exultation as his sturdiness engulfed my peaceful refuge. Reluctant to relinquish our rapturous effervescence, he shrouded me in his supple wings by a prattling brook. Against his supple musculature, I eased into a restful slumber. I was awakened by the rising sun and found myself under the cozy down in my *Abri Sûr* chamber.

I related my angel encounter to Professor Olivier Augustin, and these were his parting words before we left *Safe Haven*.

"The human psychic and physique are capable of encounters beyond rationality. When your mind, body, and spirit are free from earthly constraints, the impossible becomes possible."

Yours truly,
Young

In My Master's Chambers (Chapter Twenty-Eight)

"What unites us is unconditional love."
Victor Angel Triqueros

Third Week of November 1968
La Sultana, Marrakech, Morocco

The two days we spent at La Sultana was nothing short of consequential. In the late nineteenth century, this exquisite hotel was the home of Caïd Azzi Boujemaa. It was a gift from Sultan Moulay Ismael, the then ruler of the Alaouite dynasty to Boujemaa for his devotion and loyalty. Boujemma's son lovingly restored many of its original features during the French protectorate, and this address became synonymous with glamorous society balls and parties organized by his coquettish French wife, Odette.

In 1968, La Sultana entertained many royalties with its hospitality, elegance, and charm. It was in this resplendent establishment that I received a summon from Sheik Dr. Fahrib to his chamber.

An Abd delivered the message when my chaperone and I were relaxing in a fragrant rose petaled pool. My Valet read the note aloud.

Young, come to my chamber at 9 PM this evening.
Fahrib

"Have you any idea why the sheik asks for you?" Andy inquired.

I shrugged my shoulders.

Without uttering another word, Andy planted a kiss on my lips.

He declared, *"I'll make love to you now if not for this summon. But you must remain chaste for His Excellency."*

"You, Mr. Valet, you don't have to remain chaste. You're not being sent for. I can cherish you," I remarked.

Without waiting for a response, I gulped his firmness below water.

He moaned with delight and laid against the pool's edge with my head on his groin. My lover's masculinity never fails to excite me. Not only was Andy many women and gay males' fantasy man, but he was also my dream beau, and I was the lucky lad whom he gave his heart to. Heartened by his love, I was delighted to pleasure him with my oral expertise. Although my lover's rapturous expressions heightened my desire to envelop him in my core, I knew I had to be chaste for the sheik.

I suckled his stiffness as he savored my devotion. His hypnotic stares and heaving torso ignited my prurience to throb incessantly. His groans grew lustier as my oral action intensified. No longer able to withhold his release, he coated my mouth and his athletic frame with his gleaming virility.

I lapped at his supremacy with enthusiasm before I lowered my orifice back onto his engorgement to rouse him to another burgeoning explosion. His seed filled my throat to overflowing capacity before we shared his passion in a lingering kiss.

This man was my world and mine his. We were the Yin and the Yang, the Moon and the Sun and most importantly, the Neophyte and the Virtuoso that forms the whole. As my harem services drew closer to its finale, I was becoming like my mentor in more ways than I could envision. I was merely glad to be of assistance to my kind-hearted instructor and my benevolent patriarchs. They, who'd taken me under their wings in guardianship and guidance. I was grateful to return the favor with carnality;

especially to my beloved Valet, who had loved me unconditionally since we met.

My chaperone was unenthusiastic when it came time for me to proceed to my Master's suite. I had to remind Andy of our E.R.O.S. commitments, and I discerned that the mannerly doctor required a pair of listening ears than a sexual liaison; even though I had a hunch that my sympathetic ear might lead to an erotic rendezvous. I assured my lover that my heart was always his and I must console my patriarchs to the best of my ability.

In The Sheik's Boudoir

Andy waited at the lounge, when Malik, one of Fahrib's bodyguard guided me into my Master's bedchamber. I was not surprised to hear melancholic music emanating from the other side of the ingress. Malik knocked on the closed door before he ushered me in.

Fahrib continued on his fiddle when I entered. I kept silent until he finished with the pensive melody. He motioned for me to sit next to him when I noticed woeful tears on the sides of his rugged face.

He muttered, *"I'm glad you came."*

"Why wouldn't I. I will always be here for you, sir," I replied.

"Your cheerfulness and avidity never fail to chase my blues away," he remarked.

I kept quiet. I did not know what to say. Fahrib cupped my hand to his and played with my nimble fingers. He lifted my hand to his lips and kissed my fingertips affectionately.

"Oh, the tenderness of youth." He paused before he added, "I wish I could possess again. I wish it would never end. Those short years are now so far behind."

I spoke, "Your Excellency, you have everything life can offer."

He broke into a smile. "That's what many would say. They'll understand my predicament if they're in my shoes."

Silence followed. He resumed, "Shahria and Roya are acting out again. Their bickering is out of control."

He paused before he continued, "I'll be a happy man if I have a loving relationship like yours and Andy."

"You have, sir. With Prince P," I commented.

"He is making love with another as we speak," the Arab uttered sadly.

Once again silence fell in the room before the doctor re-commenced, "He's off with the jinniyah, Mariam."

Another round of silence followed.

"Here I am, in sorrow when it was I who gave him my blessing to be with the woman. Oh, how I wish P would love me as I love him," the aristocrat murmured wistfully.

"Of course, the prince loves you. True love is unconditional. The more love you give, the more love will return to you," I consoled.

"I wish it is that simple, Young." He wept. "In my culture, the love I have for P is taboo. Our intimacy will forever remain a secret. It's a case of don't ask, don't tell."

"When you become Emir, you can change that way of thinking," I chirped.

He burst out in laughter.

"That's what I like about you. Your purity of spirit is contagious. Unfortunately, many circumstances forbid my faith and culture to change. Maybe in the distant future but certainly not in my lifetime," Fahrib expressed lamentingly.

"You can be the first to path the way for change," I declared enthusiastically.

"Your exuberance never ceases to lighten my burden. Maybe I'll make you the counselor of my country," he said amusingly.

He pulled me to him and kissed my lips. He expressed when he released his grip, *"Where is your Valet? I want to see the both of you make love."*

Taken aback by this unexpected request, I answered, *"He is in the lounge waiting for me."*

The sheik had opened the door to wave Andy in before I could finish talking.

My guardian asked surprisingly, *"Your Excellency, is there anything the matter?"*

"Come in, Andy. I want to watch you and Young make love," the patriarch announced.

A look of astonishment washed over my chaperone's face before he replied, *"Most certainly, sir. I'm happy to be of service."*

Love To Love You

My Valet never fails to amaze me. He could switch on his virility at the drop of a hat as if by divine command. No matter the circumstances, Andy's piercing eyes and studly handsomeness induced me to ardency I find difficult to resist. His tenderness captured my soul the moment our lips met. I melted into his shielding arms as if in a protective cocoon. Our kisses soon turned to impassioned amorosity.

He lifted me onto the King and stripped me naked. I laid beneath my lover like a sacrificial lamb as his palpitating organ drummed against my briefs. His fervency strained for my oral attention.

The Arab watched unblinkingly at the unfolding eroticism. An unanticipated opportunity had arisen for my lover to fulfill his desire at the petaled flower pool, he pried my mouth open to receive his twirling tongue. He tastes honeysuckle sweet as I lapped at the swirling invasion. Like a young bird deprived of nourishment, I was hypnotized by my lover's feed. I surrendered to his every move. I needed him and him, me.

His Excellency's bulbousness bounced above my face before he inserted his stiffness into my craving mouth. His pair of dangling globes roused me to attention. I gawked at the kissing men above.

Andy lifted up my legs and spat into my twitching crevice before I had time to savor their magnificence. I craved their love that dare not speak its name, the forbidden love my Master quandary over was now played out between us.

How can this divine love that titillates, tantalizes, and arouse every fiber of our mortality be immoral? Yet, this humanly fabricated immorality had ruined many souls and induced wars among nations. And most heinous of all, this falsified turpitude continues to be used by overzealous Scribes and Pharisees to persecute this sanctified union called LOVE.

That night, our carnality triggered a consecrated trinity between us. A bond that aided the sheik to come to terms with himself. To be the man who would become king - the benevolent Emir of a nation, he would eventually lead into the 21st century.

As our heated amativeness grew in fervency, I was in seventh heaven as the recipient of two dominant alphas. I jounced euphorically as their firmnesses penetrated me effortlessly. Livid sprays of ecstatic potencies shot within my person as our triune fervidity catapulted us into simultaneous ejaculations. I laid buried within their throbbing phalluses. It was within this divine blissfulness we shared our fill in a three-way kiss.

It was close to dawn by the time my chaperone and I left the doctor's boudoir. Andy held my hand to his lips and sealed it with a kiss.

"You, boy, better tell me what transpired in your Master's chamber?" he teased delectably.

Stay In The Present (Chapter Twenty-Nine)

"Worry never robs tomorrow of its sorrow; it only saps today of its joy."
Leo Buscaglia

Third Week of July 1968
Simpson's-in-the-Strand, London, England

I was delighted to see Uncle James after several months of absence. The evening before my mother's arrival in London, I had a heart-to-heart talk with my English guardian. He had kindly invited Andy and me to sup with him at one of London's oldest English establishments - Simpson's-in-the-Strand.

This restaurant started life in 1828 as a smoking room and soon became a coffee house. Around 1850 Simpson's achieved notoriety for its traditional English cuisine, particularly roast meats. From the mid to late nineteenth century this was the most important venue in Britain for chess tournaments. When the Savoy Hotel group acquired the property at the end of the century, this prestigious institution a purveyor of traditional English food and chess ceased to be a feature.

P.G. Wodehouse labeled Simpson as *"a restful temple of food,"* while others, the likes of Charles Dickens, William Ewart Gladstone, and Benjamin Disraeli called it *"a large, well-appointed establishment."*

In 1968, the traditional English roast we ordered was carved in front of us on a silver dinner trolley by a liveried waiter who kept eyeing my handsome Valet.

"Andy, you are quite the object of our waiter's affection," Uncle James teased.

"He's everyone's lover," I jested.

"But, Young is my true love," my chaperone declared expediently.

My perceptive uncle noticed the insidious glance I had given my lover before he remarked wittily, *"Now, boys, tell me the truth."*

My Valet and I stared at one another, not knowing what to say. James looked at my chaperone for a response.

Andy, being a respectable gentleman related to my uncle of our time in the Lake District, our visit to his ex-lover, Albert's ancestral home, and last but not least our sojourn to see Dr. Olivier Augustin, the angelologist in Cornwall. Along the way, he imparted to James of his and Albert's attraction to one another. In spite of that, he maintained that I was, and will always be the love of his life.

When he finished, my surrogate father directed his question to me. *"If that is indeed the case, why are you obdurate about Andy's confession of love for you?"*

"Sir, I am not obdurate about Andy's love for me, but that I've been forewarned by Dr. Olivier Augustin to be cautious of a wolf in sheep's clothing among us," I recounted.

James burst into laughter. He opined merrily, *"Just because an angelologist warns you to be cautious, doesn't mean that the person you are to be heedful of, is Albert. Did the professor identify the 'wolf' as Albert?"*

Caught off guard by my uncle's analysis, I did not know how to respond. After all, Olivier had made no mention of Albert, except when he uttered those words his gaze was fixated on both my Valet and his ex during our St. Michael's Mount tour.

The Englishman resumed, *"You, boy, are worrying much about nothing; especially when your beloved has given you his solemn promise that you are his true love."* He paused before he added, *"That said, worrying can be helpful if it spurs you to take action to solve a problem. But if you're preoccupied with the what-ifs, then worry becomes a problem. Unrelenting doubts and fears can be paralyzing. They can sap your emotional energy, and send your anxiety levels soaring, and may interfere with your daily life."*

"Uncle, I have a more pressing matter to worry about, than to doubt Andy's love for me," I confessed.

"Tell me what is worrying you, boy?" Uncle James pressed.

Since I did not know where to begin, I kept silent.

"You know you can ask or tell me anything. I promised your mother that I'll do my best to assist you, while you are in my care," my surrogate father affirmed.

Touched by his kindheartedness, I muttered, "I know my mother is in London to whisk me away from Andy. She'd gotten wind that I am having a homosexual affair with a boy. Is that true?"

My guardian gave a hearty laugh.

"That is indeed true, and it was I, who told her about Andy. Most importantly she is here to see her darling son and to meet his mannerly beau."

"Why then, is she bolting me, with her female entourage to ten countries in Europe for two weeks; if she intends to get to know Andy?" I questioned skeptically.

"She misses her son and wants to spend time with you," my guardian answered on my mother's behalf.

"Knowing my relatives, they're likely to convince her that my homosexuality is a sin. Especially Aunty Ping Yee, Ying Yee, and several of my cousins. To my knowledge, they're staunch Methodist, and they do not condone my kind of sexual preference," I countered.

James acknowledged. *"Although that is true, you should evince to them that you have come into your own and you have the right to love whom you choose. Young, remember that positive actions will always speak louder than words."*

"That's well and good. But, I worry about the outcome. Most significantly, I hate being away from Andy, and I have nothing in common with my female relatives anymore," I pronounced sadly.

"Your mother is a worldly and a well-traveled woman. She understands you more than anybody else, besides Andy," my uncle remarked.

"It's hard not to worry," I opined.

Andy, who had thus far remained quiet, expressed, *"My dearest, the answer lies in your beliefs in the negative and the positive about worrying. On the negative side, you may believe that your worrying is going to spiral out of control, which will drive you crazy, and may damage your health.*

"On the flip-side, you may believe that your worrying will help you to avoid bad things; like preparing you for the worst and then coming up with solutions. In my opinion, your worrying shows you're a caring and conscientious person."

"Andy, you're so philosophically intelligent," I expressed.

Uncle James denoted, *"Andy is in part correct. Negative beliefs or worrying about worrying add to your anxiety. Much like worrying about getting to sleep will keep you awake.*

"But, positive beliefs about worrying can at times be damaging. It's tough to break the worry habit if you believe that your worrying protects you. To stop worrying, you must give up your belief that worrying serves a positive purpose. Once you realize that worrying is the problem and not the solution, you can regain control of your worried mind."

He paused before he rejoined, *"Young, you can train your brain to stay calm and look at life from a more positive perspective."*

"How can I train my mind to do that?" I inquired.

My surrogate dad explained, *"Let me cite you an example: daily, I have tough decisions to make as the CFO of The Hong Kong and Shanghai Banking Corporation (HSBC), and it is not easy to be productive if I allow worries and anxiety to dominate my thoughts...."*

My Valet asked before my uncle could finish. *"What techniques do you use to rectify that, sir?"*

James responded smilingly, *"It doesn't work to tell myself to stop worrying; at least not for long even if I can distract myself for a moment. I can't banish those anxious thoughts for good. Trying to do that often makes these thoughts stronger and more persistent.*

"Thought stopping often backfires because it forces me to pay extra attention to that very thought I want to avoid, thereby making it seem even more important. However, that doesn't mean there's nothing I can do to control worry. A different approach is needed. This is where the strategy of postponement of worrying comes in. Rather than trying to stop or get rid of the anxious thought, I give myself permission to have it but I put off dwelling on it until later."

He took a breather and sipped his **Sauvignon Blanc before he resumed,** *"Postponing worrying is effective because it breaks the habit of dwelling on worries when I've other more pressing matters to attend to, yet there's no struggle to suppress the thought or judge it. I simply save it for later. As I develop the ability to postpone my anxious thoughts, I realize that I have control over them."*

Andy inquired curiously, *"How do you stop thoughts of worry from reemergence by deferment?"*

The CFO answered, *"There are three steps I take to accomplish this goal.*

"First and foremost, I create a 'worry period.' I choose a set time and place for worrying. For me, it is in my living room from 6:00 to 6:30 PM so that it is early enough for me to not be anxious before dinner and bedtime. During my worry period, I allow myself to worry about whatever is on my mind, while the rest of the day, is a worry-free zone.

"Secondly, if an anxious thought comes into my head during the day, I make a brief note of it and then continue about my day. I remind myself that I will have time to think about it later. Therefore, there isn't any need to worry about it for now.

"Lastly, I go over my worry list during the appointed worry period. If the thoughts I had written continue to bother me, I allow myself to worry about them. But only for the time I've set aside for my worry period. If those worry thoughts don't seem important anymore, I cut short my worry period to enjoy the rest of my evening."

My Valet exclaimed, *"What a brilliant way to deal with worry and anxiety. I'll definitely give your technique a try."*

James gave an acceding nod before he added, *"You see, boys, worrisome thoughts and problem-solving are two very different things. Problem-solving involves evaluating a situation, before coming up with concrete steps to deal with it, and before putting the desired plan into action.*

"Worrying, on the other hand, rarely leads to solutions. No matter how much time I spend dwelling on the worst-case scenarios, I am no more prepared to deal with them should the actual event happen."

I queried, *"How then, do you distinguish between solvable and unsolvable worries?"*

"Young, It is much easier than you think. If a worry pops into my head, I start by asking myself if the problem is something I can actually solve. I ask myself these questions:

Is the problem something I am currently facing, or an imaginary what-if?

If the problem is an imaginary what-if, how likely is it to happen? Is my concern realistic?

Can I do something about the problem to prepare for it, or is it out of my control?"

He sipped his wine before he continued, "Productive, solvable worries are those I can take action on right away. For example: if I'm worried about my bills, I could call my creditors to see about flexible payment options.

"Now, unproductive, unsolvable worries are those for which there is no corresponding action. Like: What if I get cancer someday? Or what if my kid gets into an accident?

"If the worry is solvable, I start brainstorming by making a list of all the possible solutions I can think of. What I try not to do, is get hung up on finding the perfect solution. I focus on the things I can change, rather than dwell on the circumstances or realities beyond my control. After I've evaluated my options, I draw out a plan of action. Once I have a plan, I can start to do something about the problem. This way I feel less worried."

My lover questioned, "How do you deal with unsolvable worries or, to put it differently; a worry I cannot solve?"

"Andy, you're not a chronic worrier, but if you are, it is vital for you to tune into your emotions. In the majority of cases, worrying helps a person avoid unpleasant emotions. Worrying keeps one in one's head - like thinking about how to solve problems rather than allowing him or herself to feel the underlying emotions. Yet, one cannot worry one's emotions away. While a person is worrying, his/her feelings are temporarily suppressed. As soon as the worrying stops, the feelings bounce back. Then, the person *start worrying about his/her feelings, like: 'What's wrong with me? I should not feel this way!'"*

James paused when our waiter arrived to fill our wine glasses. When he departed, my uncle resumed, *"It may appear alarming to embrace one's emotions because of a person's negative belief system. For example, I may believe that I should always be rational and be in control and that my feelings should make sense. Or I shouldn't feel certain emotions, such as fear or anger.*

"The truth is that emotions, like life, are complex. They don't always make sense and are not always pleasant. But as long as I can accept my feelings as part of being human, I will be able to experience them without being overwhelmed, and I can learn how to use these emotions to my advantage."

I remarked gesticulatingly, *"Uncle, it is difficult to accept uncertainties when I don't know the outcome."*

"That is indeed true. The inability to tolerate uncertainty plays a huge role in anxiety and worry. Chronic worriers cannot stand doubt or unpredictability. They need to know with a hundred percent certainty what is going to happen. Worrying is seen as a way to predict what the future holds, to prevent unpleasant surprises, and to control the outcome. The problem is, it doesn't work.

"By thinking about all the things that could go wrong doesn't make life any more predictable. You may feel safer when you're worrying, but it's just an illusion. Focusing on worst-case scenarios won't keep bad things from happening. It will only keep you from enjoying the good things you have in the present. So, my dear boy, if you want to stop worrying, start by tackling your need for certainty and immediate answers," my surrogate dad counseled."

"*Practice mindfulness. Remember the spiritual practices your teachers - Monsieur Alain Dubois and* **Señor**

Victor Angel Triqueros taught you?" my valiant Valet reminded.

My English guardian continued, *"Worrying is usually focused on the future, on what might happen and what you'll do about it. The centuries-old practice of mindfulness can help you break free of your worries and redirect your focus back to the present. This strategy is based on observation and release, in contrast to the previous techniques I mentioned; that of challenging your anxious thoughts or postponing them to a worry period. Merging these two strategies together will help you to identify the roots of the problems and will assist you to be in touch with your emotions.*

"By not ignoring, resisting, or controlling them, and through acknowledgment and observation of the anxious thoughts and feelings, one then views the worrisome thoughts without immediate reactions or judgments, from an outsider's perspective."

Just as we were wrapping up our "worrisome" discussion, our traditional English roasts arrived on our silver platter for us to dig in.

"My dear fellas, let go of your worries. When you don't control your anxious thoughts, they will pass; like clouds moving across the sky. Stay focus on the present, pay attention to your ever-changing emotions, and always bring your attention back to the present," were Uncle James Pinkerton's final words on the subject.

"And by the way, your lovely mother is simply glad to be with you. She is here to get to know the young gentleman who loves her son unconditionally," my surrogate dad reassured before he dug into his food.

By Hook or By Crook (Chapter Thirty)

> *"Knowledge is not a series of self-consistent theories that converges towards an ideal view; it is rather an ever increasing ocean of mutually incompatible (and perhaps even incommensurable) alternatives, every single theory, each fairy tale, each myth."*
>
> Paul Feyerabend

Mid-September 2014

I did not hear from David or Andy until the middle of September. David's email arrived a day after Andy's message. This was what my ex Valet wrote:

Hello Young,

I'm sorry I had not responded earlier. I was down with a pancreatic infection and had to be treated at the local hospital. Since I turned sixty, this has been a lingering problem. My doctor says it is a hereditary disorder. My father suffered from it, and so did my great-grandfather. The chronic abdominal pain comes and goes, and left me fatigue. It is under control, and I feel better. So much about me. Let us discuss something more entertaining than my illness.

Young, during the early years of my life I was skeptical of your angel experiences. I am older and wiser and realize that there are many preternatural experiences beyond human comprehension. For a brief period, I had doubts about my mentorship abilities to you and Albert. I consulted Dr. Ericson Müller, Daltonbury Hall's

Psychology professor. He said that I have nothing to worry about.

Although angel sightings are not everyday occurrences, they do happen; especially to gifted individuals who possess high IQs. Dr. Müller advised that some E.R.O.S. recruits retain eccentric qualities that set them different from an average student.

I remember an incident when you came to me for advice when you were a Big-Brother (BB) to Helius. At one of his recruitment tests, you mentioned that this potential E.R.O.S. candidate encountered an otherworldly entity. You had ventured into the woods with him for a clandestine liaison, and he saw a naiad watch the both of you as you frolicked in the lake.

You remember you came to me for advice after your encounter? You asked if Helius' sighting was legitimate, and I advised you not to tell anyone about the incident until I spoke with Dr. Müller. I also mentioned your angel and fairy sightings to the professor.

These were the doctor's words: *"Seek to understand before taking action, yet trust your instincts when action is called for. Do not avoid danger from fear, and never seek out danger for its own sake. At no time conform to fashion from fear of eccentricity, and not ever be eccentric from fear of conformity."*

That moment forward, I liberated myself from any judgment of experiences I knew little and had never encountered. Instead, I strived to understand and to educate myself about these mystical occurrences; to better comprehend their significance and nature. And be able to guide those endowed with this unique talent.

I envy people, like you, who can see beyond our worldly horizon and suffice supernal experiences.

I look forward to David's take on this topic.

Andy

XOXOXO

Late November 1968
Ali Ben Youssef Medersa, Marrakech, Morocco

We went sightseeing with Driss, the few days we were in Marrakech. Our friend and guide took us to several historical monuments. One of them was Ali ben Youssef Medersa. This mind-boggling Hispano-Moresque decorative institution was once the largest Quranic learning center in North Africa, and it remains among the most splendid in the region to this day.

This medersa (theological college), affiliated with the nearby Ali ben Youssef Mosque was once the lodgings of nine hundred students in its one hundred and thirty-two dormitories. Despite its nineteenth-century upgrades, this institution gradually lost its students to its collegiate rival - the Medersa Bou Inania in Fez. To this day, this old seminary continues to echo its magnificence and studious serenity to tourist and visitors alike.

As our entourage passed through the medersa's entryway; the inscription above, read: *"You who enter my door, may your highest hopes be exceeded."* Surrounding this fourteenth-century blessing was a series carved Atlas cedar cupolas and *mashrabiyya* (wooden lattice screen) balconies. The expansive courtyard boasts a five-color *zellij* wall with stucco archways, cedar windows, and a marble *mihrab* (niche in a mosque indicating the direction of Mecca).

I was given an unanticipated lesson on Theological Voluntarism in these erudite halls.

Out of the blue, Leon blurted, *"What do those words mean?"*

We looked puzzlingly at the lad when he pointed to a sizable Arabic calligraphic placard on a wall. Beneath the plaque was the French translation. It read: *"Commandes d'Allah que toutes choses sont bonnes, mauvaises, le bien et le mal."*

Driss translated the verse into English: *"Allah commands that all things are good, bad, right and wrong."*

Señor Triqueros contemplated before he spoke. *"It is a meta-ethical statement which proposes that an action's status is morally good, bad, right and wrong are God's commandments."*

Aaron, Leon's Valet, questioned, *"Isn't there a theory known as the Divine Command that relates to this ideology?"*

"You're very perceptive, Aaron. There is such a theory. It is known as Theological Voluntarism," my teacher responded.

"What does the theory propose?" Andy inquired.

"The theory asserts that what is moral is determined by what God commands and that for a person to be moral, he or she has to follow Allah's commands. Followers of both monotheistic and polytheistic religions in ancient and modern times have accepted the importance of God or Allah's commands in establishing morality. Numerous variants of this theory have also been presented by historical figures such as Saint Augustine, Duns Scotus, and Thomas Aquinas. Recently, an American analytic philosopher of metaphysics, religion, and morality; Robert Merrihew Adams proposed a 'modified divine command theory' based on the omnibenevolence of God in which morality is linked to human conceptions of right and wrong," Victor explicated.

Overhearing our conversation, Ms. Saadoune voiced, *"There are professors at the Sorbonne that challenged this theory. In one of our seminars Professor Pierre Perrault argued that even if God/Allah's command and morality correlate in this world, they may not do so in other possible worlds.*

"Besides, the Euthyphro dilemma, proposed by Plato, presented a conflict that threatened to leave the morality subject to the whims of God or to challenge his omnipotence. The divine command theory has also been criticized for its apparent incompatibility with the omnibenevolence of God, moral autonomy, and religious pluralism; even if some scholars attempted to defend the theory from these challenges."

We stared dumbfounded at the female Muslim libertarian. None of us knew of this musicologist's extensive philosophical knowledge until now.

Aaron broke the silence. *"What is the Euthyphro dilemma? Do enlightened us,"* he entreated.

"The Euthyphro dilemma was proposed in Plato's dialogue between Socrates and Euthyphro. In the scene, Socrates and Euthyphro were discussing the nature of piety when Socrates presented the dilemma. The question was: 'Is X good because God commands it, or does God command X because it is good?'

"Is the pious loved by the gods because it is pious, or is it pious because it is loved by the gods? — Plato, Euthyphro.

"The Euthyphro dilemma can elicit the response that an action is good because God commands the action, or that God commands an action because it is good. If the first is chosen, it will imply that whatever God commands must be good: even if he commanded someone to inflict suffering, then inflicting suffering must be moral. If the latter is chosen, then morality is no longer dependent on God, thereby defeating the divine command theory."

Mariam paused to look at our reactions before she resumed, *"Additionally if God is subject to an external law, he is not sovereign or omnipotent. That would challenge the orthodox conception of God or Allah. Proponents of the Euthyphro dilemma might claim that divine command theory is obviously wrong because either answer challenges the ability of God to give moral laws."*

We stared at the female, speechless.

Triqueros dissipated the quietude. He commented, *"The divine command theory is featured in the ethics of many religions, like Judaism, Islam, the Bahá'í Faith, and Christianity. This theory is also a part of several older polytheistic religions."*

He paused for an opinion. None came.

Victor resumed, *"In ancient Athens, it was commonly held that moral truth was tied directly to divine commands, and religious piety was almost equivalent to morality. Although Christianity does not entail divine command theory, it is commonly associated with it. It is a plausible Christian theory because the traditional concept of God as the creator of the universe supports the idea that he created moral truths. This theory is supported by Christians; that God is all-powerful, therefore God created moral truths rather than moral truths existed independently of 'Him.' This would be inconsistent with 'His' omnipotence."*

Before anyone could counter, the professor recommenced, *"We can have a lengthy and never-ending debate on this subject, but for now, I suggest we spend our time wisely and enjoy the historical beauty of this medersa. By hook or by crook, the ancients might enlighten us as we peruse these primordial halls of distinction."*

Mid-September 2014
David's Email to Me and Andy (Part One)

Hi guys,

Sorry I haven't been in touch sooner. I was away in the Netherlands for a family vacation and to attend my school alumnus reunion. At the event, I caught up with an ex-fellow secret society member, Boriss. The two of you might find his information interesting. He said that the Enlightened Royal Oracle Society/Valkyrian Templers Abbey is still in existence, but its mission has transformed. Although sex education continues to be a part of the progressive curriculum and remains a student exchange organization; the recruits concealed assignments are no longer a part of the program. E.R.O.S. is no longer the fraternity we know and experience. Now that we are living in a different day and age, the old had made way for the new.

    Young, regarding your angel encounters, you are the only person I know who profess to have an intimate relationship with a seraphic being. I am envious of your enlightening experience, and I wish I am as venerated as you; to bask in such reverential bliss. The closest I came to witness a Supernatural occurrence was at my second Household. This incident was associated with magick.

End of July 1968
Romantik Hotel Wilden Mann, Lucerne, Switzerland

My mother's arrival in London town was nothing short of a Chinese culinary fanfare. Like many dotting Asian parents of her day, she and her entourage delivered luggage full of Malaysian nosh and munchies to me; as if I was an undernourished child, deprived of healthy sustenance. Although I missed the spicy Malaysian cuisine, I was not an avid cook and the dry goods ended in Uncle James' kitchen than within my rumbling stomach.

    The two weeks, ten countries European tour was a whirlwind of unimpressionable activities. All I recall were ascending and descending the forty-seater tour bus at this or that famous historical site. We scrambled pass diachronic monuments at lightning speed, only to stop for photo ops before we headed to the next destination. Every meal was an Asian déjeuner instead of savoring each town and country's native gastronomical savoir-faire. I felt as if I had never set foot out of Kuala Lumpur.

Atop this wearisome sojourn, I missed Andy desperately, and I longed for the trip to end so I could return to my lover. My aunties and cousins did nothing to ease my trepidations, especially when they bantered for information about my beau. Even though I countered their advances with grins and smiles; and allowed their speculations to run havoc; my brain was taxed. By the end of the day, I was mental, emotionally and physically drained.

I would sneak out of my hotel room for a walk on the wild side after they had retired to bed. My night escapades were my temporary satisfaction before I resumed another day of fraudulent countenance to their never-ending chitter-chatter.

Mrs. Foong, like any intuitive mother, detected my gloom, no matter how well I forge a smiley face. One evening after a hearty Chinese meal, we had a heart to heart chat.

Conversation with Mom

"You've grown into your own," mother remarked earnestly. *"Are you enjoying school?"*

"I can't wait to return to Daltonbury Hall," I answered cheerfully.

"Do you miss Andy?" she questioned.

I nodded and looked away sheepishly.

"James told me a lot about Andy. He said he's a wonderful man and is good for you. Is that true?"

I nodded again and remained silent.

"You must introduce Andy to me when we return to London," mother evinced.

I blurted doltishly, *"You'll like him, mom. He is intelligent, charming, elegant and..., I love him."*

Mother gazed at me before she remarked. *"From James' description, I have no doubt that I will grow to like this young man."*

She paused before she added, *"My dear boy, I want you to be happy. If Andy makes you happy, I'm fine with this relationship; even if your father is peevish by your homosexuality."*

"Did you tell dad about Andy?" I queried.

"I haven't told him anything." She wavered before she assured, *"And I'm not going to."*

I breathed a sigh of relief.

She continued, *"He doesn't need to know. The less he knows, the better."*

As if a gust of wind had dissipated the dead weight in my psyche, my anxiety evaporated instantaneously, and my buoyancy returned with a vengeance. I wanted to leap with joy and to give my mother a bear hug, yet I remained solemn to appraise my stroke of good fortune. I had indeed matured from an exuberant adolescent to a dignified young adult; my mentors and guardians would be proud of. That evening, I felt blessed by the gods in more ways than one. Especially to my dearest mother who had given me more than her fair share of unconditional love.

My psychotic jubilation lasted for a brief second before mother inquired, *"What are your plans after you graduate from Daltonbury Hall at the end of this year?"*

Taken aback by this unexpected question, I muttered, *"I, err..., plan to remain in school to be a Big-Brother to a Freshman. Then I will apply to several UK art colleges to pursue a degree in fashion design."*

I waited for my mother's reaction. None came. She beseeched me to continue.

"You know, mom, fashion is my love, and nothing will stop me from becoming a fashion designer," I asserted.

"You know your father will not approve of your career choice. That said, leave the old man for me to deal with. I'll help you achieve your goal. He is a handful, but I'll convince him to come around; even if he kicks up a big fuss and accuses me of spoiling you to the nth degree," my mother ascertained.

"Thank you, mom! You are the best mother I can ever wish for. You know me better than I know myself," I accredited my beloved mother.

"I love you very much. It is my motherly duty to see you happy," Mrs. Foong affirmed. "Now, tell me more about Andy."

Caught off guard by her request, I did not know how to begin.

She emboldened, "I know he is a gallant young man and he loves you very much."

I nodded.

"I love Andy very much, mom. I miss him terribly," I declared woefully.

I plucked up the courage to ask my mother. "I thought you came to separate my lover and me."

"I will only do that if Andy treats you horribly. Since James gave me an excellent report of your boyfriend, I want to meet him in person."

I declared, "Mom, you will love Andy like I do. He is the most altruistic person I've ever met. He's kind, gentle, loving...."

Mother interjected, "I know, I know. Even though your aunties and cousins have reservations, I am open to meet the boy. But first, I must hear directly from you that you're truly in love with Andy before I agree to see him."

She hesitated before she questioned, "What do you plan to do when Andy goes to university? Is he pursuing his higher studies in London, to be with you?"

I did not know how to respond. I prevaricated, *"We will make that decision when the time comes. For now, we are happy to be together, and your approval means a lot to us."*

She said amusingly, *"I haven't given my final approval yet. I have to meet the boy before I can bestow my blessing."*

"Mom, I know you will. You're the best mother ever!" I quipped and kissed her cheeks.

With that, we bid each other *bonne nuit* so we could have a good night's rest in readiness for another day of maniacal traveling.

Under Kapellbrücke (Chapel Bridge)

I bounced out of the Romantik as light as a lark. My week of worries was for naught. As per Uncle James' advice, my mother was merely happy to spend time with *moi*.

It was midnight when I skipped chipperly towards the wooden footbridge that spans diagonally across the Reussin, in the city of Lucerne. This unique bridge, named after the nearby St. Peter's Chapel contains several interior paintings dating back to the 17th century. The Kapellbrücke, more commonly known as the Chapel Bridge was and remains to this day the oldest wooden covered bridge in Europe, and the oldest surviving truss bridge in the world. This renowned structure is Lucerne's symbol, and by day it is one of Switzerland's main tourist attraction.

When night falls, this bridge transforms itself into a sleazy pick-up joint for men seeking the company of other men. Ari, Andy's brother, had mentioned to us the sordid activities that went on under the infamous Kapellbrücke.

My overactive libido strived for attention after a week without my lover's company. I remembered Ari's mention of this tawdry site and to discover firsthand if his report was factual; I proceeded to give this venue a try.

I noticed the silhouette of an attractive man, leaning against a wooden balustrade under the dim lights along Chapel Bridge. The sensual aroma of his cigar drew me to him.

He gave me a seductive grin, and he muttered in heavy Swiss accented French, *"D'où viens-tu?"*

I had no clue what he said.

"I don't speak French or German," I answered in English.

He exhaled a puff of smoke before he replied, *"Je ne parle pas anglais, mais il n'a pas d'importance. Vous êtes très mignon."*

Not comprehending a word, I shook my head and shrugged my shoulders.

Without warning, he pulled me to him and probed my mouth open to receive his invading tongue. Although I was astonished by his precariousness, I welcomed his macho belligerence. We kissed salaciously. Words were not needed as we hankered in our web of erotic desires.

He released his hold and beckoned me to follow. We sped towards his chalet above the city in his Thunderbird. I was already in awe by the man's raunchy prowess. He pulled me to him the moment he unlocked the chalet door and ripped our clothes off before he pushed me onto the sofa. We resumed our urgent kisses and roused one another to ecstatic elation. His craving tongue explored every crevice of my youthfulness while I buried my face against his hairiness to inhale and savor his masculinity. I coveted his supremacy as much as he yearned to dominate my tenderness. We merged like the bold and the emboldened and crave to be united like the attracting poles of a magnet.

Our foreplay burned like a flaming passion when he whipped out a pair of handcuffs and cuffed me to the King.

I surrendered to his imposing authority as he laps and bit at my reddened nipples. We were lost in the rapturousness of the moment when surges of shuddering agony and ecstasy radiated from my swollen perkiness. He had fastened a pair of nipple clamps onto my sauciness. His throbbing stiffness drummed against my palpitating erection.

Our French kiss served only to titillate his hunger to perforate my being before he lifted my legs onto his muscular shoulders. My twitching enthusiasm urged him to action. I was delighted to supplicate to his engorgement when he spat on his palpitating bulbousness to ease his ascendancy into my welcoming refuge. I clung to his burliness as his masterful countenance plowed into me with unbridled providence. We fused into a fiery orb of heated ardor. My shuddering hollow quivered to his gliding stroke. Although we spurned each other to conserve our amatory passion, our fervency took hold. With shattering exultations, our gushing potencies erupted onto and into our wanton physiques.

We did not terminate our licentiousness until the first light of dawn. Only then did we dressed hurriedly for my deliverance to L'hôtel Romantik before my tour departed for the next town and country. But most importantly, before my mother and her entourage discover my night's sexcapade with a stranger, whose name I never knew.

Femme Fatale (Chapter Thirty-Two)

"It is a man's own mind, not his enemy or foe, that lures him towards the evil temptress."

Buddha

Last Week of November 1968
Menara Gardens, Marrakech, Morocco

Señor Triqueros had organized a field trip for the E.R.O.S. recruits and our chaperones, with Driss as our guide to a traditional desert garden at the foothills of the Atlas Mountains. This tranquil landscape contains a vast water basin that serves as a reservoir for irrigation of the surrounding olive trees. This was also a place where Marrakechians go to find equanimity, away from the hustle and bustle of city living; where they can enjoy a day's outing and to admire the scenic Atlas mountain in the background.

In 1147 during the reign of Almohad, the Menara Gardens were constructed by Caliph Abd al-Mu'min. The gardens' name came from the Menara colored pyramid-shaped roof of the Menzeh Pavilion, built during the 16th-century Saadi Dynasty. In 1968, this picturesque park was and continued to be a favorite venue for couples to enjoy a romantic rendezvous.

No sooner had we set up our picnic accouterments under a shady olive tree, our teacher and guest educator, Driss, illuminated our group about the infamous Moroccan femme fatale - the fabled jinniya, Aisha Qandisha, also known as Aicha Kandida or Quandisa.

As we watched couples canoodle on rowboats and families frolic in the 16th-century pavilion; Triqueros asked our guide, *"Now that you've gotten to know Mariam better, what do you make of her?"*

"She's smart, beautiful and liberal. I'm sure many of my Moroccan compatriots would be fascinated and fearful of this unique specimen," the male model replied.

"In my culture, many men would encapsulate her as the mythical Qandisa," he added.

The Señor interposed, *"Ahh! Illuminate us about this storied being?"*

"There are copious legends of this jinniya. As a child, I was told of her existence by my grandmother. Aicha Kandida is a malicious cannibalistic water jinni who lures men to do her bidding. She is described as a beautiful woman, only to reveal her true nature as a hideous, gigantic predator when angered.

"She lurks around the banks of the River Sebu and in the Sultan's Palace grounds, waiting to charm unaccompanied foolish single men. Once the contact is made, there is no escape.

"That said, there are also stories about the jinniya's magnanimity. Men who willingly gratify her are released, unharmed and laden with bountiful gifts," Driss irradiated.

I questioned, *"How did she come into being? Is she created by Allah or by the devil?"*

The model declared, *"Some myths hold her to be the daughter of Sidi Shamharush, the king of the jinn. It is said that her mother is human, and her father is an Ighud (the shepherd of the wind). They copulated in a forest, and their offspring were given the human name of Aisha and a devil's name – Qandisha.*

"I believe that Qandisha is a version of Astarte, who is an older Middle Eastern goddess known as Ishtar. From the Bronze Age through to the classical Hellenic era, she was worshiped as a fertility goddess."

My teacher commented, *"When I was a psychology student I had the opportunity to explore the Hadmadsha's history and practices. According to this* confraternity; *many moons ago Aisha Qandisha fell in love with Ahmed Dhughi, one of the patron saints (Sadi) of this religious brotherhood. Women were bewitched by the trance-like music of Sadi Ahmed's flute and drums.*

"There were accounts of Zawiya males who were drowning in sexual and romantic problems, but when they heard the Hamadsha's musical performances, they were successfully cured of Qandisha's possessional spells."

Joshua asked, *"Who are the Zawiya males?"*

"J (Joshua), Zawiya is an all-male Islamic monastery school. In Arabic, the word زاوية *zāwiyah means an assembly or a group or circle of like-minded compatriots,"* Barry, the boy's Valet answered.

The Señor jested, *"Very good, Barry! Your years in harem services have served you well."*

Driss remarked, *"In my culture, the idea of love-possession is viewed differently than in the west. It's less poetic than the romantic-love I experienced in Paris. In Morocco, men infected by the love bug are described as possessed by a jnun."*

"What is a jnun?" Emily enquired. *"Is it the same as jinn or jinniya?"*

"They are les diables or les invisibles," the model explained in French/English.

Before any of us could question the meaning of *les diables* or *les invisibles,* Professor Triqueros explicated, *"You are partially correct, Emily, in your supposition. To put it in simple terms; jnun are people who are from below the ground or those who are from below the river. They are invisible beings with whom humans share the earth, and the only female that falls in this category is jinniya Aisha Qandisha."*

Our guide added, *"In Morocco, they are known as the pervasive creatures who can take on human form. Usually, men are the victims of Lalla (Lady) Aisha. She dwells near wells and waterways and can transform herself into a seductively attractive woman or as a hideous hag. If the victim is unaware of her cow or goat feet before she plunges an iron knife into the ground; his soul will be struck, and his spirit will then belong to her until he is released from her bondage. He'll eventually become impotent and lose interest in mortal females. He'll also suffer a variety of physical or psychological dis-ease until his soul is reclaimed through the intervention of a healing group; like the Hamadsha."*

Andy queried, *"Where can the infected locate the Hamadsha?"*

"Members of the Hamadsha are found in most northern Morocco neighborhoods. At one time or another, many of their members were possessed by Qandisha or other jnun before they joined the group. They alleviate the victim's possessional effects through notable trance-inducing musical performances and via a series of sacrificial rituals," the Moroccan commented.

He continued, *"The majority of hearsayers report that the victims of Lalla Aisha are those who had previously experienced failed love affairs, or estrangement from a spouse, or from the traumatic death of a close family member."*

Jennifer, Emily's Big-Sister, remarked, *"This sounds like a Moroccan ethnopsychiatric support group."*

"In many ways, it is," our professor stipulated. *"It's a Moroccan ethnic and cultural aspect of mental illness. The Aisha legend has an underlying Freudian theme - the conflictual relationship between love, sex, beauty before danger, madness, and chaos sets in. Aicha Qandisha represents something so irresistible that men are driven insane in the pursuit to possess her. She ignites an all-*

consuming love that is literally – possessive. Her enchanting stature expresses the irresistible temptation of beauty, which is often accompanied by the paralyzing fear that its power may wholly consume the beloved."

I chirped excitedly, *"In other words, she is the Demon Lover."*

"Clever evaluation," my teacher praised.

Before I could savor the professor's compliment, Driss announced, *"I want to share with you, my friend's story."*

Tajj: A Story of Love-Obsession

He began, *"When I lived in Marrakech, my then twenty-four-year-old pal, Jaul, suffered a mild form of unrequited love which he attributed to magical influences.*

"At the time, he was a teaching assistant at the Islamic school I attended. He first met Nora in a Marrakech suburb; after a day of Ramadan fasting when locals enjoyed night walks after breaking fast. The two were engaged soon after. A few years later, they decided to terminate their engagement, but Jaul was worried about repaying her dowry. He believed that her family had installed magic (suhur) in his food during the breaking fast meals that caused him to be obsessed (tajj) with Nora. Around the same period, he also experienced impotence and found himself handing over a significant amount of money to Nora's family. To forget her, he spent whatever money he had left on booze, while the girl's family continued to pressure him to turn over his entire salary to them.

"When Jaul mentioned his dilemma to his father, he took him to a fgi – a Quranic and practical Islamic religious expert. The fgi examined Jaul's hand (muhalla) before he wrote down the boy's predicament and his future

onto his client's palm. The religious expert confirmed that Jaul was indeed under a magical spell. He then performed some ritualistic counterspells to dissipate the conjuration.

"Jaul had not resolved his problem when I left Marrakech for Paris. That was four years ago."

After the model finished the story, Victor analyzed, "There are many accounts regarding infatuation where pathological feelings of love are overwhelming, and the implications of supernatural governance come into play. In my field of psychology study, I have come across cases where the male's inability to deal with his infatuation is often blamed on his beloved - the female and her family.

"Despite Jaul's obsession with Nora, his inability to reconcile himself to marriage, is an extreme form of a male love/infatuation dilemma. The male is sexually and emotionally drawn to a beautiful young woman but obstacles; in the form of family opposition or the lack of economic resources, gradually induced the man to suspicion and hostility towards the woman. This is when antipathetic emotions and physical symptoms manifest. In many cases, the male attributes his experience to magical disposition. Concepts of magical influences and poisonings permeate within many popular cultures. Out of fear these eldritch circumstances are often treated with *prudence* by the concerned parties. Like Jaul's father's intervention by the fgi's white magick to counter Nora's family's black magick."

Driss finalized, "When I was growing up in Marrakech, many were afraid to mention Quandisa's name. Nowadays she is the butt of Moroccan jokes and songs."

I questioned pensively, "How does Mariam fit the role of Aisha Quandisa?"

The group laughed at my disparate inquiry.

"Young, have patience. Time will reveal the answer to us," the Señor opined.

True to my teacher's words, the denouement was slated to us in less time than was expected.

Could It Be Magick? (Chapter Thirty-Three)

"Magick is in your heart."
Andy Finckenstein

Second Week of August 1968
Chinatown, London, England

My time with my mother and her entourage flew by quickly. Traveling through ten European countries and twelve cities within a two weeks period was a dull experience. No lasting memories except for some minor highlights that lingered within my psychic.

Upon our return to London, Uncle James treated us to a traditional Chinese banquet in honor of my mother and her entourage. In truth, it was my surrogate father's scheme to introduce my lover to Mrs. Foong in a favorable environment. After all, who could resist a delicious feast, especially my mother and her relatives.

No sooner were we seated in the Chinese restaurant, Mother remarked in Mandarin to James, "安迪很帅 *(Andy is very handsome).*"

The Englishman chuckled before he translated Mrs. Foong's observation to my chaperone, who looked away coyly. My Big-Brother had not anticipated such an unexpected pronouncement, coming from an elegant Chinese lady who happens to be his boyfriend's mother. That was one of the times I witnessed his modesty during our time together. He gave me an irksome glance. I burst out in hilarity at his diffident expression. The females at our table stared at me as if I had gone bonkers while Uncle James shushed me to be quiet.

Mother said to me,
"我可以看到你为什么这么好看的年轻人如此迷恋 *(I can see why you are so enamored by this good-looking young man)."*

My relatives giggled at the matriarch's declaration. Andy's embarrassment was ominous.

Suddenly, my lover responded in broken Mandarin, "谢谢冯太太 *(Thank you, Mrs. Foong)."*

I stared at my Valet, astonished by his ability to utter the Chinese syllables and wondered how he knew to vocalize the words. When my surrogate dad gave me a devious wink, I knew that he had secretly given my chaperone a crash course in Mandarin. He had prepared Andy for his first meeting with my mother and her entourage.

My gallant Big-Brother had worked his magic within his heart, and in the process, he had also installed an excellent impression upon the cultivated Mrs. Foong and her entourage. At the end of our ten-course meal, the females had taken up Andy's offer; to accompany them on their shopping spree the following day.

By the end of my mother's London visit, she had accepted her son's boyfriend. Dearest Mommy had fallen head-over-heels with my lover's hypnotic charm. My anxiety finally dissipated when Mother presented Andy with a gold pendant to thank him for looking after *moi* and invited him to visit Kuala Lumpur. Although I did not voice my concerns to Mrs. Foong about my father's objection to our homosexuality, I knew she would find a way to convince her husband to be civil if my lover got to meet my old man. I was merely glad to be reprieved from not having to see my father for another year.

Mid-September 2014
David's Email to Me and Andy (Part Two)

A bizarre incident occurred when I was stationed at the جراند بافيليو (Grand Pavilion), my second Arabian Household in Riyadh. Shabana, my patriarch - Mustafa bin Sultan Ali's second wife had problems conceiving after a year into their marriage. She desperately wanted a male child to succeed her husband's fortune. Unfortunately, after months of devotional prayers, Allah had not been kind to her. She secretly sought the help of Amira, a Moroccan thaumaturgist. Without Mustafa or any of his wives' suspicion, Amira operated undercover as Shabana's handmaiden.

    The nights when Shabana was in attendance to her husband, she would secretly release his seed from her vagina into a bottle before she gave to Amira to cast a fertility spell. The magic content would then be smeared onto one of the E.R.O.S. recruit's penis when he copulated with Shabana in secret.

    When the thaumaturgist was later tried by the Saudi Commission for the Promotion of Virtue and Prevention of Vice for Shabana's murder, she confessed that her grandmother had trained her to be a witch. By performing the smearing act, she had convinced Shabana that Mustafa's potencies would magically be transmitted into her womb via another man's deposit; whereby she will bear a male heir in her husband's image.

    The sorceress had Shabana consume a daily magic potion of various bestial productive organs. This concoction made her mistress ill that resulted in her death. Amira claimed that Shabana's illness was a positive sign that her mistress' viscera was changing to accommodate a revised productive system and that her charm had worked.

That was before the woman's demise. Not only did her magick land her in prison; she was sentenced and beheaded by the Saudi authorities after a prolonged trial.

She was convicted of practicing witchcraft based on such evidence as books on witchcraft, vials, and bottles full of "unknown" liquids used primarily for sorcery. Most western news reports implied that Amira was a victim of persecution by the Saudi government. One of Amnesty International directors declared: *"The charge of sorcery has often been used in Saudi Arabia to punish people, generally after unfair trials for exercising their right to freedom of speech or religion."*

No Western reporters had considered that the victim was practicing witchcraft, or the reason witchcraft is regarded by the desert kingdom a crime punishable by death. In the West, there is a societal need to place this seemingly inexplicable incident in a right context such as the violation of human rights rather than examining this Islamic tradition that includes the belief, practice, and prohibition of magick.

The practice of Islamic magick is prevalent throughout the Muslim world. It is manifested in the theological concept of jinns inhabiting the sphere of the Muslim occult. Furthermore, magical beliefs can constitute an existential and political threat to Islamic religious leaders, thereby provoking severe punishments and strict prohibitions of any practice that are not sanctioned by the Saudi authorities. Conversely, I believe that political leaders, such as Iran's president Mahmoud Ahmadinejad, the Taliban leader Mullah Omar, and the Pakistani president Asif Ali Zardari have employed magical beliefs to advance their political agendas.

Witch Hunt

You see, guys, throughout the Muslim world the belief in witchcraft, sorcery, magic, ghosts, and demons are widespread and pervasive. Magical beliefs are expressed in the wearing of amulets, the consultations of spiritual healers and fortune tellers, shrine worship, exorcisms, animal sacrifices, and numerous local Islamic customs and rituals that provide protection from the evil eye, the demons, and the jinns. Fears associated with these paranormal entities are widespread. They range from hauntings and curses to illnesses, poverty, and everyday misfortunes.

On the other hand, magical practices that are intended to bring good fortune, health, increased status, honor, and power also abound. To my knowledge, these mystical beliefs are not relegated to rural or poverty-stricken areas. They are observable in every segment of society regardless of socioeconomic status.

A popular Saudi Arabian custom is fortune telling. This practice differs vastly from its Western cousin; that is generally relegated to the status of a carnival act to explicitly predict the future. In the Arab world fortune telling focuses mainly on spirit protection and family counseling, rather than prediction and prophecy. Apart from cards, dice, palms, and coffee grounds readings, other activities include selling amulets to ward off evil spirits and to provide advice for marital problems.

These fortune tellers operate from shop fronts or outside of mosques and shrines. They are rarely consulted to prophesize the future. Their clients are females or the elderly who seek guidance to deal with family issues.

Although Muslim clerics denounced all magical practices as un-Islamic, the punishment for fortune-telling is not as severe as witchcraft and sorcery. While sorcery is viewed as the intentional practice of malevolent black magick; fortune telling is perceived as the use of magick to acquire unseen knowledge.

Quranic Occult

To fully comprehend contemporary witch hunts and the prevalence of magical beliefs within the Muslim world, it is necessary to understand the concept of jinn. Jinn is viewed as the Islamic explanations for evil, illnesses, health, wealth, and position in their society; together with all the mundane and inexplicable phenomena in between. The word jinn, also known as jinnee, djinn, djinni, genii or genie is derived from the Arabic root j-n-n which means to hide or be hidden; like the Latin word occult which means hidden.

In many western cases, occult practices are marginalized and relegated to pagan traditions or the mystical aspects of religious traditions. But, in Islam, jinns are an integral part of Islamic theology. According to the Qur'an: God created humans from clay, angels from light, and jinns from smokeless fire. Although the belief in jinns isn't one of the five pillars of Islam - a person is not considered a Muslim if he or she does not believe in their existence. As recorded in the Quranic missive, both humans and jinns are the only two intelligent earthly species. While jinns are often described as angels and demons, they are complex intermediary beings who, like humans, possess free will and can embrace goodness or evil. They are required to worship God, and their deeds will be decreed on Judgement Day.

Shayatin (devils) are evil jinns and *Iblis* (Satan) is their chief. They can shapeshift into humans or animals. In the Islamic tradition: dogs, urine, feces, and blood are intrinsically impure, and jinns are known to mutate to become dogs and dwell in bathrooms, graveyards, and other unclean places. Muslims also believe that evil jinns are phantom entities that can possess humans and utilize their paranormal influences over them. Many Islamic countries adjudged women to be weaker in their faith and are impure during menstruation; hence they are more susceptible to the power of jinns.

Although jinns are relegated as fantasy characters to many believing Muslims in the West, they continue to believe in their existence. Witches, sorcerers, and fortune tellers are deemed to be under the control of jinns and are referred to as "jinn catchers."

Jinns are intrinsically intertwined with the practice of both licit and illicit black magick (*sihir*). Quranic black magick is utilized by those who have learned to summon the evil jinns to serve their human purposes; while licit Quranic magick adduces Allah's guidance to exorcize the *Shayatin*. Spiritual healers who do not employ Quranic healing methods are designated as witches and sorcerers.

In Riyadh, the qualified exorcists were natives designated by the religious authorities to heal the infected. Although there are contemporary hospitals with psychiatric departments; abusive and quasi-medical practices have been committed in the name of Quranic magick.

A common practice I witnessed was the chaining of a mentally ill patient to a religious shrine for forty days to exorcize the jinn that had possessed the man. The possessed was only fed bread and black pepper. He wasn't allowed to change clothing and was forced to sleep on the ground until his release. This man did not survive the harsh treatments. After death, he was buried in an earthen mound near the shrine where he was chained.

There are western educated Muslim physicians, mullahs, and religious scholars that are against these inhuman practices but are inclined to attribute difficult cases to possession. It is without a doubt that clerics believe in the powers of jinns. They would no more question the existence of jinns than they would the Quran.

In my opinion, the Islamic strategy to win souls is through divine protection via Allah or jinns. Hearts and minds will then follow their belief system. These were my brushes with Islamic magick that left strong marks, which is difficult to dislodge after I left my harem services.

Boys, I look forward to your contributions on this magickal topic.

    Best wishes,
    David

In The Kasbah (Chapter Thirty-Four)

"Magick is the art and science of causing change to occur in conformity to will."
Aleister Crowley

First Week of November 1968
Kasbah Tamadot, Atlas Mountains, Morocco

Count Mario Conti, the Italian socialite, had friends around the world and Morocco was no exception to the rule. An invitation arrived from the Count's Italian compatriot, Señor Luciano Tempo for our entourage to reside at his country estate, The Kasbah Tamadot; located at the foothills of the Atlas Mountains. This Venetian was an interior designer and antique dealer in Carmel, California. He fell in love with the richness of Moroccan style and hospitality. While air-ballooning across the Atlas, he stumbled across a splendid villa in southern Marrakesh and took on the challenge to restore this ruined kasbah to its former glory. In the process, he added his individualistic indulgence in comfort and luxury to his fortified dwelling. Every room and surface were a feast for the eyes. While the decorative ensemble pays homage to traditional Moroccan style, the intricate details were pure Luciano Tempo. Although antiques and artifacts juxtapose in dizzying profusion, it was decorated with a sense of proportion than clutter. This interior designer had made it his life's mission to reconstruct this ancient habitat to its former glory until he sold it to Sir Richard Branson in later years and became one of the most spectacular Virgin Limited-Edition hotels in Morocco.

When we were guests at Mr. Tempo's magnificent estate, refurbishing was still in progress. In preparation for our Atlas Mountain hike, we rested our tired feet at this luxury outpost. Kasbah Tamadot was also the final destination of our North Africa tour before Andy, and I joined Tad and Curt in Buenos Aires as cheerleaders to the sportsman international polo tournament.

Kasbahs are to Morocco what castles were to medieval Europe. These bastioned domiciles once housed the region's nobility. The high crenelated walls, towers, and interior courtyards protected them from unwarranted invaders. In 1968, dotted around the southern Moroccan landscape were ruined kasbahs - some deserted and some inhabited by squatters.

Upon our arrival at Kasbah Tamadot, I was surprised to find Tad and Eberhardt. Together with another unexpected guest, they had turned up unannounced. She was none other than Prince P's American girlfriend, Anastasie. This beautiful female decided to join her prince charming in between her numerous modeling assignments. Little did we know that her arrival would lead to a feud between her and the musicologist, Mariam.

Dinner Conversations

The dining-room in Luciano's Kasbah, where the ceiling bordered with 17th-century Burmese prayer books and silver Berber wedding-belt buckles adorned with the auspicious hand of Fatima were used as napkin rings; our entourage was served a scrumptious dinner by local servants. A pair of enormous sculpted Thai fish stood guard at the edge of the central courtyard's pool, where schools of golden carps swam playfully in response. Mr. Tempo hosted this lavish soiree to honor the arrival of his princely guests - Prince P and Sheik Fahrib and their entourages.

As we watched the setting sun disappear behind the High Atlas Mountains, Tad asked our host, *"How did you chance upon this winsome place?"*

"Ahh! It's a dramatic story. Are you sure you want to hear my boring narration?" Luciano answered musingly.

We nodded chucklingly.

He resumed, *"Several years ago, I nearly plummeted to death on those very peaks (he pointed to the mountainous backdrop) during an ill-fated balloon expedition launched from Marrakech. The helium in my balloon contracted more than expected as the night air replaced the Moroccan sunshine. My companion and I fired our burners in vain. We plummeted at a rate of 2,000 feet per minute from 20,000 feet above sea level. We thought to leap into the darkness in an attempt to land by parachute, but the rocky and uninhabited ground offered little chance of survival. So we dumped weights over the sides to slow the fall."*

He paused to puffed his cigar and sip his Cabernet Sauvignon before he re-commenced, *"We hurled everything out the door. Suitcases, our clothes and a bag full of money. It was worth losing a bit of money because we managed to stop before the balloon hit the ground. We were also able to stabilize the balloon and remained afloat throughout the night. The next morning a squadron of heavily armed Algerian soldiers found us and brought us to a local warlord in the middle of the Sahara."*

"It was a sort-of-luxurious kidnapping," he jested. *"We told the warlord that we would love to go home, but he kept us as ransom. I spotted this tranquil ruin when the president of Algeria finally sent a helicopter to rescue us.*

"I decided to purchase the fortress to commemorate my air-balloon adventure. I fell in love with the property and made it my mission to refurbish this enchanted fortress," Señor Tempo iterated.

"What a magical story," Mario exclaimed. *"While we're here, I want to do a fashion shoot in hot-air balloons across the Atlas."*

"That can be arranged," his compatriot announced. *"It's a great way to see these magickal cordilleras."* Again, he pointed to the panoramic backdrop.

Two days after our arrival at Kasbah Tamadot, it was arranged that we sojourn by air balloons up the Atlas. This adventure would prove censorious to both Mariam and Anastasie as their feud took on a new meaning to the term - "superbitches."

Third Week of September 2014
Andy's Response to David's "Magickal" Email, c/c to Me

Hi David,

In response to your "Magickal" message; I suggest we first examine the term Magic or Magick. These are general names given to all kinds of arts that produce demonstrable effects in shifting the balance of the universal aura known as Cár'áll or Styrásh-cár'áll. These effects may result in a person's advantage or harm. Such a shift of universal energy/aura can either be attained through the efforts of a trained mind, through the wanted or unwanted assistance of supernatural forces or departed spirits or by an intentional or arbitrary mastery of nature's secret forces. Magick can be cast intentionally by almost anyone who can establish contact with the aura through a direct channel.

There are many aspects of magic that are unexplained, especially the kinds that happen accidentally or intentionally. Like in life and death situations where folks who have never cast spells had managed to survive through supernatural assistance, which they had somehow manufactured on their own.

One explainable example is the magical manifestation of the will. It is this principle that all magical theories are based. The first thing apprentices at the *Mages' Academy of Xima* (Institute of Magic or School of Magic) learn, is *The Sentences of Will* – the ability to master one's own will. *The Sentences of Will* are not only applicable to individuals but also to nature. Although this theory is heavily disputed among Santharian scholars; for me, it is the most probable.

The Power of Will

The main implication to *The Sentences of Will* is that the might of magick is strongly related to willpower; where the spell caster's power of imagination can determine the Magic's intensity. Therefore, mages with a lack of focus or intelligence are incapable of casting powerful or destructive spells.

Not only was the Moroccan Thaumaturgist you mentioned, perceptive; she was also focused on her drive to succeed. Amira firmly believed that her magical charms could assist Shabana to conceive an heir to inherit her husband's fortune.

The tools used by mages who lack willpower is to enhance the caster's ability to focus on his/her mental energies and to transform auras to their desired effect.

Tools commonly used by sorcerers, sorceresses, wizards, and witches are:

Magical formulas: These incantations are recited aloud when spells are cast during focus magic. Recitations are a central part of Elemental Magic; although Clerical Mages also recite short prayers that resemble magical formulas.

Spell Books and Tomes of Prayers: While Elemental Mages use Spell Books; clerics prefer to utilize Tomes of Prayers. The differences are - Spell Books contain magical formulas to cast spells while Tomes of Prayers include mantras and short prayers to wield their influences. A mage and cleric usually carry such a book with him/her to transcribes newly learned spells into their volumes.

Runes and Symbols: In physical form runes and symbols can be drawn in the air, on a piece of cloth or on the ground. The drawing of runes or symbols can transfer the caster's magical energy into these signs and channel its power into physical form. This technique is used to create *Spell Scrolls*. If these runes and symbols already exist in a definite matrix, a mage can use this mold to transcribe the spell into his/her *Spell-Book*.

Reagents: This application is usually used by Elemental Mages to cast lower level spells to achieve the desired effects. Novice mages often carry pouches with strange items like snake skins, dried rat blood, garlic, sulfur or dark earth. These are similar to Amira's vials and bottles of "unknown" liquids that you described. These items assist the caster in guiding his/her spell towards the desired direction. *Reagents* are consumed by the energies of the spell and cannot be rehashed.

Spell Scrolls: These parchments are used to cast spells instantly. This magical activation will drain less of the caster's energy. The only drawback is the *Spell-Scrolls* can only be used once before they crumbled to dust.

Artifacts: These religious relics work as a catalyst to conjure, add, disrupt or redirect other spells. They are also used to improve the defensive or offensive skills of the wearer.

Joining of Wills: This is the combination or the joining of magical strength by two or more mages to achieve a similar goal. This act adds to their willpower and to amplify their focus to become more potent. This is a technique *Weavers* (a secret mage organization who are capable of weaving strands of raw magic as a group) frequently used to release complicated magick formations.

Although these optional tools are used to cast magic easily and efficiently; nearly all spellcasters cannot do without them. In truth, the fewer tools a mage requires, the more formidable his/her willpower.

I will illuminate you further if you are interested. If you have any "Magickal" questions you would like to fire my way, I'll do my best to answer.

For now, I bid the both of you well.

Andy

Last Week of September 2014
My Questions to Andy and David's "Magickal" Emails

My dear ex-Big-Brother,

Can you tell us how you know so much about magical applications? Since when did you transform yourself into a sorcerer? Or are you a wizard?

David, was the E.R.O.S./V.T.A. recruit (the one who copulated with Shabana with Mustafa's enchanted sperm smeared on his penis) indicted, incarcerated or sentenced to death? What happened to the secret society? Was it exposed during the trial?

Both your emails are beguiling. I'm eager to learn more. ☺

Yours truly,
Young

The Pursuit of Happiness (Chapter Thirty-Five)

"There is no such thing as the pursuit of happiness, but there is the discovery of joy."
                                                        Joyce Grenfell

Third Week of August 1968
Rules Restaurant, London, England

The week Andy and I spent with my surrogate dad and my mother flew by quickly. My lover was super-attentive to the beloved Mrs. Foong. She, in turn, wasted no time to shower my Valet with praises for his gallantry. Andy's gentlemanly charm had won over my mom and her coterie. After mother and her entourage departed to Malaya, Andy and I stayed with Uncle James for an additional day before we returned to Daltonbury Hall.

The evening before Andy and I were scheduled to leave for school, the three of us had a heart-to-heart talk at *Rules;* London's oldest and one of the most celebrated restaurants in the world.

Over two hundred years and spanning the reigns of nine monarchs, *Rules* has been owned by three families. Just before The Great War; Charles Rule, a descendant of the founder, thought of moving to Paris. By sheer coincidence, he met a Briton by the name of Tom Bell, who owned a Parisian restaurant called the *Alhambra*. The two men agreed to swap businesses. During the war, Mr. Bell, an officer in the Royal Flying Corps left the running of *Rules* to Charlie, the Head Waiter, who had served Charles Rule for many years.

During the second world war, *Rules* structure was reinforced with thick wood if German bombs fell on its premise. The restaurant also remained open from 1PM to 3PM to offer the compulsory rationed meals at five shillings and was the only eatery to serve copious rabbits, grouse, and pheasants that were not distributed.

It was in this historic establishment that Uncle James enquired of my lover, *"Andy, what are your plans for the future?"*

My Valet answered without a thought, *"To look after Young."*

"That's well and good but what is your plan when you leave Daltonbury Hall at the end of the year?" the Englishman queried lightheartedly.

"I applied to several universities in Australia and New Zealand to pursue an engineering degree," Andy replied.

"How do you plan to look after Young when the both of you are oceans apart?" my uncle queried.

"I hope Young will go with me Down Under to pursue his fashion studies," my lover opined.

Although I knew my chaperone had plans to further his education in engineering, I did not expect him to drag me to the opposite end of the world, where fashion was a non-existential humdrum byproduct instead of a celebrated art form like London, Paris or Milan.

I was immersed in thoughts when Pinkerton directed his question to me, *"What are your thoughts on this, Young?"*

I replied halfheartedly, *"It's all too sudden. I've to sleep on it."*

My lover glared at me incredulously as if I had committed a crime by not agreeing to his proposition immediately. I felt guilty and avoided eye contact with my chaperone.

"*This is an important decision for Young. He should have time to think it over,*" James declared.

I announced suddenly, "*Like Andy, who had given his time to care for me, I also wish to be a Big-Brother and mentor to a new E.R.O.S. recruit. I like to volunteer my time to prime a Daltonbury Hall freshman before I enroll to a fashion college.*"

My surrogate father opined, "*That's a great conviction I cannot dispute. I admire your intrepidity. How do you feel about this, Andy?*"

"*I can't disagree with Young's altruistic certitude. I guess I'll have to be a Big-Brother for another year to wait for this chap to complete his mission. Then we can depart Down Under for our further education,*" my lover remarked.

My uncle evinced, "*Andy, you have to follow your passion instead of putting your life on hold. If your heart is not fully engaged in the pursuit of your dreams, you'll not be happy with yourself and Young.*"

"*I'll be happy wherever Young is. I cannot do without him,*" Andy proclaimed.

"*Ahh! The beauty of young love is much to be admired and misprized. I suggest you, guys consider your propositions carefully before jumping to a conclusion you'll regret,*" James advised.

Just then, a waiter arrived to take our order.

As soon as the man departed, Pinkerton resumed, "*Andy, you are an intelligent chap. I'm sure you are aware that happiness is elusive, and it is also a state of well-being that encompasses living a good life. In short, with a sense of meaning and deep satisfaction.*

"*From my experience, happiness is not to feel good all the time. An even-keeled mood is psychologically healthier than a mood in which one achieves great heights of happiness regularly. After all, what goes up must come down. I call this 'The Up-side of Feeling Down.' Negative emotions do us great favors. They save us from ourselves. In my line of work, I've asked many of my clients and friends what makes their lives worth living? They usually cite things that they find meaningful, such as their work or relationships instead of their mood. That's why I want you guys to be sure that the decision you make is the right choice for the both of you."*

"Your advice is an obeisance I'll take to heart, sir. Do illuminate us further," Andy commented.

"Andy, you are such a gentleman. Young is lucky to have you," my uncle remarked zealously.

James gave me a mischievous wink before he resumed, *"While living below the poverty line makes it hard to be happy, happiness is not about being rich or being able to afford everything you want to purchase. Money can't buy happiness. The exception to this rule is when you spend your hard-earned money on experiences with other people.*

"For example, if you took the bonus you earned and went on a new and exciting weekend getaway with your friends or family, then you might feel happier. However, this is rarely the way people choose to disburse their windfalls. Most likely, they would use the money on themselves to give their egos a boost. While this excites them temporarily, it is only a matter of time before their expectations change to fit their new budget. Before they know it, they are just as happy or unhappy before they received the bonus.

"Third, and certainly not the last: Happiness is not a destination. The adage, 'Are we there yet?' is often applied to discussions on happiness. As if a person works towards happiness and suddenly one day it 'arrives' at his or her doorstep. On the contrary to popular belief, unless you are one of the few and far between, who won the genetic lottery and is naturally happy; it takes regular effort to maintain happiness.

I questioned, *"Uncle, so far you have listed three items that happiness isn't. What, then is happiness?"*

My surrogate dad gave a hearty laugh before he explained, *"One technique to be happier is to keep a habitual gratitude journal of happy life events. Be thankful for all the positive and negative occurrences that life brings. This will help you discover the meaning of happiness."*

"Is it that easy?" I asked puzzlingly.

Pinkerton responded cheerfully, *"Happiness is a combination of how satisfied you are with your life. An excellent example is to find meaning in your work or career. It is also a matter of how good you feel on a day-to-day basis. To put it directly - our life changes and our mood fluctuates, but our general happiness is often genetically determined. The good news is, this can be offset with consistent effort.*

"Think of happiness as your weight. If you eat the way you want and is active, your body will settle at a specific weight. But if you choose to eat less and exercise more, your weight will adjust accordingly. If that new diet or exercise regimen becomes a part of your everyday life, then you'll stay at this new weight. If you go back to overeating and chooses not to exercise, your weight will return to where it started. The same applies to happiness.

"In other words, with consistent practice, you can control how you feel. You are able to form life-long habits for a satisfactory and fulfilling life."

My Valet interposed, *"When I was at the Bahriji (Oasis) School, one of my professors taught us the seven habits of happy people."*

"And what are they?" James inquired.

"These were the pointers Professor Henderson gave:

Relationship - Express what is in your heart. **He counseled that people who have one or more close friends** *are happier, and it doesn't matter if we have an extensive network of close relationships or not. The difference is how often do we engage in the group activities to share our personal feelings. He termed this as 'Active-constructive responding.' It's the ability to show genuine interest in what people say and to respond with encouragement. This, he advised, is a powerful way to enrich relationships and cultivate positive emotions.*

Acts of Kindness – Cultivate kindness. *The professor commended people who volunteer or care for others on a consistent basis. He discerned that they are happier and less depressed. 'Caring' can involve volunteering as part of an organized group or club or it can be reaching out to a colleague or classmate who is lonely and/or struggling with an issue. Like what we, as Big-Brothers and Valets are to our charges.*

Exercise and Physical Well-being – Dr. Henderson also advice to keep active and eat healthily. He instructed that regular exercise is associated with improved mental well-being and lower depression. He went on to explain that the ancient adage, 'sound body, sound mind,' and a 'gut-brain axis,' are the links to counter depression. These actions make a person happier and well-balanced."

I queried before Andy could continue. *"What is 'gut-brain axis?"*

"'Gut-brain axis' is the biochemical signals that take place between the gastrointestinal tract and the central nervous system," my uncle clarified.

"Young, please don't ask so many questions and let me continue," my lover admonished.

He resumed, *"That brings me to Flow –* Find your flow. *Dr. Andrew stated that if we are deeply involved in reaching a goal, or activity that is both challenging and well suited to our skills; we merge into a happy state called flow. He went on to cite examples of activities such as playing sports, an instrument, or teaching; these can produce the experience of 'flow.' Flow is a type of intrinsic motivation. 'You do what you're doing because you like what you're doing. If you learn only for external, extrinsic reasons, it is unlikely you'll remember what you did.'*

"The fifth habit: Spiritual Engagement and Meaning. Henderson revealed that spirituality is closely related to the discovery of a deeper kind of happiness that generates a higher meaning in one's life.

Strengths and Virtues – *'Discover and use your strengths,'* my ex-professor advised. The happiest people are those that have discovered their unique strengths; such as persistence, critical thinking, and virtues. By applying those strengths and virtues for a greater purpose than for one's personal goals, we can achieve 'Authentic Happiness' to realize our potential for lasting fulfillment.

Positive Mindset – *His final words on happiness are to treasure gratitude, mindfulness, and hope.* Similar to your advice, sir; my mentor stated that grateful people show greater positive emotions, a significant sense of belonging, and lower incidences of *depression* and stress."

"Andy, you don't need me to give you advice on happiness. You know it already," my surrogate dad articulated amusingly.

Our "Pursuit of Happiness" topic transmuted to other matters of the day when our scrumptious food arrived.

Sexual Starvation (Chapter Thirty-Six)

"The pain of sexual frustration, of repressed tenderness, of denied curiosity, of isolation in the ego, of hatred poisoning all love and generosity, permeates our sexuality. What we love we destroy."

Germaine Greer

First Week of November 1968
Kasbah Tamadot, Atlas Mountains, Morocco

I was summoned to the *Majesty*, my Master's chamber, the evening of his and my tutor's return. He was in a flutter when I entered. He paced around the room and muttered to himself.

The moment he saw me, he seethed, *"How can Mario do such an underhanded thing to me?"*

"Do what underhanded thing to you, sir?" I inquired.

"He stole Kalf from me the moment I left for Buenos Aires. Do you know that he and Kalf are an item?"

He did not await my reply before he fumed, *"He is aware I desired the lad for myself, yet he went ahead and stole him from under my nose!"*

Before I could comment, he resumed irefully, *"I should have known not to trust that bastard. As soon as my back was turned, he's up to no good. I'll never forgive him!"*

"I'm sure Mario would consult you in such an important matter. It is an oversight on his part. I've no doubt that a word with him will resolve the situation," I said soothingly to subside his anger.

"Kalf told me that the rascal pursued him relentlessly. When he refused his advances, he forced himself on him. This is outrageous!" The athlete vociferated.

I was shocked to hear such a proclamation, especially when the three males had a blithe liaison before my Master's departure to Argentina. I found his pronouncement a challenge to comprehend.

"Have you spoken with the Count about this?" I questioned.

"I don't need to. I know for a fact that, that bastard Italian is the wild-type and he'll deny any wrongdoing," the Arab huffed.

"How can you be sure? Shouldn't you give him the benefit of the doubt and listen to his side of the story?" I proposed.

He countered, "I trust Kalf more than I trust the scoundrel. He has a history of manipulating his conquest before he ditches them. I have no respect for that man."

"I thought the both of you were the best of friends?" I remarked.

"Not after this! It's over! I want nothing to do with that scoundrel. He is contemptuously disgusting!" my Master declared.

I inquired curiously, "What exactly did Kalf tell you?"

"He said when he refused his advances, the rogue raped him and held him captive," the Arab revealed.

"This man you described doesn't sound like Count Mario Conti I know. He had never laid a hand on me without my consent. Are you sure Kalf is telling the truth?"

The moment I voiced my consternation, I knew I shouldn't have. Since my Master was deeply infatuated with the Moroccan, my controversial comment only added insult to injury.

I quickly rephrased my question, *"Although, I do not doubt Kalf's narrative; wouldn't it be prudent for you to hear Mario's side of the story?"*

The athlete exclaimed before I could continue. *"I'M NOT SPEAKING TO THAT SCUMBAG!"*

"If you are agreeable, sir, let me speak to the Count. Tomorrow, I'm working with him on the air balloon photo shoot. I'll ask him in private, and make sure that our group has no knowledge of our conversation," I assured.

"Do what you want, boy. I don't trust the Italian any more than I have credence with a hypocrite," my Master evinced agitatedly.

I moved closer to him and ran my fingers along his half unbuttoned shirt. My hand traced his beard line, down his muscular chest and to his hairy navel. His impish smile indicated that my seduction had eased his vexation. Tad courted my investigation with a passionate kiss. I reached to cup his bulbous globes. His strong palpitations pronounced his readiness to relinquish his indignation to embrace lust.

As my oral expertise worked its magic on my Master's erection, his livid demeanor transformed to loving affections. He was unwilling to relinquish the euphoria I had licentiously bestowed on his masculinity. He lifted me onto the bed to cherish my tenderness as if I was Kalf, the boy he desires to possess. For now, I was a convenient substitute who held the proficient skills to satisfy his carnal pleasure.

On the other hand, I greeted our eroticism with unrivaled ecstasy. After all, I was a well-groomed E.R.O.S. recruit, explicitly trained for circumstances such as the one I found myself in.

Starved of sexual nourishment, the seasoned athlete devoured every part of me. His pent-up sexual tensions had burrowed its way into a fist of fury; when all he required was a liberation of venereal energies that had engulfed his person.

    I nuzzled my face between his fuzzy buttocks as he begged my tongue to jab into him with gusto. I was more than willing to oblige when my lingua prowess swirled around his twitching orifice. My Master was in seventh heaven as I feasted on his privates. Like a suckling infant, I guzzled on his dangling roundnesses and devoured his throbbing protrusion with cherished devotion. When he could no longer relinquish my lubricious sanctity, he flipped me onto my back and plunged into me. My inner sanctum welcomed his onslaught and urge him towards the point of no return, while his massiveness stroked me to cries of triumphant provocations. The athlete poured forth his repressed libation into my receptive incubator. Not only did his release stimulate my sprightliness, but it also restructured his fiery comportment to his usual exuberance.

    My Master had fallen into a peaceful slumber by the time I left the *Majesty*. As I proceeded towards the suite I shared with my Valet, I was determined to get to the bottom of the feud between the photographer and the athlete.

Early October 2014
Andy's Reply to My Query, c/c to David

Hi boys,

    Hahahaha!

    Young, I am not a sorcerer or a wizard. I fell into a deep depression when I moved to Australia. My condition worsened, and there were days I could not get out of the bed. I also suffered from insomnia and binge-ate.

    The doctors could not diagnose my problem. Instead, they prescribed me with a variety of antidepressant and sleeping pills to temporarily alleviate the complications. These drugs made matters worse and made me bilious.

One of my rowing pal, Paul, suggested I visit a native Sharman who could perform miracles on people with similar conditions like mine. It was Sharman Yarran who illuminated me on aborigine magick and magical applications. He diagnosed my problem the instant he set eyes on me. He asked if I have intimate friends in Australia. I told him that I left Canada after several disastrous relationships and I wanted to start afresh in Casterton. I had just joined the local rowing club, and Paul recommended him to me.

He shook his head and remarked, *"It's been a while since you had sexual contact with a person. Your dis-ease is from the lack of physical intimacy."*

I did not respond.

"You need to kiss, spoon, to hear someone else's heartbeat, and to feel the touch of their hands on your body. To put it mildly, you require the intimacy of an affectionate human to disperse the negative energies that have invaded your mind, body, and soul.

"Although I can temporarily alleviate your suffering, you, yourself must release your internal negativity back to nature. I'll recite a healing incantation and perform a cleansing ritual to drive out the fatalistic forces that had lodged in your system," Yarran analyzed.

He instructed me to sit cross-legged in the middle of a fiery circle before he encircled the ring and sprinkled holy water into the fire before he delivered an Aboriginal chant. As soon as the water hit the flames, uncanny bluish-green vapors surrounded me. I fell into a trance.

I journeyed back in time. In my fugue state, I witnessed the discontentments, arguments, unhappiness, regrets and a host of antipathetic emotions from past relationships that surfaced like phantom apparitions to suffocate my advancement. Suddenly, a pair of loving hands reached for me like your hands, Young that held me before you fall asleep. You pulled me from the rut and lifted me to serenity, where I thrive in harmony.

When I came out of the trance, the fiery ring had dwindled to ashes. Sharman Yarran held my hands and enquired as to how I felt.

"I feel relief," I answered.

"You're suffering from severe sexual frustration. I suggest that you find yourself an affectionate partner to share the beauty of life," he advised.

That evening while I laid awake in bed, I delineated my relationship failures. These were what I surmised:

I had bottled up many unresolved emotions when I left New Zealand for Canada. I had not mentioned any of my inner turmoils to anyone. I thought I had gotten over my messy breakup with my New Zealander boyfriend, Toby, but all I did was run to another country to evade my unresolved issues. I thought that my adverse predicaments would rectify itself over time. I did not suspect that it would manifest into a sexual intimacy issue.

When I got to Alberta, I was fully engaged in my engineering position and buried myself in work. I ignored everything around me and plunged into my new job with heart and soul. I had little to no contact with anyone except my colleagues, who were folks whom I would never discuss my relationship countenance. When I plowed through another detrimental separation with a French Canadian boy, Guy, my dis-ease caught up with me. Again, I ran away post-haste to Australia without confronting my precipitations.

My failed relationships had me heading in the opposite direction from any potential intimacies. Although I had casual encounters, they did nothing to satisfy my longing for that particular person. I'm sure you can guess who that person is, Young? ☺

The build-up of this defeatist energy added insult to injury. It manifested as manic depression and left me little choice but to tackle my trepidations head-on. Yarran assisted me to inspect myself truthfully and openly. I spoke freely about matters of the heart, soul, and mind with him. He became my confidant.

He initiated my return to the dating arena. That was how I met Albert, my life partner of eight years who recently passed away from AIDS-related complications.

Well guys, so much for my "Magikal" experience. I look forward to your responses.

For now, I bid thee au revoir.

Andy

Mentorship (Chapter Thirty-Seven)

"Mentoring is a brain to pick, an ear to listen, and a push in the right direction."

John C. Crosby

End of August 1968
Daltonbury Hall, England

I was glad to be back at Tolkien Brotherhood, the fraternity dormitory I was assigned to Daltonbury Hall. Andy had returned to Kipling Society where he belonged. The week before classes resumed for the Fall semester, I was summoned to the headmaster's office. Although I knew that my final Household assignment was at وكر الذئب *Aldhdhib Dann (Wolf Den),* Tad's palatial mansion in Riyadh; I also wanted to inform the principal of my desire to become a Big-Brother.

When I arrived at Dean Dawson Higgins' office, Andy was already waiting outside the chamber. Since it wasn't customary for Big-Brothers (BBs) or Valets and their respective charges to meet the principal together, I was astonished to see my Valet. After all, the principal/student audience was a private session, and a third party would be a privacy intrusion. I was eager to find out my chaperone's present.

The moment Andy closed the office door, Dean Higgins motioned us to sit across his large oak desk.

He began, *"It is nice to see the two of you back at school. How were your summer holidays?"*

My Valet answered, *"Thank you for asking, sir. Both Young and I had a beautiful summer in the Lake*

District with my auntie, and with our respective parents in London."

"That is excellent! Let's get down to business," Professor Dawson expressed.

My Valet and I glanced at one another. We wondered if we had done something indecorous, but none came to our minds.

The dean continued, *"Young, it is brought to my attention that your E.R.O.S. services are coming to fruition. You graduate after the Fall and Andy, your notable contribution as a Big-Brother cum Valet has been conscientiously recorded.*

"My questions to the both of you - what are your plans after you leave Daltonbury Hall?"

My BB looked at me before I spoke, *"Since I entered Daltonbury Hall I'd grown by leaps and bounds. I like to thank you, sir, for giving me the opportunity to experience life outside of school."*

Dr. Higgins gave an appreciative smile before he declared, *"It is our responsibility to provide and equip our students with a comprehensive education to face the challenges of the outside world. And you, young man, have passed the stimulus with flying colors. The question remains - what is your plan for the foreseeable future?"*

"I would like to give back some of my time to groom and mentor a Freshman," I responded earnestly.

"That is altruistic of you, son." He paused before he resumed, *"Being a Big-Brother is a demanding post. The chosen candidates will undergo three months of intensive training and examinations. Several of our staff members and current Big-Brothers are heading the inculcation programme,"* the headmaster articulated.

"I understand, sir," I explicated.

The headmaster resumed, *"Before I can give my permission for you to proceed with your BB application, you'll have to meet with the mentorship committee for approval. If the consent is granted, I will forward you the application forms to complete. Before you leave for the Bahriji (Oasis School), you'll be notified of an appointed meeting.*

He turned to Andy for a response to my inquiry.

"Sir, I would also like to stay on for another term as a Big-Brother/Valet," my chaperone announced.

The principal did not appear pleased with my Valet's pronouncement.

"Andy, for the past three years, you've been an excellent mentor to several Freshmen, especially to Young. In my opinion, it is time for you to pursue your career and to seek higher accomplishments?

"Don't get me wrong, your unwavering support to Daltonbury Hall and the Enlightened Royal Oracle Society mentorship programme hasn't gone unnoticed. We are grateful for your munificent contributions, but you must also consider what is best for you. The advancement of your university education is as important as your philanthropic benefactions," the elder counseled.

He added, *"Your parents approached me to inquire about your future plans. They would like to see you enroll in a renowned engineering university or college. Although the decision is entirely yours, I'm acting as a messenger to deliver their intentions. A word of advice before I let the both of you go; trust your instinct, and the correct decision will manifest."*

As soon as Andy closed the office door, he vociferated, *"Why can't my father leave me alone, instead of meddling in my life!"*

I was surprised to hear those words from my respectful Valet.

"You shouldn't be so defensive. Your parents are concerned about your future, and they want the best for you. After all, they are paying for your education, aren't they?" I remarked.

"If they truly love me, they will accept you and my sexuality," my Valet voiced irritatingly.

To soften my lover's dejection, I commented, *"Frauline Maria and your siblings are cordial to me."*

"Yes, but not like your mother, who accepts me with an open heart," he discerned.

"You haven't met my father. He is like your dad, he cannot come to terms with my homosexuality," I declared. *"Yet, you counsel me, not to be so hard on my old man. I'm now reversing your excellent mentorship to entreat that you be not so strident to your father like I did with mine. As you are well aware, the older generation views the world differently than we. There'll always be a generation gap between parents and their children."*

"Me-Oh-My! Since when did you grow up and mature into this judicious stripling?" my Valet teased.

"You once said to me: 'Mentoring is a brain to pick, an ear to listen, and a push in the right direction,'" I quoted my chaperone.

He corrected my statement. *"That extract is not from me but by John C. Crosby, the late American politician from the state of Massachusetts."*

With that affirmation, my lover departed to Kipling Society while I returned to Tolkien Brotherhood to meet my new roommates for the very first time.

Early October 2014
David's Reply to My Query, c/c to Andy

David's message arrived a day after Andy's response. He wrote:

Hi guys,

I feel for you, Andy. Depression is not to be scorned but to be resolved with solicitous cognizance. When I mentored William, a young charge at my boarding school, I encountered a similar situation with this adolescent. I coached him back to health from a nervous breakdown.

Before I lurched into a daunting anecdote, I will answer Young's query about Anthony; the E.R.O.S./V.T.A. recruit who copulated with Shabana with Mustafa's 'enchanted' sperm on his penis. ☺ To cut to the chase, the lad disappeared from Riyadh as rapidly as he had appeared. The E.R.O.S./V.T.A. officials in Saudi Arabia made a deal with the local authorities to not bring charges on Antony. With the blink of the eyes, he was back at his boarding school; as if he had never set foot at the Grand Pavilion in Riyadh. Such were the E.R.O.S./V.T.A. authoritative influences in the Middle Eastern bureaucratic establishments.

The Enlightened Royal Oracle Society/Valkyrian Templers Abbey continued without a care in the world; as if this incident never occurred. I'm confident that the E.R.O.S./V.T.A. elders from across the board took precautions against future mishaps of this nature from ever happening again.

Since there was no trace of Antony to be found, the case rested solely on Amira, the sorceress. As an example, to those who dare to delve in Quranic black magick, she was executed.

Back to my charge, William. He was one of the sweetest fellas I ever knew when we met. He had a beaming smile and a glowing personality any boy his age would envy. Atop that, he took to his harem challenges like a fish to water. No one suspected that this radiant gem was manic depressive. Will was a shining example by day, but when night fell, he locked himself in his room and wallowed in negativity. Any movements outside would trigger his terror. Trepidations engulfed his person and left him paralyzed.

But when the dawn appears, he would regain his ebullience. He kept his Jekyll and Hyde personality in check until I became his BB. In the beginning, he refused to room with me until the school authorities made it mandatory that Big-Brothers had to keep vigilance on their charges twenty-four seven. It was then that I noticed his chameleonic transformation.

At first, I did nothing because I did not wish to jeopardize his prospect for the E.R.O.S./V.T.A. selection but when the nights became too intense, I knew I had to help the lad. I informed the school authorities of his maniacal symptoms. I was glad of what I did even when the lad was temporarily confined to a mental asylum. Eventually, William functioned generally through medical supervisions and treatments. Unfortunately, he did not make it into the Enlightened Royal Oracle Society/Valkyrian Templers Abbey; even though the lad had no idea, he was being considered. Yet, I felt guilty to eradicate his chance to a practical educational experience.

I had to consult my school's psychotherapist shortly after Will's admission into the mental institution. I wanted to be sure that I made the right decision to inform the school authorities of William's condition.

This was Dr. Rufus, my psychotherapist explanation:

"You just failed a big test and are bummed about it. Or, you're going through a bad breakup and feeling down. We've all been there. In our day-to-day life, everyone experiences ups and downs, but as time moves forward, our mood becomes better, and we resume our usual self again. Unlike the average population, individuals living with mental disarray cycle through extreme mood swings that cause disruption to their daily life.

"Bipolar Disorder, Manic Depression, and Bipolar Affective Disorder are synonymous with one another. The classic symptoms of bipolar disorder are the periodic changes in mood, alternating between periods of elevated disposition (mania or hypomania) to bouts of depression. A person living with bipolar disorder may feel energetic, abnormally happy, and make reckless decisions during his/her maniacal states. But, during depressive spells, he/she may feel an overwhelming urge to cry, experience feelings of hopelessness and have a negative outlook on life. Hypomania is a less severe form of mania; where a person generally feels pretty good, with a better sense of well-being and productivity.

"Not only does the bipolar disorder patient feel 'down in the dumps,' his/her depressive state may lead to suicidal thoughts that could transform to feelings of euphoria and a never-ending vivaciousness. These extreme mood swings are frequent. The good news is that there are treatments that can keep a patient's moods in check, thereby allowing the sufferer to live a productive life."

Dr. Rufus also stated the manic symptoms which I listed below:

Extensive periods of feeling "high" with overt elation, gaiety, and immensely friendly disposition.

Extreme irritable feelings.

Easily distracted.

Having racing thoughts.

Talking rapidly.

Have focusing problems; like jumping from one thought to another when conversing.

Undertaking numerous new projects without the ability to complete the assignments.

Restlessness.

Signs of boundless energy.

Sleep negligence and not feeling tired.

The sufferer's unrealistic belief that he/she can achieve the impossible.

Engagements in impulsive, pleasurable, and high-risk behaviors; such as poor financial investments, indiscriminate sexual indiscretions, excessive shopping sprees.

Inflated self-esteem.
Grandiose feelings.
Acute agitation.
Drastic goal-directed activity.
A high sex drive.
Making grand and unattainable plans.
And last but not least, a detachment from reality – psychosis that includes delusions or hallucinations.

Below is a list of depressive symptoms:

Feelings of sadness, tearfulness, hopelessness, and a sense of emptiness for the most part of the day and on a daily basis.

The sufferer takes no pleasure or interest in his/her day to day activities.

He/she also suffers weight fluctuations that include significant weight loss or weight gain.

Sleep disturbances of either sleeping too much or insomnia.

Restlessness or slowed behaviors.
Suicidal thoughts or attempts.
Guilt feelings and worthlessness.
Inability to concentrate.
Indecisiveness.
Enervations and fatigue.
A loss of interest in activities the sufferer once enjoyed.
Anxiety and uncontrollable crying.

Before the doctor sent me on my way, he stated amusingly, *"You, David, you do not suffer from any of the symptoms I'd listed. My prognosis is that you are suffering from a case of guilt which you will overcome in due course. If your guilty conscience persists after six months, then come back to see me. Otherwise, you are cured."*

That my friends were my close encounter with Manic Depression Disorder. ☺

Yours truly,
David

A Dead Ringer Scuffle (Chapter Thirty-Eight)

"I'm not saying they are weak, but they brawl like a couple of bitches on a balloon flight."
                                        Curt Simon Eberhardt

Second Week of November 1968
Above the Atlas Mountains, Morocco

As the air balloons that carried our entourage lifted off from solid ground, I could see clearly from high above. I shared the carriage with the balloon operator, Tanjo, my Valet, Andy, and Mario, the fashion photographer. We glided across Asni (Kasbah Tamadot's nearby town) towards the peaks of the Atlas Mountains. The distant view of Marrakesh resembled Lego bricks crafted into toy-size city blocks. The unbearable lightness of being washed over my person as I busied myself assisting the photographer. Lighter than air and freer than the soaring birds, we sailed on top of the world towards the snowy peaks. It was a sentiment I could never experience on the solid ground.

I plucked up the courage to ask the Count.

"Are you enjoying Kalf's company?" I asked.

He gave me a sheepish grin as if he would rather not discuss his boyfriend. I did not pursue the topic.

After a while, the Italian confided, *"Kalf is not the easiest person to be with."*

"Why?" I queried.

He fiddled with the various dials on his camera and did not answer. When he did, he said, *"It is difficult to predict his mood swings. One minute he could be affectionate, but with a blink of the eyes, he would give me the cold shoulder. I don't know what he's playing at? I find this type of behavior abhorrent."*

"Have you spoken to Tad about this?" I questioned.

He shook his head in anguish.

"Tad is worse. He avoided me like the plague when I approached him. I have no idea what's with the man? Maybe, he's disgruntled that the Moroccan chose me over him."

I tested the waters to get the photographer's response. *"That might be one reason why my Master hasn't been happy since his return."*

"What did he say to you?" the Italian inquired curiously.

"I'm not supposed to divulge my Master's private conversations to anyone," I replied.

My statement stirred the Count to probe further.

"You can tell me, boy. It'll be our little secret," he pledged.

"Can we trade?" I quipped.

"What kind of trade?" the photographer responded with interest.

"If I tell you what my Master revealed; will you impart to me what you did with Kalf?" I sallied.

"What do mean by what I did with Kalf? I don't understand your implication?" the Italian expressed puzzlingly.

I added, *"A little bird told me that you took the Moroccan against his will."*

"What!" he exclaimed. *"I would never do such a thing to anyone without their consent; let alone Kalf. He is old enough to make his own decisions with who and whom he chooses to sleep with."*

He drew me to him and vociferated, *"Who's been spreading such damaging rumors about me? It better not be you, lad!"*

He released his grip when I shook my head.

"It's not me, sir. My Master told me...." Before I could finish my sentence, Mario glared at me sharply.

He voiced angrily, *"It's Tad, isn't it? He is the one spreading this vicious rumor about me because Kalf desired me more than that scoundrel."*

I vindicated, *"He meant no harm, sir. He was concerned about Kalf's wellbeing...."*

Again, I was silenced before I could complete the statement.

"That bastard who calls me his best friend; is nothing but a jealous rumor mongering liar. When I see him, I'm going to thwack that rogue good and hard!" the Count announced ferociously.

My Valet who was then assisting the balloon operator, turned our direction to witness a fuming photographer spilling obscenities about his best friend. Andy scowled at me as if it was I, who had initiated this raunchy pandemonium. I shrugged my shoulders when he came to cool the commotion.

Suddenly, Tanjo gave a loud shriek and pointed his finger at the adjoining air balloon that toted the two female models, who were the subjects of our morning shoot. From a distance, we saw the couture-clad women tearing at one another's throats. Their balloon attendant tried desperately to keep their air-carriage afloat while he tempted to separate Mariam and Anastasie from throwing one another off the edge. The operator was petrified that the wobbling dirigible would collapse under the furor.

Mario, not one to miss a chance to capture some dramatic shots, whisked out his camera and began to click away at the female combatants. Andy and I stared agape at the unfolding scene.

The prince and the sheik shouted through their megaphones in their floating baskets from the opposite direction. They tried to unfazed the hostile females but to no avail.

The winds of change had steered the balloons into the clouds. Enveloped by the cumulonimbus, we could not see the various carriages, let alone witness the catfight that happened a few moments ago.

Tanjo counseled, *"We should return to base immediately. A thunderstorm is brewing in the rippling clouds."*

Our swashbuckling photographer demanded that we sojourn forward. Andy stepped in to reason with the Count. After much persuasion, he agreed to return to the station.

We were wet from the torrential downpour by the time we touched solid ground. The rest of our entourage were already in the building when we entered. Prince P and Sheik Fahrib had sundered the feisty women to different chambers.

Like Raquel Welch in her wet pre-historic garb in *One Million Years B.C.;* the women's ethereal ensembles hugged like seductive Amazonian armors to their lissome physiques. They were ready for battle if the conflict arose again.

When Andy and I entered, Prince P was in the midst of consoling his American girlfriend as she teetered for equilibrium to the feisty brawl, the perilous thunderstorm, and her close encounter with death.

Their air balloons had drifted straight into the eye of the cyclone. Thanks to P, Fahrib, Tad, Curt, Victor, and the operators; the two females and their operator had managed to escape unharmed from the calamity. The three airboats had trussed itself together and pulled one another to safety. It was a narrow escape, and the trauma had drained their insouciant selves to assess the unpredictability of their mortality. This harrowed experience proved to be a turning point in our lives.

As we regained our composure, a series of precipitous noises were heard in the corridor. The men rushed out, only to witness a round of fisticuffs between my Master and the photographer. They hurled and punched at one another like boxers in a boxing ring.

Curt and the sheik rushed to hold back the Sportsman, while Andy and Triqueros tore Mario away from Tad. In confusion, the Count's cuff hit Kalf and sent the Moroccan to the ground. The lad scrunched up in agony and cursed the Italian for his offensive action. He shouted a string of allegations of rape, incarceration, and used as a boy-toy against his will by the Italian.

All eyes turned towards a shocked Mario. Silence fell over us. No one knew what to make of the accusations; let alone the scuffle between the once inseparable bosom pals. If another round of assault would resume, we hurriedly curtailed the explosive situation and ushered the pugnacious trio in different directions.

Andy and I did our best to calm my Master but to no avail. He swore revenge on Mario for his vituperative belligerence towards the apple of his eye. While the Count avowed that he had never violated or imprisoned anyone against their will, let alone the Moroccan.

This exploit ended his bromance with the athlete. The feud between the Playboys continued after Tad had terminated his cursory affair with the quacky bipolar Kalf.

We achieved little success even though my lover and I did our best to amend the men's relationship. The duo finally made peace on a sunny day in the merry month of May 1969. Their bromance resumed with a vengeance as if nothing repugnant had ever happened.

On the other spectrum, Mariam and Kalf bonded like a couple of long-lost siblings. Both had similar aspirations to grip onto the men that succored their physical beauty for them to climb their respective ladders of success. Not only did their clutches resulted in woeful goodbyes;

their dramatic exits also engendered P to shy away from future intimacies with women, and Tad avoided any long-term affinities with potential life partners.

The musicologist moved on to greener pastures after her breakup with the prince. Unfortunate for Kalf, he was back to square one when his fleeting dalliance with my Master ended. The Moroccan revamped himself as a tour guide to wealthy visitors to the Maghreb. That was the last I saw of the femme fatale and the boy toy.

On the contrary, Anastasie made a hasty decision to marry the bisexual prince. By providing P with an heir, she thought she could tether his straying eyes, but sadly, that was not the case. Instead, her speedy resolution caused more damage than an advantage. Subsequently, their child custody litigations flew its fugly colors between the American and the Bahraini Royal family. It ended poorly for both parties.

We disbanded our sojourn up the Atlas after that detrimental air balloon incident. The prince and his entourage returned to Bahrain; while the Sheik, my Master, and our cortège headed to Buenos Aires to bolster Tad's forthcoming Polo tournament. As for the photographer and the supermodel, they left for Paris; where Andy and I rejoined them later for the grand Swarovski fashion presentation.

Second Week of October 2014
My Message to Andy and David

Wow! Both your emails overwhelmed me. I'd no clue that you, my beloved ex-Valet/lover suffered such a traumatic meltdown after we parted ways. My heart reaches out to you.

Our separation wasn't easy for me either. Although I did not suffer a nervous breakdown, I ventured down some disreputable alleyways; as you read in A Harem Boy's Saga – II – Unbridled.

Srihan, the Sri Lankan E.R.O.S. recruit was the only bipolar sufferer I encountered. I know little about Bipolar Affective Disorder except for that incident, and from your account, David.

That leads me to a question - has either of you encountered mythical creatures? I'm curious to know your thoughts on this subject. ☺

Young

Being A Big-Brother (Chapter Thirty-Nine)

"You learn more about life from observing your Big-Brother than from reading a book."
Dr. Richard Lichman

Second Week of September 1968
Bahriji (Oasis) School, Dubai, United Arab Emirates

I couldn't help but wonder how I would fare as a mentor to a Freshman as I contemplated my future Big-Brother's role. At that precise moment my Bahriji fencing instructor, Dr. Richard Lichman bumped into me.

"Young, nice to see you back at the Bahriji," the professor greeted.

I remained quiet when I acknowledged his salutation.

"Why are you looking so glum on this beautiful morn?" he chirped.

"I'm unsure if I'm up to the task as a Big-Brother (BB)?" I replied noncommittally.

"You have the makings of an exceptional BB. There's nothing to worry about," Professor Lichman emboldened.

"Come, have a fencing match with me. I'll demonstrate the X-factors to be a premier Big-Brother," Richard suggested flirtatiously.

I nodded and followed him to the fencing studio.

Fencing Skills

As we changed into our dueling outfits, the professor remarked, *"Big-brothers are like these protective clothing we wear before tournaments. BBs take on a protective role when it comes to the well-being of their young charge, like a lion to its cubs. With his Big-Brother around, Little-Brothers (LB) will never have to worry about creepy men."*

As we stood *en garde* to commence our combat, my instructor inquired, *"Do you remember the person who introduced you to sports and fitness?"*

"My Big-Brother Nikee," I answered.

"That's correct. A Big-Brother can influence his charge to tap into his competitive side. This skill becomes an asset when his Little-Brother tries to succeed in his career path. A BB provides his charge with great insights into the male-dominated world of competition. He will help develop the boy's self-esteem and leadership skills," Richard advised.

Lichman threw me a *feint* without warning. I parried his attack.

"I almost got you. You've to keep your emotions in check when you play the role of a comforter to your LB, especially when he's in a tricky or tragic situation.

"You'll also have to be a defender cum bodyguard and be ready to jump to his aid at a moment's notice. A Big-Brother is his LB's knight in shining armor before his Prince Charming shows up," he expressed amusingly.

Before Richard could complete his sentence, I *remised*. This time around, it was Lichman who countered with a *touch*.

"Got ya there, son," my opponent declared facetiously before he added, *"A BB knows all his Little-Brother's shameful moments. He'll never expose his secrets even if he teases his charge mercilessly. His charge is safe with him because he knows his Big-Bro is his biggest supporter and will brag about him to his friends."*

He paused before he re-commenced teasingly, *"Like Andy is to you."*

I countered with an unexpected *riposte*.

"Ay! You caught me off guard, you crafty devil!" The fencing instructor conveyed.

"You will make a superb Big-Brother. As soon as I get a little too self-assured, you brought me back to reality by a stop-thrust.

"This is definitely a mortifying moment. You were an awkward kid when I taught you, your first fencing move. Now, you're a pro like me," he declared before we ended our gregarious duel and headed to the shower stalls.

Our manhood stood to attention like they did in the past as sprays of sparkling aqua cleansed our athletic physiques. This occasional fuck-buddy of mine gave a flirtatious wink that play was a welcome finale to our combative engagement.

"When your charge feels like the world is crumbling at his feet and he feels as if he cannot do anything right; you, the BB will always be there to catch him when he falls because you never want to see him be anything but unhappy. A Big-Brother will always be there for his charge." Professor Richard Lichman concluded before our evening of fun and games.

Third Week of October 2014
Andy's Response to My Email, c/c to David

Y oung,

You always come up with unconventional topics like encounters with mythical creatures.  The only mythical creature I've encountered is you. You are a unique specimen in a positive way. You are also one fantastical being I'm trying to figure out. Although I don't dwell on the past and had come to terms with our separation; I'm still mystified by the "real" reason you rejected my life partner's proposal. I promised to care for you, but you chose differently.

Over the years, I've failed miserably to find for someone like you. Although I had a couple of successes, they were short-lived. It was your idiosyncratic modus operandi that attracted me to you. After that, I could not omit you from my life.

Don't get me wrong, I'm not trying to win you over from your life partner of twenty-one years. You are happily married, and I respect that. I'm merely reiterating the promise that I'll always be here for you as your ex-Big-Brother and Valet whenever you need my guidance and love.

You have a best friend in me forever.

Love,
Andy

Third Week of October 2014
David's Response to My Email, c/c to Andy

David's email arrived a few days after Andy's message. I couldn't help but simper at their responses.

David's email:

Hi guys,

You two lovebirds should message each other privately and not have me involved. I don't mind reading your lovey-dovey chitter-chatter. Why don't the two of you have a romantic liaison and get it over with, rather than pining over a lost love? ☺

Below is my response to Young's "serious" question. I do have a tale to tell. LOL!

When I vacationed with my family in Nova Scotia in the Fall of 1967, I encountered *Evangeline, A Tale of Acadie*. This epic poem was composed by the American poet, Henry Wadsworth Longfellow. The poesy follows an Acadian girl named Evangeline and her search for her lost love Gabriel. It was set in the period of the Expulsion of the Acadians.

The Legend Of Evangeline

"Our perception of the past is often an illusion, a mirage created as much by the biases of the creators of historical records as by the biases of historians themselves. While historians cannot divest themselves altogether of their personal outlook, molded as it is by environmental factors, they can at least attempt to pierce the veil of subjectivity surrounding their chosen topic."

This is a quote from Carl A. Brasseaux - *In Search of Evangeline: Birth and Evolution of the Evangeline Myth*.

According to Longfellow, Evangeline is a harrowing but fictional account of two lovers. Evangeline and Gabriel were separated on their wedding day during the expulsion of the Acadians from Acadia (present-day Nova Scotia, Canada). In 1755, the English Governor of Canada issued an ultimatum to the Acadians to swear allegiance to the British Crown and to forsake their Catholic faith or be exiled. Those who refused were forced to leave and herded onto ships without regard to family ties.

Upon Evangeline's arrival in Louisiana, she learned that her beloved, Gabriel was in the Atakapa district. Soon she began her journey there and found that Gabriel had left the region in a grief-stricken state. The woman wandered through the American frontier to search for her lost love.

She eventually gave up her search and joined the *Sisters of Mercy* in Philadelphia and dedicated her life to the service of others. Years passed before she found Gabriel on his deathbed. He died in her arms, and she died soon after.

Longfellow had heard the story of Evangeline and Gabriel from a Rev. Horace Lorenzo Connolly at a dinner party. Longfellow did not want his poem to be a documentation of historical events even though he consulted with Thomas C. Haliburton from the Historical and Statistical Account of Nova Scotia.

Other Versions

One of the first Louisiana writers to re-tell the tale was Sidonie de la Houssaye. She used the story in her 1888 novel, *Pouponne et Balthazar*. She details the story as a family legend handed down by her grandmother. In this story, Pouponne Theriot is separated from her fiancé Balthazar Landry during the deportation. Through the period of exile and resettlement, she cared for her fiancé's elderly father and remained faithful to her betrothed. Balthazar attained the rank of Captain in the French army and returns with an education before the couple wed.

The best-known version of the Evangeline story is *Acadian Reminiscences: The True Story of Evangeline*, a novelette by Felix Voorhies who was a district judge and member of the Louisiana House of Representatives. Voorhies' story, published in 1907, is about Emmeline Labiche and Louis Arceneaux, the "real" Evangeline, and Gabriel. According to this version, Emmeline and Louis tried to flee the village of St. Gabriel in old Acadia before the deportation but were caught by the British and were subsequently separated. Emmeline was exiled to Maryland before she arrived in Louisiana with a group of Acadians led by Rene LeBlanc, the former patriarch of St. Gabriel.

According to Voorhies, Emmeline and Louis reunited beneath the oak tree by Bayou Teche in St. Martinsville. By that time, Louis was married to another. Emmeline lost her sanity. Heartbroken, she withered away and died.

The Truth Behind the Myth

This story came to be a thinly veiled historical account until the 20th century. Evangeline and Gabriel were widely accepted as fictional characters. Carl Brasseux, the assistant director of the Center for Louisiana Studies at the University of Southwestern Louisiana, released a book in 1988 to put this traditional tale to rest.

Rev. Jean-Marie James, a pastor at St. Martin de Tours Church in St. Martinsville said, *"Longfellow wrote a beautiful poem, but poetry is not history. Evangeline could have existed, but there was nobody to write history except the pastor of the church who recorded baptisms, marriages, and funerals."*

Since history is defined as recorded past events, none of these stories can be authenticated. Even if Evangeline, or Emmeline Labiche, did not exist, there were plenty of folks who lived, suffered and died as she did. It is likely that the legend persevered because of its romantic appeal and its testimonial to the enduring spirit of Love.

The reason I'm relating this tale to you, guys, is: I hope the both of you will not become the likes of Evangeline and Gabriel; only to reunite on your deathbeds. Conciliate your past differences and get back together while you still have time to reconcile.

I will leave this rigmarole and say no more.

Yours,
David

PART THREE

Argentina - Buenos Aires
Saudi Arabia – Riyadh, Mada'in Saleh مدائن صالح
England - Isle of Wight, London
Brazil - Rio de Janeiro

A Puppet on Strings (Chapter Forty)

"The truest characters of ignorance are vanity, pride, and arrogance."
                                                      Samuel Butler

Third Week of November 1968
The Plaza Hotel Buenos Aires, Argentina

Our arrival at the Plaza Hotel was nothing short of fanfare for the athlete and his entourage. The presence of Sheik Fahrib, one of Sharjah's heir apparent added cloud to this historic establishment. Ernesto Tornquist, the local landowner, banker, and the creator of this monument spared no expense to welcome his distinguished guests. We were greeted by an assortment of well-known Latin American music, played by a big band as our motorcade drove up the hotel's driveway. When the *Himno Nacional Argentino* (Argentine National Anthem) was performed in the elegant foyer, fashioned by Alfred Zucker (of New York Metropolitan Opera House fame), we stood at attention.

In 1968, the Plaza Hotel Buenos Aires was the most elegant and contemporary building in South America. All the rooms were centrally heated with telephone and elevators accessibility. The furniture was imported from Thompson & Co. and Warin & Gillow of London. Statues by Gustav Heinrich Eberlein stood to salute visitors as they entered the great hall. Last but not least, the Spanish artist Vila y Prades enticed guests, the likes of Edith Piaf, Luciano Pavarotti, Indira Gandhi, Charles de Gaulle, and Theodore Roosevelt into the building's inner sanctum with his scrumptiously painted ceilings. This Grande Dame was then and still is one of the most luxurious accommodations this side of South America.

At La Biela Café

La Biela took his name from the Connecting Rod in the engine of a vehicle that transforms a swaying movement to make the car or train runs smoothly.

La Biela is also Buenos Aires historical **café that began life more than a hundred and fifty years ago. Not only was the venue and decorations impressive, but it was also a place for the well-to-do for a social time-out.**

It was in this institution, I circumvented my Master's inamorato; the neurotic and arrogant Kalf. At La Biela, his haughtiness took on a life of its own and little did he suspect that his conceitedness would be his downfall.

In the event of a rainy day, Tad had given the lad a credit card for safe keeping. Instead, the Moroccan used the plastic as if it was free money. **He bought everyone drinks at** La Biela **as if he was a big spender while the athlete was in practice for his upcoming polo tournament.**

Eberhardt remarked, *"I wonder how long his superciliousness will last?"*

My Valet negated, *"We all want to be confident. It is a quality that helps us build strong relationships with others, get things done, and move forward in our work and life."*

My teacher countered, *"It is well and good to have confidence, but if we let it go overboard, confidence can turn into something dark."*

"What is that something dark?" I questioned.

"Arrogance," Curt replied. *"Arrogant people never admit they make mistakes, and when they do, they try to deflect attention to others."*

Even though my Valet knew the answer, he parried, *"And what do humble people do?"*

My teacher declared, *"They readily admit and accept their mistakes, apologize, and learn from them, but this is not Kalf's way."*

I gazed at the Moroccan and quipped, *"He should demonstrate accountability and be responsible for his actions; rather than to deny any wrongdoing and cast the blame on others but himself."*

"You are absolutely correct," the educator commended.

"That fellow should communicate and behave respectfully, instead of flaunting his self-importance," my chaperone remarked.

"He is the height of arrogance. He believes that he knows all the answers and doesn't want to accept the input of others," **Eberhardt** opined.

I chirped, *"Shouldn't he be open-minded and be willing to learn something new?"*

My professor resumed, *"In my opinion, the lad should demonstrate gratitude, give praise and recognition where it is due. Humble people habitually recognize great contributions and find it easy to say thank you and acknowledge someone for the way they make a difference in the world."*

He sighed before he added, *"But I don't see that in the Moroccan."*

"He doesn't practice forgiveness, let alone gratitude," **Andy** remarked.

"My words of advice to you, Young is to ask for honest feedback and act on it," my professor advocated. "My mentor once said that feedback is the breakfast of champions. To do a better job; we need feedback from others. Make a habit to ask for frank, direct, and to the point **criticisms**. When you get them, don't just sit and do nothing. Act on it."

I commented wittily, *"I'll take your advice to heart, sir and act on it."*

And acted on it, I did. I approached Kalf to obtain his egotistical point of view.

A Talk with The Moroccan

Since the teenager was footing the bill, Kalf was preening from the attention by the new E.R.O.S. recruits and their chaperones. They had latched onto the big spender like bees to honey. The Moroccan looked at me cynically when I approached.

I complimented, *"Kalf, I'm glad to see you so radiant."*

He gave me a duplicitous glance to my sudden interest in his wellbeing.

I spoke, *"I come in peace. Can we let our bygones be bygones, so we can start anew?"*

"I'm not like you, I don't forget the past that easily," he grimaced. *"I'll never forgive you for standing in my way."*

I explained, *"I mean no harm. I was doing my Master's bidding to bring Mario, him and you together."*

The lad mocked, *"I'm regarded as a boy toy to those who profess their love for me. While you are everybody's pet, and they love you unconditionally."*

I was shocked by his disclosure before he lashed out loud. *"You get all the good things in life while I, I get nothing but scornfulness. I hate you!"*

His confession brought on a shockwave to those around us. Silence fell over our entourage.

"I didn't know you feel that way about me?" I declared. *"We can be friends rather than enemies."*

The boy broke into tears. I reached to comfort him. He pushed me away and continued to sob. His good-time mates watched without coming to his aid.

Even though it was not my fault that he felt lesser than me, I apologized, *"I'm sorry you feel that way."*

I reached to console the lad again. This time he did not brush my hand away. Instead, he leaned into my chest for solace and wept uncontrollably.

Kalf's pals scattered like ants and dissipated in the face of a dilemma. I was left with the neurotic Moroccan.

A Heart to Heart Chat

Kalf confided in me his inner fears under a tearful face.

He professed, *"I'm never good enough for my parents."*

"You mustn't think that way. You are doing well, and I'm sure they are proud of you," I muttered soothingly.

"You don't know my parents. Ever since I was a child, they nagged me to be what I am not," the Moroccan declared.

"All parents want their children to do well and succeed in the world," I heartened.

"My parents want me to be like my brother, Bushr, a man's man. I tried to imitate him and failed miserably," he announced dishearteningly.

"You are your own man and is living the life you created for yourself. Isn't that a good thing?" I encouraged.

He rebuked my comment. *"My old man wants me to repent from my sinful ways and fulfill my filial duties as a cogent son of Islam. He wants me to marry and produce heirs to continue my family's name."*

"Can't your brother do that?" I inquired.

"Yes and no," the boy uttered.

I beckoned him to continue.

He mumbled, *"Bushr is married, but he is childless. Although he sees other women outside the marriage, he treats them as playthings to be had and discarded at will."*

I discerned, *"Did your brother treat you like a plaything when you were a child?"*

He nodded and looked away ashamedly. It dawned on me that the root cause of the Moroccan's bad behavior was due to his abusive and overzealous family and religion. Subconsciously he had taken on the role of an object to be used and discarded at whim. His fears had become his reality and manifested as neurotic dramas. This revelation brought on a new understanding I had of the Moroccan. My heart reached out to the teenager with compassion.

"You have to understand yourself before you can relegate your fears," I proposed.

He looked at me puzzlingly and did not comprehend my suggestion.

Silence shrouded our exchange.

He finally whispered, *"Will you help me?"*

"Of course, I will," I responded wholeheartedly.

That day marked a new beginning of my relationship with the Moroccan.

A House of Cards (Chapter Forty-One)

"Human rights are praised more than ever and violated more than ever."

Anna Lindh

Mid-September 1968
Aldhdhib Dann الذئب دن *(Wolf Den),* Riyadh, Saudi Arabia

My Master sent a chartered helicopter to collect my Valet and me from the Bahriji. As soon as we touched down *Aldhdhib Dann (Wolf Den),* Tad's ancestral home in Riyadh, several Abds (Arab boy servants) collected our luggage and showed us to our lodging. I was amazed by the size of the property; not to mention the twenty-bedroom mansion, together with several outbuildings that housed Tad's relatives and a staff of forty.

A pristinely kept swimming pool and a well-equipped gymnasium awaited the athlete's use when in residence.

A twenty-car garage housed luxury models of the latest sports and sedan vehicles that any automobile junkie would envy.

A man-made lake with frolicking swans and mandarin ducks glided buoyantly within this manicured oasis, surrounded by an extensive variety of fruit and flowering trees. This desert sanctuary also harbors an aviary and a zoo, filled with exotic animals; cared for by a crew of gardeners hired by the *Maison* keeper, Jean-Pierre Saad. This knowledgeable French-Arab horticulturist, hired by Tad's father, Abdul Kabir Hafiz was born and raised in Paris, and Riyadh.

Besides, maintaining the grounds at *Aldhdhib Dann*, Jean-Pierre also worked closely with the Horticulture Science Department at the Université Paris-Sud in the developments of hybrid plants. Andy and Curt Eberhardt took to Jean-Pierre instantly. The men had a lot in common, and one of them was the quest for spirituality in nature.

Although Tad has many enlightened people as friends, he was the complete opposite. The athlete's primary objective was to make money, and the more, the merrier. Sports was his channel to fame and fortune, and he trained energetically to be the best in his game. His trainer was also my private tutor, Herr Curt Eberhardt who was an accomplished sportsman in his own right.

Herr Curt Eberhardt

Tad recruited the German as his full-time trainer when they met at a sports event in Munich. Besides being my Master's coach, Curt also doubled up as a private tutor and translator to the *Aldhdhib Dann's* household, especially to the E.R.O.S. recruits. The sportsman was already at *Wolf Den* when Andy and I arrived.

"Welcome to the 'House-of-Cards,'" he jested when we shook hands.

My Valet and I looked perplexingly at him and wondered what were in store for us at our new ménage.

He said cheekily, *"Don't worry guys, you'll maneuver through this minefield in no time."*

We stared at the German in bewilderment.

"Oh, don't look so worried. I'm being silly," the sportsman remarked mischievously. *"Come, let me show you the property. Tad asked me to be your guide."*

We got to know the professor better as we proceeded to the various destinations.

House of Cards

I asked, *"Why do you call Aldhdhib Dann, a house-of-cards?"*

"I was joking. Don't take my pronouncement to heart," my instructor answered.

"There must be some element of truth," my Valet opined.

Curt glanced at us dubiously before he declared without much divulgence, *"There is always something new and surprising in this household every day."*

Andy probed, *"Cite an example so we can be better equipped to handle such occasions when they arise."*

The sportsman grinned slyly before he resumed, *"There was a commotion in the East Wing yesterday."*

He paused and held his hand to his heart before he continued, *"Allah bless her heart! Our patriarch's younger sister, Miss Yasmin refused to eat."*

"Why?" I chirped.

"The young lady was protesting her rights to date a Eurasian man she met at a conference in Riyadh," my teacher revealed.

"What happened then?" I inquired.

"They force-fed her," my teacher replied.

My chaperone questioned, *"Who are they?"*

"They were Yasmin's three male relatives. The men held the girl down and forced food into her mouth. She convulsed. Then they locked her and her ladies-in-waiting in her boudoir," the German stated.

"How inhumane!" my lover voiced. *"Why didn't Tad and the other relatives intervene?"*

"Tad's mother, Najiyah and a couple of his siblings did intercede. But Abdul Kabir, the senior patriarch refused to budge when Tad and Najiyah begged for

leniency. After all, it was Abdul Kabir who ordered the deed," Eberhardt expressed despondently.

"That's barbaric!" Andy exclaimed.

"That is correct. My advice to the both of you is to keep your affections discreet. Most of the Aldhdhib Dann residences are not like your Master," Curt counseled.

"In Saudi Arabia, women's rights are subject to the whims of men. My friend and student, be vigilant when it comes to women's issues." The German cautioned.

"Is that the reason you warned us to maneuver through the Aldhdhib Dann minefields with discretions," I pegged.

My tutor nodded before he dispensed these final words. *"There is a fine line between what is acceptable and what's not, in this country. Be mindful of the way you behave. You'll notice that your Master is quite a different person when he's in his home turf."*

We proceeded to the aviary and the zoo to be acquainted with Allah's animal kingdom and with the horticulturist cum zoologist, Jean-Pierre Saad.

At the Aviary

My mind wandered to the story of *The Nightingale* as we strolled through the avifauna refuge to marvel at the plumed birds of paradise.

"These songbirds have beautiful voices, but they can't sing their ballads to the world," I admonished.

The men looked at me with consternation before my Valet enjoined, *"Indeed, that is true. But they are protected from the woes of the world."*

"I'm sure Allah didn't create them to be held captive in a cage; no matter how large, spacious and airy the oubliette," I negated.

"You are correct. Although traditions are hard to erase, these feathered creatures are showing signs to make themselves heard," the horticulturist commented.

"The birds are screeching to be released and to fly free. Rather than be caged for a few to appreciate their graces," I concurred.

Andy and Curt gave me unseemly glances to indicate for me to shut up. On the contrary, I felt emboldened.

I evinced, *"I'm sure you are familiar with the story of The Nightingale by the Danish author Hans Christian Andersen. It is about a Chinese emperor who prefers the tinkling of a bejeweled mechanical bird to the songs of a real nightingale."*

"Me raconter l'histoire à nouveau. Il semble que j'ai oublié. (Tell me the story again. It seems I have forgotten)," Jean-Pierre sallied.

He was having fun with me.

I began, *"Once upon a time, there was an emperor in China who learns that one of the most beautiful creatures in his kingdom were the songs of a nightingale. He commanded that the nightingale be brought to him. One of the kitchen maids directed the king's men to a nearby forest where the nightingale resides. The songbird was captured and forced to sing for the Emperor. Unlike the uplifting songs she chirped when she was a free spirit, her ballads turned sad and melancholic. Soon, the emperor grew enervated of her disheartening arias.*

"One day the emperor was given a bejeweled mechanical bird, and he lost interest in the real nightingale. He cast the bird back into the forest as a piece of garbage. Shortly after that, the mechanical bird broke down, and the Emperor was taken seriously ill. The real nightingale learned of the emperor's condition and returned to the palace. She sang her healing songs to the

dying sovereign. 'Death' was so moved by the bird's ballads that he granted longevity to the emperor."

As soon as I finished iterating the tale, Saad quipped amusingly. *"What is the moral of this story, young man?"*

Before I could speak, my Valet intervened, *"The moral of the story is that beautiful melodies and well-sung arias can heal despondent spirits."*

Andy covered my allusion if my outspokenness might endanger my position at the *Wolf Den* before I began service.

"I see. It's a revelation I must take to heart," the horticulturist teased.

Without publicizing the nuances, he was aware of our double entendre.

Just then, Curt Eberhardt suggested we visit the zoo. We followed.

The Zoo

The *Aldhdhib Dann* zoo compressed of engendered species from every continent. A cornucopia of clacking noises pierced the visitor's ears with unintelligible perplexities within the fenced acreages. I had no clue when or where our tour began or ended since their disconcerting sounds threw me into a state of confusion. I would have gotten lost in this lush labyrinth of wild blue yonder, if not for Monsieur Jean-Pierre Saad's guidance. The ferocious competed with the domesticated. This zoo was in and of itself a reflection of the dissensions within *Wolf Den*; where members wrangle for prominent positions in this ever-changing desert-scape.

This oasis was picture perfect of a resplendent sanctum to the credulous visitant. Generations of Hafizes had transformed this expansive property into what it is now. It was Abdul Kabir Hafiz, Tad's aging father who commissioned the zoo and the aviary. This elderly patriarch was soon to conjoin a fourth wife, Jamila, who was forty years his junior.

Tad Abdul Hafiz, the second in line to inherit this vast seigneury had spent a significant amount of time away from the estate. The best way for this intransigent athlete to escape his dysfunctional family was through his sports.

"Are you off to la-la land," my chaperone jolted me back from my daydream.

I commented, *"This is an impressive property."*

The horticulturist replied, *"This land has passed through four generations of Hafizs. It was first acquired by Tad's great-great-grandfather, Sulaiman Yusef Hafiz before it was built upon by his son and heir, Zayn Abraham Hafiz. But it was Dawud Arib Hafiz, Tad's grandfather who added to the original property. Dawud, an avid landscaper, redesigned the grounds to accommodate a lake and appended an extensive array of fruit and flowering trees. He developed what we see now. But it is the current owner, Abdul Kabir Hafiz who created the aviary and zoo."*

"C'est Magnifique!" Andy exclaimed.

"Who added the swimming pool and gymnasium?" I gagged and affixed, *"Let me guess. Master Tad Abdul Hafiz?"*

They laughed before Curt announced jestingly, *"We better return to the house before this lad decides to relate another ambiguous fable and have us guess the tale's moral."*

I had not thought to evoke another narrative to punctuate our zoological exploration until then.

I proclaimed, *"I do have another story to tell."*

The men eyed me with perspicacious scrutiny to indicate, *"Here goes the wise guy again."* I launched into the story of *Animal Farm*.

As soon as I finished, Jean-Pierre announced, *"It is an ingenious story that will illuminate the listener to act on what's right within humanity's framework. Treacherous deception and revolt would cause more harm than good."*

He directed his gaze at the creatures in the zoo. *"The good thing is; we care and look after these animals with providence and protection."*

"Is that so?" were Professor Eberhardt's sardonic words before we returned to the main house.

Tango Buenos Aires (Chapter Forty-Two)

"What would life be without a little Tango?"
            Bernard Tristan Foong

Last Week of November 1968
The Plaza Hotel, Buenos Aires, Argentina

"Come, let's celebrate!" My Master exclaimed after his team's polo practice win at the Campo Argentino del Polo, popularly known as the 'Cathedral of Polo.' This Buenos Aires multi-purpose stadium and home to Campeonato Argentino Abierto de Polo is the most crucial polo event in the world that Tad would participate in a week.

"What's the joyous occasion?" Andrico, one of our E.R.O.S. compatriots, asked.

The athlete replied cheerfully, *"When in Buenos Aires, we do what the Porteños do. We Tango!"*

The Arab grabbed hold of Kalf to demonstrate a mock tango. We stared at him as if he was bonkers.

He announced blithely, *"We are going to a milango."*

"What's a milango?" Jeddi, Andrico's BB inquired.

Tad did not answer but continued to dance around the room.

Professor Eberhardt elucidated on the athlete's behalf, *"There is Tango, and there is Milango. Milango houses are found throughout Buenos Aires. These are venues where Porteños go dancing."*

He sipped his wine before he resumed, *"The scene is genuinely romantic. The men stay on one side of the room and the women on the other. When a song starts, the men approach the women to dance."*

Andy exclaimed excitedly, *"I love it! Such chivalry."*

"Can men dance with men and women with women?" I inquired.

Curt burst into hilarity before he commended, *"Is that not what your Master is doing?*

"I was about to say before you and Andy interrupted. A woman is free to decline a dance, but dance partners do change throughout the night. Every segment of society become one in the dance hall; be they young, old or middle-aged. I've never felt anything sensually invigorated than in a milango."

The athlete stopped his dance.

He commented spritely, *"Milangos are special places. I describe it as an organized event where people go to tango. Now, a Milango is not to be confused with a Milonga – which is a type of tango music and a distinctive style of dance performed solely to that music. Milangos are filled with merrymakers, dancers, and spectators. They're there for a good time; to watch and be watched."*

"Sounds fun!" Ileen, the female E.R.O.S. recruit cried.

"I can't wait to tango," she declared.

"There are definite hierarchies in a milango, and everyone has a role to play. Maestros travel and teach around the world while tangureros are stage performers. Then there are the DJs, live orchestras and tango singers who keep the dance floor moving. Last but not least, the event organizers provide the spaces for the dance patrons," our Master explained.

"Oh! I forgot to mention the tango 'sharks' who prey on tourists and newcomers and the old milongueros who use to rule the floor, but now they are there because milangos are their second home," he added.

"Who are the tango 'sharks'?" I questioned.

Tad and Curt burst out in laughter. Both men responded almost simultaneously, *"They are men who behave creepily and inappropriately when they dance with the opposite sex."*

"What about men who dance with the same sex? Are they also called tango 'sharks?'" I asked.

My tutor quipped, *"They're called tango 'whales.'"*

"Why?" I queried.

Our group burst out in guffaws at my naiveté.

My Valet responded amusingly, *"Your silly boy. Your teacher is pulling your leg. Men who prey on handsome male dancers are often fat and obese, like whales."*

"Are these predators always fat and obese?" I countered. "What if the tango 'whales' are handsomely virile? What do you call them?"

More laughter ensued before our patriarch pronounced, *"Let's go while the night is young."*

At Confitería Ideal, Buenos Aires, Argentina

At the stroke of midnight, the night was indeed young at *Confitería Ideal*. This two-story building had been in operation since 1912. Founded by Don Manuel Rosendo Fernández, a merchant from Galicia; he decorated this distinctively European looking *milango* with original French bohemian armchairs, marble staircases and a bar of Slavonic oak boiserie specially carved by Slavic craftsmen. The floors, ceilings, and windows were highlighted with decorative Fleur-de-Lis design. Fourteen imposing pillars, two grand pianos, and old mirrors gave this establishment a luxurious ambiance that any well-dressed patron would be proud.

Famous personalities, the likes of Jorge Luis Borges, Adolfo Bioy Casares, Luis Sandrini, Juan Domingo

Perón, Evita and Joan Manuel Serrat have passed through this hall with fanfare. So did Maurice Chevallier, Maria Felix, Robert Duvall, and Yoko Ono who tangoed deep into the wee hours of the morning.

I felt like I had traveled back in time to a Belle Époque era when tango ruled Buenos Aires. Men in formal garb and women in figure-hugging gowns strutted and swaggered while patrons at side tables studied their techniques. The scene resembled a 1940s romantic movie that had wrapped me around its fingers to lured me onto the dance floor. I couldn't help but marvel at the ostentatious crowd even though I've been warned not to look too closely at anyone unless I knew what I was doing.

My eyes caught sight of a suave tuxedoed man who was by the bar with a drink, and a cigar in hand to entice a potential dance partner onto the floor. I fell under his spell.

Before I had a chance to gather myself, he had swept me onto the pristine dance floor.

I gasped and whispered, *"Sir, I have no idea what I'm doing."*

"Follow me, and you'll be fine," he said seductively.

Off we tangoed from one end of the room to the other. Adrenaline surged into my head as if I had drunk glasses of champagne. I was intoxicated and beguiled by this eroticism as he whirled and twirled me like a ragdoll. Not only had his decorous movements glided me along with ease, but his debonair refinement also inveigled me to lean against him for support. I had no idea where I procured my competence, but I knew he was no ordinary dancer but a hoofer.

When the music concluded, I leaned against him to catch my breath before I inquired, *"Are you a maestro?"*

He grinned and replied mischievously, *"Do you want me to be?"*

Before I could respond, Andy was by my side.

"Hi, I am Andy, and you are...?" My chaperone introduced.

"Everyone here calls me Franco."

He extended his hand to shake my guardian's before he announced, *"Nice to meet you, Andy. And...?"* He looked at me for a respond.

My Valet announced authoritatively before I could answer. *"I am Young's chaperone. I'm here to ensure he doesn't step out of line."*

Andy shielded me from the stranger since the man had whisked me away, unannounced. I detected a hint of jealousy in my guardian's voice.

"Young is a good dancer. I would like him to study with me," the Argentinian expressed.

Before I could answer, my guardian replied, *"We're in Buenos Aires for the Campeonato Argentino Abierto de Polo. Young wouldn't be here long enough to study with you."*

I interposed, *"I will love to learn to tango. Will you teach me?"*

"I'll be happy to give you some lessons during your stay," Franco declared cheerfully.

Andy gave me a lugubrious glance before he granted me permission. I kissed my lover to thank him for his amenability. I smiled at the dance instructor. He gave me a knowing wink.

While we were talking, I noticed a beautiful woman dancing with Tad while Kalf looked on with dejection. I went to the Moroccan. Without a thought, I pulled the boy onto the dance floor and began to tango with him. Neither the lad nor I had any idea what we were doing, but he was glad I came to his rescue, even though he was stunned by my action. Like a pair of waddling ducklings, we whisked around clumsily. Not only had our ebullience cheered up the crowd, but it also enlivened some revelers to take to the floor. We had fun, whirling and twirling even though the

Moroccan was apprehensive about our moves. He soon dropped his guard and went with the flow.

That evening was one of those rare occasions where I witnessed the reticent Kalf coursed through an invidious situation without a care in the world. The night air had enveloped us with hypnotic romances and seduced our heady selves to tango until dawn before reality erupted with violent storms where we least expect.

End of October 2014
My Message to David and Andy (Part One)

Hi fellas,

Me-Oh-My, I didn't anticipate such an outpour of support and concern from the both of you. I'm flattered! LOL!

Andy, I am grateful for your love and friendship. You can assure that I'll do the same for you if you require my assistance. You can count on me. ☺

I also want to thank you, David, for your superb effort to physically reunite Andy and me; even though we'd already reconnected cognitively. I'm sure when the opportunity arises, the universe will bring us together. That includes you, whom I have yet to meet in person. As always, the streams of life will guide me to go with the flow. ☺

Back to some serious discussion. I do have stories to share about my encounters with mythical beasts. Here is one…

Pride and Prejudices (Chapter Forty-Three)

"Pride and prejudices are the children of religious ignorance and bigotry."
Tad Abdul Hafiz

Third Week of September 1968
Mada'in Saleh مدائن صالح (Cities of Saleh), Saudi Arabia

My Master was indeed a different man in Saudi Arabia. His regimented schedules amazed my Valet and me to the nth degree. Unlike his party boy behaviors when abroad; now, he embodied the paragon of proper comportment. He and Eberhardt would do laps at his Olympic size pool at 5 AM daily. From seven to nine AM, they worked out at the gymnasium. Breakfast was served to him at precisely nine-thirty AM before he headed to his sports practices, rehearsals, and other athletic activities until 5 in the evening. His personal time was between six to eight PM before his dinner with his family or business-related associates. He retired at 11 PM before he resumed the same procedures the following day.

Henry and I were the only E.R.O.S. recruits stationed at *Wolf Den*. Our tutorials with Professor Eberhardt commenced at nine-thirty every morning without fail, except on Holy Friday which was our day off and when the athlete attended mosque with his family. This was also the day of our field-trips to historical places in the Saudi Kingdom. During our excursion to the ancient *Mada'in Saleh* مدائن صالح *(Cities of Saleh)*, also known as

Al-Hijr or *Hegra*; I had a chance to ask Professor **Eberhardt** about my Master's demeanor transformation.

Curt had organized our visit to *Hegra* through his archaeologist friend, Dr. Benjamin Liberman. He was a part of the *Al-Hijr's* excavation team. This ancient rock-cut architectural Nabatean kingdom, second only to Petra in the north is relatively unknown to the larger world. Back in 1968, the prohibition by the Saudi government on the veneration of objects and artifacts hindered archaeological activities to minimal. This "Stoneland" and its nearby vicinity were primarily inhabited by Bedouin tribes. We were fortunate to visit this comparatively untouched locale before it was declared a national treasure in the early seventies.

Our teacher's ingenuity to visit these essential vestiges was a feat before survey permits were finally granted. A private helicopter ferried the six of us from *Aldhdhib Dann* to Al-Ula village, where *Al-Hijr* was located. There, we met Dr. Liberman who acted as our guide.

As our entourage listened to the archaeologist's analysis of the sites' historical developments; I found a private opportunity to ask my professor.

"Why didn't our Master come to Hegra with us?" I enquired.

Eberhardt responded casually, *"He has plenty to do before we leave for Rio."*

"Rio!" I exclaimed. *"You mean Rio de Janeiro, Brazil?"*

"Yes, boy, Rio de Janeiro, Brazil," he answered lightheartedly.

I added, *"Why are we going to Rio?"*

"He's been invited to be a judge at the Miss Brazil beauty pageant," my teacher replied.

"How did he get to be a judge at a beauty pageant?" I questioned.

The German said amusingly, *"Young, your Master is an international sportsman. He receives many invitations to national and international events. Being a judge at a beauty extravaganza is one of his obligations."*

I inquired, *"He's not the Master I know when he's abroad. He behaves differently in Riyadh. Why is that?"*

Eberhardt sallied, *"Is that so?"*

He paused before he continued, *"Your Master has a lot on his mind. Besides, he must be physically and mentally ready for his upcoming tournaments. I'm here to ensure he's in shipshape for these challenges."*

"Like dealing with the Aldhdhib Dann's womenfolk?" I quipped.

"Shush! Not so loud, you scalawag. I'll wallop you if you divulge anything improper to strangers about the Aldhdhib Dann household," he cautioned.

"Then tell me what's up with him?" I pressed.

He pulled me out of earshot before he chastised, *"You, boy, better watch your tongue and not air any Aldhdhib Dann's dirty linens. You get me!"*

"I heard squabbles outside the library last night. What happened?" I evinced curiously.

My teacher whispered guardedly, *"You must promise me to keep this to yourself."*

I nodded and crossed my heart to indicate my sincerity.

Women rights

My Valet was at our side just as my tutor was about to commence.

"What's going on? I heard your teacher shushing you," Andy inquired.

Curt declared, *"I reprimanded this chap not to be nosey."*

"What's he prying at now?" my chaperone questioned.

"About Tad and the Aldhdhib Dann's womenfolk," I announced.

My statement caught the professor off-guard. Left with little choice, he revealed his cognizance to us.

He began, *"Miss Yasmin acted up again last night. She and several of her female cousins had joined a women's rights activist group. They protested against having a male 'wali' accompany them everywhere."*

"What is a 'wali'?" I asked.

My teacher explicated, *"A 'wali' is an official guardian. Typically, he is the father, brother, uncle or husband. Although guardianship is not enshrined in Saudi laws; government officials, courts, businesses, and individuals usually act on it. That means women require their 'wali's' consent for significant activities; like traveling, obtaining a passport, getting married or divorced and the signing of legal contracts."*

Curt added, *"Miss Yasmin's father and eldest brother, Ali had spoken strongly against her participation in such a controversial group. They tried to stop her from attending the meetings, but the young lady refused to budge. They locked her in her boudoir and refused to release her unless she changes her stance. She went hysterical and tried to kick down the door."*

I gasped, *"What happened after that?"*

*"Tad stepped in to soothe the uproar, and **Najiyah** stayed to console her indignant daughter,"* my tutor stated lamentably.

Just then, Dr. Liberman yelled from a nearby vicinity for us to tack along. The archeologist was delighted to have an engrossed party in Jean-Pierre Saad, Henry, and his Valet, Louis. They hung on Benjamin's every word as we meandered through rock corridors, wells, tombs, and burial sites; while Eberhardt, Andy and I continued our conversation out of earshot.

Curt commented, *"You already know, Young; members of the opposite sex cannot mingle freely. Though, there are a few exceptions, like in hospitals, banks, and medical colleges."*

"Can women attend universities and colleges?" Andy enquired.

The professor denoted, *"They are allowed entrée to all women higher learning institutions, but co-education is a no-no."*

I chimed, *"I know they wear a black abaya when they leave the house. Are they allowed to dine with men in restaurants?"*

"Most eateries have allocated sections for 'families.' These areas are separated by dividers from all-male parties. Females are required to enter and exit restaurants through separate entrances from the men," my teacher disclosed.

"Do women get a fair hearing in court and do they receive an equal inheritance?" My Valet questioned.

"That's the million riyals (Saudi Arabia currency) question. As the saying goes: the testimony of a man equals that of two women. The fact is, a woman's legal position in this country is like that of a minor. It is sad that she has little control over her own life.

"In regard to your question of inheritance; under Sharia inheritance laws, daughters receive half the amount awarded to their brothers. Sometimes, they are omitted from their father's will altogether and impelled into poverty," Eberhardt informed.

"No wonder Miss Yasmin and her activists' petition for their rights," I cried.

"The good thing is, King Faisal bin Abdulaziz Al Saud is determined to modernize the country. I hope Saudi

women will soon be granted the rights they deserve," my teacher responded sanguinely.

We fell in line with our entourage without any eyebrows being raised.

End of October 2014
My Message to David and Andy (Part Two)

...In the early months of 1970 I mentored a Daltonbury Hall Grecian-Italian Freshman from Rome named Helius. We were out riding and came upon a forest pond when he related legends and myths from his country.

"Why did your parents name you Helius?" I asked.

"When I was a child, my Grecian father told me the tale of Hēlios, Helius in Latin. My name means Sun, East, Day and Sunshine."

He paused before he added, *"My dad told me that Hēlios was a handsome Sun god, and his crown was the sun's shining aureole. Led by Pegasus and four flying horses, Hēlios rode his gleaming chariot across the sky, every morning to circle Oceanus (god of the Seas) before returning to the East at nightfall.*

"Father named me Helius because I'm the very image of Hēlios," the lad proclaimed.

Just then, from the corner of my eyes, I caught a flash of white among the trees. I thought little of the mirage and remain focus on Helius.

But when I stared into the boy's eyes, I saw a radiant winged horse reflected in his pupils. I followed Helius' gaze but saw nothing except greeneries. I returned my attention to my charge.

"Did you see a white winged horse?" I questioned.

"What white winged horse?" he fibbed.

"I'm pretty sure I saw a winged horse reflected in your eyes a few moments ago," I attested.

The lad looked flustered but remained silent.

I pressed, *"Tell me what you saw."*

He denied his phantasm and said he saw nothing but trees. I did not believe him.

"You are lying. Tell me the truth. I'm your BB, and you can confide in me. I'm not here to judge but to provide guidance and mentorship. We must trust one another if we are to bond," I counseled.

"Like Andy and you?" he quipped.

"What do you mean, about Andy and me?" I responded gushingly.

The boy declared, *"The love between the two of you is legendary."*

Taken aback by his remark and I went quiet before I expressed. *"Don't avert the topic. I want to know what you saw. It is not about Andy and me."*

I held Helius hand to mine.

"You must always tell the truth. I cannot assist you if I don't know the whole story. Our bond would not be genuine if you lie or tells half-truths. As your BB and friend, I'm here for you. Our friendship will develop if we are honest with one another," I advocated.

Like a fresh bloom, he opened himself to me.

"Will you promise not to tell anyone what I saw?" he pleaded.

I promised him I will never break my pledge until now. This is Helius' story…

The Tango Of Love (Chapter Forty-Four)

First, I caught your vision
Then, I sensed emotion
Next, I felt the passion of my Love for you
Your lips were so inviting
I dreamt of pure delighting
My heart felt so excited
By sweet love from you
I want to hold you now
I want to hug you now
I just want to kiss and squeeze you tight
I plan to show you now
How much I do adore you now
Tonight we will dance the Tango Of Love
When I smelt your scent
Filling up the whole room
I had to ask all the flowers to leave
The ice cubes were all melting
From passion emanating
Deep in my heart from love for you
I want to squeeze you tight
Kiss, and hug, and treat you right
Swim with only you in Love's delight
I plan to show you now

How much I do adore you now
Tonight, we will dance the Tango Of Love."
Tango Of Love - lyrics
by Monty Guy

Early December 1968
Tad's Suite at The Plaza Hotel, Buenos Aires, Argentina

Kalf and my tango puttering had rustled my Master's concupiscence to watch his boyfriend and me perform a sexual "Tango" for his private amusement. I was summoned to his suite two nights before his polo tournament.

Although I had no idea why I was called to his chamber, I had a presage that my convoke was erotically connected. As was the norm, I refrained from ejaculation when I received my Master's request. My Valet and I were groomed and poised for action an hour before the appointed time. As we waited in our room, I asked my guardian, *"Do you know who the modish lady is? The one who danced with Tad at Confiteria Ideal."*

Andy replied, *"I believe her name is Katherina and she is an accomplished ballroom bailarin and a fashion model."*

I opined, *"She's elegant and dances beautifully. Is Tad dating her?"*

"You can ask your Master when you see him," my Valet answered before he added, *"Why do you want to know who she is?"*

"I wonder if Kalf knows the nature of their relationship and what he thinks of her?" I remarked.

My chaperone counselled, *"It's best not to ask too many questions. The complexities will play out by itself. Time always impart results."*

I negated, *"Señor Triqueros taught me that Time is a human contrivance. There is no Time in space."*

"That is correct. But if you hold firm and wait, the result will eventually reveal itself. In other words, time will tell," Andy enjoined.

In My Master's Chamber

Sensual music enticed us into Tad's suite as he ushered us into his boudoir. Kalf, dressed in a half-open bathrobe laid on the king while the muscly athlete held him in an affectionate embrace. No words were required. We knew that my Master's summon was an erotic participation in a ménage à quatre. Andy gave me a willful glance to join the duo on the bed. I stripped naked and stood next to the mattress when my summoner pulled me down to kiss his lover. I prised open his lips to receive my swirling tongue. Like an enlivened doe, eager to espy my upending gesticulation, the Moroccan abided in accordance. His vulnerability reminded me of my youth when I too was seeking ardor in the arms of the handsome and the dominant, to care and protect my precariousness. A susceptibility that could shatter into a thousand pieces and engender the saddened heart to ossify into an impenetrable bastion of abhorrent repulsion to those who proffer succor.

I held the boy's lips to mine and as our passionate kisses melted in synchronicity to the rhythm of our yearning hearts while Tad and Andy worked their oral magic on our throbbing protuberances. They oscillated between cherishing our plumpness to delving into our inner sanctums of carnal delights. These erotic pleasures propelled us to euphoric ecstasies as we revolved around one another; embracing roles that were at once anomalous but rewarding.

A sight I had not witnessed until now was my Master's wonted machismo reduced to acquiescence by Andy's assertiveness. The athlete's fervent submissiveness abated to his master's dominance like his caprice was his mandate. He complied to my Valet's gesticulations with aplomb. Aroused by this unexpected development, I also took on an alphaness I never knew I possessed. I plunged my bulbousness into Kalf's mouth as he gusted for air from my unflagging onslaught. Governed by my unyielding demands his covetousness had fashioned him, my slave.

I commanded, *"Stop whining like a child and get on with it!"* I whacked the boy's face.

His puppy-dog eyes stared at me unflinchingly, craving for my approval. *"You like it, don't you! Now, get it nice and wet!"* I ordered before I landed another blow on his cheeks. I pulled my organ away to tease his craving as he begs to pleasure my palpitations.

Tad, whose hands were already cuffed behind, knelt before his master. With wanton immodesty, he too implored for his master's assertiveness as Andy smacked his bearded face and spat into his mouth before he jammed his stiffness back into the Arab's willing oral orifice.

I had fostered my lechery on the Moroccan as I observee my guardian's supremacy. I wrestled the boy's on the king and pried his defying legs apart before I jammed my tongue into his inviting crevice. In one fell swoop, I plunged into him. He cried in rapturous elation. Before long, his tightness gave way to my formidable invasion as I plowed into his love's cavern with abandonment. I rammed into his uncharted territory while my rousing mind exploded in a billowing barrage. Like a heady roller coaster, my concupiscence exhilarated as I stroked the lad with unbridled jubilations. Like an obedient slave, Kalf, tilted his bottom to meet my thrusts. Not only did his amatory whimpering invigorate my explosive velocity, but it also stimulated my ecstatic lubriciousness to consummation. I flipped the boy onto his back and mounted him like an untamed stallion, as I hurtled towards the cliff of no return.

Galvanized by Andy's erotic performance I bulldozed my way to nirvanic transcendence; while Tad, the complaisant pig-bottom cried for more as his master drove into him unyieldingly.

The sight of the athlete French kissing his lover hurled me over the threshold. Gushes of my molten potencies filled the Moroccan to dribbling capacity as his spasming sphincter milked for more.

Andy released his jubilance into my Master's welcoming bifid as we merged into a four-way kiss with the duo. The Arab's simultaneous outpour coated his caressing palm with wholesome potencies before he fed them to Kalf and me.

Before long, our lasciviousness also enkindled Kalf to spew his abundance onto his taut belly. Tad lapped up his lover's fecundities to share between us. Although we laid spent, our active carnality did not subside until way past the witching hour. Only then did my chaperone and I returned to our suite; exhausted yet ready to dance our very own Tango of Love.

End of October 2014
My Message to David and Andy (Part Three)

"I first saw him when I was six years old," Helius confided.

"We lived in a remote part of Italy when I was growing up. Behind our house laid an untouched forest and a stream. When the maids and my nanny hung up the laundry in the rear lawn, I would go down and play by the water; where a great variety of wildflowers carpeted the forest floor in the early months of spring.

"One day when my nanny was helping the servants, I sneaked into the forest. That was when Petronius revealed himself to me. At first, I noticed a flash of white from the corners of my eyes, but when I looked carefully, there was nothing but trees and wildflowers. I continued to explore the area, but every time I bend to pick the flowers, the glint

would zip by. Finally, I sat by the stream to ascertain that my eyes were not playing tricks.

"Out of the blue, a winged stallion materialized. I've never seen such a fantastical creature except in fairytale books. The white horse bobbed its head to beckon me. I stood frozen, yet its kind and loving eyes attracted me towards him."

I queried, *"How wide was his wingspan?"*

"At least eight to ten feet when outstretched," the boy replied before he added, *"Petronius is significantly bigger than an average horse. Maybe I was small then, and he appeared larger. He lowered its head for me to pat as if in acknowledgment of my panjandrum."*

"Panjandrum!" I exclaimed.

Helius elucidated, *"I'm from the Godly realm, and Petronius pays his respect to me."*

"How do you know you're from the Godly realm and how did you know the horse's name?" I enquired bafflingly.

"My father told me I was an unconventional baby, and I am blessed by the gods," my charge stated spiritedly. *"To answer your other question: The name Petronius was marked on the side of his mane."*

"What happened after you pat him?" I questioned inquisitively.

"He nudged me to mount him, but my tiny frame did not enable me, so he indicated for me to hold firm onto his hair. In one fell scoop, he lifted me onto his back with his snout and took to the air. I clung to him for balance," Helius iterated excitedly.

I questioned, *"Didn't your nanny look for you?"*

"She panicked when I was nowhere to be found. From above I saw her scurrying for help," the lad answered musingly before he added, *"Petronius didn't fly very far. Since the commotion was at the back, he circled*

and dropped me in front of our house, so no one would notice his presence.

"Nobody knew I had returned when I entered the front door until I placed the wild bouquet by my mother's dresser. Only then, had nanny spotted me standing by the window."

I declared, *"Did you tell them about your encounter with Petronius?"*

"I told dad when he came to say goodnight, that evening."

I oppugned, *"Didn't your nanny asked where you'd gone?"*

"I told her I was playing in the front garden."

I probed, *"What was your dad's response when you told him about Petronius?"*

"He said he was glad the deities found me and sent Petronius to be my guardian against harm, and that I should keep my present and future mystical experiences to myself; otherwise people will think I'm demented," my charge iterated.

"Have you told anyone besides your dad and me?" I inquired.

Helius shook his head.

"I confided to you because I have a presentiment that you too have had otherworldly encounters," Helius surmised.

"What makes you think that?" I expressed.

The boy said lightheartedly, *"It takes one to know one."*

"We must discuss this further," I finalized.

Dear Andy and David, there is more…

A Peculiar Request (Chapter Forty-Five)

"A change of scenery can help alter everything."
                                                             Drew Pomeranz

Last Week of September 1968
Aldhdhib Dann دن الذئب *(Wolf Den),* Riyadh, Saudi Arabia

Since the females were housed separately from the men's residences, I seldom saw the *Aldhdhib Dann's* womenfolk except in passing or when they were chaperoned by their 'walis' to the city. I chanced upon a pretty lady in a floral hijab on one occasion. Her perspicacious eyes spotted Andy and me as her vehicle rounded the men's compound. My instinct told me that the young woman was Yasmin, the nonconformist. As her sedan disappeared out of the driveway, she gazed at us.

I did not pay much attention to the happenstance until later after the household had retired for the night. I was awakened by a series of rustling noises below Andy and my bedroom window. I went to investigate to make sure that the zoo animals had not escaped from their confines. I noticed some movements in the shrubbery. Under scrutiny, a slender figure in black waved at me. My curiosity took flight, and I climbed down the egress by our balcony wall. I was surprised to find the female I had happened upon that morning. She gesticulated for me to be quiet and to follow. Just when I was about to move, my chaperone peered out of the window. He was awakened by my disappearance. I waved for him to join us. The intruder shushed us to be silent.

She arrived at a discreet location away from the mansion. When we were safely hidden from view, Andy voiced, *"We'll be in trouble if we are found with a female, especially in the middle of the night."*

Yasmin responded in perfect English. *"No one knows we are here. I need your help. Will you help me?"* she implored.

Before either Andy or I could answer, the female whispered, *"I know the two of you is the answer to my prayers. Please say you'll help me."*

"What is it that you want us to do?" my chaperone questioned.

My guardian glanced at me. Lost for words, she did not know what or how to present her request.

I said puzzlingly, *"We can't assist if we don't know what you want?"*

She uttered, *"Will you convince my brother to take me to England when he leaves in a week. I want to go shopping in London."*

My Valet and I looked at each other in bewilderment.

"Can't you ask him, yourself? Why do you need us to relay such a straightforward message?" I queried.

My guardian stated before the female could answer, *"I'm sure Tad or your relatives will take you shopping where and whenever you desire."*

"I need to be in London with my brother, Tad. He is the only person who understands me. He's more likely to take me if the both of you put in a good word on my behalf," Yasmin professed.

I queried, *"What are you planning to buy in London? Have you been there before?"*

"Of course, I have been to London. I want to return to experience the freedom of that country," she proclaimed.

Andy inquired suspiciously, *"You woke us in the middle of the night to ask us to appeal to your brother to take you shopping in London?"*

"I have no choice but to wake you at this hour because my father, Abdul and eldest brother, Kaleb forbid me to have any contact with strangers and foreigners," she said defiantly.

"Abdul and Kaleb are Muslim traditionalists, and the women in my family have little say in our lives. But Tad is a worldly man and believes that we should be treated respectfully.

"Unfortunately, he travels regularly, and we are left in the care of our patriarchs whom I have little reverence," Yasmin opined woefully before she added, *"Tad is a good man, and I want to spend more time with him."*

"I'll do my best to persuade your brother, but I can't make any promises. He has a mind of his own and is not easily influenced by others," I deduced empathetically.

Although Andy was aware of my noble intentions, he gazed at me questioningly as if I should have given Yasmin's request further consideration before I agreed to help.

When the young lady entreated my Valet, he nodded and said he would do the same as me.

When we parted, we promised the female that we would not disclose our meeting to anyone.

Within Our Chamber

As soon as we were out of earshot, Andy opined, *"I have a hunch that there is more to Yasmin's intentions than just a shopping spree in London."*

"I am sure she has good reasons," I replied.

"You are so trusting, and you believe what people tell you, without hesitation," he commented.

"If you are uncertain of her intentions, why did you agree to put in a good word for her?" I asked.

"Because of you, my love. I didn't want to thwart your kindheartedness and be the sullen guy to mar her travel plans," my lover reflected.

"We'll talk to Tad and see what he has to say. It is up to him to decide. At least we kept our word," I replied and finalized. *"Maybe our efforts are for naught."*

First Week of November 2014
David's Message to Me, c/c to Andy

Young,

I can't wait to read the rest of your caper with Helius. Although your story seems far-fetched, I'm all ears. After all, there are many anomalous encounters in this world that humans have yet to comprehend. So, I'll give you the benefit of the doubt before I comment.

All the best, my friend.
David

Andy's Message to Me, c/c to David

My dear chap,

I'm not astounded by your mythical encounters. After all, you'd angels, and fairy experiences during our time together. I'm roused to know the rest of your Helius and Petronius story.

Unfortunately, my connection to the numinous spheres is solely mystical than mythical, but I admire your ability to tap into your sixth sense and wish I am gifted like you.

Remember Albert, my ex-charge? He also had encounters with angels and avowed that he'd a chance meeting with a unicorn. When I was at Canterbury University in New Zealand, I received a lengthy email from him. He swore he came close to patting Boaz, the unicorn. Below is what he wrote:

Albert's Story:

Andy, you'll never believe what I saw in the early months of autumn, 1972. A glimmer of white, flashed through the trees when I strolled in the woods nearby Sissinghurst Court. When I stop to observe the area, I saw nothing but foliage. I continued into the woods.

Suddenly, I spotted the silhouette of a dazzling white horse grazing in a thicket. This equidae had a spiral horn on its forehead. I rubbed my eyes to make sure they weren't playing tricks before the beast sensed my presence. It did not bolt but stared at me with cognizance.

I approached the steed to pat the beast's sparkling mane. A sudden sound frightened the animal. His forelegs rose in perturbation, and I noticed the inscription on the underside of his thorax before he sped away at lightning speed. The words on its torso were - *Dominum Nomine Booz.*

It took a while for me to regain my composure before I returned home to decode the markings. This is an English translation of the Latin words - *Dominum Nomine Booz* is *Boaz (Swiftness)*. I named that unicorn, *Boaz*.

Sadly, I never saw *Boaz* again.

Guys, what do you make of Albert's encounter with *Boaz*?

Andy

The Game Of Kings (Chapter Forty-Six)

"Whether it's his beloved 'Game of Kings' or his magical success in business and self-promotions, Tad Abdul Hafiz does not know how to lose."

Curt Erick Eberhardt

December 1968
Campo Argentino del Polo, Buenos Aires, Argentina

"*T*he King of Games" – *Let other people play at different things but The King of Games is still the Game of Kings.* This verse, inscribed on a stone tablet from China to the West, sums up the ancient history of what is believed to be the oldest organized sport in the world. For most of its two thousand five hundred years of existence, Polo was indeed a game of Kings. Even though the precise origin of polo is obscure and undocumented, there is ample evidence of the game's regal place in Asian history. Although no one knows where or when stick first met ball after the tribes of Central Asia domesticated the horse; it was likely that the use of light cavalry throughout Asia Minor, China and the Indian sub-continent popularized this rugged horseback game. As conquering and re-conquering armies swept back and forth across the world, polo became the noblest sport of Kings, Emperors, Shahs, Sultans, Khans, and Caliphs from both the ancient and the contemporary world. Throughout the centuries, real and fabled monarchs together with their legendary horsemen were portrayed as heroic warriors, dexterous hunters, and exceptional polo players of masterful prowess.

The King of Games was introduced to South America by British cattlemen, and Argentina rapidly became the mecca for polo aficionados. In this land of the gaucho, boys who grew up on *estancias* (estates) play polo as soon as they learn to ride. Consequently, many top-ranking players are Argentines. It came as no surprise that Tad Abdul Hafiz's opposing team consisted of the Heguy brothers, Alberto and Horacio, and **Juan Carlos and Alfredo, the Harriott brothers. This handsome quartet of sport's tabloid superstars were** polo protégés of the Coronel Suarez Club, an adjunct of a market town at the southwestern extremity of the Pampas; some 300 miles from Buenos Aires. Every December, as many as thirty thousand polo fans gather to witness the Argentine Open, the world's most prestigious polo tournament at Campo Argentino del Polo.

Who Is That Woman?

This was the question Kalf raised while we mingled at the fancy pre-tournament soiree, a few hours before the contest. As I followed the Moroccan's gaze, I spotted a beautiful female in a red hat that tilted at a calculated angle to match her Valentino carmine colored ensemble. An outfit I had seen in the latest edition of Harper's Bazaar. Even though she looks like a fashion model, her poise gave her métier away. I recognized her instantly. She was the same woman whom I saw at *Confitería Ideal* who danced cheek-to-cheek with my Master. She held on to Tad as if he was her beau while she hobnobbed with the who's who in the international polo league and the athlete made no effort to deter that perception.

It was little wonder that Kalf was seething with jealousy while I tried to calm his nerves. As much as I tried to talk the lad out of a confrontation with the female, he did the opposite. The Moroccan swaggered to Katherina's party when my back was turned. He seized a glass of bubbling champagne from a passing waiter and splashed the drink on the unsuspecting bailarin. Time stood still as we looked on in horror. Silence fell over the crowd before the carmine clad lady screamed in agitation. Her attacker bellowed profanities at the baffled socialite. Impulsive anger clutched my Master. He punched his boyfriend in the face and hurled him to the ground before the athlete kicked his paramour's belly. With Tad's sensibleness relegated to the rear, he shouted, *"You worthless bastard! I should never have taken you in."*

The throng was horrified by this unexpected pandemonium. My gallant Valet rushed to assist the mangled Kalf, while Herr Eberhardt helped the disarrayed Katherina to rejigger out of her soaking garb. Tad's team members heaved the athlete to the locker room to recuperate before the championship. Andy and I carted the injured Kalf back to the hotel and left the rest of our delegation to witness the tournament.

Maybe it was my Master's emotional, and psychological perturbation or his team efficaciousness; Tad's delegation loss the trophy to Coronel Suarez. This rattled the Arab's consternation further. The following day he returned to his suite drunk and tossed the Tunisian out of the chamber they shared. A series of livid profanities followed, whereby the athlete ruled that he was done with Kalf. In bitter resentment, Kalf swore revenge at this injustice before he disappeared hastily. That was the last Andy, and I saw the Moroccan.

Not only did our Buenos Aires sojourn ended in shambles, but I also acquired the role of a sympathizer when Tad summoned Andy and me privately to his suite. Even though Herr Eberhardt had cautioned us that Tad Abdul Hafiz does not know how to lose, we were unprepared for the circumstance that follow.

When we entered, the athlete was in a state of dishevelment. With his palms on his face, he sobbed like an egocentric child and cursed his polo opponents for their nonpareil win.

"*The game is rigged!*" he vociferated sourly.

Andy and I looked at one another in silence. We did not know how to respond.

My Master continued, "*The Asociación Argentina de Polo (Argentine Polo Association) made sure that the **Coronel Suarez** had an advantage over us.*"

"*What makes you infer that?*" my guardian enquired.

"*My gut feeling,*" he paused to drink from a bottle of whiskey.

He resumed, "*My team is the best, and yet the Heguy and the Harriott brothers took the cup. There's no justification except that the organizers wanted their country to win,*" the Arab instigated wryly.

"*I'm sure it's a fair and honorable competition,*" I blurted absurdly.

"*Bollocks! Before the game began, the press was already making claims that **Coronel Suarez was a sure win**,*" my Master exclaimed.

He slammed down a sports paper on our side. The headlines read: *Coronel Suarez set to win.* The article went on to document the accomplishments of the Argentinian team. It said: "*During the captaincy of Coronel Suarez; the Harriott brothers – Alfredo and Juancarlitos won the Argentine Open twenty times and with countless other trophies at home and abroad. The Argentine team took the United States Cup of the Americas in four successive bouts. And for five consecutive years, the Coronel Suarez lineup which comprises of the Harriott and the Heguy brothers, Horacio, and Alberto Pedro; boasted a 40-goal handicap; the only one in the world.*"

Andy remarked judiciously, *"This looks to me like a candid sport's news report."*

"Bunco! It's bullshitting hogwash to convince the populace that **Coronel Suarez** *is the best team in the world,"* the Arab deplored.

When I observed the distraught man clearheadedly, a realization washed over my person. His devastating polo loss was a pretext for a more profound underachievement. His inability to maintain a stable and amorous relationship. As much as Tad basks in his playboy image; deep within, he pined for a loving intimacy like Andy and I shared. But his station, religion, and upbringing would not permit the man to be his real self. His sporting accomplishments were façades to camouflage his inner discontentment. When he fails in an athletic contest, he saw his defeat as a personal weakness. This realization provided me the empathy to soothe my Master. What Tad needed was a loving consolation and not a systematic analysis of a *Game of Kings* from my Valet.

The Art of Loving

While Andy was busy analyzing the accuracy of the newspaper article, I began to massage my Master's shoulders to relax his weary joints. His tautness unknotted to my loving touch, and his tenseness eased to my every move. My guardian soon discerns that the athlete's disgruntlement was pent-up emotions. When my nimble fingers caressed my Master's lumbar region, Andy followed my lead and orchestrated a series of head massages to ease the man's inner turmoil.

Without uttering another word, our loving touch had alleviated his animosity. In the process, our raiments had also slipped away to bare ourselves from the illusionary masquerade society demanded of us. We felt at one with the cosmos as creation had intended. With our resplendence revealed, so did our vehement copulation. We intertwined like coruscated serpents shedding our skins to impart the new and to rediscover our liberty. The freedom that mankind had so cleverly concealed throughout the dawn of civilization.

Through the universal language of intercourse, our entwined souls rendered a thousand words as we journeyed unhurriedly through the aleph of time. We shifted our alphas and omegas in synchronicity; to heave, and sigh as we pleased and to gratify one another to our points of no return.

We surrendered to the sensual delights of our raison d'etre. Our sexual rigidity gyrated between abutted tenderness and erotic firmness. As we transitioned from rugged masculinity to feminine silkiness, our surreptitious emotions vaporized before we careened towards our impending release with transcendent mastery.

While the athlete delivered his repressions back Boreas' way, I unleashed my honesty into my Master's unbridled freedom as Andy sounded his call to the wild. Drained from societal restraints, we laid unruffled in each other's embrace before Tad drifted into a restful slumber.

Only then did my lover declared soulfully, *"It's incredible how sex can heal dis-ease."*

Upon his words, we crept out of my Master's chamber and returned to our soothing boudoir for a peaceful night's rest before we departed for London, the following day.

Feud (Chapter Forty-Seven)

"Some of the hardest people to cut off are family members. But sometimes they are the ones that need to go."
                                          Andy Finckenstein

Early October 1968
Aldhdhib Dann دن الذئب *(Wolf Den),* Riyadh, Saudi Arabia

While Henry and I listened attentively to Professor Eberhardt's lecture on *"The Rationale of Reasonable Disagreements,"* a pandemonium was brewing down the corridor near the *Aldhdhib Dann's* library. Our teacher continued his lesson uninterrupted, unaware that an explosive family discord would soon detonate.

Eberhardt counseled, *"Societies are rife with disagreement about matters of ultimate importance, such as religious, moral, economic, and political significance. These are consequences of human reasoning which are limited by cognitive and environmental factors. If we are to remain free, we must learn to accommodate these disagreements.*

"For us to do so, we must figure out if our disagreements are reasonable or otherwise. A free society should tolerate and extricate the beneficial qualities from equitable disputes and dismiss the unreasonable arguments."

We paid no attention to the strained voices that resonated some distance from the study. We stayed focus on our teacher.

He resumed, *"People on both sides of a disagreement are often sufficiently informed, reflective, sincere, and bear one another no animosities. Yet their reasonable dispute would persist."*

Henry's Valet, Louis, who was browsing a periodical nearby, chimed, *"John Rawls, the liberal egalitarian philosopher, held that reasonable disagreements exist due to six features of human psychology, reason, and institutions."*

Before Curt could respond, Andy interrupted, *"Rawls termed the features as the 'burdens of judgment.'"*

My professor posted, *"Since the both of you are versed with the 'burdens of judgment,' can you tell us what they are?"*

Louis commented before my Valet could reply. *"First and foremost, the evidence on the disagreement is both conflicting and complex.*

Secondly; even when we agree on the relevant considerations, we may disagree about their weight.

Third: our concepts are merely moral and political theories. They are often vague and vulnerable to being undermined by hard cases.

Fourth: the way we assess evidence and weight values are shaped by the unique, total experience that each of us brings to the table.

Fifth: we often find different kinds of normative considerations on both sides of an issue, thereby making an overall assessment difficult.

Sixth and by no means last: any system of social institutions is limited in the values that it can attempt to defend or further. And many hard decisions have no easy answer."

"Well explicated, Louis. You should be my teaching assistant," our tutor quipped.

The rumpus outside was more pronounced, so our teacher halted the lecture to evaluate the commotion. He was in a quandary upon his return and advised us to remain in the library. Though he was thwarted by the ruckus, he recommenced his address.

"It is inherent that religious, moral, and political disagreements involve complex reasoning and evidence. People can examine the same evidence and come to different conclusions. The same holds true when weighing different arguments and other considerations. Anyone who has taken an introductory ethics course knows that our moral concepts are vague and subject to hard cases. Likewise, is our political ideas. When pressed many people will admit that their beliefs are based on their unique life experiences. Reflecting on this fact could help them substantiate that the diverse other might have a good reason for believing and acting as they do," Curt conjugated.

My guardian interposed, *"F.A. Hayek also offers an account of the sources of disagreement that is similar to Rawls' but is richer. Hayek stated that dispute about the relative weight of moral values will lead to evaluative pluralism; even if the 'scales of value' of rational, ethical people are inevitably different and often inconsistent with one another. He further developed an original account of the 'burdens of judgment.' He inferred the mind as a system of rules that organize subjective perceptions in cognitively unique ways. The brain itself is an order of a set of events taking place in some organism and in some manner related to, but not identical with, the physical order of events in the environment. The result is that different minds will map the world differently; for their knowledge of the world is inevitably subjective, limited, and distinct from the understanding of others."*

"Andy, for Hayek, each person only possesses a tiny, distinct piece of knowledge about how to create functioning social order. I think we can conclude from this that our reasons to accept the rules that comprise that order will, consequently, be radically situated and

subjective," the professor declared as the external outburst got more robust.

Our teacher pressed on, *"The Rawlsian and Hayekian 'burdens of judgment' suggest that disagreements about matters of ultimate import are frequently non-culpable. People who reason well concerning their evidence can come to dramatically different conclusions about not merely political and policy issues, but about which forms of life have ultimate value. Given their unique life histories, people are rationally entitled to affirm entirely different views about complex issues. We can reasonably disagree about many matters, including a vast number of political problems and their underlying normative and empirical suppositions.*

"The 'burdens of judgment' also imply that we're going to have trouble recognizing a reasonable disagreement even when there is one. Since our perspectives are so limited and different, we will have difficulty understanding how others can disagree with us. The same contestable, ambiguous facts that should lead us to recognize reasonable disagreements can prevent us from seeing that they are consistent in the first place."

The library door burst open as Professor Eberhardt wrapped up his statement. Tad and his eldest brother, Ali, tore into the room to retrieve texts from the Quran, religious and political books to support their tempestuous feud.

The brother's indignations against each other baffled us. No one dared to intercede especially our professor who stood dumbfounded by their rage. Like lightning bolts, they came and went in a flurry, and left us dazzled in the wake of their wrathful rivalry.

I was confident that a duel would be forthcoming if Tad had remained in *Wolf Den*. Luckily, the athlete's duties called. Three days later we found ourselves in London at my Master's townhouse with Miss Yasmin in our midst.

My teacher terminated our lesson as soon as the squabbling duo departed.

The educator evinced perplexingly before we were dismissed, *"Given what had transpired, we should return to our respective chambers to regain our equipoise. Tutorials will resume tomorrow.*

"The topic for tomorrow's lesson will be 'Reasonable and Unreasonable Disagreements.'"

November 2014
My Message to David and Andy (Part Four)

Hi guys,

This is the final segment of my Helius and Petronius enumeration.

When I probed my charge further to his experience with the flying horse, he put his fingers to his mouth to indicate for me to be quiet before he let out a series of whistling sounds that resembled bird calls. Low and behold, the ephemeral horse I had seen in Helius' pupils materialized into form. The animal observed us from across the pond. I stood bewildered before I clenched the enormity of this encounter.

This mysterious beast revealed himself to me because he trusted my integrity. I was honored to be accorded the cachet to testify its divinity. This pearlescent skinned creature glowed like a rainbow, and its eyes were as vibrant as the blazing sun.

Before I could grasp the encounter, Helius had mounted the horse and was airborne. I watched agape as they encircled me. Helius whispered into the creature's ear when they landed. He lowered his head and pawed its foot my direction.

My charge announced, *"Petronius is delighted to make your acquaintance."*

Flummoxed, I did not know how to react.

I kowtowed to the beast. *"I am esteemed to meet you, Petronius,"* I muttered.

He nodded in acknowledgment.

Helius commented cheerfully, *"We communicate via telepathy. Like you, with the preternatural beings, you'd encountered."*

"Would you like Petronius to take you for a flight?" the boy asked.

I nodded.

"Hop on Big-Brother," the lad sallied.

I soared through the air like I was on the back of an angel. Similar to the experiences I had encountered under the influence of LSD at Andorra's Campos de Fresa para Siempre (Strawberry Fields Forever) and during my hallucinatory dream when I blacked out at A*RGOS*, the BDSM establishment in Amsterdam. But this encounter was real, and I had Helius to avowed its authenticity.

Dear fellas, this was just one of my candid encounters with a phantastical beast. ☺

Love and hugs,
Young

The Uniqueness of Being Human
(Chapter Forty-Eight)

"Uniqueness is something my father pounded into me."
　　　　　　　　　　　　　　　　　Helius Sol Mardas

December 1968
Daltonbury Hall, Isle of Wight, England

That year, I did not return to Kuala Lumpur to spend the winter break with my family. Instead, I was at Daltonbury Hall being groomed for the role of a Big-Brother. I was one of twelve students recruited to enter the school's Big-Brother programme.

　　Although my final days at *Aldhdhib Dann* were not as smooth running as with my other Arab households because my Master had fallen in love with me even though I could not return his approbation. He wanted me to stay for another term, but Andy was at the ready to whisk me away at the drop of a hat as soon as my service at *Wolf Den* concluded. Tad had summoned my guardian and me to his study before we left. He was close to tears.

　　"I am sad for us to say goodbye. You two are my friends and supporters of my convictions; especially when it comes to prorating advice to delicate matters," my Master conceded.

　　He wiped the tears from his eyes before he resumed, *"Young, I am very fond of you, but I realize that nothing can deter the love you have for your Valet."*

　　The Arab glanced at my chaperone. *"Andy, I'm revered to know an honorable gentleman like you. Take good care of this lad. Otherwise, I might steal him from you,"* he joked.

My Master hugged us for a farewell salutation before he handed us a couple of packages.

"Go, before I change my mind and insist you stay for another term of service," the man opined and waved us away, in case he changed his mind.

Tad's chauffeur dropped us to Waterloo Station to board the train for Portsmouth Harbour before we caught the ferry to the Isle of Wight.

Not only was my lover delighted that my harem ordinance was behind us and he could have me to himself, but he was also relief that I no longer have to share my eroticism with another.

Although my Master was capricious, he was a benevolent man and did his best in the face of difficulties. I had grown accustomed to his idiosyncrasies and found him to be prepossessingly unique even when I had to tread with caution when his temper flared. He was a lost boy who longed for love but was afraid to commit. When his intimacies failed, he exonerated the blame on the other. This gave him an excuse to vindicate his guilt and resume his playboy stature before the procedure repeated itself.

In some ways, I felt downhearted that I could not do more to help this athlete, who had achieved so much in the field of sports but accomplished so little in his quest for love. While love and munificence had fallen onto my lap without much exertion; he craved with earnestness for this affectionate indulgence with chagrin.

Andy once said, *"Young, you cannot help others until you can help yourself. Once you've effectuated that, the universe will reveal its secrets in more ways than you can fathom."*

The BB Inception Ceremony

My lover was elated when Daltonbury Hall selected him to be one of three instructors, together with two professors. They were to edify twelve students including me in the Art of Big-Brothership. That year, my school's BB programme had carefully handpicked the appointed twelve from a pool of twenty Volunteers. We were notified of the selection before our winter break and were adjured to remain at Daltonbury the week before Christmas for an inception ceremony.

"We welcome the twelve eventual Big-Brothers into our midst," announced BB Joshua from the podium.

"We are honored to be your advisers, friends, and compatriots throughout your big-brother internship. If you have any queries or concerns, do not hesitate to approach our two advisory professors - Dr. Baron Struss, and Dr. Richard Kron or Big-Brother Andy, Solomon and me for guidance," he informed before he introduced the mentors.

He continued, "I am the person I am today because of Professor Struss and my ex-Big-Brother, Lucas, who mentored me when I was a Freshman at Daltonbury Hall."

Joshua passed the microphone to Solomon who announced, "I believe this is true for the twelve of you since you have chosen to donate nine to fifteen months of your time to foster the well-being of the incoming Freshmen. We were fortunate to have a Big-Brother take us under their wings and to show us the ropes. I'd like to thank and honor the mentors we had throughout our teenage lives. And to reflect on the importance of the positive and empowering effects of mentorship. The great thing about being a mentor is that anyone can be one, but you must make the decision and take the initial step. Therefore, it is appropriate for Dr. Kron to highlight the reasons for mentorship."

Professor Kron took the mic and cleared his throat before he heralded, "First and foremost, I'd like to thank all of you for being here to take up the challenge to be a

Big-Brother. You boys have the potential to change a young person's life. Do not be intimidated by the weight of that mission. As Solomon mentioned, anyone can be a mentor. You don't have to be wise to change a life.

"When I was thirteen-years-old I was matched with a life-changing mentor. My ex-Big-Brother James Schiffer, now Parliamentarian James Schiffer was then an astute Daltonbury graduate destined to enter the law faculty at Oxford University. At the time, I had no idea what a barrister did, even though the word sounded impressive. Growing up, I did not know many people like James. To have him in my life and to witness his examples gave me a new sense of life's possibilities and the potential to be more than I could be."

Professor Struss interjected when Dr. Kron took a sip of water.

"Nowadays, so much of our mental energies are spent on ourselves such as our hopes, fears, anxieties, our next Big Plan, and our goals for the future. Having a mentee will force you to not think of yourself and to concentrate on your charge's hopes, fears, and plans. This will transcend your egotism on a consistent basis. By focusing your energies on helping someone else, you provide a valuable service; both to your charge and to yourself. Perhaps, during the process, your mentee will help you realize that your fears aren't as insurmountable, or your plans are as all-important as you think they are," Baron expressed.

Professor Kron chimed before Struss could continue, "Besides, your charge will help you stay hip. There's nothing like having a young person in your life to keep you from turning into an old fogey."

Dr. Struss evinced jokingly, *"You mean like you, Richard?"*

We laughed at their facetiousness.

Baron recommenced, *"You, guys, are also helping to build a better, more stable society. One-to-one mentoring helps create happier, more stable adults, which benefits the community at large. According to a study undertaken by our school to measure the impact of our Big-Brothers program, lads with Bigs were:*

46 percent less likely to use illegal drugs than kids, not in the program.

27 percent less likely to use alcohol than kids, not in the program.

52 percent less likely to skip school than kids, not in the program.

37 percent less likely to skip a class than kids, not in the program.

Apart from that warm, fuzzy feeling from being a mentor, it also has a measurable positive impact."

Richard interposed, *"Boys, you may end up with more than just a mentee, but an added member of your family.*

"All the years when James Schiffer and I paired up, we've been through a lot together. From joyous celebrations to grand adventures, and through difficult times. These were special moments we'll never forget. I was honored to be the Best-Man at his wedding, and I also stood at his side when he was sworn into Parliament. On the other hand, James was there at my graduations from Daltonbury Hall to Oxford University. When I lost one of my best friends in a plane crash, he was the one who consoled me. We were there for each other through good and bad times. In short, James wasn't just a mentor; he is a part of my family, and I can't think of him in any other way."

Professor Struss clutched the microphone and concluded, *"The life you end up changing could be your own. Even if it's a bit of a cliché, it doesn't make it any less accurate. Your decision to become a mentor will lead to a* series of events, experiences, challenges, rewards, and opportunities you cannot foresee. These will force you to learn, evolve and despite yourself, will become a better human being. The world needs more mentors; more shining beacons like all of you who will help our Freshmen to navigate the perilous challenges of our ever-changing world. It is important to remember that your charge can also serve as a beacon to you; by assisting you in your own difficulties. Even if they do this in the most innocent ways without consciously realizing it. They will remind us of what really matters.

"Ultimately, mentoring is not a one-way process, but a two-way street. It has the potential to change and transform not just one life but two. It is an adventure that you will learn much about yourself with stories to last a lifetime. Its rippling effects have the potential to change the world and/or save it."

"If you ask me, it is not a bad return on your investment." These were Professor Kron's final words.

Second Week of November 2014
David and Andy's responses to Me

Hi Young,

Wow! You must be over the moon to ride on a flying horse. Is the Helius and Petronius narration real or did your active imagination run havoc? Just checking to make sure you are all there. LOL!

If this is a real story, you are the first person I know who rode a winged horse. It must have been an exhilarating experience. Wish I could ride one too. ☺

Blessings!
David

Young,

You are a genuinely unique individual. All my other lovers pale in your presence. I'm not staggered by your encounter with a flying horse. Ever since I've known you, there is a uniqueness about your being, a certain *je ne sais quoi*, I find difficult to pinpoint. Stellar entities are drawn to you like bees to honey. Perhaps it's your sweet innocence and untainted wiliness. I, for one, am captivated by your definitive attributes. That said, I look forward to reading more of your mythical experiences.

Love,
Andy
XOXOXO

Astute Resolutions (Chapter Forty-Nine)

"It is not a good idea to forecast, or double guess the fates; you will always be fooled."

Iman

First Week of October 1968
Tad's Townhouse in Mayfair, London, England

Our lesson on *Reasonable and Unreasonable Disagreements* did not recommence until a couple of days after our London arrival. The devious Miss Yasmin had tricked her brother, Tad, Andy and me. She had convinced us that she needed a change of scenery when it was her elopement strategy to marry Josef, the British Eurasian, she was secretly dating in Riyadh.

Although my Valet and I did not have to convince my Master to scurry his sister away from *Aldhdhib Dann,* the athlete's livid dispute with his conservative brother, Ali, prompted his decision to liberate Yasmin from the clutches of their traditionalist father and overtly religious brother. Tad would not be able to forgive himself if he had left the female in Riyadh. Little did he realize that his artful sibling had another plan in mind no matter how latitudinarian he was. As soon as we set foot in London, she vanished into thin air.

Tad was furious with Yasmin and with himself for being double-crossed. He was at a crossroad. Besides having to garner a credible explanation to his hidebound parents, he also had to report a missing person to Scotland Yard. Thanks to the astute Curt Eberhardt, my Master uncovered Miss Yasmin's whereabouts without police intervention. Since the athlete had to attend to several essential sports engagements; my professor, Andy and I interceded and solicited a deal with the female to return to her brother's care, and Tad would give her away to Josef at their wedding.

My Master was enraged when he heard the bargain, but the three of us convinced the Arab that this was the best solution for all involved. After all, Tad's family had nothing to lose but much to gain. Josef was an accomplished financier, and his family was of solid standing. Yasmin would be well cared for in regards to financial stability and in love. The hurdle the athlete had to face was to convince his conservative family that this union was a marriage made in heaven.

Under the guise of our lesson - *Reasonable and Unreasonable Disagreements,* Professor Eberhardt vindicated us that the master plan for this complicated transaction was in fact straightforward. All that was needed was to have one's head screwed on the right way.

Reasonable and Unreasonable Disagreements

Our German professor commented as we gathered in the townhouse dining room. *"In every relationship, be it personal or professional, there will always be disagreements. There is never a situation where people understand and agree with one another all the time. That is a fantasy and not a reality."*

He added, *"As an educator and trainer, I spend a lot of time with students and clients. I help them deal with communication breakdowns. Many disagreements amount to transmissions decline, and over the years I'd ascertained seven efficient ways to deal with disagreements."*

BB Louis chimed, *"Do enlighten us, professor."*

Curt gave us a sly smile before he elucidated, *"It's really very simple.*

First and foremost: seek to understand. People tend to disagree when they don't understand one another. When one party is busy wanting to be heard and doesn't spend the time to understand; disagreement happens. Most of us are more alike than different. When you realize that, you will start to accommodate, tolerate or even appreciate a different viewpoint. Therefore, seek to understand, acknowledge and be open-minded to listen to the other person.

Then, look beyond your own provocations. Many disagreements stem from someone being triggered by something that's been said. What is provoked is usually fear and the awareness of one's limitations. Whatever had happened in your past, you must find a way to get past those vexations. Remind yourself that you're in a new situation and that person does not mean to harm you."

Andy injected, *"Third and certainly not last;* is to seek out similarities and not differences. Personally, I find that the best way to resolve a disagreement is to look for common grounds. When I concentrate on the variances, the gap becomes extensive; but when I search for common grounds, it bridges the vacuity even though at times it may be a stretch."

Our tutor promulgated amusingly, *"Thank you, Andy. That is indeed true, but you forgot to mention that one has to be a good listener. In any conflict, it's crucial for both parties to be heard. That means it is essential to be a good percipient, to be unbias and nonjudgmental. A good auditor gives his or her full attention; asks for clarification if necessary and listens to different opinions without being defensive or argumentative. The best way to monitor this is to be silent. That's when you learn to take responsibility for your own feelings. In heated disagreements, it is easy to make accusations, lay blame and fabricate excuses.*

"To work through the blame game, you have to be honest with yourself and to take responsibility for your feelings and presumptions that may have contributed to the communication breakdown."

Eberhardt continued solemnly, *"Make a commitment to yourself. During an intense disagreement, it is not uncommon for one or both parties to have a foot out the door. If you want to honestly get to the heart of the matter, be sure that the other person understands your commitment to the relationship. Even if you have an issue with their behavior, you have to keep that matter separate."*

Louis expressed, *"It is wise to use positive language. None of us want to be called names, to be singled out negatively or to hear all the bad things they had done in the past. If you speak in negatives, the other person's feelings will get hurt, and they will shut down. But if positivity is brought into your iteration, then it is likely that you will be heard, and the disagreement can be resolved rapidly, smoothly and efficiently."*

My Valet counseled, *"Disagreements are a way of life, but they don't have to cause havoc. The next time you boys encounter a conflict, try these techniques and see if you can resolve the problem faster and more efficiently."*

Professor **Eberhardt** repossessed therein.

"Generally, reasonable disagreements come in two varieties – normative and empirical. A reasonable normative dispute concerns the identification and application of moral principles and values. For example, both parties might disagree about the relative importance of deservingness. Are any of us in a cognitive position to make that determination and to justify our temptation to surmise that those who disagree with us have made a culpable mistake?

"On the other spectrum, unreasonable disagreements happen frequently. One irrational normative

dispute is the rejection of the moral equality between races. Someone who forthrightly affirms that Middle Easterners are more morally crucial than Caucasians probably cannot hold his/her position with adequate reflection, honesty, and goodwill. It is easy to imagine someone from a previous period in human history who thought as much, but nowadays such a belief cannot survive adequate rational scrutiny, nor is the notion compatible with possessing a moral character," the professor advised.

He paused before he professed, *"Unreasonable empirical disagreements are more common, such as advancing family ties and fanatical religious beliefs. No adequately informed person can firmly believe that the above-mentioned holds truth when confronted with evidence.*

"As I've noted, the identification of reasonable disagreements is difficult. Due to our cognitive biases and our limited means of determining why others advocate their positions. Consequently, we tend to deduce that our adversary holds his/her belief because of some culpable failure/failures on his or her part. It is a failure of reflectiveness, information collection, and/or a fundamental insensitivity to underlying moral value. Yet, our cognitive limitations and biases will lead us to overestimate the frequency of unreasonable disagreements. Therefore, we should resist the temptation to condemn others for their differences."

Three Steps in Reasonable Disagreements

Before Curt Eberhardt curtailed that morning's tutorial, he stated, *"I'd like to finish today's lesson by explaining how you can recognize a reasonable disagreement when one presents itself. Imagine that you find yourself in a moral or political dispute with another and you regard the conflict as unreasonable (on their part). There are three valuable facts to reflect upon.*

Number one: your cognitive limitations are significant and are likely to affect your judgment that your opposer has made a culpable error in defending his/her position. Although, it is tough to know why people believe what they reckon; take a moment to pause and reflect on your biases and limitations, and how it could hamper your judgment.

Secondly: ask yourself whether you have enough information and have engaged sufficiently in your reflection about the mental state of your interlocutor. Is he/she rational and reasonable in his/her supposition? If you have trouble with your discernment, apply the principle of charity and assume that the discrepancy is due to non-culpable factors.

Last and certainly not least: act on the principle of charity with honesty and respectfulness. Strive to verify if the other person has useful information to support his/her arguments and if he/she is prepared to take your opinions and rationalizations seriously. If your interlocutor has flawed details or patently uses erroneous assumptions, then it is an affirmative confirmation that the disagreement cannot persist with reasonable people. Whereby, your opponent's estimation can be dismissed."

Our instructor's closing statement was, and I quote:

"If people followed this logical procedure during their moral, religious, and/or political disagreements, you'd discover that you had underestimated the frequency of reasonable disputes. Each of us is within our bubble of information and experience, and so are those with whom we disagree. Unless you break through these cognitive barriers, it is impossible to understand our adversary's point of view. Yet the first thing we do is contemptuously impugn their motives, rationality, and their intelligence. This is dangerously unwarranted."

The New Look (Chapter Fifty)

"SUDDENLY, Christian Dior arrived, and overnight we all adopted his New Look."

Bettina Ballard
(*Vogue* editor)

December 1968
The Victoria & Albert Museum (V&A), London. England

Andy and I were back in Uncle James' townhouse over the Christmas and New Year Holidays. The thoughtful Mr. Pinkerton, who knew my pertinacious love for fashion, had arranged with his friend, Ms. Joanne Brogden, to give us a guided tour of a special Post-War Paris Fashion exhibition. The presentation was held at the Victoria & Albert Museum (V&A), and our guided visit was a belated birthday gift from my beloved uncle. Not only was Ms. Brogden, an accomplished Fashion professor, she was also the newly appointed Head of Fashion at the Royal College of Art (RCA), London.

I was beside myself, on the day of our museum sojourn. I had to select the perfect outfit for the meeting. While Uncle James looked on with amusement as I dressed; my chaperone was exasperated with my fastidiousness.

Andy remarked miffily, *"Young, you're going to view a fashion exhibition. You're not an exhibit. You don't have to fuss over the way you look."*

James said wittily, *"Andy, you never know who you're going to meet. After all this lad plans to be a part of a new wave of fashion designers and an impressive appearance can often lead to impactful outcomes. He should dress the part to impress Ms. Brogden. She might be his future mentor."*

James Pinkerton's prediction did ring true. In 1973 when I entered the RCA to pursue my postgraduate Fashion studies, **Professor** Brogden became my Fashion mentor. But then in late 1968, I was merely my debonairly self, where fashion was and still is the quintessence of my being.

Upon arrival, we were greeted by a tall, good-looking gentleman at the grand museum foyer. He introduced himself as Élan Coleridge, an RCA Fashion educator.

"Professor Brogden is called away on urgent business when she was about to come to meet you. She asked me to be your guide. I hope you will not be disaffected by my presence," Élan quipped friendlily.

Not only was Coleridge tall and handsome, but he also reminded me of my Italian photographer friend and mentor, Mario. A classic aquiline nose sat atop of Élan's striking features, and his sturdy physique lends an authoritative air to the man I took too immediately.

He led us into the large hall before he began, *"When Paris was liberated in 1944, the city was on its knees. But within a decade, it had regained its status as the world capital of style, romance, and allure. When I was in Paris in 1947; much of the city was still infected by its war-weary shabbiness. It cast a sad shadow over the grandeur of this ancient metropolis I'd encountered as an adolescent before the war. Although the mood on the streets and the streets themselves had improved. The startling difference was the city's reputation."*

As we browsed through the Paris Post World War II photographic images, my uncle opined, *"Post World War II France was broke. A sixth of all the buildings were dilapidated and its economy on its knees. The decades of neglect were painfully obvious. Smoke-blackened stone facades, cracked stuccos, and peeling paintworks were prevalent. I was there in 1945 after Paris was liberated but sadden by its population. They were close to starvation, and the disparity between the beaux quartiers and working-class districts were in abundance. Yet a handful of wealthy Parisians, diplomats, and visitors lived in luxury. The black market was in full swing, but everyone did whatever they could to scrape by."*

James sighed and shook his head before he added, *"I felt there was a collective sense of shame that the country rolled over without a fight to the Nazis. There was also a settling of old scores, and the most visible was the meting out of summary justice where collaborators were executed or having their heads shaved. Locals staged public protests like heartening celebrations."*

Élan expressed, *"I was there when Christian Dior unveiled the New Look. France was in wartime scarcities. There were coal shortages, and electricity was rationed. For the ordinary Parisian their daily circumstances were not much better than they were during the war. Paris was also paralyzed by workers' strikes. The cost of living was astronomical, and food scarcity was acute. Corroded by years of German occupation, Parisians were blanketed by cynicism and futility. I sensed their apathy and bitterness."*

As we proceeded down the exhibition hall, the educator resumed, *"At the ateliers, afternoon showings were a handful of wealthy socialites; members of the diplomatic set; well-to-do tourists, and numerous disciples of the 'international society.'*

"The models were scrawny and petulant looking. One couturier made it a point to feed his models. 'I want them to look like human beings, not skeletons,' he said before he added sanguinely. 'And, if they have enough to eat, perhaps they'll smile.'"

James said regrettably, *"During those post-war years, the Parisian sun never seemed to rise, and the winter sky resembled a lid of iron graying the skin of my hands and making my face wan. There were few cars on the streets with the occasional truck running on wood-burning engines, and aging women on old bicycles. The heavy silence made Paris a doomed city. If I'm not mistaken, food rationing lasted until 1949. As a foreign resident, I had to queue outside the town hall to obtain coupons for everything; from food to clothes."*

Coleridge announced, *"I returned to Paris for the 1949 winter collections when the tenseness finally took a turn for the better; amidst some bitter strikes in the Parisian dressmaking industry."*

"How did fashion transform the city's tension?" I queried.

"Fashion was what pre-war Paris was synonymous with. The garment sector employs some thirteen thousand skilled artisans in highly specialized workshops. The Nazis failed miserably to move the industry to Germany. France was desperately short of foreign currency, and wealthy overseas women, especially Americans, were more than happy to pay a fortune for their clothes. You see, Young, couture is a high-profile and exportable manifestation of l'art de vivre for which France stood," the Fashion professor counseled.

He continued, *"Shortly after the liberation of Paris, Lucien Lelong, Robert Ricci, and a group of French artists and designers developed a plan for Paris to recapture its position as the world capital of haute couture. They created a hundred and seventy figures, each a third the size of a real person. These were used to display the first post-war Paris collections; complete with jewelry, designed to scale by Boucheron, Cartier and Van Cleef. The dolls are shown in le Petit Théâtre de la Mode, aptly translated as a miniature theatre, with sets designed and constructed by the likes of Jean Cocteau and Christian Bérard.*

"The little couture show opened at the Louvre in March of 1945, and immediately attracted more than one hundred thousand visitors, and raised a million francs for the French war relief fund. That year, it also showcased in Barcelona, London, Leeds, Copenhagen, Stockholm, and Vienna before crossing the Atlantic to New York and San Francisco in 1946. In December 1945, the devaluation of the franc acted as a powerful incentive for tourists and buyers to travel and splash out in France. Buying couture had never been so reasonable!"

We finally arrived at the haute couture fashion display of post-war Paris.

I questioned, *"Why did it take two years after the Paris liberation for Christian Dior's New look to happen?"*

"Young man, things don't change overnight. It takes time for the spirit of change to gain momentum," Uncle James declared.

We checked out the beautiful garment displays encased in glass containers when Élan recalled, *"The lead up to Dior's first collection in the spring of 1947 was chaotic. He had an insufficient workspace, and his inexperienced staff had to use the corridors and stairs to travail. One of the designer's key models passed out at a fitting while a workroom staff collapsed under stress. Despite that, the excitement carried over into the show."*

Coleridge paused to remember, *"At the time, I was a young Fashion intern, and that show's tension was electrifying. I had goosebumps when the first model came on the runway. Her flared skirt swirled like an open umbrella within the packed room and knocked over ashtrays. That brought the audience to the edges of their seats. After several ensembles, I had a premonition that I was witnessing a unique moment in the evolution of fashion."*

The professor pointed to a beautifully attired mannequin before he advocated, *"The New Look is a reprise of mid-nineteenth century fashions with billowing skirts that nipped-in below the waists. It was a dramatic departure from the frugal and angular broad-shouldered military-like uniforms of wartime fashions. Dior's New Look was uncompromising. It necessitated intricate workmanship and sewing techniques that had disappeared during the war. Notable undergarments were engineered to create the curvaceous silhouette."*

My chaperone, who had thus far remained silent, remarked, *"It was indeed a triumph for Christian Dior. I'd read old press coverage about the New Look, and it heralded the beginning of a renaissance for French couture. The wealthy elite and fashion editors from around the world loved it. The article also noted that those who cannot afford it aspired to it. The New look was a must-have."*

"That is correct, Andy. Suddenly, Dior arrived and became an overnight success. Women around the world embraced his New Look; even when it was difficult to buy materials in quantities to copy the style. Then, there were major fashion differences between the cities and the country folks, who ridiculed the city-dwellers for their extravagance," Élan sniggered.

When our tour finally ended, Professor Coleridge said, *"As you can see from the exhibits, the New Look was not only controversial, it also stirred a riot in a Montmartre street market."*

"How so?" I asked.

"Dior's clothes were dispatched to Montmartre in large wooden crates on board a camionette. The models changed in the back room of a nearby bar. When the first mannequin walked onto the rue Lepic market, the street went silent. A stall keeper shouted insults of outrage and hurled herself on the model. Other women followed her lead and attacked the poor girl. They tore at her clothes and hair. The other models retreated hastily back to the

safety of Dior's headquarter at Avenue Montaigne," Élan explained.

When we thanked Professor Coleridge for his illuminating commentary on Paris post-war fashion experiences; he suggested we continue our conversation at a nearby pub so he could be better acquainted with us. Since Uncle James had other business to attend, he left the three of us to our contrivances that ended in a propagational way I had fantasized but not envisioned as reality. The professor's alluring charisma and well-versed Fashion knowledge took my breath away. I was already infatuated with the man who would later become my Fashion mentor when I entered the Harrow School of Art & Technology and the Royal College of Art to pursue my Fashion studies.

Third Week of November 2014
My Reply to Both, David and Andy

David, your open-mindedness is one appealing quality that got you selected into E.R.O.S./V.T.A. As you are aware, our education taught us to be truthful in all matters; including the iteration of fantastical beasts encounters by the society's recruits. LOL!

That said, I have a question. During your years of service, did you ever contemplate leaving any of the Arab households or E.R.O.S./V.T.A.? Did that notion ever enter your mind? If so, what were the reasons behind the rumination or reflexions?

Young

Andy,

I am rendered speechless by your loving tributes to me. You never fail to awe me with your accolades. I am humbled by your trust. There are times I do not feel I deserve such eulogize from an intrepid man like yourself. You always remind me to be myself; even though it is difficult to live up to your expectations at times. I am a mere mortal feigning as an angel while you are the manifestation of perfection - God. LOL!

My dear ex, I am sure the readers of *A Harem Boy's Saga* would be interested to know more about your life, after our amicable separation. Do enlighten us with your insightful sagacity.

Love,
Young

Beauty Pageants (Chapter Fifty-One)

"Beauty pageants teach the exact same skills that sports do: goal setting, 'can do' attitude and performance under pressure. Except in pageants, you wear nicer shoes."
                                                            Tad Abdul Hafiz

Second Week of October 1968
Copacabana Palace Hotel, Rio de Janeiro, Brazil

Tad's entourage made a three day stop in Rio de Janeiro before we headed to Acapulco, Mexico, where we reunited with Sheik Fahrib, Prince P, and their respective entourages to witness the 1968 Olympic Sailing Competition. As documented in chapter one - The Perfect Storm.

In the early nineteen sixties when Brasilia became Brazil's national capital, Rio de Janeiro was about to lose its vibrant luster; even though beauty pageants continue to reign supreme in this South American metropolis. The Miss Brazil World or Miss Mundo Brasil, in Portuguese, was and still is an annual beauty contest that aims to select the best candidate to represent this Federative Republic in the international Miss World contest. That year, it was held at the infamous Copacabana Palace, the most opulent hotel in Rio.

The hotel's history began in 1923 when President Epitácio Pessoa adjured the hotelier Señor Otavio Guinle to construct a monumental masterpiece. The French architect Jose Gire was entreated to model a Mediterranean style hotel like that of Hotel Negresco in Nice and the Carlton in Cannes. From that moment forward, the Copacabana Palace became a symbol of Rio.

Although the Copacabana Palace hotel added historical value, tradition, and luxury to this effervescent city; Copacabana beach was then relatively unknown to the international set. That changed in 1933 when the Hollywood movie *Flying Down to Rio* discovered Copacabana and its Palace Hotel. With Fred Astaire, Ginger Rogers and a host of chorus girls dancing on the wings of an airplane over Copacabana beach above the Palace Hotel, this establishment's Golden Book soon registered the signatures of Tyrone Power, Henry Fonda, Errol Flynn, Bing Crosby, Douglas Fairbanks Jr., and Walt Disney.

In 1938, this traditional institution inaugurated its Golden Room and made it Copacabana's number one show venue in Latin America. The world's biggest names flocked here to perform. Dionne Warwick, Josephine Baker, Ella Fitzgerald, Marlene Dietrich, Ray Charles, Edith Piaf, Lena Horn, Gilbert Bécaud, Nat King Cole, Sammy Davis Jr., Tony Bennett, and Ray Charles had made their appearances through its revolving doors and added glamor and éclat to its already vivid reputation.

In 1949, the old Copacabana Theatre Casino transformed itself into a state-of-the-art, five hundred seat Copacabana Theatre. In a market heavily dominated by foreign acting companies and European playwrights, this new theatre became the venue for new and upcoming Brazilian productions.

Since its inauguration, this sumptuous operation was and continues to be the stage of significant political, cultural and social events. In the process, it transformed Copacabana into one of the most famous districts in the world.

In 1968, the year we arrive marked Señor Otavio Guinle's demise. His widow, Dona Mariazinha took over the Hotel's management. She was determined to continue her husband's legacy by hosting the 1968 Miss Brazil

World beauty pageant. One of the most flamboyant events ever held in Latin America.

Tad Abdul Hafiz, a leading sports figure of his time was one of a handful of celebrity judges invited to partake in this internationally broadcasted occasion. The moment my Master set foot in Copacabana Palace, an army of journalists, reporters, and photographers descended on him. These obstreperous bunch muscled Curt, Andy and me to a corner as they fought to canvass with the athlete.

It was Andy who spotted Count Mario Conti in deep conversation with an elegantly dressed couple at the hotel bar. When the photographer noticed our presence, he motioned for us to join him before he introduced the pair to us.

Señor Roberto Pisani Marinho extended his hand to greet us before uttered amusingly, *"Call me Roberto. Everyone calls me Roberto."*

"This is the great Brazilian actress, Natalia," the Count introduced the lady next to him.

Señor Marinho continued, *"We are discussing the positive and negative aspects of international beauty pageants. We'll like to hear your opinions?"*

Neither Curt, Andy nor I had any knowledge of the inner workings of the beauty pageant industry, we kept silent.

"Roberto, you are the head of Globo, South America's largest commercial TV network, and a seasoned beauty pageant organizer; give us your insights to this multi-million-dollar industry," Mario announced.

The media mogul gave a hearty laugh.

"Mario, my friend, you know more about the beauty and fashion industry than any of us. Why don't you enlighten us?" Roberto remarked.

The business tycoon paused before he added, *"I will tell you that one positive aspect of beauty pageants is that the participants can definitely become good public speakers and be excellent performers in front of large crowds. When a girl keeps her cool in front of a huge group, she can express herself freely. These are valuable training for contestants who want a career in music, broadcasting, or jobs that require her to speak with confidence. I've seen their comfort level rise with their pageant experience."*

The actress chimed, *"But one of the downsides of beauty pageants are the participants can turn shallow and be hung up on the beauty aspect. It is great to win a beauty pageant, but it can also make her obsessed with her looks. Thereby making her conceited.*

"The positive aspects of the competition are shoved aside when the public shower winners with so much attention. They can easily become overconfident. In my opinion, contestants should use this once in a lifetime experience to build their positive qualities."

Conti injected, *"Natalia, you are talking like a seasoned thespian. I'm sure the level of fitness and discipline it takes to participate in beauty pageants will help a contestant get her body in ship-shape. Pageants are grueling work. This experience will provide a lass the opportunity to take her fitness level to peak condition, and to gain knowledge and patience which will serve her well."*

"Not to mention the grand prizes, scholarships, and travel opportunities for the winners. To see the world, do charity work, and make tangible benefits internationally. Often, the cash prizes assist the victors in funding their passions," Roberto commented merrily.

"That is indeed true for the winner. But the losers go away with a loss of confidence and a negative outlook on the experience. Those who are determined to win and come away empty handed, often feel depressed and desolate. If they don't have a strong support network, the defeat can affect them in an unhealthy and

counterproductive way. The positives gained from participation are often lost in self-pity," Natalia expressed.

For the first time, Eberhardt remarked since we joined the group. *"I have nothing against beauty pageants, but I am concerned for children's participation. Like their adult counterpart, they experience the negative results that come with losing. In my perspective, children are not mature enough to handle jeopardies. They are more likely to take a defeat hard, and a loss of self-confidence. In my opinion, to have them focus on their looks and be judged by it can be harmful. If they are to enter beauty pageants; their parents and mentors should educate them on the pros and cons of winning and losing."*

Roberto exclaimed assuringly, *"Well said. I couldn't agree with you more. Perhaps, I should start the first male beauty pageant in Rio."*

He glanced at my teacher, Valet and me as if we were likely candidates.

The tycoon recommended, *"The beauty pageant experience helps a candidate towards her goals. The challenge, confidence, and self-esteem she gains remain when she requires it in the future. Contests that require contestants to demonstrate a talent usually encourage unfocused individuals to take an honest approach to themselves and to realize that looks and talent do go together. Atop that, to answer tough questions on the spot can improve a contestant's ability to think quickly and accurately."*

The actress expressed, *"Beauty pageants are expensive. Travels to and from cities are not cheap. The gowns often cost an arm and a leg, especially for penurious participants. Not to mention the physical strain to obtain the 'perfect' body which can lead to an eating disorder and excessive cosmetic surgeries. It's not easy to stay focus on her goal and to care for herself simultaneously. I applaud those contestants who can avoid the pressure and enjoy the stressful experience."*

The Count finalized, *"Natalia, there is no easy solution for pageant contestants when their fate is in the hands of the judges. The best result she can expect is to apply the positive factors to herself. Beauty is a pleasant quality to possess and to win a pageant is a bonus. At the end of the day, beauty pageants are forums to help contestants increase their important characteristics."*

By the time Tad made his appearance at our side, the paparazzi had dispersed. Our conversation had veered to other matters, such as a night out to paint the town red which was the photographer and the athlete's favorite pastime.

The Milliner (Chapter Fifty-Two)

"Romance is the glamour which turns the dust of everyday life into a golden haze."

Carolyn Gold Heilbrun

Mid-December 1968
Élan Coleridge Studio, Kensington, London

Our drink at a nearby pub led us to Élan's millinery studio. Although Coleridge was married and lived with his wife in the country, he had rented a studio in the heart of Kensington to produce his one-of-a-kind hats. I couldn't help but marvel at the man's creative genius where hats in every color, shape, and delineation filled his workroom.

As much as he liked me, Élan was more interested in my Valet whom he doted with pensive adulation. My Valet, not one for the limelight, offered me to the professor as if I was a sanctified lamb for his taking. Although I was reverential of the handsome professor and desired to know everything about hat making; I was hesitant when my lover confabulated me as an amatory gift to the man. When we were introduced, Andy was the one who had eyes for the milliner, even though the sexual attraction between us were mutual. Yet, diffidence had shadowed my chaperone. It was an attribute I had not seen in Andy until then. I had no clue that within his self-assured composure existed timorousness.

As much as I fancied Élan, I was more intrigued by his hat making skills than his strive to bed us. Unlike my Valet and I, who were able allurers, the milliner's come-hither dictums appeared contrived. There were moments when Andy and I suppressed our sniggers at his attempts to bare ourselves for his pleasure. Instead, I took the reins to have some educational amusement before I reeled him in, to regain his candidness for our tryst.

"How did you become a hat maker?" I inquired curiously.

"My mother was a lover of hats. I was awed by their magical qualities to transform a woman's look and emotions when she dons a hat for the different occasion," the man responded with a glint in his eyes.

"Does that apply to men?" I quipped.

He glanced at us before he replied, *"Of course it does, especially on a well-groomed male, like the ones before me."*

My self-conscious chaperone replied, *"Young is the fashionista, I'm only his tag along."*

"Ahh! But you are equally primed like this aspiring fashion designer," the milliner looked at us enticingly before he resumed, *"When I was growing up, I was very awkward. My classmates would make fun of my height, build, and a hooked nose. They nicknamed me Eagle's Beak. One day, when I was harassed, a good-looking sergeant in uniform came to my aid. From that moment forward, I became obsessed with men in liveries; especially servicemen in full regalia."*

"So, you have a fetish for uniform personnel?" I sallied.

My comment hit the man's core. He announced inexcusably, *"Yes, I do have a weakness for good-looking men in uniforms, especially soldiers and sailors."*

I wisecracked, *"I presume you'll like to see us in military and marine getups with matching headgears?"*

The man gave us a devious look and proceeded to rummage through a closet. He extracted an infantry uniform and a sailor's outfit before he handed them to us.

Little did I know that I had stuck my foot in my mouth. My guardian stared at me bafflingly. I was equally perplexed by this sudden turn of events. He handed Andy the naval ensemble and passed me the soldier garb.

"Will you put these on? I want to see you in them," he entreated.

My lover and I did as was told. Andy motioned to me to discard my brief like him. Élan's pupils dilated when he adjusted the sailor cap on Andy's head and the beret on mine. His expression was that of hallowed adoration. He could not keep his eyes off us when he proceeded to tantalize our protruding loins.

Like Coleridge, my chaperone was similarly emboldened by the image of me in an army outfit. As if my Valet had just encountered a sexy trooper, he French kissed me passionately. Élan's lips soon merge with ours in a three-way lock as our luring tongues swirled like intertwined serpents in heated passion. My lover in uniform transformed my ardor for him multifariously. In marine regalia, his rugged handsomeness amplified trifold as his tilted Dixie Cup fell seductively over the edge of his eye. This unanticipated illusion stimulated the hat maker and me to attention below the waist. Within our pants, our eager palpitations drummed incessantly as we stroked each other while in lock lips stance.

As if by divine postulation, our nimble fingers reached to unzip the other's pants before they inched their way towards each other's masculinity. This rousing foreplay had unhinged Élan's awkwardness. In its place rose a sturdy specimen that could gratify any hot-blooded male; be they bi, gay, or straight.

While Coleridge buried his bearded face between my lover's bubbly derriere, I gravitated towards their massiveness. Andy swooned as he thrust himself towards the swaddling provocation while their prodigious double entendres filled my mouth to the brim. I was in seventh heaven and craved for more.

Before I knew it, the professor had laid us on his daybed. He wasted no time to drive his bodacious tongue into Andy's crevice, while I swathed Élan's bootylicious rump and sucked his towering protuberance in readiness for him to penetrate my lover's inviting hollow.

This was one of those rare occurrences where Andy permitted his masculinity to be possessed by another dominant male. The milliner's mannish chest of fur ran down his navel and beyond. Like my lover, I welcomed this sturdy specimen into my sacred sanctuary without vacillation. Since my beloved was usually the dominant participant in our naughty assignations, Andy's acquiescent contentment was a rare but congenial treat to witness.

I savored the rapturous sight and sounds that emanated from the duo as I laid beneath the men to impel them to euphoria ecstasies. In the opposite direction, my lover's mouth galvanized me to emphatic exuberance as he swiveled his oral fissure between my twitching cavern and quivering bulbousness.

Suddenly, the masterful Élan flipped me onto my back and plowed into my willing crevice. My squeals of delight aided the man's blissful exhilaration and propelled him towards the point of no return. He pulled himself away only to jab himself into my lover's anal orifice. Coleridge could no longer contain himself. His sacredness poured into Andy's inner sanctum before he hefted back on me to deliver his velvety residuum into my convulsing void.

Andy could no longer withhold his enthusiasm. He furrowed inside my shuddering hollow and spilled his molten lava deep into my already overflowing haven. Both men slumped on me from buoyant depletion. Their leaking residues threw me over the edge. I exploded onto their hairy torsos before they lapped at my creamy outpour to shared my remains in an ecstatic three-way kiss. Although spent but rejuvenated we cuddled in tender affection and vowed we would do this again soon.

While Élan pledged to show us a secret fraternity where devotees of uniformed men met for prurient activities; my chaperone and I also swore that we would never utter a word of our tryst to anyone. The hat maker did keep his promise, and so did my Valet and me. The talented milliner is now dead and buried, and I am sanctioned by Andy to reveal this mysterious rendezvous within the pages of A Harem Boy's Saga – V – Metanoia; a memoir by Young.

Mid-December 2014
A Private Message from Andy to Me

Hi Loverboy,

Sorry for my late response. This past week was a roller coaster. During one of my rowing practices for an upcoming race, I was carted off to the hospital. The doctor diagnosed my recurring bladder pain as pyelonephritis. Although there is no cause for alarm, as it can be treated with antibiotics; I am grounded in the race which I wanted to participate. I'm stranded without much to do, except rest and to heal.

Hence, I have plenty of time to catch up with my correspondence. Young, you are too kind to paint me in such a holy light. I cannot get the credit you'd portrayed me in your memoirs. I am merely an ordinary guy who did his best to be a proficient Big-Brother/Valet to those under my supervision. And be a rectified lover to you simultaneously. I care about your wellbeing and continue to cherish our subliminal time together.

Now that I am older and wiser, I'm glad I did not drag you to New Zealand. You would not be a happy camper without your Fashion aspirations to govern your divine motivation to be an accomplished designer. Neither would I be satisfied to remain in London when I desperately needed to escape my homophobic father.

As much as I missed your presence during those problematic university days, I also understood that we had different paths to follow. I was overjoyed when I learned that you were accepted into Harrow College of Art and Technology and to the London Royal College of Art. I knew Uncle James had pathed the way for your apparent acceptance to both institutions. Your precursory introduction to Ms. Gay Yates (fashion lecturer at Harrow College of Art and Technology) and Élan Coleridge (fashion professor at RCA and celebrated milliner) were indications that James had planned these meetings circumspectly for your acceptance into both prestigious institutions.

Your uncle was a good man and an excellent mentor to us. His sound advice for you to remain in London and Paris was of sound judgment. Although at the time I resented him for keeping you in the United Kingdom.

You must be wondering why I am making a point of telling you all of the above. Maybe, I am a reminiscing fool or someone who is looking for a riposte to see you again before my days are up. Either way, I will always be your boosterish fan. When push comes to shove, I would like to see you face-to-face instead of our current long-distance communications. I don't mean to be assertive, but I would love to see you again when you are ready for us to meet. After all, it has been forty-five years since we parted ways. Do consider my proposition. ☺ I look forward to your thoughts.

Love,
Andy
XOXOXO

Terma Centaurs (Chapter Fifty-Three)

"To the moralist, prostitution does not consist so much in the fact that the woman sells her body, but rather that she sells it out of wedlock."

Emma Goldman

Second Week of October 1968
Centaurs (Terma), Copacabana, Rio de Janeiro, Brazil

Full of beautiful women and XXX behaviors; Rio de Janeiro's *Centaurs* had enticed celebrities, sports stars and to anyone willing to pay a fee to experience this scandalous Terma. Our entourage arrived at this establishment with much fanfare and kissy-faced welcomes under the auspice of Señor Roberto Pisani Marinho, a regular at this sin palace.
    In Brazil, a terma is a bathhouse that consists of spa facilities, health and fitness amenities, massage services, a bar and by no lesser means; brothel ministrations. A nightclub was cleverly installed within *Centaurs* to facilitate customers for easy access to potential playmates. Although prostitution is legal in the República Federativa do Brasil, and there are no laws forbidding adults from being professional sex workers; it is illegal to operate a bordello or to employ sex workers. To enjoy an erotic night out without any government officials breathing down their necks, nightclubs and termas became stomping grounds for locals and tourists alike. These establishments have never been raided until the 21st Century after Brazil claimed victory in the 2002 World Cup; when one of the

soccer gods, well known for his sexual appetite, chartered Rio's most popular terma for a private party. Orgiastic video images of the player and his copulating partners were glaringly displayed all over the establishment. This stirred the authorities to perform a spurious cleanup of what has always been one the country's implicit attractions.

That night when we were at *Centaurs*, the place was packed with international male revelers and bootylicious sex workers of every conceivable surgically enhanced bosom and booty sizes.

Tad, Mario, and the spirited Roberto disappeared in separate directions with several ardent ladies of the night while Curt, Andy and I were left at the bar to espy the patencies of this rattling enterprise. Women with beautiful faces and stunning bodies gravitated in our direction as we avoided eye contact with these magnificent creatures of the night.

Sergio, the handsomely gruff barman, sensed our trepidations and drifted our direction.

"Where are you guys from?" the bartender inquired.

"Germany and the United Kingdom," **Eberhardt** answered on our behalf before he added, *"And how long have you been working here, Sergio?"*

"Four years. I've seen many displays of grandiosity during my time here. Anyone with money can live big at Centaurs," the Camarero answered preposterously.

Just as he was about to continue, he was waved away.

He resumed unapologetically upon his return, *"One evening, a rich dude shelled out several thousand dollars to reserve the master suite along with twenty girls. The gangbang, the strap-on, the 'naked walk through the house,' are everyday occurrences here."*

The man was called away again.

When he reappeared, he commented musingly, *"We nicknamed this prim and proper patron, Couve-flor (Cauliflower). Whenever he is here, he would hire two girls and have them shove Chokitos (a texturized chocolate candy bar) up his ass. To satisfy himself, the girls had to order him to eat the Chokitos out of his own butt while they spanked him in the process."*

Andy queried, *"Are you not fazed by this brazen display of sex for sale?"*

"I am a Carioca (a native of Rio de Janerio). In Copacabana, prostitutes are everywhere. When I was an adolescent, I would take girls to the water tower of my building and have sex with them. Everyone does it, including my schoolmates and we talk openly about our experiences. When we were old enough, we graduated to fast fodas (fast fuck) houses," the Brazilian announced proudly. *"Sex is in our blood. Every Carioca loves a good whoopee."*

I inquired, *"Has any of the patrons tried to get you to have sex with them?"*

The barman responded cheerily, *"Of course they have. They want to pay me to sleep with them or to watch me fuck the girls they paid for."*

"And…, do you?" I asked.

The Mixologist laughed-out-loud. *"Being a staff of this institution, I am forbidden to bed the customers. But…, there are ways around it."*

I stared at the rogue and waited for more. He did not respond until he returned from another round of his chores.

"There is always The Clube," the bartender advocated.

"What is The Clube?" my Valet asked.

The Camarero answered wickedly, *"Sometimes, I go there after work. It is a men's sauna near the area where the travesties (transgender sex workers) hang out.*

"One night, a man was pounded by a group of travesties in skintight dresses and high heels. The fool had the temerity to pickpocket one of their friends. When the guy tried to pull the trick again, they took their revenge."

Before we knew it, two Garotas (lassies) had settled themselves on either side of my tutor and my Valet. Gio, one of the females overheard the last part of our conversation and vented in broken English. *"We are cut off and the misconstrued people in society. I'll make my voice heard. We trade bodies willingly and purposefully for a living. Instead, we are branded as pariahs. People forget we are mothers, sisters and have families."*

Curt commented puzzlingly, *"What makes you turn to prostitution for a living?"*

"Pretty boy, everyone is a whore in our own way," she quipped.

Her veracious declaration put a stop to Eberhardt's sanctimoniousness. Instead, her lurid hands worked their way around Eberhardt's curly hair before she inserted them into his semi-unbuttoned shirt. The German halted her advancement when she leaned in to kiss him.

My teacher asserted, *"First and foremost, I can't afford you. Besides, I'm not in the mood for sex."*

She made no attempt to pull away but resumed her exertion.

"I want to fuck you," she challenged.

Valentia who spoke no English mirrored her girlfriend's exploits. She also backed away from my chaperone.

Gio attested sarcastically, *"I not sexy enough for you? Or are you a homo?"*

Her proclamations did not sit well with my teacher who contested. *"My decision has nothing to do with you nor is my private life any of your business."*

Both Garotas kvetched in Portuguese before they left us in a huff.

The hawk-eyed barman announced before he gave us a mischievous wink, *"The girls like the both of you. Most likely, they'll not charge you for their services. When Gio and Valentia solicit men they like, the guys are bound to have a good time. They are excellent love makers."*

Andy questioned, *"How much do the girls charge?"*

"Their fees vary with individual customers. From not having to pay to three thousand reais per go," Sergio noted.

"How do they determine their fees?" I queried naively.

The Mixologist giggled effusively before he disclosed, *"If you are handsome, like you guys, no fees are required. But if the client is less pleasing to the eye or unattractive, their charges climb accordingly. And if they are rich and famous; then they'll have to pay an exorbitant tariff."*

I questioned, *"How much do the Garotas here earn a month?"*

"If it's a busy month, they can earn as much as twenty to twenty-five thousand reais."

"Wow! That is a pretty good paycheque," my Valet exclaimed.

The bartender added, *"That is true, but the girls also need a lot of emotional stability and equilibrium to do what they do. A Garota told me that she works four days and services four clients per day. She stops until her money runs out. Then, she gathers herself to do it again. Her dilemma is to disconnect sex from affection."*

Eberhardt bored by the elusive coming and goings of the bar suggested we proceed downstairs to the spa. Before we parted ways with Sergio, we agreed to meet the following night after the **Miss Brazil World** beauty pageant. He would be our guide to *The Clube*.

Below Stairs

The floor below housed a wet, and a dry sauna together with a cold pool next to the public shower stalls. A series of massage rooms lined the corridors. Below stairs, the ambiance was unhurried as compared to upstairs. Since females were out-of-bounds in this male-only domain, this penis exposed area resembled that of a fancy gym locker room.

Our antsiness morphed into wonderous relaxation as the three of us wondered between the furiously hot saunas and the chilling dip pool. This was indeed a comfortable venue to catch one's breath after an intensive erotic workout.

Above Stairs

Moi, the incongruous anticipant, was curious to know what transpired above stairs. Since Andy refused to let me out of his sight, I pestered him until he concerted to accompany me to the upper level. I was pleasantly surprised by the unimpassioned activities that occurred in the back room on the top floor.

I witnessed a fella muff dived into his new friend's loin while another buried his face in his Garota's oversized breasts. A third watched his partner gyrate her large booty on his lap and face. Although, these men received what they came for; the women were in the act solely for the money. After all, these performative rituals were, but an amicable sleazy exercise where the concupiscent looked to hookers to fulfill their indecorous fantasies rather than sanction their reveries to run amok.

By the time Mario, Tad and Roberto reappeared, we were ready to return to our respective beds; in readiness for a new and exciting day at Ipanema Beach.

December 2014

A Season's Greeting card and a handwritten letter arrived from David. He wrote:

Dear Young,

My family and I are vacationing in the Bavarian Alps, and we're having a wonderful time.

One sunny afternoon, I looked out the window and found Jacob, my 13 years old grandson by the lake. He appeared to be in conversation with someone or something. Yet, there was no one and nothing beside him.

When I tucked him into bed that evening, I asked him whom he talked to earlier. He turned away as if I had uncovered a secret. I encouraged him to reveal the truth and promised not to disclose it to anyone, not even to his parents.

Although when I first heard his confession, I was a little perturbed but not aghast at what he confided. He vowed that he had a dialogue with his dragon friend, Pharon who was lying next to him. They had met on several occasions.

I related your unicorn experience to Jacob. He was relieved to know that he is not the only one who encounters a mythical beast.

Jacob is an intelligent boy, and it is not in his nature to lie. I believe he is telling the truth, even though this came as a surprise to me. Since I was skeptical of your fantastical experiences with mythical beasts, I am beginning to comprehend that other dimensional forces and creatures exist and are in communication with perspicacious earthlings like you and my grandson.

Thanks to you, I have a closer relationship with my beloved grandson. One with whom he can share chimerical stories with. LOL! You will hear from me again, and about Jacob's fantastical dragon encounters.

I wish you and your partner A Joyous Holiday Season and A New & Successful 2015!

Best wishes,
David

Breaking News (Chapter Fifty-Four)

"Your pain is the breaking of the shell that encloses your understanding."

Khalil Gibran

Christmas Eve 1968
Rules Restaurant, Covent Garden, London, England

Since my arrival to London in 1964, Uncle James' annual Christmas Eve dinner with *moi* at one of the city's notable restaurants had become a tradition. Since Andy and I have never been to *Rules*, my English guardian reserved a table at this historic establishment so we could experience traditional English cooking at its best.

Thomas Rule promised his despairing family that he would reproach from his wayward past and settle down to raise a family in the year Napoleon Bonaparte began his campaign in Egypt. To the disbelief of his family, Rule opened an oyster bar in Covent Garden. Not only was his enterprise successful, but it also proved to be a lasting venture that spanned the reigns of nine British monarchs.

Charles Rule, a descendant of the founder, wanted to move to Paris before The Great War. By sheer coincidence, he met a Brit by the name of Tom Bell who was then the owner of Alhambra - a successful Parisian bistro. With a gentleman's agreement, both men swapped businesses. During the war, Tom Bell became an officer in the Royal Flying Corps, and he left the restaurant to the care of his Head Waiter, Charlie; who had served Charles

Rule for many years. *Rules* flourished over the years and continue to hail as the oldest restaurant in London and one of the most celebrated in the world today.

Throughout its extensive history, the tables of *Rules* have been occupied by writers, artists, lawyers, journalists, and actors. Great literary talents like Charles Dickens, William Makepeace Thackeray, John Galsworthy, and H. G. Wells had dined in this heritage restaurant. *Rules* had also appeared in novels and movies by Rosamond Lehmann, Evelyn Waugh, Graham Greene, John Le Carré, Dick Francis, Penelope Lively, Claire Rayner, and in the latest 2015 James Bond movie - *Spectre*.

Legions of famous actors and actresses had passed through this venerated establishment's unofficial "green room" for the world of entertainment. Its walls, adorned with hundreds of drawings, paintings, cartoons, caricatures and photographs of the stage and silver screen; from Henry Irving, Buster Keaton, Stan Laurel, Charles Laughton, Clark Gable, Charlie Chaplin, John Barrymore and a list too long to mention.

Luke, the **maître d'hôtel** who knew my uncle came to greet us as soon as we entered the restaurant.

After our introduction, the **maître d'** began, *"Rules is a patrimonial restaurant. We are here to offer the best in service, ambiance, and food. These days when everyone is deluged with similar brands, our restaurant ascribes to create something special for our customers."*

Uncle James responded complimentarily, *"And Rules does it with flying colors."*

Luke gave my uncle a friendly smile and thanked him for his patronage.

The **maître d'** pronounced proudly, *"Rules serves the best British food, and we specialize in classic game cookery, a variety of oyster preparations, and an array of pies and puddings. Our able staff is trained in game* *management controls and treatments at our High Pennines estate; 'England's last wilderness.'"*

As soon as our food and beverage orders were placed, my surrogate father enquired, *"How have you been, lad?"*

"I'm doing splendidly. Couldn't be better, sir," I replied readily.

"And you, Andy?" James inquired.

My Valet answered reservedly, *"I am good sir. Thank you for asking."*

My English guardian glanced at my lover furtively before he asked concernedly, *"Is there something that is bothering you, young man?"*

My chaperone evaded James' query and remained quiet before he feigned entrancement by the pictures on the walls. My guardian looked at me for an answer. Since I had no clue to my Valet's apprehension, I shrugged my shoulders in ignorance.

"It's an impressive artists' line-up," my chaperone declared.

Just then our beverages arrived at our table.

"To the both of you; A Merry Christmas and A Blissful New Year!" my uncle wassailed cheerfully.

For a brief second, James and I noticed that my BB's eyes had welled up.

"Tell us what's bothering you, Andy," James pressed.

Since my chaperone did not answer, Pinkerton commented wryly, *"The entertainers you see on the walls gave up a lot of their personal life to be where they are today."*

Without warning, trickles of tears gushed out of my lover's eyes.

"Andy, what's the matter?" my uncle questioned.

James and I exchanged looks of consternation and wondered what had washed over my Valet as he continued to sob woefully.

"*I'm sorry, sir. I don't mean to be such a sentimental fool,*" Andy apologized.

"*I've been accepted by the University of Canterbury in New Zealand. I commence the first term of my engineering studies this coming Fall,*" my chaperone disclosed.

"*That is excellent news! Are those tears of anticipation?*" my English guardian exclaimed.

Andy shook his head before he opined, "*I'm crying because I will miss Young terribly.*"

He held his hand to mine and looked me in the eyes.

"*Will you come to live with me in Christchurch?*" he proposed earnestly.

I stared at my lover speechless and did not know how to respond.

My uncle broke the ice and spoke. "*I am so happy for you, Andy. Your parents must be thrilled by the news.*"

My chaperone shook his head. "*I haven't told my parents or any of my siblings about my scholarship,*" he replied.

"*Scholarship!*" I exclaimed confoundedly.

He nodded before he resumed, "*Yes, the University of Canterbury offered me a full bursary to their Engineering Department for four years. I also applied to Brunel and the Imperial College in London but have not received answers from them.*"

James blazoned enthusiastically, "*Congratulations, Andy! You will make an excellent engineer. Your parents will be proud of you. This is cause for celebration instead of sadness.*"

Tears continued to fall from my lover's eyes. "*I don't want to be apart from Young. Will you be my better half and live with me in New Zealand?"* he proposed to me again.

"I..., I can't. I must pursue my fashion studies in London and Paris. There are no significant fashion institutions in New Zealand. That country is a fashion void," I blurted.

My conscientious uncle counseled, *"Andy when I was your age, I was in love with a girl named Eunice. I wanted her to relinquish her German veterinarian pursuits to join me in England. She was torn between her passion for her animal well-being and her love for me. We struggled and wrangled for weeks over my proposal. In the end, she chose her career. I was devastated by her decision, and I cried for weeks.*

"Over time, my ambition to be a successful financier obscured my despondencies. Now, I am thankful that I followed my calling. There is never a day that I am not invigorated by my chosen career.

"I'm sure the two of you will understand the momentousness of your decisions. To follow your divine provenance. Whatever you choose, choose wisely. Remember, boys, you only have one life in this physicality to achieve your derivation."

Although I was cognizant of my lover's university applications, I was not prepared for this unexpected announcement. As thrilled as I was of his Canterbury acceptance, I was also disheartened by our impending separation. Within the deepest recesses of my heart, I knew I had to remain in London to fulfill my chosen vocation. Even though I was immensely tempted to be his significant other, I could not be under his auspice for the rest of my life.

Looking back, I had subconsciously charted my path towards a career in fashion. In 1968, nothing and certainly no one could deter me from being an aspiring fashion designer. As it was then and is now, my steadfastness on Fashion had brought me many achievements and continues to propel me daily.

That evening at *Rules* was a turning point for my Valet and me. Andy's proposal had stirred a capriciousness I never knew I possessed. Even though my heart laid heavy with incertitude, I did not exhibit ruefulness at the dinner table. Where resolution once stood its ground, I was now paralyzed with dubiety and volatility.

Andy was my first love, and I loved him exceedingly and he with me. Yet our amorousness challenged the very foundation of our survival. Thanks to my scrupulous English guardian, we enjoyed a subliminal Christmas Eve dinner which otherwise would have been an ordeal. Not only did Mr. Pinkerton alleviate my BB and my pensive firmaments, but he also brought us closer.

That night Andy and my lovemaking took on a gradational magnetism that merged us into *moksha*.

Last Week of December 2014
My Email to Andy

Dear Andy,

I am sorry to hear about your ailment. I pray for your full recovery. Are you back in the saddle, rowing with your team?

I hope you had a delightful Christmas. Did you spend it with your siblings? Please send my regards to Aria and Ari.

Of course, when the opportunity presents itself, I would love to see you again and to catch up in person. I am open to suggestions even though I am unsure when our meeting will happen. LOL!

Love,

Young

Nip and Tuck (Chapter Fifty-Five)

"You know who cries the hardest in the Miss World pageant? The winner. Because she can't win again, and winners always want to."

Count Mario Luciano Conti

Second Week of October 1968
Copacabana Theatre, Rio de Janeiro, Brazil

The Miss Brazil World pageant was already in flutter mode when our entourage entered the state-of-the-art performance hall. Glitzy banderoles and festive decorations hung from floor to ceiling as if Christmas had arrived early in Rio. Roundtables filled with pageant contestants' families, friends, supporters and spectators talked animatedly in their native tongues over blaring background music.

When the larger-than-life master of ceremonies appeared before the enlivened crowd, a group of local band members was already onstage to begin one of Rio's lavish annual celebrations; the crowning of the next Miss Mundo Brasil.

Wolf whistles and catcalls welcomed the opulently attired emcee, Roberto Pisani Marinho. The same Señor whom we'd met at the **Copacabana** Palace bar the evening before. This seasoned personality knew how to work his audience. While his sincerity had the assemblage in arrant attention, his one-liners also brought them to hilarity.

When the first round of contestants paraded on the extended runway next to our table; Ms. Ina Vargas, the ultimate beauty pageant insider, commented proudly, *"Isn't Ula beautiful? I trained her since she was 14 years old."*

The Count acknowledged, *"You did a fabulous job, Ina. You sure know how to coach the participants to be the crème de la crème from thousands of hopefuls."*

"Thank you, Count. Your compliment means a lot to me. These girls were like babies when they came to me. But when I'm done grooming them, they are college graduates with diplomas in hand to conquer the pageant world," the glamorous lady responded gleefully.

She added, *"But winning the diamond-and-pearl crown comes with a price."*

Eberhardt queried, *"And what price might that be?"*

The Brazilian bombshell, Juliana Santos; pageant winner from a couple of years prior, pronounced, *"I wouldn't have won if I didn't have surgical procedures done on my face and body. For these (she ran her hands over her curvaceous body), I am grateful to my mentor who advised me to have breast, cheeks and chin implants before the pageant."*

The women gave each other knowing grins.

The beauty queen resumed, *"I work hard to have the perfect body. It's like studying for a math exam to get good grades."*

Andy questioned, *"But is it perfect if it's been surgically enhanced? Are pageant contestants allow to have cosmetic augmentations to compete?"*

The two females giggled as if they shared a secret understanding.

"My darling," Ina replied jovially, *"Like steroids in sports; surgical enhancements are the indecorous secret of the pageant world. It is not banned or frowned upon in our circle.*

*"It is common for contestants to remove a rib or two to make their waist smaller, to have breast augmentation, nose reshaping or eyebrows lifted. Not to

mention dental amelioration. These are de rigueur procedures."

The swimwear parade began when Ms. Vargas finished her explanation. Rounds of applause, wolf whistles, and catcalls; especially from the men, emboldened the contestants down the catwalk.

As the participants strutted by, Juliana asserted with pride, *"When a fashion model sashays down the runway, it's about the clothes she is wearing. But in a beauty pageant, the woman is the center of attention. The clothes are secondary.*

"I am 23 years old, and I already had eighteen surgical procedures. I had breast implants, cheekbones bioplastic sculpting, silicone remolding in my chin, a sharpened jawline, pinned back ears and liposuction on my waist and back. These improvements are totally subtle. They don't leave marks or scars on the way I looked before."

My teacher inquired, *"If the augmentations are so indistinct, why do you bother putting yourself through the agony? Surgeries can go askew under a surgeon's hands."*

"Cosmetic enhancements can assist us to reach our goals. I want to be a spokeswoman for women who don't feel pretty or perfect. If she tries, she too can fulfill a dream she wants to realize," Ms. Santos attested.

"Sometimes, I feel like I am studying to become a doctor. I work on my figure to get it to where I desire it to be. My current profession is to compete in other international beauty pageants. My doctorate is in body measurements," the ex-pageant winner mused out loud.

My Valet queried, *"How can you be proud of your body if it's not really you?"*

Juliana riposte, *"I work very hard to be in shape. I follow a strict diet, work out, and cosmetic augmentation regimen so I can be proud of myself. Besides, there are no rules against the use of cosmetic enhancements in beauty competitions. The only rule is to be born a woman."*

The **evening wear parade and the** final round of the 1968 **Miss Mundo Brasil were in full swing**. Sparkling gowns with plunging necklines in vibrant shades peregrinated down the catwalk to the bossa nova song – *Garota de Ipanema (The Girl from Ipanema)*. Sung by none other than the international **Brazilian** superstar singer, songwriter, and guitarist, João Gilberto.

I was glued to the contenders' splendiferous dresses as they floated by. Yet, my ears were also eavesdropping on our table's conversation.

Like me, Mario, the accomplished fashion photographer oohed and aahed as each contestant undulated to the rhythmic sensuality of *The Girl from Ipanema;* as if the song was written and sung especially for them.

The Count commented, *"I know some people don't respect beauty contests, but this event is truly spectacular. Besides being beautiful, these girls are also intelligent. It takes quick-wittedness to answer the questions* **Roberto posted to them.***"*

The pageant groomer declared blithesomely, *"Girls under my wings are trained on posture, fashion, makeup, public presentation, speech eloquence, and attitude. I don't endorse anorexia, but I do run a brutal selection process. Once, I turned away a high fashion model because she refused to gain weight. Beauty queens are not skinny rabbits.*

"My proteges signed official contracts that neither my staff nor I encourage them to undergo cosmetic augmentations and they must inform my agency if they had had work done. My girls' health and well-being is my concern, and we, pageant organizers don't want to be sued for supporting nip tucks. Before-and-after photographs are bound to surface if a contestant hits it big. If a participant's cosmetic surgery goes awry, there will be a significant

scandal and my agency, and I will suffer the consequences. **That said,** *I am sure there are at least ten women on stage tonight who had augmentations on their physiques."*

I blurted, "But Juliana mentioned that she would not have won the crown if you had not encouraged her to have cosmetic surgery."

"Be careful what you say, boy. Ina did not pursue me to go for the operations. I went willingly. It was my then trainer and mentor who counseled me that some enhancements would improve my chance to win." Ms. Santos corrected my proclamation.

She continued pragmatically, *"Millions of people from around the world watch this annual contest. The winner will achieve overnight stardom. She will grace international and national magazine covers and be invited to co-host a variety of media programs. She will also be the spokesperson for dozens of commercial products. The financial rewards are immense. That is the reason contestants go through great lengths to snatch the title."*

Andy intimated, *"Aren't beauty pageants a showcase for male fantasies of what an ideal woman should look like?"*

"I beg to differ," Ms. Vargas countered. *"I took Juliana into my fold because she is self-assured and her confidence commands attention in front of the camera."*

She looked to the photographer for his approval before she recapitulated, *"For the most part, Juliana's physique is natural and not sculpted. She is five feet nine inches tall with a dancer's body. She towers over most of the men around her; except for you guys at this table. She commands attention when she walks into a room."*

Ms. Vargas had the final word before **Señor Marinho** crowned the 1968 **Miss Brazil World winner - Señorita Martha Maria Vasconcellos, who would become the 1968 Miss Universe.**

"I took a rough gem and created Juliana, the ultimate beauty queen. I brought her to life, and along the way, I make some minor changes to the unpolished diamond. By the time I am finished, I had created a brilliant," Ina deliberated with satisfaction.

The First Week of January 2015
My Response to David's Christmas Letter

Hi David,

I am glad you bonded with Jacob, your grandson, via a shared interest in fantastical beasts. From your description of the lad, he sounds like an intelligent young man. Like my ex-Little-Brother (LB), **Helius**. From my experience, people who encounter preternatural creatures are gifted communicators between our world and other parallel realms. These individuals possess high intelligence quotient and are exceedingly sensitive to their surroundings. I am speaking for myself. LOL!

I hope your relationship with Jacob continues to strengthen and you can be a mentor to him in everything. He sounds like a sweet adolescent. I look forward to hearing more of his mythical encounters. Keep me posted.

Best wishes,
Young

I Don't Know How To Love Him
(Chapter Fifty-Six)

"There are three constants in life... change, choice, and principles."

Stephen Covey

New Year's Eve 1968
Catacombs - Earl's Court, London, England

After ringing in the new year with Uncle James at the River Restaurant in the luxurious Savoy Hotel; Andy and I, like most young bucks in the late 1960s, made our way to the steamier side of town. We went clubbing in our formal attire. Our garb was out of context to the customary denim and jeans, the BLUF (Breeches and Leather Uniform Fanclub) dress codes or the unisex getups that gay men embraced so fervently.

A crowd had already gathered outside the *Catacombs* when we arrived. Back in the late sixties and seventies, this hedonistic establishment located in Earl's Court had a long tradition of sybaritism and was a haven for beer-drinking backpackers from Down-Under. This neighborhood was also the heart of London's gay nightlife.

It was at this dingy underground dance club that gay Londoners new to disco were introduced to Donna Summer's famous hit – *Love to Love You Baby*. It became their national anthem. This discotheque was also the hangout for the well-known English comedy actor, Kenneth Williams. He had been spotted regularly to flounce down its rickety stairs with an entourage of "sisterly" comrades.

Like every fluid metropolis, London continues to attract the LGBTQIA plebeians of its day; even when the once predominantly 'gay districts' had moved to other areas. Earl's Court was and still is a place of notoriety for its transient population. Back in its heyday, this was the stomping ground for Australians and New Zealanders on temporary visas. The sizeable Victorian mansion blocks in the vicinity offered cheap rentals to many trampers and acquired the nickname – Kangaroo City.

It was at the *Catacombs* that Andy, and I met Michael, a good-looking New Zealander who had rented one of these outposts. As we stood in line to enter the overcrowded nightspot, the New Zealander struck up a conversation with us.

"*Are you guys local?*" the mustachioed man queried.

"*We are from the United Kingdom and are visiting my charge's guardian in London,*" my chaperone responded pretentiously.

The leatherman stared at us before he remarked, "*You guys are not dressed for the Catacombs.*"

My Valet was about to comment when the turquoise-pink-haired doorman waved us in. He apparently liked what he saw. We jumped the queue to Michael's chagrin who had already waited an hour to enter.

The quirky doorman who was attracted to Andy, commented as we passed through the threshold, "*Handsome, you look cute in a tux. I'll talk to you as soon as I get a chance. Meanwhile, have fun, boys!*"

Whiffs of amyl nitrite permeated throughout the space when we entered the dimly lit basement. A sea of bobbing heads and semi-naked bodies greeted us as if we had stumbled into Satan's abyss. Candlelit cubicles lined the dance floor periphery. These areas were for exhausted revelers to recharge before they took to the floor again.

We headed to the bar since the booths were fully occupied. I was overcome by an urge to order a Pimm's No. 1 (a gin-based fruity liqueur). Little did I realize that this cocktail would have me in nausea.

Since Andy's university acceptance announcement, my heart had laid heavy on my future's variability. His imminent departure and my incertitude to remain in London had me in a tailspin. I was torn between my career resoluteness or to follow the man I love, and alcohol offered me a temporary release from these imperceptible issues.

Although Andy cautioned against my alcoholic requisition, when his back was turned, the barman took my order. My lover and Michael chatted animatedly when I took a sip of the Pimm's. After the third sip, my head spun like the vinyl disc at the DJ booth. The enticing music and the unprincipled carnality drew me to the dance floor. Before I knew it, I had discarded my clothes amidst a group of semi-naked men. Under the revolving disco lights and the men's enticing physiques sent me into a daze. A pair of hands pulled me away from the obstreperous assemblage when I was about to blackout. I was rushed out of the club to regain my composure. Refreshing air filled my intoxicated lungs. Michael threw his leather jacket over me while Andy wrapped me in his arms.

The New Zealander suggested, *"Both of you should come to my flat to chill until this chap is strong enough to make it home."*

We followed the man.

At Michael's Bedsitter

Michael was a neat freak. Although his accommodation was tiny, the compartmentalized cupboards, shelves, and drawers were methodically organized to house his leather wear and regular work clothes. I would never have guessed this New Zealander to be a Leather-Queen if I had met him at the florist or supermarket where he works.

The soothing music and the strategically placed floral arrangements added an artsy feel to his bedsitter. As we sat on the bed, his nimble fingers reached to fondle my guardian's groin while his other hand caressed my buttocks. Our lips soon met in a three-way lock. His captivating eyes observed our tongue dance like a captive hawk as we relished our intimacy with urgency. Prompted by our captive kisses, our manhood sprang to attention. Not only did Michael's masculine leather garb enlivened my concupiscence, but it also conjured my imagination to fantasize to what lay beneath that **commanding** uniform. Our French kisses sent me into an aphrodisiacal abyss I found difficult to resist.

Although BDSM (bondage, dominance, and sadomasochism) was not new to me, Michael's passivity to Andy's advances ensnared my fascination to chronicle our liaison on camera. I whipped out my portable and snapped away at our steamy tryst as they sucked my hardness to throbbing velocity.

My camera framed the couple's lubriciousness as if I was witnessing my lover and my intimacy. Out of the blues, lamentations of despondency gushed to the forefront. Emotional surges of our impending separation flooded my quivering physique. I wept as the rousing eroticism played out before me.

When my lover noticed my snafu, he whispered, *"Are you okay?"*

"I'm overjoyed to witness your pruriencies," I lied.

The duo resumed their passionate amorosity. Droplets of disquietude trickled down my eyes as I continued to photograph the dominant and the submissive's electrifying coitus.

The leatherman in harness and jock wasted no time to envelop my Valet's palpitations into his anal orifice while his oral fissure engulfed my stiffness with enthusiasm. He pleaded for more when I held his cranium firmly on my groin. The New Zealander groaned in ecstasy as we plowed into him without clemency. No longer able to maintain his fiery avidity, his deliverance sprayed onto the bed. Andy's massiveness exploded into the submissive's twitching derriere before his heaving torso slumped against the New Zealander's sudoriparous hind. Precipitated by their spritely intensities, I blasted my cherished pride into the leatherman's oral void which he devoured with glee.

We laid quietly on the Queen to savor the afterglow. Michael's smoldering cigarette cast an eerie glow in the shadowy darkness while my guardian and I dressed to return to the posh side of town. The New Zealander was keen to see us again and arranged to meet a couple of nights later at Club El **Sombrero**. Unbeknownst to the leatherman, Andy and I had left the following afternoon for Daltonbury Hall to commence my new term and my Big-Brother training programme under my Valet's tutelage.

First Week of January 2015
Andy's Response to My Message

Yes, I am back in the saddle after several weeks of slow recovery. Ari came to visit and stayed for a week. It was nice to catch up with him. He enquired about you and sends his regards.

I am glad to know that you are open to visiting me in Australia. I will be delighted to show you the country I call home and will be honored if you'll stay with me. We can catch up on the old and the new. I'll be at the airport waiting for you when you notify me of your arrival.

I look forward to seeing you again.

Sorry for this brief message. I am on my **way** to the hospital for my medical follow-up.

Talk soon.
Andy

A Cut Above the Rest (Chapter Fifty-Seven)

"When you look at me, when you think of me, I am in paradise."
William Makepeace Thackeray

Second Week of October 1968
Ipanema Beach, Rio De Janeiro, Brazil

Shortly after the crowning of the new Miss Brazil World, Mario, Tad, Roberto, the winner - Señorita Martha Maria Vasconcellos, and the 1968 Miss Mundo Brasil runner-ups, together with a host of other pageant judges and hangers-on disappeared on a time-honored celebratory afterparty. Andy and I were left to our contrivances. Although we had agreed to go to the *Clube* with Sergio, the night was young; and under the hypnotic glow of the October moon, we strolled along the infamous Ipanema Beach.

In the day, this sun-drenched strip welcomes sun lovers from around the world, and its subcultures of leftists, hippies, and artists are as diverse as Rio itself. Back then, my chaperone and I were unaware that to the **East of Rua Farme de Amoedo was** Praia Farme; a notorious playground for men who prefer men or trannies who sought the company of muscle *bears* (slang for hairy gay men). This sordid area had acquired the reputation of *Barbie Land. Barbie* - an argot used by Cariocas for waxed or unwaxed muscular homosexuals.

As we ambled hand in hand and barefoot along the cool ocean's edge, frisky Andy kicked at the ripples and soaked me from head to toe. In playful retaliation, I pushed my lover into the water. He dragged me along with him. We splashed at one another like a couple of delinquents. Before long, we were frolicking in the water like frivolous jaybirds.

An odd feeling gushed through me when Andy pinned my hands on the sand. I stared at my handsome guardian and wept. Not knowing what overcame my person, I shut my eyes tightly. As if I was unworthy of his love, I dared not look at his flawless self.

"What's the matter, Young?" my lover inquired.

I did not reply. I was afraid to open my eyes to behold my guardian's beauty. When he planted an impassioned kiss on my mouth and laid on top of me, I responded in kind. Even though his mind probed my serendipitous quiddity for answers; I had no riposte to my melancholia. My recalcitrant tears continued to flow as my lover's gentle caresses soothed my wistful heart.

We French-kissed for what felt like an eternity.

I whispered, *"I don't deserve you, Andy."*

He stared at me before he chirped, *"You are being a Silly-Billy. What do you mean you don't deserve me?"*

"You are every person's dream boy. Why am I the lucky one to have you? I don't deserve your love." I sobbed.

My lover held me to him before he planted another kiss on my lips. His action stirred our already hardened manhood to palpitate.

I stared at him unflinchingly and brushed a stray curl from his princely face.

"I don't know what I'll do without you?" I murmured.

"You wouldn't be without me...," he paused before he resumed, *"Unless you choose to ditch me."*

My guardian laid a finger on my lips to prevent me from speaking. Instead, he encircled his tongue around my protruding nipples. I arched my back to greet his sensual titillations with hedonistic delight. His hand careened towards my tender bottom to tease my twitching hollow.

I would give myself to this handsome Apollo, anytime and anywhere, and Ipanema beach was no exception to the rule. Little did we realize that spying eyes were observing our every move, a short distance away.

Andy's beauty was beyond compare under the glimmering October moon. I was the luckiest boy who had captured the heart of this demigod. As my lover's nimble fingers razzed the smoothness of my skin, my undeserving apprehension continued to course through me. While the undulating waves caressed our naked souls to impassioned lubricity, his loving touch and tender kisses lured our youthfulness to throbbing urgency.

I was in seventh heaven when his mightiness perforated my sanctum of delight. We remained motionless, encased in his cocoon of love. Our mind, body, and spirit merged to the Oneness of Being under the oscillating waves. This empyrean coitus unified us to unimaginable bliss. Our souls coiled like intertwined serpents before our crowns burst into a "thousand lotus petals." Time stood still as we amalgamated within Sahasrara's sensual currents. Our immobility had divinely impelled us towards nirvana. Torrents of my Apollo's sacred oblations poured into my beatified sanctuary while my libations spritzed onto our already dampened torsos. Our lips remained locked in subliminal ecstasy. We were reluctant to relinquish this sanctification until sanity regained its grip.

As we lay by the water's edge, Andy whispered, *"You, boy, is a cut above the rest."*

"And I say the same of you, Apollo," I teased.

A small assemblage had gathered in the shadows when we stood to dress. A couple of *bears* and she-males had circle-jerked while spying on Andy and me. Although no tenebrous observers traversed our path, they were awed by our sacred eroticism. Their eyes followed as we passed them in silence.

We did not meet Sergio at the *Clube* but returned to *The Palace* to be readied for Acapulco the following day; as I had documented in A Harem Boy's Saga – V – Metanoia; a memoir by Young, chapter one - *The Perfect Storm*.

The Third Week of January 2015
David's Message to Andy and Me

Hi guys,

Time flies by quickly, and before we know it, January is almost over.

Shortly after my return from our **Christmas vacation, I suffered severe stomach pain and was rushed to the hospital. I've been diagnosed with stomach cancer and is undergoing treatment to eradicate the cancer cells from spreading. Thank goodness, I discovered this malice at its early stage. The good news; it is treatable.

This distressing experience fostered me to reevaluate my life and to devote more time to my family, especially to my grandson, Jacob. As I mentioned to Young in my previous email; I bonded with the lad through our shared cognizance of fantastical creatures. I hope you and Andy will befriend Jacob? He is fascinated by Young's preternatural experiences and has questions regarding this topic. As you know, my knowledge on this subject is limited and am unable to answer his queries. He is badgering me for your email and Facebook addresses so he can connect with you.

I hope this is not too much to ask. I look forward to your responses.

Best wishes,
David

PART FOUR

England - Isle of Wight, Daltonbury Hall
France – Paris
Netherlands – Utrecht, Amsterdam

What Is Love? (Chapter Fifty-Eight)

"Youth is the gift of nature, but age is a work of art."
                                                            Stanislaw Jerzy Lec

Early in January 1969
Daltonbury Hall, Isle of Wight, England

My final term at Daltonbury Hall was hectic with my upcoming "A Level" examination to prepare, and my month-long Big-Brother training programme. John, my ex-roommate was the teaching assistant to my Big-Brother/tutor, Hanns.

This Eurasian ex-wild child had matured beyond his eighteen years of age. Besides being debonair, and decorous; John's worldliness could rival any gentleman in both the Western and Eastern hemispheres. He was my first buddy at Daltonbury, and we were glad to revitalize our friendship. Although our relationship started on rocky grounds due to my jealousy between him and my then ex-BB/trainer, Nikee; we had settled our differences. On the occasions when we were back to school from our various Household assignments, our friendship flourished and picked-up where we left. We were rooming together again before his graduation as an official Big-Brother.

My handsome twenty-year-old Big-Brother cum educator, Hanns, was a strapping bisexual Norwegian. Besides being an avid skier and ice-hockey enthusiast, he was on his final leg of Big-Brothership before he headed to the University of Pennsylvania to study medicine. I was delighted to be under this BB's tutelage.

The evening after my return from London, John and I had a chat at the student's recreational facility.

"How are you and Andy getting along?" he enquired.

I replied enervatedly, *"I'm not looking forward to his departure to New Zealand."*

I paused before I added, *"It is hard being in love."*

Silence followed before my roommate responded, *"You know, Young; love is the most powerful emotion a person can experience, and almost nobody can define what love is. It is difficult to understand love because the word itself is not the same as the feeling."*

"What do you mean?" I queried.

He resumed, *"You see, the word 'love' is often used as an expression of affection towards another: like I love you, but it also expresses pleasure: such as I love chocolates. To make things more complicated, love also represents a human virtue that is based on compassion, affection, and kindness. In other words, a state of being that has nothing to do with something or someone outside of yourself. For me, is the purest form of Love."*

He paused to garner my countenance before he commented, *"Do you know that in ancient Greece, there are seven words to define the different states of love?"*

I nodded.

"When I was in Athens with Andy, he told me the four Greek words for love: Storge (affection), Philia (friendship), Eros (Romance) and Agape (Unconditional Love or Charity). But he did not mention the seven states of love. What are they?" I questioned inquisitively.

"I don't need to tell you the first four since you already know them, but I will mention the other three. Ludus (Playful, young love or flirting), Pragma (Longing-lasting love) as in a longtime married couple, and Philautia (Self-love).

"The love you feel for Andy is not the same as the love you feel for your mother. The love for your lover also changes throughout the relationship. You feel different emotions in different situations and people, yet, the word 'love' is used loosely. I may say 'I love you' to two different people, but the meaning and feeling are entirely different," he declared.

"I know that," I muttered.

"But do you also know that a person's feelings are controlled by the right brain and language is by the left?" he added.

I shook my head in ignorance.

"For the sake of argument; you say the word 'love' twelve times a day in different circumstances. The 'love' word loses its power because your left brain cannot comprehend the excitement of 'love,' that your right brain feels. Therefore, we need to know the seven feelings of love before we repeat the 'love' word constantly. You see, Young, awareness is the secret to love," John promulgated.

He continued, *"First and foremost, do not abuse the word 'love.' Use alternative words to express an emotion. For example; I enjoy chocolates rather than I love chocolates, or I have a passion for my job instead of I love my post.*

"Enjoy, love and passion are three different emotions. Therefore, it is essential to learn the true meaning of these words; not merely to communicate with someone, but to experience them. Words are powerful instruments in communication with others and yourself. Words you use also create awareness and your reality. If words are used wisely, you'll learn to recognize the kind of loving emotion you are feeling. Then you are able to enjoy the different kinds of love more profoundly."

"Wow! I didn't know the different 'love' expressions have such significance," I exclaimed.

"Love is not something you acquire or don't uncover, but a practice of a lifetime. If you don't have love within, you'll never find it in the exterior," my friend counseled.

"That, I am aware," I opined.

He interposed, *"Words are agreements to express ideas or feelings. Although the meaning of the word 'love' is not absolution but a personal interpretation; the group of emotions associated with love is difficult to fathom. It is even more difficult to express to another.*

"The creation of a word can give rise to an emotional feeling. Sometimes lovers create words to express how they feel for each other. These created words become an agreement or memories for the people involved. Special moments are conjured up in the lovers' minds when these words are used."

I evinced, *"In my culture, there are many words to describe an emotion instead of one."*

The teaching assistant stated, *"In other languages there exist many words that relate to love that express different emotion than in English. Once you are aware of these words and recognize the feeling; then you can have a better grip on the experience."*

"A Chinese word that comes to mind is Yuan-fen. It is a love relationship established on the principles in the Chinese culture," I conveyed.

"Throughout my travels with the various households, I've learned many new expressions of love. There is the Yaghan word – Mamihlapinatapai, which means a look shared by two people who desire intimacy which neither could fulfill. Then there is the Brazilian Portuguese word – Cafuné, which means running your fingers slowly through a person's hair. In Nordic - Forelsket translates to a first timer's euphoria when he/she falls in love. There are also French words like - Retrouvailles that describes the happiness of seeing

someone again after a long time and La Douleur Exquise; the agony of the heart when he/she desires someone they cannot have. In Arabic - Ya'aburnee illustrates the hope that you will die earlier than your beloved, so you don't have to live without the beloved. Finally, the Portuguese word - Saudade chronicles the feeling of longing for the loved one who is unavailable," John adjudged.

"I know the word - Saudade. It happened in Amsterdam to my ex-patriarch, Dr. Sheik Fahrib, and his beloved, Prince P," I voiced.

My friend admonished, *"'Moments' are essential in other cultures. That is the reason they have words like these to express their feelings. Young, my advice to you, is not to use one word to define your love for Andy but to recognize the varied forms of love and abide by them."*

He added, *"Love is emotion in action. You can learn how to feel and cultivate your love to encompass the different types of love. Appreciate the love you feel and then share that love with others. The love between two entities begins when the interaction is based on truth, trust, and respect. These criteria are essential for mutual love to grow between both parties. When both partners reciprocate the love they give, their bond will grow by leaps and bounds."*

Little did I realize that my first lesson in Big-Brothership training had begun in the recreational facility that evening.

On our way back to our dormitory, John asserted, *"Once you understand the workings of love, falling in love with someone becomes easy. The difficult part is to stay in love. If it is difficult to remain in love. It is also likely that the person you are in love with is not the love of your life, but a temporal amatory experience. True love is beautiful, and if it is not; the chances are it's not real. It is time to move to greener pastures when love fades away, and you don't feel the passion any longer."*

These were his final words before we bid each other goodnight, *"The important question for you is - are you experiencing love or are you not?"*

I excused myself for a solitary stroll; to ponder his final remark before I retired to our dormitory to begin another frantic school day.

Second Week of January 2015
My Reply to Andy

Dear Andy,

Do you remember the four loves you taught me when we were touring Greece in 1967?

Since then, my knowledge of the word 'love' has ameliorated prodigiously. LOL! Please correct me if my comprehension of romantic love is incorrect. ☺

Brain scientists tell us that love is involuntary. It is a craving for a specific person. In the early stage of romance, it is healthy and natural to "lose control." Love will make a person do strange things. It is a physical addiction and to treat it like addiction can assist us to understand love.

As you had mentioned in the past, the ancient Greeks termed love as "the madness of the gods." Whereas contemporary psychologists define it as a strong desire for emotional union with another person. The word 'love' means different things to different people.

I have taken the liberty to quote some descriptions of love:

A songwriter wrote; *"Whenever you're near, I hear a symphony."*

In Shakespeare's words; *"Love is blind, and lovers cannot see."*

Then there is Aristotle who professed that *"Love is composed of a single soul inhabiting two bodies."*

Andy, I am aware that romance is one of three primary brain systems:

The sex drive or lust - the craving for sexual gratification that enables a person to seek a range of potential mating partners. Passion is not necessarily focused on an individual, and a person can have sex with someone whom he/she isn't in love with.

Romantic love or attraction is the obsessive thinking about and craving for an individual and can evolve to enable a person to focus his/her mating energy on one individual at a time. Kabir, the Indian poet, wrote, and I quote: *"The lane of love is narrow; there is room for only one."*

Attachment - the feeling of profound union with a long-term partner. This enables one to remain with a mate and to enjoy the benefits of living together.

These feelings interact in numerous ways to create myriad forms of loving.

Let's take attraction. Whether it is called romantic love, obsessive love, passionate love, or infatuation, human of every era and culture had and continue to be affected by this irresistible power. The intensity of romantic love in most relationships lasts from six months to two years before it transforms into an attachment. Romance is the beginning of love and has the most effect on human behavior. I have listed below, the behavioral traits of the early-stage of romantic love:

Special meaning; where the romantic partner is the center of the world, and the besotted likes anything his/her mate likes.

The beguiled has difficulty sleeping due to his/her intense and embedded energy.

The infatuated also suffer a loss of appetite and mood swings from separation anxiety.

The enamored craves for emotional and sexual unions and becomes intrusively possessive.

You may wonder why I am prattling on about romantic love. The traits of your previous emails inveigled me to suspect that you wish to rekindle our old romance. My question to you, Andy, *"Are you falling in love with me, again?"* ☺

    Your beloved ex,
    Young
    XOXOXO

Friendship (Chapter Fifty-Nine)

"My best friend is the one who brings out the best in me."
Henry Ford

Second Week of January 1969
Daltonbury Hall, Isle of Wight, England

Unlike my formal Bahriji School training to the Arabian households, my Big-Brothership inculcations were relatively informal. Besides, Hanns and Andy being my official Big-Brother educators; John, the teaching assistant (TA), also acted as my provisional advisor if I required precipitated counseling. Since we were buddies and rooming together, he was accessible for convivial confabulations. This TA proved to be a valuable aid especially when it came to dishing out guidance over my disquietude regarding my lover's imminent departure. I was glad to have sympathetic ears to confide in while the thrice-weekly Big-Brothership theoretical vernaculars were delivered by both supervising professors, Dr. Baron Struss, and Dr. Richard Kron together with Hanns and Andy.

Friendship

During one of our tri-weekly meetings, Hanns brought up the topic of friendship.
  The instructor inquired, *"Can anyone tell me the meaning of friendship?"*
  John announced, *"The dictionary defines friendship as a state of being friends and being in friendly relation to*

a person or between persons. It is an affection that arises from mutual esteem, goodwill, friendliness, and amity."

"*That all sounds well and good, but it doesn't cover the fact that true friendships are relationships that are unconditional and can survive the test of time,*" Hanns declared.

The instructor turned to me for my opinion.

I pondered before I replied, "*Friendship is a combination of affection, loyalty, love, respect, and trust. It also includes having similar interests, mutual respect and an attachment to one another.*"

Andy expressed, "*I need true friends to experience friendship. The emotional safety provided by genuine friends means not to weigh my thoughts and measure words. True friendship is when someone knows me better than him or herself, and in a crisis, will take a position in my best interests. Friendship is long-lasting and goes beyond just sharing time together.*"

The Norwegian lauded our input.

He commented, "*Friendship means different things to different people. For some, it is the trust that someone will not hurt you, and for others; it might be unconditional love or companionship. Whatever your definition: friendship is generally considered to be a mutual and agreeable relationship between two or more individuals.*"

He paused before he added, "*A person who has a true friend has found a priceless treasure.*"

Andy injected, "*Friendship is not one-sided. It takes two individuals to negotiate the boundaries of a relationship. The fellowship will not survive if only one person makes an effort to sustain the alliance without the assistance and recognition from the other.*"

"*Precisely. It takes positive and negative experiences to define a personality. To build friendships, it is essential to be akin with those who are compatible with you on an emotional and psychological level,*" Hanns stated before he pronounced, *"That brings me to my next question; how to be an honorable friend to your assigned charge?"*

Before any of us could comment, John answered, *"Be a good listener to your Little-Brother (LB)."*

Both educators chuckled.

"That is an excellent beginning, John," **Andy voiced.** *"Perhaps the easiest and most direct way of being an attentive BB is to ask your charge how his day went. Have daily conversations with him and listen to what he has to say."*

The Norwegian enjoined, *"Practice at being an active listener. Whether it's a brief check-in or a heart to heart talk; the conversations are learning opportunities where you get to know your LB and have a meaningful discussion. Go into the conversation with the intent to improve mutual understanding and respect between the two of you."*

My Valet added, *"Give your charge your full attention and allow him to speak without interruption. Acknowledge and respond thoughtfully to what he tells you without judgment. This will encourage your LB to confide in you and to keep the conversation open."*

I questioned, *"What if his confessions involve conflicts with fellow schoolmates or bullies?"*

"That's a good question," Hanns acknowledged. *"My answer to you is to **advise him to resolve the conflicts maturely and honestly.** Most adolescents have squabbles and small fights. A Big-Brother should avoid having big, dramatic arguments with the bully/bullies or his fellow schoolmates. This means being the bigger person. Advise your Little-Brother to tackle the issue/issues by confronting his opponents sensibly. This will help him feel respected and supported by you. It will also assist him to learn to stand up for himself."*

"What if his uncompromising antagonists continue to harass my charge?" I catechized.

"If your LB is unable to resolve a conflict on his own, you can then reach out to other authoritative figures for guidance. This could be your advisors or staff members in the school. Conflicts between adolescents are often minor and can be worked out between themselves. A Big-Brother should also install in his charge that there is no shame to reach out to someone of authority. This will denote your charge that there is no shame to ask for help when required," Andy counseled.

Hanns asserted, "Andy, although that is true, I would also advise a Big-Brother to watch out and stand up for his Little-Brother in tricky situations. If the bullies would not listen to reason and continue to pick on the boy, the BB should step in to mediate. Do your best to stay on your charge's side and work with him to resolve the dilemma. Having your LB's back will show him that he has your support."

John advocated, "I find that citing my personal experiences can support a charge. I don't dispense advice unless it is asked for. Otherwise, I may come across as being pushy. Citing from personal experiences on how I manage to resolve or deal with an issue shows my empathy and support for my LB; especially when it comes to romantic and sexual relationships."

The Norwegian interjected, "If your LB asks you for romantic advice, I will encourage him to talk about the specifics of the situation and his feelings. A Big-Brother can offer his perspectives on how to have a healthy, responsible, romantic liaison with a person or persons." He snickered and added, "Especially if the BB has had a few experiences that taught him valuable lessons about romance, sex, and love."

Before my educators terminated the meeting, my Valet finalized, "Last but not least, comfort your Little-

Brother when he faces a challenge. He will experience a range of trials and tribulations, will encounter difficulties and may fail in his attempt to do something extraordinary. Do not shame him for his failure and make him feel bad. Instead, you, as a Big-Brother should comfort, support, and encourage him to get back on track."

End of January 2015
My Response to David and C/C to Andy

I hope you are doing well and have recovered from your cancer treatment. My partner and my prayers are with you.

Jacob, your grandson, wrote to me when I befriended him on Facebook. He is a sprightly fella. The lad told me about his encounter with **Pharon** in his lengthy email. He wanted my advice about preternaturality and for me to keep his queries anonymous. On the contrary, he said he has no objections if I wish to publish our correspondence. I am confused by his incertitude.

Below is his message to me:

Hi, Mr. Foong

David, my granddad, is a friend of yours He told me your extraordinary adventures with fairies, angels, unicorns, etc. I am intrigued by your experiences and would like to know more about them. I also have preternatural encounters I would like to share with you and to get your advice.

One afternoon when I was cycling home from school, I met Phron in the forest near my house. That day, I had not tidied my room, and I knew my mom would harp at me for not doing my chore. So, I stayed away until she left for work before I sneaked in to finish my task.

I sensed something lurking in the shadows when I was in the woods. I thought it was a stray animal hiding behind the trees. Although I saw nothing, I felt I was being watched. I didn't find anything when I went to check out the area. I was about to leave, I heard the anguish moans of an animal. I smelt an otherworldly aroma I'd never detected before even though the pitiful cries persisted. I stayed quiet to see if anything would reveal itself. Nothing happened, except the groaning sound.

Soon, I got bored and was about to leave when a blurry apparition showed itself. Although I was taken aback I did not bolt. An odd feeling told me that the wraith was hurt and needed help. Out-of-the-blue a small dragon appeared a short distance from me. I was dumbfounded. I noticed its injured foot that bled severely. The creature licked my hand when I bound the wound.

I read the animal's mind. He wanted to be my friend and was grateful for my help. That was how Phron and I became pals. Later, I fed the dragon dog food, when I returned to the forest to check on him. He ate everything. I did not tell anyone that I had befriended a dragon in case they would think I'm cuckoo. Granddad David is the only person who knows of Phron, and he told me about your phantastical encounters.

I am relieved to know that I am not the only person who has a relationship with an otherworldly creature. I hope we can share our extraordinary experiences.

Thank you for friending me on FB. I look forward to your reply.

Cheers,
Jacob

Helius' Despondency (Chapter Sixty)

"Courage is fire, and bullying is smoke."
Benjamin Disraeli

Third Week of January 1969
Daltonbury Hall, Isle of Wight, England

A week after my return to Daltonbury Hall, Professor Baron Struss introduced me to Helius. The erudite educator knew the Freshman, and I had a lot in common, so he arranged a meeting after one of my regular classes. Even though I was unaware that I was thrown into the deep as part of my precursory assay to my Big-Brothership survey.

Like me when I first entered the boarding institution, Helius was a shy, quiet and an introvert boy. He was bullied by a couple of older boys in his previous school before he came to Daltonbury. Although John was the Freshman's temporary BB, the adolescent's sagaciousness drew him to me like a bee to honey. The lad was unaware that I was a Big-Brother in training and he would be under my care when I passed the leadership programme. John, Helius and I roomed together at Tolkien Brotherhood. This Greco-Roman youngster was as inquisitive as me. He would pose vacillating questions to obtain my response whenever we found ourselves alone.

He asked at one of our ancillary meetings, *"How do you define bullying?"*

I replied nonchalantly as I was in the middle of schoolwork, *"Bullying is when someone hurts or scares another person repeatedly."*

He continued, *"Have you ever been bullied?"*

Curious to his inquiry, I asked, *"Helius, are you being bullied?"*

"No!" Helius exclaimed.

"I hope not since your BB John watches over you, 24/7," I remarked.

He paused before he resumed, *"How do you deal with bullies?"*

Roused by his line of questioning I turned to him and explain, *"Before I answer your questions, let me clarify the inappropriateness of bullying. This intentionally hurtful behavior involves an imbalance of power. The one being bullied feels alone, depressed, scared and feels he or she has nowhere and no one to turn to for help. Bullying includes name-calling, inflicting physical pain, exclusion, public humiliation, dangerous pranks on the innocent and defacing the victim's property."*

I paused to observe the lad's reaction.

After a moment's silence, he muttered, *"A couple of older boys in my previous school called me a milksop and a sissy when I don't do what they ask of me. They were mean and spread malicious rumors about me being a cross-dresser."*

"Did you confront them to put a stop to their spitefulness?" I asked.

"When I challenged them, they hit me and threatened to strip me to see if I was a boy or a girl. They ganged-up and forced me to do their bidding. When I refused, they damaged my locker and stole my pocket money," the Freshman confided.

"Did you report them to your teacher or your parents?" I enquired.

"They threatened, if I told on them, they would smash me to a pulp. I was scared and told no one," Helius expressed regrettably.

*"If a situation like this happens at Daltonbury, you must inform your BB or a teacher. It may seem scary to tell

someone. By telling, you will not only get help, but it will also make you feel less afraid. If you are being physically bullied and is in danger, you must speak with a trusted counselor immediately," I advised.

"Can I come to you if I get bullied?" he implored.

"Of course. You can tell John and me if anything like this happens. We are here for you," I asserted.

"If you'd told an adult before and they haven't done anything about it, inform someone else you can trust. Tell the person what transpired; who did the bullying, where and when did it happen, how long had it been happening, and how it made you feel. If you had told your BB, teacher or counselor, ask them what they will do to help stop the bullying. It is their job to help keep you safe. The elders at Daltonbury are concerned about bullying, and they will assist you. Keep telling until someone comes to your aid," I counseled.

The boy questioned, *"Why do bullies, bully?"*

"A typical reason is that a bully lacks attention from a parent and lashes out at others to be noticed. Often, they are kids of negligent parents or parents under the influence of drugs and alcohol.

"Sometimes older siblings can also be the cause of the problem. If they had been bullied, they are more apt to harass a younger person to empower themselves. Parents can also be bullies because they are angry or do not handle conflict well and their children turn to this kind of disruptive behaviors because they learn them at home. It is a conditioned action that can be unlearned," I admonished.

Helius commented, *"Proteus (Pro), my older half-brother is aggressive and dominating, but he is not a bully. I know he loves me even if he doesn't admit it, but Pro will have a fit if he finds out I like boys. He'll say I deserve to be bullied."*

I consoled, *"Some boys are just more aggressively dominating and impulsive by nature. It doesn't always* mean that they are bullies. I am sure Proteus means you no harm. He may not understand your sexual preference, but that doesn't make him think you deserve to be bullied in school. For all I know, he may come to your aid if you told him the truth. The truth will always set you free."

I looked at him for a response. None came. So, I continued, *"Bullies dominate, blame and use others. They lack empathy and foresight and have contempt for the weak. They crave power and attention. They see weaker boys as their target and seldom accept the consequences of their actions. Most bullies don't understand how wrong their behavior is and how it makes their victims feel."*

While we were in the middle of our "bullying" discussion, John entered and heard parts of our conversation.

The teaching assistant chirped, *"No matter what kind of bully someone is, they have not learned kindness, compassion, and respect,"*

"Are there different kinds of bullies?" the adolescent questioned.

John listed, *"Social bullies have poor self-esteem and manipulate others through their malicious gossip and spiteful lies. The detached bullies plan their attacks. Often, they are affable to everyone but their victims. On the other hand, the hyperactive bullies who don't lack social skills but misbehave and cause physical injury to their prey."*

"Wow! I didn't know there were so many different types of bullies. Although the bully I encountered comprise of all that you mentioned," the Freshman recounted.

John continued, *"I was once a bully, and the reasons I gave myself were:*

Bullying made me feel stronger, smarter, or better than the person I bullied.

I lashed out at others because my parents didn't give me sufficient attention.

I wanted to hang out with the right crowd and harassment was what they did, so I imitated their malign actions.

I was jealous of the person I harassed.

Last but by no means least, I thought that by intimidating others, I could keep others from bullying me.

"It is at Daltonbury that I came to realize that bullying isn't cool. It's an act of meanness and has harmful effects on the lives of those I bullied."

Helius inquired, *"How does one deal with bullies?"*

John sensed something was amiss.

He responded solemnly, *"Helius are you being harassed? Is that why you want to know how to deal with bullies?*

The Freshman went quiet. We looked at him for an answer. He was in tears when he finally confessed.

He muttered sobbingly, *"Since my arrival at Daltonbury, there is a Junior who picks on me continuously."*

John and I looked at one another before the teaching assistant pressed, *"Helius, tell us who is intimidating you?"*

He continued to weep but kept quiet. I put my hands around his shoulders to comfort the boy before I cited my bullying experience at the Methodist Boy's School in Kuala Lumpur. I also adduced that my bullier ended up being my lover before his parents dispatched him to a boarding academy in Ireland.

After I finished, John relayed, *"Helius, there's a lot you can do if you're harassed. The first thing is for you to work it out with the bully, that is if you don't feel at risk, scared or physically threatened. The more empowered you are and can solve the dilemma yourself; the higher the chance for you to stop him from bullying you.*

"The bully wants you to react, and his goal is to strip away your power to make you sad and scared. If you show him that you are not intimidated, he'll lose interest

because he cannot rob your power. He wants to get you angry, but if you don't become indignant, the bully will lose his control."

The Big-Brother paused to get the boy's reaction. None came.

"Daltonbury Hall's Big-Brothership programme gave me self-confidence and pride. I turned from being a bully to help those who are being bullied.

"Bullies are human like us. The only difference is that you are not a bully. Bullies act the way they do because they lack attention or parental love and nurturing. They are insecure, and bullying makes them feel powerful. They look for a reaction from you, and if they aren't given the satisfaction, they lose interest," John reaffirmed.

I commented, *"John, can you give us some pointers on how to handle a bully."*

"Picture your bully on his head with his body stretched like he's in front of a distorted mirror. The verbal abuses he threatens you with are warbled and incoherent, and he had turned yellow with pink stripes. Or envision a protective shield around you. Then visualize all the nasty things the bully verbalized had bounced off this ginormous buckler," he advocated jestingly.

The BB turned to his charge and counseled, *"Stay confident, lad. Bullies pick on those whom they think are weaker than them. You might be scared, but stand up to them, and they will stop."*

I stated, *"My advice to you, Helius, is to vociferate loudly to the bully – 'LEAVE ME ALONE,' or look him in the eye and say something silly. In my experience, a bully feels empowered to intimidate a person, but he will seldom harass a group. Hang out with your friends when you see the harasser approach.*

"If these tactics don't work and he continues to intimidate you, it is time to seek help. Like you are doing now. The both of us care about you and will assist you, but

we also want you to be able to stand up for yourself to defend your rights."

John supported, *"Do not think it's your fault that you are in the wrong. Nobody deserves to be bullied. The problem will not disappear if you keep the harassment to yourself. Make sure you report the issue to the relevant authorities. Telling is not tattling. It's the right thing to do. You must also remember not to skip classes or extracurricular activities because you're scared of the bully being there. No matter how dire you think the problem is, do not hurt yourself. Nothing is so hopeless that it cannot be resolved."*

The lad finally plugged up the courage to reveal his bully's identity. Although John and I were stupefied, we were not surprised. After all, this malicious teenager had caused harm to several of our friends when he played the role of Tinker Bell at our school's 1967 Christmas pantomime. We'd thought the Junior had turned over a new leave, but we were wrong. He was still the boy who wouldn't grow up, the one and the same Samuel Luke Libernhan. The once, shy and timid lad when he first arrived at Daltonbury Hall. Sam and I were pals until his vindictiveness jeopardized his entry into the Enlightened Royal Oracle Society; even though he had no idea, he was one of the few shortlisted for an illuminating education of a lifetime. His viciousness had returned. It was up to John and me to report his transgression to the school authorities.

With heavy hearts, the three of us arranged to meet Dr. Baron Struss, and Dr. Richard Kron, to inform them of Helius' tormented predicament.

Catharsis (Chapter Sixty-One)

"Being nasty to others was my way to vent."
                              Samuel Luke Libernhan

Last Week of January 1969
Daltonbury Hall, Isle of Wight, England

The afternoon before our meeting with Professor Struss, and Dr. Kron, I cornered Samuel when I passed him by the corridor. He was his usual buoyant self.

"*How are you, Sam?*" I enquired.

"*Splendid! Couldn't be better,*" he responded.

"*Do you have time for a chat? I've been busy with my studies and haven't had time to catch up with you lately,*" I commented.

"*Sure!*" he replied.

As we proceeded to the recreation room at Tolkien Brotherhood, I inquired, "*What have you been up to since your return to Daltonbury? I'm glad the school reinstated your suspension after the prank you played at the pantomime.*"

"*I've been busy catching up with schoolwork,*" he answered amiably.

"*I care about your wellbeing, Sam,*" I stated.

"*Do you really?*" he scoffed before he taunted, "*Or are you simply 'concerned' for the next batch of incoming Freshmen?*"

"*Samuel, that is an unfair comment. I care about my friends, and you for one should know,*" I countered.

"Oh! Don't I know! You claim to be my friend, and when I was suspended, you or Andy didn't bother to come to see me," he declared indignantly.

I explained, "We were away on our student exchange assignments. We would have come to visit you if we were in England."

"That's your excuse," he voiced.

I sat on a nearby bench so we could converse in private.

I began, "Sam, you are a Junior at Daltonbury. Didn't your expulsion teach you a civics lesson to be reverential to your fellow students? Instead, your apathy has led you to recriminate others rather than to better yourself...."

He stopped me before I could continue.

"You can talk. You and Andy have everything you desire while I am left in the lurch. I hate the both of you and those whom you care about," the Junior berated.

I interrupted, "Sam before you proceed to say things you will regret; I want you to cogitate your actions. Not only did your unethical behavior injured your fellow schoolmates and got you in trouble, but it also jeopardized your selection to a once in a lifetime student exchange programme. I suggest you reflect on your actions rather than inculpate those who care about you. Hopefully, you will grow up and learn from your mistakes."

"You and Duc are the same. All this reflection bullshit is nothing but to make yourselves feel superior," the Junior denounced.

I expounded, "You should have taken your ex-BB's advice prudently, then you wouldn't have been suspended. Samuel, you are an affable and simpatico young man, don't allow your indignation to disparage you. Be responsible for your actions and be significant. You'll garner genuine respect and admiration instead of false venerations through the harassment of others."

My scrupulous demeanor stirred a recognition within the Junior. He sputtered and broke into tears. *"I hate you, hate you, hate you!"*

I consoled the lad like a callow puppy deprived of affection. He sobbed in bereavement. When he stopped crying, I offered, *"Sam, how can I help?"*

Silence followed before the Junior muttered, *"Will you still be my friend if I tell you a secret?"*

"Of course, I will. But you must realize that you are responsible for your actions. No one can solve your problems except you. To blame others is a lame excuse for impulsive behavior," I commented.

He nodded.

"I've been bullying your roommate, Helius," he confessed.

"Why?" I asked.

"Because he gets your attention and I don't," the boy declared.

I was taken aback by his rationale.

I remarked, *"Helius is not my charge. John is his Big-Brother even though the three of us room together."*

"I know, but the Freshman gets your attention when he's in need, and I don't," Sam muttered sheepishly.

I expressed, *"I am your friend, and you can approach me when you are in need. I'll do my best to assist and support you. Are you having problems with your studies or extracurricular activities?"*

He shook his head before he responded, *"I like to hang out with you and Andy."*

"That is fine with me. Would you mind if Helius joins us?" I inquired.

"I like Helius. He's a friendly chap even though he's in a world of his own," Sam evinced.

I smiled mischievously before I suggested, *"Sam, the right thing for you to do is to apologize to Helius. Tell* him you are sorry, and you will not harass him again. Then ask for his friendship."

The lad thought for a moment before he nodded.

"I will apologize to Helius. Hanging with him will be interesting. Will you put in a right word for me? I might grow to like him," Samuel conveyed.

"Have an open heart and mind. You will be amazed that the both of you have more in common than differences," I maintained.

"Well chappy, are you ready to have a cup of tea at the Hobbit?"

We proceeded to the cafeteria to catch up on our latest and greatest. With Helius' despondency resolved, John, Helius and I canceled our meeting with the student counselors.

Early February 2013
Andy's Personal Message to Me

oung,

Although I am not on Facebook, I befriended Jacob. He sent me an endearing message which I answered with words of encouragement. My email response to Jacob was c/c to you and David.

To your question: *"Am I falling in love with you again?"*

Let's start with this checklist below:

An article by the social psychologist Grace Cornish, states that relationships that are built on friendships are more likely to succeed. She claims that it can be an embarrassment to declare one's undying love for a friend, only to find that he or she is not interested. She also posted some key points to evaluate the situation before one plunge into a love proposal too hastily.

Young, you can also check your perceptions and tell me your opinion. ☺

According to the erudite Dr. Cornish; romantic love consists of three ingredients: attraction, closeness, and commitment.

Attraction is the chemistry - the part of love that makes you feel flushed, out of breath and jittery around the person you are in love with.

Closeness is the trust, caring, and acceptance that develops between two people who share their private thoughts and feelings.

Commitment is the glue that binds the lovers together through dark times, arguments and difficulties.

She advocated that the above mentioned must be present for real romantic love to occur and the chances that closeness and commitment already exist in a close friendship.

My dear Young, may I also suggest you take an honest look at your feelings. Evaluate whether you really feel an attraction to me or are you mistaking the closeness and commitment of friendship for real love. When you are sure about your discernment, then proceed.

Friendships can develop into something more without either person being aware that it is happening. Maybe they have puerile names and phrases for one another, or their friends are continually teasing them about becoming a couple. Perhaps they communicate with one another regularly.

This begs the question; are you feeling the romantic tug? Maybe, I am. LOL!

Both of us must take an objective look at the situation to make sure we are not falling victim to wishful thinking. If it genuinely feels right, ask for my thoughts. I might make the first move. ☺

The psychologist also indicated to take a step back to move forward. If I have romantic feelings, but you don't,

I am in an unbalanced relationship. She suggested that I should back off and become less available. I should cultivate other friends and spend time away from the person I desire. I can then bring the balance back to the friendship by asking for favors.

For example, I might ask you to assist me with a task or chore. If you agree, then I should be thankful for your attentive behavior and acknowledge my gratefulness with a Thank You note or a personal gift. If you are nonreciprocal, it is a sign that you are not interested in advancing our friendship to courtship.

Cornish's advice is to introduce the subject of dating. Once the both of us feel the relationship is balanced and comfortable, it is time to consider dating possibilities. She said that some might jump for a kiss right away while others might prefer a direct conversation. And there are those who choose to drop hints.

Select the approach that best fits both parties. Avoid doing anything unnatural or out of character, and to trust one's instinct. Then take the risk and go with the flow. ☺

Love can appear in the most unexpected situation. You or I may have concerns that our friendship will suffer if we proceed down the path of romance. Here is where the good doctor gave some common indications that friendship is turning into romantic love:

Body language reveals how someone feels.

An example: If I am romantically interested, I may lean towards you when we converse, or I may create opportunities for physical contacts. Mirroring is another subtle body language. It is imitating the other person's style and pace of movement. If I gaze at you with wide eyes, laugh at all your jokes (even if they are not funny), and I display signs of priggishness; these, she listed as typical flirtation signals.

Oh, I forgot that we were already taught to identify these signs at the Bahriji School eons ago. LOL!

Do either of us experience giddiness, a loss of appetite and can't think of anything but the object of our affection? If so, you and I are in love.

Young, I'm sure you are aware that when a person is attracted to someone; the brain releases dopamine that causes those happy, excited feelings, and triggers an increase in testosterone which boosts sexual desire. If you and I are preoccupied with thoughts of each other and experience butterflies in our bellies when we are around, close, or communicating with each other; these are telltale signs that we see us more than just friends.

For a friendship to turn to love, the feelings must be mutual. We may find excuses to spend time together, or we may be in constant contact via emails. If our messages are turning flirtatious or suggestive, this is a definite sign that a romantic bond is at work. It is easier to drop hints about each other's feelings from afar than in person. LOL!

Finally, you or I may witness one another's love interests revolving in and out of our lives, and the both of us were there to lend each other a sympathetic ear after a breakup. You may also have played matchmaker to set me up with one of your pals, and vice versa. Whatever part we played in each other's love lives before, things will differ if we are falling in love with one another. I may become quiet, moody or irritable or show suspicious behavior if you talk to another guy. You may feel the same. If neither of us has any desire to date other people and would rather spend time together, this is an unequivocal clue that we are becoming more than friends.

Well, my dearest ex, I'll leave you to ponder over my answer to your million-dollar question. Hahaha!

Love, hugs, and kisses,
Andy
XOXOXO

The Lightness of Being (Chapter Sixty-Two)

"Skepticism has never founded empires, established principals, or changed the world's heart. The great doers in history have always been people of faith."

Edwin Hubbel Chapin

Mid-February 1969
Daltonbury Hall, Isle of Wight, England

A couple of days after my talk with Samuel, the Junior took my guidance and apologized to Helius. Although the Greco-Roman lad accepted his bully's apology, he was skeptical of Samuel's sudden change of position and remained aloof when they were together.

One afternoon when Andy, John, Helius and I were out riding, I asked the Freshman, *"You're standoffish with Sam when he is with us. Is everything alright?"*

The boy replied unenthusiastically, *"I don't trust Samuel."*

"Why?" I inquired.

He took time to respond before he declared, *"He tolerates me because he wants to be with you and Andy. I don't believe his apology is genuine."*

"Are you still afraid of him?" I questioned.

The lad remained silent.

"Helius, do you know the meaning of fear?" Andy asked.

"It's a dangerous feeling I have when I am in peril," the Freshman answered.

"That is partially correct. Fear is an emotion that tells you to avoid or escape an ongoing or impending situation. It could be external, natural and subconscious. These fearful worries can drive our trust away," my Valet indicated.

John posed, "Is Sam threatening you again?"

The boy shook his head.

"Not at all. In fact, he's overly pleasant," Helius remarked.

"Why are you skeptical of his motive?" I enquired.

Before the lad could respond, Andy remarked, "Do you know, Helius; that fear is the main factor that keeps many from living their full potential?"

"How so?" the Freshman chirped.

"You see, the fear of the unknown can cripple the level of excellence a person can achieve. Although the positive side of this trepidation is that it keeps you alert and aware, but it also wastes an opportunity for you to develop a lasting friendship that can lead to many fruitful possibilities.

"If your apprehension gets in the way before you give Samuel a chance to make amends; you're already declaring yourself a loser. Calculated risk-taking is a significant step, and you never know where this friendship may lead to for the both of you," Andy advised.

John injected, "If you are panicky that your friendship with Sam is already doomed, you had failed before you even start. A strong bond is when both parties are confident that they are supportive of one another in good and bad times. Every measure is a risk. Some uncertainties are successful, and some are not. My advice to you, Helius, is not to let your fear of failure stop you from trying."

I chirped, *"My way of overcoming fear is to know the reason for my anxiety. Ignorance is often a wall without foundation. It whispers that I cannot progress because the wall is strong, but the truth is; this self-imposed wall can be demolished quickly, and I can achieve more than I can ever imagine."*

My Valet propounded, *"There is a light within each individual that shines magnificently, yet we forget it exists. This connate radiance is the core of our essence, and it is available for us to access anytime. It is our fears, negativities and emotional baggage that overshadow this lightness. We convince ourselves that this is the person I am, and I'm meant to be this way. The truth is; we need to release the weight that weighs us down and limits us to our full potential.*

"It is our birthright to be joyful and trusting. Often the ego holds us captive and insists that we are our thoughts, fears, personalities, and dramas. In verity, each one of us is a radiant soul on earth, to shine our light and share your gifts with the world."

We stopped and stared at Andy assiduously for him to continue.

"Life is not about anguish and victimhood but the lightness of being," he counseled.

"You referred to the lightness of being. What exactly is it?" I questioned.

My Valet answered lightheartedly, *"Young, our deepest fear is not that we are inadequate, but we are powerful beyond measure. It is not our darkness but our light that frightens us. Most of us are petrified to open our hearts to our authentic self. We are accustomed to believing that it is unsafe to shine our light and show our greatness. Apart from a few, most people are conditioned to suppress who they really are; in case they upset others or appear arrogant."*

Helius muttered, *"What is so arrogant about connecting to spirit and to allow our essence to radiate and impact others?"*

My guardian gave a hearty laugh before he replied, *"You tell me, Helius. If I wasn't mistaken, a moment ago, you were concerned about Samuel's motive of wanting to be your friend."*

The Freshman went quiet.

Andy resumed, *"Do you remember when we were kids we were full of light and love; only to have our spirits squashed along the path of growing up."*

None of us uttered a word.

My Valet continued, *"Playing small, or as I refer to it as 'diminishing our light,' is not helping anyone. When we are not in our 'light' self and allow fear to take over love; we appropriate insecurities and anxieties."*

John queried, *"How do we free ourselves from our negative beliefs and perturbations?"*

"Good question, John. Our dis-ease will be transformed by acknowledging and embracing the light within and around us. What I advocate is not wishful thinking but transformational healing. Our illumination is a gift from the spirit and is a part of the universal soul," my Valet advocated.

"You haven't answered my question. How?" John pressed.

Andy simpered, *"All you have to do is visualize yourself, or the situation that requires healing and surround it with light. Close your eyes and imagine yourself embraced by the radiance of love. Visualize the negativity dissipate while the brilliance lifts your spirit to revitalize and energize you cellularly."*

Helius enquired, *"Can I use this transmogrifying technique on another person?"*

Andy adjured smilingly, *"Of course you can. Envision your amatory light penetrating the person or situation that requires your mitigation energy. Sanction his or her fears and gloom to be dissolved for positivity, creativity, and joy to regain its rightful place. Remember, Helius, the power of light can correct that which is in our mind.

"My advice to you is to permit yourself the universal gift of happiness, peace, and lightness. Illuminate the things that do not serve and support you. By enabling your unique light to radiate, you are also entitling others to shine their light. You'll be amazed that all the brilliance in the world cannot compare with the dazzle that is within each of us."

"Can we perform a group radiation session now?" I quipped jokingly.

Second Week of February 2015
David's Message to Andy and Me

Hi guys,

Thank you for friending Jacob. He is an inquisitive and intelligent young man. As you've discovered, he has many questions he wants answers.

I admit that I helped him draft the message to the two of you. He wrote and rewrote the draft several times before he presented it to me for correction. I edited some of his phrases and words before he finally settled on the message you have on your computers. He takes after me in being a perfectionist and articulacy; both traits I take pride in. ☺

Thank you, guys, for your concerns. I am on the road to recovery. Hopefully, I am done with this wretched disease and am able to return to my customary self sooner than later. Young, thanks for the Get-Well e-card. Deeply appreciated.

Do keep me in the loop to your correspondences with Jacob. I like to follow his progress like a fuddy-duddy granddad. ☺ Then we'll have subject matters to talk about when we communicate.

Have yourselves a Happy Valentine's Day.

David

February Thirteenth, 2015
My Message to Andy

My dear ex,

You certainly know how to revert my question back in my direction. You crafty devil. ☺

I did a review on the checklist you provided as per your recommendation. Below are my findings:

Attraction – like the beginning as it is now, I find your wittiness, worldliness, tenaciousness, and last but by no means least, facetiousness extremely attractive. As much as I am drawn to you, I don't feel flushed, out of breath and jittery; as mentioned in your checklist. But I do look forward to reading your emails; to better comprehend your line of reasoning, and to gain valuable insights from your reasons.

Closeness – I understand you trust, care and accept me for who I am. We have this closeness since the day we met. These same attributes also made our separation steep and strenuous, oh-so-long-ago. It is indisputable that our propinquity will remain for the rest of our lives.

Commitment – although I am unsure if you are in a committed relationship with another; I am with Walter, my life-partner of seventeen years. Even though we joke about having a triplet relationship with you - like you and I had with Oscar, back in 1966; Walter and I are devoted to one another. Nowadays, I am incredulous to a triplet relationship working out to the benefit of all parties involved. As is often the case, one person is left unfulfilled and will eventually part for greener pastures. So, my sweet Andy, you can mull over my observation and tell me your thoughts. ☺

Body language – Since we are oceans apart, this is a question neither of us can answer. Our communications have thus far been via emails and long-distance correspondence.

Giddiness and a loss of appetite and can't think of anything but the object of our affection? I don't believe so. My weight remains at 160 pounds, and I consume the same amount of food as I regularly do. So, my friend, there is no 'love' symptoms in this area. LOL!

Butterflies in my belly – none here. Hahaha!

I have truthfully answered the questions on your checklist. Now it is your turn to examine your feelings and respond to the million-dollar question you'd so cleverly hurled my direction. ☺

    Love, hugs, and kisses,
    Young
    XOXOXO

Romance, Love & Sex (Chapter Sixty-Three)

"Purity brings freedom, life, love, and a sense of stability and fortification for which every human heart longs."

Eric Ludy

Third Week of February 1969
Tolkien Brotherhood Dormitory, Daltonbury Hall, England

Since Helius' arrival at Daltonbury Hall, he was under John's care and observation. Instead of taking to his Big-Brother, this sprightly lad gravitated to Andy and me. The adolescent would slide into my bed to cuddle on the nights when he felt lonely and homesick. Like an altruistic brother, I embraced this young confrère with equanimity, so he could sleep unperturbed in my arms. There were occasions when I felt Helius' hand on my morning wood when I was in a shallow slumber. I did not move away, nor did I brush his hand aside since it was natural for males to have erections. I wanted the lad to feel unsullied.

John was visiting his parents in London when my Valet came to spend the night. That evening, Andy, Helius and I nuzzled in bed together.

The Freshman queried, *"John keeps telling me to play the field and not be attached."*

He paused before he resumed, *"I don't understand why neither of you gets jealous?"*

"What's there to be jealous of?" I answered.

The Greco-Roman remarked, *"The two of you are devoted to each other, yet you have sex with other guys. Don't you get jealous?"*

Andy replied mischievously, *"That's because we learn to separate love, romance, and sex and contained them in apropos packages."*

"How do you do that?" our confrère questioned.

"First and foremost, you must recognize that romance, love, and sex are three different words with different implications; even if these terms can be wad together to have a single denotation," my Valet replied.

"The word romance often indicates fun, frolic, innocence, and immaturity.

"Love, on the other hand, offers an acute sense of responsibility and cohesiveness from the involved parties. Love is the aspect to which romance culminates into a sexual or nonsexual connection and cannot be determined or measured by anyone. Love is an emotional sentiment," Andy added.

Helius chirped spiritedly, *"What about sex?"*

We chuckled at the boy's enthusiasm.

I declared, *"Sex happens when both or more parties are attracted to one another. When the participants permit their indigenous selves to experience the interconnectedness between them and when deep-rooted immoral beliefs are cast aside to allow our untainted essence to emerge; intercourse becomes an electrifying experience."*

"Tell me more," the adolescent implored.

My lover denoted, *"Boy, before you jump the gun, let me finish my romance explanation."*

The Freshman nodded.

*"For romance to bloom into blossoms of love, the partners must be mentally and emotionally secure. One vital component is to sanction personal space, exchange

one another's thoughts, and to spend time together. Without these elements, the partners will drift apart.

"These supportive components are healthy for building a love attachment. It is imperative for partners to understand each other's thought process for a smooth and comfortable relationship to flourish," my chaperone counseled.

I added, "Romance demands mutual responsibilities, recognition, and innocence from the lovers. You see, Helius, passion cannot remain static, it must progress to a love attachment or friendship; and in some cases, it will terminate altogether. Love can't fly without the innocence and fun of romance."

"Can we get to the sexual aspect?" Helius pressed.

"Would you like Young and I to demonstrate with you the erotic beauty of intercourse?" Andy answered beguilingly.

Although our confrère's countenance was irrepressibly enthusiastic, he nodded sheepishly. Without further ado, my Valet planted a passionate kiss on the boy's lips before I joined in to partake in a memorable tour de force.

My lover's affectionate kiss on Helius' tender lips stirred us to libidinous excitements. Eager to suffice to Andy's prowess, the boy reciprocated with amatory avidity. I was engulfed by our unmitigated sensuality as our lips met in anticipation of what was to come. My Valet's dexterity stirred in me a tenderness I could not disregard. Mirages of our impending separation flashed across my mind. I wanted our affaire de coeur to last forever, yet my rationality forbade me to throw caution to the wind and to follow him to the Land Down Under. Since Andy's imminent departure weighed heavy on my mind; and my internal conflict had whipped me into many sleepless nights. As much as I love this chivalrous lover and wish to accompany him to the ends of the world; my desire to forge a life as a fashion designer proved stronger with each passing day.

As I observed my guardian's copulation with our young confrère, a cognizance washed over my person that Andy would be okay without my presence. Little did I suspect that we would wither without each other's love and support.

My lover's masterful dominance over Helius' youthful physique reminded me of my lover and my first encounter. With the passing of time, the passion I felt for my guardian had not diminished but had grown stronger and more potent. Not only had our reverence bonded into an inextricable whole but our devotion to one another had also solidified. No person or parties could sunder us but rendered our connection more concrete.

My fondness for my friends flowered like blossoming perennials in our garden of earthly delights as our concupiscence thrust us into an inseparable entanglement. The Freshman's hypnotic moans and my lover's arousing groans threw us into a collective roar of rapturous release.

Our fountains of youth poured forth as we offered our overflowing libations to honor the self and to those we cherish. We amalgamated into a Oneness-of-Being in a three-way kiss, like we did when we commenced our sojourn of love and sex.

Third Week of February 2015
My Reply to Jacob, Bcc to David and Andy

Hi Jacob,

Thank you for reaching out to me. I am fascinated by your encounter with Phron. I hope your friendship with your dragon pal will last a lifetime. Very often when we grow older, our ability to discern preternatural entities are blindsided by mundane concerns. I pray that this will not happen to you and you will continue to experience the splendor and rapport with other life forms from different universes.

I am blessed to have encountered praeternatural beings. These unparalleled experiences had provided me the insightful knowledge that other realms exist beside and around planet earth. I was fifteen when I chanced upon a sprite kingdom at Bassenthwaite Lake in the English Lake District. I documented my praeternatural encounters in A Harem Boy's Saga – V – Metanoia; a memoir by Young. I hope you will someday read my autobiographical series and gain some insightful information to help you better understand your exceptional experiences.

My advice to you, Jacob is not to allow temporal rules of behaviors side-track your intuition. Let your instincts be your guide. Play by your directive and listen to your inner voice. By doing so, you will come to appreciate your uniqueness and experience many extraordinary adventures that will usher humanity to a better comprehension of the unknown and as yet untapped universes.

These are exciting times where humanity is going through a quantum leap. New explorations and discoveries of our origins and methodological perceptions are reassessed and re-examined to reposition our long-held worldview. These findings will help us understand the scope of our earthly mission and our interactions with entities from uncharted planets.

I believe that our praeternatural encounters are not novel experiences but ongoing interactions between earthlings and otherworldly species. Besides humankind being interconnected, I am also confident that we are interrelated with other numinous genres. That is why we can interface with them through telepathy and mind communications.

My ex-tutor and renowned Zentologist, Professor Alain Dubois once proclaimed, *"Many things within our limited minds have yet to be illuminated; which we can only access with a purity of heart and innocence of spirit."*

Jacob, be confident of your preternatural encounters and don't be dissuaded by those who deem your authentic experiences as the imaginations of the young. Be childlike but never childish.

I look forward to our correspondence and wish you and Pharon all the best. Please send my regards to your granddad, David.

Aloha,
Young

Bitten by The Love Bug (Chapter Sixty-Four)

"Infatuation is when you find someone who is absolutely perfect.
Love is when you realize that he/she is not perfect, and it does not matter."

Bernard Tristan Foong

Early in March 1969
Daltonbury Hall Indoor Swimming Pool, England

Helius took on a different demeanor after our tryst. The lad was on his toes and in his best behavior. He dressed and groomed handsomely whenever my lover and I were around. Although, Helius had no knowledge that our rendezvous was also a case study of his erotophobia and/or erotophilia inquest, entrusted to Andy, John and me by the E.R.O.S. recruitment board; we were worried that the Freshman might be infatuated by the both of us.

As we watched Andy's game of water polo, Helius' stare never swayed from my Valet when there were other distractions. Like the Senior could do no wrong the Freshman applauded his every move. The adolescent also agreed with everything I said and did, even if my actions were brazenly ostentatious. I was curious about Helius' unusual behavior, so I asked the lad, *"You've been behaving terribly odd. Are you alright, Helius?"*

The Freshman stared at me adoringly before he replied, *"I love you and Andy."*

"What do you mean?" I questioned.

"I admire the two of you. You are my heroes. I look forward to being with you guys daily. I'm your devoted fan," the boy lauded.

I eyeballed the boy as if he was out of his mind before it dawned on me that this Greco-Roman adolescent was infatuated with Andy and me.

I expressed, *"Helius, do you know that infatuation is an unreliable foundation for a healthy relationship?"*

"What do you mean?" he questioned.

"Often, when we idolize someone, it is a protection of our inner pain and despair. Helius, infatuation is like a drug-induced 'high' that temporarily elevates us out of our depression," I explained.

He ogled at me as if I spoke in tongues.

"Infatuation is a defense mechanism, an unconscious strategy for avoiding pain. You may think I am crazy to say that infatuation is a way to ward off anxiety, but that is often the case," I added.

"I'm not infatuated, but am truly in love with you and Andy," the boy responded lividly.

I shushed him not to be so loud before I indicated, *"Infatuation can also be a result of projection."*

"What do you mean by a result of projection?" he remarked.

"Projection is another form of defense mechanism. Aspects of yourself that you've kept hidden from your consciousness and are unable to identify. Traits such as confidence, success or charisma that you've disowned; but possessed by your objects of infatuation. By attributing significance to these traits, you see them as outside of your personal reach," I ascribed.

Helius leered at me while I continued, *"Another form of projection is when you impute to others an extraordinary ability to provide you with a feeling that you aren't giving yourself."*

Before I could continue my elucidation, the Freshman queried, *"What kind of feelings?"*

"Like sentiments of unconditional love and acceptance. Many people do not treat themselves with respect and unequivocal acceptance. Our disowned traits make us easy targets for infatuation, especially when your objects of infatuation hold your abandoned features," I imbued.

The adolescent asked, *"Do I own those infatuation patterns you described?"*

"That my friend is a question that only you can answer. My advice to you is to help yourself to reintegrate your 'shadow' aspects and to embrace them wholeheartedly. Utilize mindfulness and self-observation to understand what you have renounced," I counseled.

"Teach me how to do that?" the boy expressed.

"Ask yourself who are you infatuated with? What are their qualities you admire? Are you preoccupied with the highs and lows of idolizing someone and then you see them fall from grace? These are significant clues to the forsaken parts of yourself. Until you are conscious of these fragmented portions, these foibles will have a hold on you," I recommended.

Just then, Andy scored a direct hit. We stood and cheered. Helius expressed when we resumed our position, *"What if my infatuation isn't reciprocated?"*

I replied conscientiously, *"Just because you're infatuated, it doesn't mean there isn't a premise for a solid friendship. But you must separate passion and love. Figure out what you value in your friends and in life. A fulfilling relationship is based on values and not an obsession. Be conscious of your decision and select friends and compeers with the qualities you esteem. Otherwise, you'll have to wait for your crush to stop itching before you realize that the wait was a waste of time."*

The Freshman opined, *"How do I know if my infatuation will materialize into something substantial?"*

"From experience, boy. Things will happen naturally once you own all your positive and negative attributes. Practice self-love and don't rely on others to fill the gaps. That said, it doesn't mean that you stop appreciating the fantastic qualities in others. Quite the contrary; you'll discern them openly, and no one will then be put on the pedestal to be worshipped," I answered assiduously.

Needless to say, my lover's team won hands down, especially Andy who scored bigtime for his polo league.

Dinner at the Hobbit

While Andy and his teammates went to the nearby village for a celebratory bash, I was left in the company of John, Helius, and Samuel. Over dinner at *The Hobbit*, John inquired, *"Did you guys enjoy the match? It's a shame I couldn't be there to see Andy's team win."*

Samuel chirped, *"I wasn't there either. I was in class."*

John looked at his charge when the Freshman announced cheekily, *"Today, I had an all-important lesson on infatuation from Mr. Foong."*

"And what did Mr. Foong teach you?" Sam quipped.

"I always thought infatuation was part of love, and they complemented each other until Young informed me that they cannot coexist," Helius divulged.

John glanced at me searchingly and wondered what I told the adolescent.

I announced, *"Many are convinced that they're in love with someone because they are infatuated with and think about their object of infatuation obsessively. They are besotted with that person and have difficulties managing their daily chores. I cited that this intense fixation is not true love but hidden phobias of our 'shadow' self."*

Samuel voiced mischievously, *"Do enlighten me about the differences between infatuation and love?"*

John propounded, "*Simply put:*

Infatuation happens instantly while Love is a slow process.

Passion wants physical affection while Love desires a deeper connection.

Crush makes a person act irrationally while Love calms him or her down.

Obsession is intense and short-lived while Love has a warm and lasting effect.

Fixation is reckless with emotions, but Love is solicitous and compassionate.

Calf-Love has ulterior motives, but genuine Love is filled with good intentions.

Desire brings out obsession and jealousy whereas Love brings out understanding and trust from the parties involved.

Infatuation is shallow. Love is deep.

Crush is a selfish and draining performance in as much as Love is kind and energizing.

Passion often makes a mountain out of a molehill, but Love does not make a fuss over insignificant issues.

Obsession is the idea of being in-love while Love is loving the person genuinely for who he or she is.

Fixation is possessive. Love is generous.

"Wow! That's a mouthful! I didn't know the differences are so extensive," Samuel exclaimed.

"There is more, do you want me to continue?" the BB expressed.

I interjected, *"Please continue. I'm sure Helius will like to know."*

The Freshman nodded in agreement.

John recommenced, *"Infatuation isn't built on solid foundations while Love is constructed on substantial grounds.*

Passion holds grudges, but Love forgives.

Infatuation thrives on playing cat and mouse games while Love thrives on sequential connections.

Desire is delusional whereas Love is real.

Obsession has unrealistic expectations while Love has pragmatic standards.

True Love is mature in as much as Puppy-Love is childish.

Love is entrenched in friendship whereas Crush is rooted in desire.

Love springs from self-assurance. Infatuation swells from insecurity.

Passion makes a person vindictive. On the contrary, Love makes a person altruistic."

Samuel voiced, *"How much more is there? I can't remember everything you said."*

John asserted amusingly, *"The more reason you need to know the rest of what I have to tell you, Sam."*

"I can replay everything to you. I have tape recorded this and my conversation with Young if you want to relisten to it," Helius proffered flippantly.

"Helius, you crafty devil. I didn't know you have a tape recorder on you," I vociferated.

The Freshman sniggered before he crowed, *"I have tricks up my sleeve you don't know about."*

"Boys, will you let me finish my infatuation spiel before you get carried away with your titter-tatter," John blazoned.

"The final components that differentiate Infatuation and Love are:

Crush is undefined whereas Love is exclusive.

Passion is self-destructive in as much as Love can heal many wounded hearts.

"Most importantly Obsession thinks love should be perfect, but Love knows otherwise. Love is not worried or in the least bit concerned about perfection because no one is perfect," the BB broadcasted.

"Yaay! It's finally over!" the Junior exclaimed excitedly. *"Can we return to a time-honored conversation?"*

"Not so fast, Sam. I want you to listen to Helius' recording of Young's infatuation rigmarole, so you'll get our invaluable wisdom into your thick head," John taunted the bullheaded Junior; to which he responded by biding us, *"Goodnight mates! I'm out of here."*

In The Blossoming Gardens Of Osborne House (Chapter Sixty-Five)

"Platonic or Divine Love: The boy is so handsome! God has created him so beautifully!
Erotic or Earthly Love: The girl is so hot! I wish I could kiss her!"

Ziaul Haque

Second Week of March 1969
Osborne House Gardens, Isle of Wight, England

A few days before Andy and I left for Paris to attend the Swarovski Fashion Extravaganza; BB John, Lucas, and Andy together with their respective charges, Helius, Samuel and I took a bicycle tour around the Isle of Wight. The island was awash with the diaphanous aroma of blossoming spring flowers as we cycled to Osborne House. This Italian Renaissance-style palazzo was the former residence of Queen Victoria and Prince Albert. Following the Queen's demise, the property was bequeathed to the State and became the Royal Naval College training institute. During World War I, it was used as an officers' convalescent home before it was renamed King Edward VII Retirement Home for military and civil service officers. Back in 1969, the lower floors of the mansion and its extensive grounds were open to the public.

As we laid out our picnic accouterments under a large oak tree within this historic estate, Helius enquired, *"Young, can I go to Paris with Andy and you?"*

His Big-Brother, John chimed before we could respond, *"Helius, aren't you going home for Easter?"*

"I would rather be in Paris than Rome," the Freshman replied.

Samuel commented enthusiastically, *"Can I go to Paris too?"*

John responded searchingly, *"Boys, why do you want to go to Paris when you are supposed to spend time with your families? Besides, you are not invited to the Swarovski fashion presentations like Andy and Young."*

Samuel's BB, Lucas injected, *"I wouldn't mind being in Paris for Easter. That city is beautiful and terribly romantic this time of year."*

"Don't encourage the Junior and the Freshman. Otherwise, they'll be pestering Andy and Young to bring them along," John chastised before he added, *"Lucas, you may or may not know that this lad (he gazed at Helius) is infatuated with Young and his Valet."*

"Is that so! Well, maybe we should have a discussion on romantic and platonic love," Lucas declared vehemently.

Samuel chirped, *"I'll tell you the difference. Romantic love is gooey and kissy-face while platonic love is unafraid to put up a fight."*

We burst into laughter at his elementary evaluation before Lucas interjected, *"Sam, your assessment is partially correct. Platonic love is not chary of a scuffle, but on the contrary; romantic love is more than being gooey and kissy-face. It is about being able to compromise."*

The BB paused before he added, *"You see, when you love someone platonically, there isn't fear of conflict. There is nothing 'to break' or 'tarnish.'*

"The fight may last a day or longer, but you'll make peace because you understand each other, and you grow during that time apart. But when you love someone romantically, the relationship is then based on

compromises. It is imperative to you for the other person's happiness. You feel content when your lover is blissful. Their needs precede yours, and any unresolved negativities will feel heavy and irksome to you."

John opined, *"My perspective on platonic love is to tell it like it is; whereas with romantic love I want to spare my lover the unpleasantness."*

"You mean to sugarcoat and to lie to your partner?" Andy countered.

"That is not what I mean, Andy. If I love someone romantically, it matters how I make them feel. If I have a topic that is difficult to relate, I will think of the best way to deliver that message, and minister that message to their emotional criterion," John clarified.

I remarked, *"When I love someone platonically, I'm unabashed if I hurt their feelings because as a trustworthy friend, it is my job to tell it to them straight rather than spare them the predicaments. If they need a shoulder to cry on, I'm there for them. For me, platonic love is a case of the ride or die while romantic love is until death does I part."*

Andy voiced, *"Where did you learn that biker jargon - ride or die?"*

"From Haalib and Azil," I sniggered.

"Those spoiled brats who got Narnia and Albert in trouble. I hope they are better behaved after their Switzerland's rehabilitation," my chaperone exhorted.

"I pray so. After all, Sheik Fahrib, the princely heir to the Sharjah throne should be able to control his nephews' disrespectful behaviors," I adjured.

Lucas directed us back to the discussion before we got sidetracked.

"Young, your description is a unique way to say that both kinds of love are everlasting. What happens when someone you love romantically or platonically committed a

crime and killed a person? Will you help them bury the body and lie in the court of law?" the BB asserted.

Andy expressed, *"That's a significant decision for my conscience to choose. It'll depend on the circumstance and the factors related to the crime."*

John avowed, *"This is indeed a weighty question. When I love someone platonically, that love is in my life. I will tend to the situation, but I will also assess and acknowledge the outcome.*

"on the other hand, romantic love has endless possibilities. It requires planning, creativity, options, and decisions. Agreements between the parties involved are vital."

Helius who had not commented until now, conveyed, *"Loyalty is a crucial element in platonic love. It is long-lasting, and it keeps me grounded."*

"That's correct, Helius. Contrarily, romantic love is sensitive, volatile and delicate. A whimsical adventure filled with fiery passion that is both satisfying and priceless; that is if you and your romantic partner have similar raison d'être," I averred.

I observed the Freshman's expression before I continued, *"Helius, romantic love will sweep you off your feet when you least expect it. It is a different emotion to infatuation. When romantic love hits, you will sense it in your heart.*

"A word of caution, when you try to cross the line from platonic to romantic, be prepared for rejection. Rejection sucks when romantic love is unreciprocated."

My Valet enjoined, *"You can save yourself a lot of heartaches when you understand the difference between friendship and relationship. If you find yourself falling in love with a friend, make sure your lust is not a fleeting avocation. Otherwise, it may lead to an explosive situation, or it may turn out to be in your favor. Either way, it is a painful recovery. The nature of the friendship will change.*

"If you feel that your emotional bonds are mutual and can last, then make a proposal; but be prepared to face rejection and the possibility of losing his or her friendship. However, if both your connection is secure and he/she reciprocates, then it is a right call."

Lucas counseled, *"If you feel that the feelings are not mutual and you value having the person in your life, you can also choose to wait for the right circumstance before you propose.*

"As per Andy's input, the dynamics of the friendship will change. It is likely that the romantic relationship won't be as laid-back as the friendship, and jealousy may raise its ugly head. Be smart and be honest with yourself and weigh both negative and positive possibilities. A word of caution, if you are considering a romantic relationship with your best friend, infatuation should be the last thing on your mind."

Helius he burst into tears at the mention of infatuation. We were taken aback by his emotional outpour.

"What's the matter, Helius? Are you alright?" John inquired and stepped in to console his charge.

"I don't know what to do? I'm in love with Andy and Young," the Freshman cried.

We looked at one another in bewilderment before Andy soothed, *"Helius, Young and I love you very much. We treasure your comradeship. As you are aware, I will be leaving for New Zealand in a few months. You can come visit me anytime."*

I vindicated, *"Helius, you are very dear to me. I value our friendship and will assist you in any way possible. You can approach me for help. I'll be there for you."*

"Does that mean the both of you are not in love with me?" the boy questioned.

Andy and I nodded.

Samuel laid his hand on the Freshman to comfort him.

He whispered into Helius' ear, *"Love is sturdy, unwavering and unfazed. It takes a lot to shake up a relationship. The surprises in the world will pop up, but our link will remain solid."* He kissed the weeping adolescent on his lips.

This astonishing revelation was more surprising than Helius's confession. We stared at the Junior, not knowing what to make of this mystifying turn of events.

Sam continued to confess unapologetically, *"I had eyes for Helius the day he entered Daltonbury, but I didn't know how to handle my dubiety. I wrestled heftily with my homoerotic feelings. In exasperation, I bullied the Freshman. I thought I could ditch my licentious thoughts by accosting the object of my affection. Instead, my harassment threw me into profound disarray. Most nights, I cried myself to sleep. I hated myself for hurting the person I want to love."*

The Junior paused to wipe his tears before he resumed, *"After Young confronted me, I finally make peace with myself. Thanks to all of you, I learn to cherish the object of my affection rather than to destroy the person I love."*

Unable to contain his tears, Samuel held Helius' hand and planted an affectionate kiss on his palm.

"Will you forgive me, Helius?" he muttered and gazed at the lad.

The Freshman was as baffled as the rest of us. He remained silent when Sam announced, *"I love you, Helius. Will you accept me as your boyfriend?"*

Silence fell over our party. None of us knew what to say.

The adolescent quipped, *"Sam, I forgive you, and I will be your boyfriend as long as you don't bully me."*

We burst into merriment.

John sallied, *"The two of you are so endearingly special and a treasure to be with."*

Lucas said concernedly, *"Why didn't you come to me for advice, Sam? I could have helped you through your blustery predicament."*

"I know you will provide me with sound advice, but I need to come to terms with myself, my sexuality and to reconcile with my emotional upheaval. No one can help me but me," the Junior explicated.

Without further ado, Samuel kissed Helius passionately in front of us and threw the Freshman into a state of unanticipated discombobulation.

We cheered and congratulated the loving duo as we frolicked within the blossoming gardens of Osborne House.

Put On The Ritz (Chapter Sixty-Six)

"I love Paris in the Springtime."

Cole Porter

Mid-March 1969
Ritz Paris, France

The smell of spring was abloom in and out of the Rolls Royce, courtesy of the Ritz Paris, that came to collect us at the Roissy. As Big-Brother John had predicted, the Freshman and the Junior pestered Andy, and I to take them to the City of Romance. The lovebirds inveigled that they would learn treasured lessons of love from the seasoned amorati - my lover and *moi*. And what better place to ascertain that *affaire de coeur* but in *La Ville de L'amour* (The City of Love). In short, they did not want to return home for their Spring recess. Neither Samuel or Helius have been to the French capital before, nor do they have knowledge of my Valet and my Enlightened Royal Oracle Society's assignments, we were careful not to reveal our secret avocations to the boys. Even though the pair were currently under E.R.O.S. observation and Samuel was once a potential candidate until he jeopardized his recruitment admission; we had no intention of disclosing the fraternity's secret activities to our charges.

After Samuel's *kokuhaku* 告白 (Japanese for Love Confession) to Helius, the Junior had metamorphosed from a rogue to a gentleman. Not only did their union bond their relationship, but Samuel also took on the protector's role to his lover. He had matured from his prankish self and was conscientiously perceptive to his boyfriend and friends. His transformation prompted John, Andy and me to re-nominate the lad's entrée to the Enlightened Royal Oracle Society. The E.R.O.S. authorities' pronouncement was for the three of us to further monitor the Junior. To make sure that he would not fall back into his disruptive habits. The best way to surveil his conduct was to engage Sam in assay situations. If his reciprocal actions prove to be propitiously sanguine, E.R.O.S. committee would then consider his ingress. Although my Valet and my time in Paris was a vacation, we were also on a covert mission to review the Junior and Freshman's behaviors.

My ex-private tutor and sports trainer, Herr Curt Eberhardt greeted us at the lobby of the Ritz Paris. After a solicitous round of French salutations, Eberhardt enquired jovially, *"Who are these good looking boys you have with you?"*

"Let me introduce - Samuel and Helius. It's their first time in Paris," my chaperone established.

"They are our Daltonbury Hall schoolmates," I injected.

"Are the two of you a couple?" the Sportsman queried.

Since Sam had never been subjected to such an inquiry, he did not know how to respond. He turned away abashed.

On the contrary, Helius directed his response to the professor. *"Do we look like a couple?"*

Curt declared amusingly, *"Boys, I'm pulling your legs. Come with me, our party is expecting you in the Floral Garden."*

He beckoned us to follow.

In the Floral Garden

When we entered the private *jardin*, workmen were busy working on the finishing touches to the Swarovski Fashion Extravaganza. As if I had stepped into a magical wonderland, large pink Madonna lilies enticed me into the diaphanous marquee. Tiny Swarovski crystals encased the center of each blossom like glittering jewels ready for pollination while gleaming swan-shaped crystals hung like sparkling birds above our heads.

A pristine runway sat in the middle of the enormous chamber. Its peripheries adorned with rubicund lilies with pellucid Swarovski "pollens." As if expenses were left unchecked, images of oversized Swarovski Swan emblems lured the consumer into the company's sybaritical universe; where fashion, beauty, elegance, and sophistication reign supreme.

Neither Andy, our companions nor I had witnessed such polished prodigality. We were blown away by this scrumptious display of unrestrained grandeur.

Mrs. Andrea Swarovski was next to us before we could absorb the rich details of this fantasyland.

"I'm glad you boys made it to Paris. I wasn't sure if you were coming?" she promulgated.

Although she was aware that my chaperone and I would not miss this once in a lifetime event, I realized that her air talk was uttered by one who had one too many. Mario stepped in before her tipsiness took hold.

The fashion photographer chirped excitedly, *"Nice to see you guys again."*

He noticed our charges and added, *"And who are these two gorgeous young men?"*

He ogled at Samuel and Helius.

The boys looked away in embarrassment.

"This is Helius and Samuel, our schoolmates. It's their first time in Paris," Andy introduced.

Before my chaperone could continue, the Count offered, *"I'll be happy to show these gorgeous specimens the City of Romance. Let's have dinner at Au Chien Qui Fume. I'm sure they'll love the place."*

Like Mario, Tad was also smitten by our friends.

The athlete chimed, *"Au Chien Qui Fume is an excellent start. After dinner, we'll go to G for some fun."*

There and then, Andy and I made it a point to inform the Count and our Arabian patriarchs in private, that our charges were as yet, not E.R.O.S. initiates but were under the fraternity's observation.

"Young, come with me. I would like to introduce you to the best fashion show choreographer and organizer, Galvin Seamon. I'm sure the both of you will have a lot in common," Mario, the fashion savant, announced.

We left our charges in the company of Andrea, Tad, and Curt, and followed the Count backstage.

At the back of the marquee was a sizeable enclosure with rows of clothing racks, portable tables, and an assemblage of full-length mirrors. While the tables toted a cornucopia of beauty items; from wigs, hairpieces, and hair accessories to assortments of makeup products; the mobile trestles along the peripheries held a significant number of sparkling gowns carefully covered in transparent garment bags.

An animated maestro directed a contingent of cackling models, hair, and makeup artists at the far end of the room. While the artists perpetuated the model's specific aesthetics to each participant, the choreographer dispensed the show's procedures to his team.

As soon as the doyen saw the Count, he approached our group and greeted the photographer with kisses on both cheeks.

The maestro inquired cheerfully, *"Qu'est-ce qui vous amène en coulisse, mon cher ami? (what brings you backstage, my dear friend?)"*

"*J'aimerais vous présenter deux de mes amis, d'Angleterre (I like to introduce you to a couple of my friends from England)."*

The Count gave the man a pat on the back before he resumed, *"C'est Young et son chaperon, Andy. Les jeunes n'est mon fashion protege. Je crois que les deux d'entre vous ont beaucoup en commun pour discuter (This is Young and his chaperone, Andy. Young is my fashion protege. I believe the both of you will have a lot in common to discuss)."*

The virtuoso greeted Andy and me with pecks on both cheeks as he did with the Count.

"I am Galvin. Call me Gal. It is nice to meet fresh faces in the industry. I've been in fashion for many years," he declared in thick French-accented English.

"I've known Mario for a long time, and we've collaborated on many projects. I'll be happy to assist you," the Frenchman added.

The seasoned fashion doyen glanced at his pal for his reaction.

Since I was enthralled by the workings of a major fashion presentation, I complimented the maestro sheepishly, *"I am bedazzled by your sweeping production before it has even begun."*

"It's going to be a fabulous show. Tout simplement FABULEUX!" Galvin answered jovially and threw his hands in the air to emphasize his vehemence.

I took the opportunity to ask Monsieur Seamon, *"How do you even begin to arrange an elaborate show like this?"*

"From experience, boy. From experience," Galvin replied exuberantly.

Before the doyen could explain the inner workings of putting together a prime fashion event, Andy pulled Mario aside to inform him of Helius and Samuel's status quo.

They left the virtuoso and me to our fashion talk.

As soon as my chaperone and the Count departed, Monsieur Seamon resumed enliveningly, *"Putting on a ritzy fashion event is exciting. It's like an artist creating a masterpiece. First, I meet my clients to discuss their needs, desires, and what they want to achieve from the presentation. Then we work on a theme and concept. This really gets my creative juice flowing."*

Gal paused to catch his breath before he continued, *"For an established fashion company like* Swarovski, *I took their firm's emblem – The Swan and decorated the ballroom's interior with swan-shaped crystals to showcase the Swarovski logo. I also worked closely with the fashion designers they collaborate with, to come up with the presentation's overall theme."*

I chirped, *"It must be an effortless endeavor to put on a show when money is no object."*

The man declared precariously, *"Here is where you are wrong. All shows have a budget. I have to prove my worth and convince my client that I am the right person for the job, and I can deliver the product within or below the cost of the allocated amount."*

He smiled mischievously before he resumed, *"First, I sell them on my creativity. I jot down a list of ideas that complement and will create a media buzz for the corporation; even if my vision may seem absurd or impossible to accomplish. Then, I select two to three cohesive and impactful concepts to present to the client...."*

He paused to recollect an event he had done.

"A few months ago, I did an impromptu fashion event in New York for Christian Dior's designer, Marc Bohan. Everything was kept a secret until the last minute when distinguished guests and reporters received a personal call to tell them where to show up. Suddenly, everything came to life at this abandoned railway station –

the music, models, and backdrop materialized in a split second," the maestro recalled.

"*Without the paparazzi getting wind of it, I prepared that event for a month and managed to keep it under wraps. It was fun to pull off a phenomenon like that and make it a success,"* Galvin announced proudly.

"*Did the Dior customers like your extemporaneous function?"* I inquired.

"*Of course, they did. The presentation is everything. I conferred with Marc, Dior's business associates, their marketing and public relations team and they loved my killer proposition. They know my love and enthusiasm for fashion, and I'm known for my excellent show productions,"* the virtuoso proclaimed before he added, "*After I landed the gig and with the approved budget, I look for the best people in my industry to work with. Like the front and back of house showrunners, the head dresser and crew, essential hair and makeup experts, and a sharp sound and lighting company. Last but by no means least, a skilled graphics and printing house, and a competent social media firm which most established fashion brands already have. Like a jigsaw puzzle, all these factors must gel together to create my presentation vision."*

I questioned, "*What happens after you've formulated your team?"*

"*I prepare the posit for the company to approve and sign off for production work to begin. I work with the venue personals to coordinate load-in and out schedules, and union rules and restrictions that may apply. I make sure that the stage design is appropriately scaled and impactful within the allocated space. It is crucial to have sufficient room in the press-pit for the paparazzi to set up their media equipment without hindrance,"* the maestro advised.

"*Wow! That's a lot of work to handle,"* I expressed.

The choreographer specified, *"That's not all, boy. I also work closely with the promotion and marketing team in the pre-show press coverage. The guest list is imperative especially when we have to accommodate celebrity and VIP clients and significant store buyers.*

"For the fashion show to flow smoothly, I create a 'show-flow' chart for the front and backstage crews."

"What is a 'show-flow' chart?" I questioned.

"It is a communication outline of what is to happen, when, and who is responsible for what. It is also a general information sheet for the show's run through. It comprises of dates/times/venues for model fittings, and it also consists of visual information on how the clothes, accessories are worn by each model," Seamon explained.

I posted, *"How long do fashion shows generally last?"*

The organizer enjoined, *"Usually, it is between seventeen to twenty minutes to present fifty to seventy 'Looks.' No more than half-an-hour.*

*"At the **Swarovski** show you will see tomorrow; each model has three changes. Since everything happens at lightning speed, the front and backstage coordination must work like clockwork. Under my supervision, no mistakes are allowed."*

I inquired curiously, *"Does the same format apply to haute couture fashion shows too?"*

"That is an astute question, young man," the maestro remarked before he counseled, *"Haute couture presentations is a unique case. Couture houses can afford to hire one model per 'Look.' Most likely, there will be fifty to seventy models in one show without clothing changes for the mannequins."*

The Count and my Valet returned before the maestro could continue his fashion counseling.

Mario joshed, *"You guys are still at it? I knew the both of you would have a lot to talk about. Unfortunately, I must snatch this cutie away to rejoin our entourage. I'm sure he will corner you tomorrow after the show with more questions."*

I thanked Monsieur Seamon for his valuable advice. He gave me a devious wink and whispered in my ear, *"Je vais réclamer mon droit de consultation à une date ultérieure (I will claim my counseling fee at a future date)."*

Before I left, I winked at the rogue. He gave my buttocks a flirtatious slap and send me on my way.

The Power of Love (Chapter Sixty-Seven)

"In the house of lovers, the music never stops, the walls are made of songs and the floor dances."

Rumi

March 1969
At Au Chien Qui Fume (Dog That Smoke), Paris, France

As soon as our party was seated at *Au Chien Qui Fume,* Helius enquired, *"Why are there so many pictures of dogs smoking on the walls?"*

Mario broke into laughter and expressed, *"Haven't you notice that Paris is a city that loves dogs?"*

The tipsy Mrs. Swarovski added, *"Way back in the 20s, the owner of this restaurant showed off his cigar smoking poodle and pipe puffing griffin to his customers. Soon the restaurant became known as* Au Chien Qui Fume *- Dog That Smoke."*

"Are you kidding?" Samuel chirped in disbelieve.

Andrea resumed amusingly, *"It's true. This is part of the restaurant's charm to have the walls covered with pictures of dogs smoking."*

Tad declared, *"This restaurant has been here since I could remember. It serves a plethora of delicacies, like its mouthwatering oyster and shell dishes. The excellent selection of wines is beyond compare."*

Mario asserted, *"Back to the question of dogs; they are not only man's best friend, but they are also man's best love. Their loyalty is irrefutable. I can't say that of humans."*

Samuel gave Helius a smirky smile as if he would never betray his boyfriend. The Freshman looked away shyly.

My Valet commented, *"So sweet! The heroic beauty of young love."*

Andy glanced at me as if to refer to our affaire de coeur. I avoided my Valet's gaze. Although his statement held truth, there were instances when I doubted if I could reciprocate my lover's, unfading love.

"Love is many splendor things. It touches us in a variety of compassionate, romantic, sensual, and companionable ways. Not only are these varied manifestations life-enriching, but it is also profoundly transformational," Eberhardt imbued.

"That is indeed true," Andy seconded before he added, *"I attest to that."*

"Is that so," Tad sallied. *"Andy, share with us your experience."*

My lover began, *"For me, the power of love is a chrysalis. It is a* **safe haven where radical transformation happens before something new and gloriously beautiful emerge."**

"Like a caterpillar morphs to a butterfly?" the Sportsman razzed.

Andrea chimed, *"Tad, it is obvious that you've never been in love. I'm intrigued to listen to Andy's interpretation of the transformational power of love."*

My Valet resumed, *"These new* **metamorphosizes** *are* **not premeditated or forced. It is a natural process where Young, and I are aware of our** *changes.*

"Although I have no clue how universal this transformational love is; I do know it is real and powerful. I found it, or it found me when I least expect it. My encounter with transformational love came at a time when my personal life was falling apart.

"I started to live authentically and in harmony with myself. That was when I gained a new perspective on life and was able to bring that authenticity into my interactions with others. When I am open and forthright about my life, others recognize the changes in me, and my life was directed to love."

"You mean to Young?" the Count joshed.

All eyes turned my direction. I remained silent.

Curt came to my rescue. He stated, *"Love has a way of healing past wounds. These invisible traumas could be from our dysfunctional parents, friends or ex-lovers, and we can carry this inert pain within. Like poison eating at our core. But in the face of love, healing is possible."*

Samuel voiced, *"When I was a child I desperately needed my parents and friends acceptance, but I found none until I met my most loving and supportive friend, Helius."*

Tad gave a hearty laugh before he wisecracked, *"Are you sure yours is not puppy-love?"*

The Junior glanced at the Sportsman loathsomely.

"Aww, I'm sorry. Did I hurt the little boy's feelings?" the Sportsman mocked.

Eberhardt jumped in to dissipate the pernicious air. *"You know, our self-image is primarily influenced by those close to us. We, humans, are imperfect, and through our own failings, and the careless handling of our heart by others; our self-image becomes tarnished and distorted.*

"My dear Samuel, fear not, for love has the power to clear out the grime. It will provide you with a sparkling mirror to see yourself positively. Your sense of self will be re-calibrated."

Andy heartened, *"Fear of rejection can play havoc within the mind and create a barrier to authentic intimacy. Love certainly gave me security, acceptance and enabled me to be honest and in doing so, I am able to love unceasingly. With fear out of the way, I can concentrate on getting to know my lover intimately."*

I was astonished by my chaperone's confession. To me, Andy was God's perfect specimen. In my eyes, this handsome Apollo could do no wrong and surely needed no acceptance from himself or anyone. I was blown away that a lesser mortal like me could provide this demigod the transformational love he avowed. Once again, his divulgence sparked a state of turmoil within my core. My decision not to accompany him to New Zealand would break his noble heart. Images of our impending heartbreak overshadowed the scrumptious dinner that had arrived at the historic *Au Chien Qui Fume*. I was already charred, not by the dogs that smoke but by self-mortification.

Last Week of February 2015
Andy's Response to My Message

Hi Loverboy,

I'm glad you did the checklist. I hope you discerned that our relationship spans far beyond romantic love. Although passion is our birthright, there are also many barriers that stand between us and the intimacy we seek. I'm sure you realize that self-love is the most transformative love of all.
I have another quiz for you.
How do we harness our inner power to experience the love we're seeking?
My answers:
We often look for love externally and overlook the need for self-love. There is a correlation between how we feel towards ourselves and how others feel about us. The more we can love our authentic self, the more we can create love through romantic relationships and beyond. Since our

separation, oh-so-long-ago, I've developed a mantra of self-respect and joy through meditation.

You may or may not know that I am a member of several charity organizations. One of them is the RSPCA Australia. Besides regular meditation, I've also made compassion my daily practice. I nurture seeds of understanding within my heart through acts of empathy, kindness, and acceptance; thereby making myself a fertile ground to suffering and defenseless animals. By practicing compassion toward others, the world reflects that compassion back to me.

I went through a difficult period after the death of Albert, my life-partner of seven years. I lost my self-confidence and love until I found unconditional love with the animals I helped to rescue. My compassion gave me a sense of purpose. Through my own vulnerability, I regained self-confidence. I was also acutely aware of my deep connection with the animals I saved. Although I do not speak the animal's language, nor do they speak English, there is an invisible bond between us, and that mutual affinity is love. By acknowledging and cultivating unconditional love, I regained myself. I was able to reopen my heart to self-respect, compassion, joy and most importantly love.

My dear Young, even though we are oceans apart, I feel the glow of your love within and without me. I do not need to make love to you to be in love with you. Our transcendental love for one another is with us always, like we did many moons ago and so it is now.

      Forever Yours,
      Andy
      XOXOXO

What's Love Got To Do With It?
(Chapter Sixty-Eight)

"The heart that loves is always young."

Bernard Tristan Foong

March 1969
G, Paris, France

I felt like I was watching a replay of Andy and my early affinitive rapport when I observed Samuel and Helius's interactions. My heart reached out to the young lovers as they forge their uncharted path towards the love that dares not speak its name. Since those early years of artless exuberance, my lover and I had matured. In its place, I had grown by leaps and bounds in this lifestyle that was then foreign to me and had embraced the new *moi* with gusto. The once shy and uncertain sissy boy had become a confident and sophisticated young adult. Now, it was time to relegate my E.R.O.S. position and to excogitate two new recruits to my station; to guide and mentor Samuel and Helius, like Andy and my other BBs did with me not so long ago.

    As I gazed at our gyrating entourage boogying at *G*'s dance floor, déjà vu took over my person. Flashes of euphoric moments with Andy and my other chaperones coruscated my mind. I gleamed with pleasure at those treasured moments. The reverberating music, the ever-changing lightscape and the assemblage of sexy revelers sent my palpitating heart to a garden of earthly delights. As I marveled at the semi-naked perennials, a hand clasped my shoulder. I was taken aback by none other than the handsome French Moroccan actor/model I had been reminiscing.

"*Driss, what a surprise to see you!*" I exclaimed.

"*Good to see you too, ma belle,*" the model announced excitedly. "*Où est votre bien-aimé, Andy (Where is your beloved, Andy)?*"

I pointed to the dance floor where our party was boogieing.

Beside Driss was an attractive looking Eurasian man in his early-thirties whom the model introduced as his fun-loving friend, Kaalib.

The man kissed my cheeks before he declared, "*Oh mon dieu, ce qu'un beau specimen (Oh my goodness, what a beautiful specimen).*"

Driss responded, "*Il est pris, ma chérie (He is taken, my darling).*

"*Est-ce si. Je peux toujours essayer (Is that so. I can still try),*" he replied musingly.

The model pointed at Andy when he noticed the men at my side. My Valet came over to join us.

Kaalib remarked before my chaperone arrives, "*Ce qu'un bel homme. J'aimerais bien le connaître trop (What a handsome man. I like to get to know him too).*"

Driss gave his friend a mischevious wink and smiled, as if to say, "*Try if you must.*"

My chaperone and I were delighted to see Driss again. Although we'd planned to visit the actor/model when in Paris, we were preoccupied with our gang and weren't sure if Driss would be in the city or traveling the world on his many acting and modeling assignments.

While Andy and Driss were catching up, I kept vigilance on Sam and Helius. Helius was captivated by Mario's sophistication, like me when I first met the Count. On the contrary, Samuel took a dislike to the playboy's haughtiness. After all, Mario had made no qualms to come on to his boyfriend.

In the opposite spectrum, Tad played the role of Samuel's ally to perfection. His ulterior motive was to bed the Junior and what better opportunity than to use this circumstance to his advantage.

Without stirring any unwarranted upheavals, my Valet and I figured the best route to pacify this unanticipated situation. We counseled our charges to be vigilant. Unbeknown to us, the universe has its way of allaying this otherwise dangerous minefield, and our cause for concern was temporary.

Kaalib invited me to dance while Driss and Andy were in conversation. The Eurasian whisked me around the dance floor like fluttering parakeets as our disco wear shimmered and sparkled under the flashing lights. We laughed and jostled our way through the crowd. The handsome picaroon was a superb dancer and flirt. He balanced me on one knee before he swung me back on my feet to resume our frenzied footwork and guided me through the exotic uptempo song with a tango beat. Kaalib's libidinous closeness and my coquettish heat bewitched us to a passionate kiss. No one had danced with me with such fervency and panache like this extraordinary man. This danseur whom I discovered later was an avid ballroom competitor and instructor. He was in Paris for the Parisian Dancesport competition. That evening, he was out painting the town red with his fuck buddy, Driss. And what better place to see and be seen than at *G*.

What's Love Got To Do With It?

My Valet and I were surprised that the Count and the Sportsman did not invite our charges to spend the night with them upon our return to the Ritz. Although Andy had a word with our patriarchs, we did not expect both playboys to venerate our exhortations. After all, they were used to having their way and rarely do they allow another to influence their decisions. Although flirtation was their norm that evening, when it came time say *bon nuit*, they did not press the boys for more. Andy and I were relieved by this turn of events.

As for Driss and Kaalib, my lover and I invited them for a nightcap in our chambers; we shared with our charges.

As soon as we entered the room, Andy enquired, *"Did you boys enjoy your first day in Paris?"*

Samuel expressed, *"I had a great time, but I don't care for the Count. I like Tad. He is a gentleman."*

"You think Tad is nice because he paid attention to you," my chaperone remarked.

Before the Junior could answer, Helius chirped, *"On the contrary, I prefer Mario to Tad."*

We burst into laughter.

"The two of you are so cute," Driss declared. *"Young and innocent, and see the world like wide-eyed puppies."*

"I'm no puppy, and neither is Helius," Samuel retorted.

"The way people seem on the surface and the way they behave are two different things," **Kaalib** commented.

"Is that so," I mused.

The Eurasian replied, *"Observe your crush and see how they treat others. If he is always putting other people down, there's no reason that he won't treat you that way too. If he has a reputation for cheating on previous boyfriends, then you won't be immune to it, either. It's better to find someone you can connect with than to try and change someone into the person you think they should be."*

"Are you talking about yourself?" I teased.

Kaalib resumed merrily, *"I am speaking on behalf of us. First and foremost, you have to be honest with yourself and examine your reasons for wanting to be with that person. Ask yourself these questions:*

Are you going after this relationship because you want to feel mature?

Or are you doing it out of competition with your friends?

Or is it because you really and truly like this person?

"There are countless reasons why we choose to initiate a relationship with somebody, but not all of them are good. Getting into a tie for the wrong reasons will lead to nothing but pain. The person to suffer the most will be you."

"Wow! What a mouthful. It sounds like you are looking for a permanent relationship," I exclaimed jokingly.

"Aren't we all?" the danseur expressed.

Driss adjured, *"That's quite a proclamation coming from you, Kaalib; the one who champions others to play-the-field."*

The Eurasian gave the model a sly glance to insinuate for him not to reveal his secrets.

The French Moroccan resumed sardonically, *"Having sex with my crush is a great way to know him before I embark on a romantic relationship. It's the best way to find out if he is genuinely enamored by me or if he's in for a good time."*

He paused before he continued, *"It is also a good idea to find out how well he gets along with my friends. My pals will decipher this person's character; without any preconceived notion of whether he is a one-night stand or long-term boyfriend material."*

Samuel stared at Driss as if he was blabbing Glossolalia, while Helius nodded in agreement with the model's assessment.

Andy opined, *"I will spend time with my crush and get to know him. If he feels the same way as I do when we first met, then it's time to up a notch. My advice is to follow your instincts. Tease, flirt, and fuck. If he responds in kind, then it is time to take things seriously. The relationship will be more satisfying if I wait before I profess my love to him."*

"Spoken like a sage," Samuel championed.

With a roguish grin on his face, my lover recommenced, *"That said, I will also suggest not to put all your eggs in one basket. I was never good at playing the field until...."*

Suddenly he trailed off as if he remembered something he shouldn't mention.

I voiced, *"In the past, when a man showed a genuine interest in me, I would stop dating other men for one primary reason: I lacked the confidence to juggle several men at once because I doubted my self-worth. I felt sneaky and unethical and uncomfortable playing the field. I didn't know how to handle their sexual advances and was afraid if a guy found out that I saw another, he would drop me. I would immediately decline invitations from other men when I was smitten with a new man and fantasized that he liked me as much as I wanted him. Of course, it seldom worked because the new guy would sense my relationship agenda, and he would stop seeing me. If I had casual sex, I felt morally obligated to cut myself off from other guys. In short, I threw all my eggs into his basket until he disappeared."*

My Valet enjoined, *"I discovered that seeing one man at a time was a mistake. I invested time, energy and emotions in that person and later found out he's the wrong chap. I forfeited opportunities to meet a variety of men, one who could become my perfect match...."*

My lover was cut short when Helius voiced, *"Like you found Young?"*

We burst into mirth again.

Andy restarted, *"Yes, I found my perfect match in Young. As long as I am respectful of the feelings of the men I have sex with and I am truly honest with my partner; that meaningful and committed relationship is the path to true love."*

The Freshman questioned, *"In other words, by putting my focus on one man limits my opportunities to eventually meet my ideal life partner? Is that what you said?"*

We nodded except Samuel who remained unconvinced, even though he attested to our analyzation as a vital component of a healthy relationship. My lover and my testimonies prompted Kaalib to come clean.

The Eurasian acknowledged, *"Driss is correct, I enjoy making love with men I'm attracted to. It allows me the opportunity to compare the attributes and compatibility with the guys I date.*

"Some people know the traits and qualities they value in a life partner while others learn through trial, error, and heartbreaks. I am not that kind of guy who evaluates men with my intellect, even if it can fast-track me to the right man. I allow my emotions to rule the day."

The model remarked, *"Having the amorous attention from two or more men has a way of making me feel desired and empowered. It increases my confidence and self-assurance. Sexual encounters are like interviews for acting or modeling jobs. With each experience, I hone my skills and become more at ease. In the process, I learn to assess the potential of the person I bed."*

Kaalib riposted, *"I do a reality check if I fall in love quickly and obsessively romanticize the outcome of a possible relationship. I also keep a journal when I'm seeing two or more men. This assists me to curb my infatuation and sentimental longings. By documenting the men's desirable traits, and abhorrent behaviors, I can adhere to the facts and then come to a decision.*

"The men I fall for are usually handsome, beguiling and successful but lack the qualities for a long-term partnership. Therefore, I make a point to separate sex and love. After all, what's love got to do with sex?"

"A lot," my Valet quipped before he added, *"Men aren't stupid; they can sense when I am seeing another person. The fact that I have affairs with other men tells him that I am worth pursuing. If he really likes me, his competitive nature will kick in, and he will want me for himself.*

"If I also make known to him that I am bedding other guys, and he plays hard to get and decide that it is not worth pursuing; then he is not the right person for me."

The danseur announced, *"A man is NOT my boyfriend until he tells me I am the guy of his dreams. Until then I am free to have sex with all of you."*

He pointed to Driss, Andy, Helius, Samuel and me, to which we nodded and answered with an astounding YES!

Serendipitous Reminiscence (Chapter Sixty-Nine)

"Adolescence represents an inner emotional upheaval, a struggle between the eternal human wish to cling to the present and the equally compelling desire to get on with the future."

Louise J. Kaplan

March 1969
Paris, France

Not only did the Swarovski Fashion Presentation glimmered with a star-studded turnout that glittered and shimmered in haute couture gowns covered with Swarovski crystals, but it also overflowed with sparkling champagne. Bewitched and beguiled by such brilliance, I was especially enraptured by none other than the Givenchy clad Ms. Hepburn. The one and only Ms. Audrey Hepburn who wore a gown so simple, yet so elegant which she accessorized with a Swarovski encrusted necklace that showcased her gracefulness to dazzling aplomb.

Tad and Mario, the debonnaire were in their element. They hobnobbed with the who's who in the international circuit. Thanks to Mrs. Andrea Swarovski, Samuel and Helius secured invitations to this glitterati soiree. They, like me, were blown away by the glamorous sophistication that was the paragon of haute Paree, especially within the fashion and entertainment world. The boys sat dumbfounded. They gawked at the couture-clad celebrities who strutted around like bootylicious strumpets consorting for their next inordinately paid assignments. Their designer scents trailed behind like a train of invisible fluttering butterflies.

At La Tour Eiffel

The morning before the Swarovski presentation, Andy, Driss and I showed the boys, the sights of Paris. We visited the Louvre, Notre-Dame de Paris, Sacré-Cœur and last but not least, La Tour Eiffel and lunched at one of the 1930s style Eiffel Tower restaurants. As I stared at the enchanting view of Paris from this iconic landmark, déjà vu overtook me. Flashes of my encounter with Prince P and Baron Pierre had me in goosebumps.

I stepped out to the viewing gallery while my lover and friends were busy consuming their *bonne bouches* and exchanging titter-tatters. I needed alone time to reflect on these few years of my life that had flown by so speedily. I wanted to relive those aesthetic experiences and unforgettable adventures that were compelling and precarious. Escapades that would be etched in my consciousness forever.

When I observed the Junior and the Freshman through the restaurant's panes, I could not help but wonder what would become of my friends. If they were accepted into the Enlightened Royal Oracle Society, would they be resilient to withstand the trials and tribulations of their assignments or would they fall by the wayside like some of my compeers? I wanted the best for my charges and would do my utmost to mentor and groom them for their missions. Like me, I desired for them the best that youth could offer and to live life to the fullest.

Paris drew me to its enchanted bosom like no other metropolis. I was awed and floored by its sanguinary history and antiquitous romanticism. Most significantly, this *Ville de L'amour* (City of Love) is fashion's epicenter, and as an aspiring fashion designer, I was bewitched by its glamorous sophistication. Like an unsuspecting fly caught in a spider's web, I was hypnotized by its polished magnetism that cradled me like a powerful seducer.

Helius reminded me of me when I was a freshman. During our six-way liaison the night before, he was spritely inquisitive and curiously ebullient. Although in the beginning, the slenderly diffident Samuel was hesitant, he soon warmed to the sexcapade and took on the role of an assertive participant. Curious and aroused by his vivacious boyfriend, Samuel's eyes scrutinized Helius' every move as he luxuriated in his raunchy executions. The Freshman's unconstrained prurience tantalized the Junior to heights of passionate ribaldry, especially when Driss' passionate groans paralleled the adolescent's bootylicious thrust. Sam's orgasmic release hurled the model to his point of no return. The Junior remained buried in the actor's upturned booty as he shot his potencies into Helius' tenderness.

At the other end of the spectrum, Andy, like Samuel, perused Kaalib and my coitus with hawkish variability. My chaperone's ardency fluctuated like bipolar forces. When he elbowed the Eurasian's dominance over me for mastery, his mood swung from passionate endearments to emphatic aggressiveness. I detected hints of insecurities in my lover I had not witnessed before. As if he wanted me to himself, Andy tussled for my affection when I accorded the danseur entry into my inner sanctum. My Valet was at once aroused and indignant by the Eurasian and my intimacy. Even when Kaalib was into him as much as the danseur was lustful of me, tinges of possessiveness overshadowed my chaperone's buoyant self.

On the other hand, their pugnaciousness stirred my concupiscence to precipices of sexual delight. When they wrestled for my affection, I felt desired and empowered. As the men oscillated their bulbousness in and out of my orifices, I was in seventh heaven. Their lasciviousness spurred my release to jubilance when they finally deposited their love seed in *moi*.

That night we changed partners many times until exhaustion overtook us and we fell into peaceful slumbers within one another's embrace.

Andy jolted me from my serendipitous reminiscence to reality when he inquired, *"Are you OK, Young? You seem so far away."*

He plopped himself next to me and put his hand on my shoulder.

I answered contentedly, *"I was reminiscing about my life."*

He declared, *"You know, Young, since we met, you've chased my blues away. I can't live without you, and I can't bear it if we're apart."*

He caught me speechless. I could not bring myself to tell my beloved that our relationship would soon come to a close; that I had made up my mind to stay in London and Paris for my fashion education, rather than follow him to New Zealand. As I laid my head on my Valet's shoulder, tears welled in my eyes. Like fortified lovers, Andy kissed my tender lips to assure me that all is well. Yet, my irksome heart wept uncontrollably. I did not wish my lover to witness my anguish and despondency that were eating at my core. In the hope that my desolation would magically disappear, I shut my eyes tightly. Neither of us desired our affection to end. We were lost in that unperturbed moment where time stood still. But tears of sadness would not leave me alone, and when my valiant beau detected grief, I turned away quickly.

"Tell me, what is troubling you," he asked.

I did not answer, but when I finally spoke; I lied, *"Nothing. I'm simply blissful to be with you."*

He scrutinized my insincerity.

"Tell me the truth. I can tell when you are lying," my chaperone urged.

I wondered how best to break the unpleasantness to my beloved.

Just as I was about to come clean, Driss, Helius, and Samuel appeared to notify us that it was time to return to the Ritz; to dress for the Swarovski Fashion Extravaganza.

Third Week of March 2015
Jacob's Email to Andy and Me

Hi Young and Andy,

I am writing with considerable sadness in my heart. Grandpa David died of cancer a week ago. He was cremated, and we scattered his ashes on top of his mountain retreat. Not only did I lose a caring grandfather, but I also lost a sympathetic and supportive mentor. David was the only person who knew and understood my friendship with Pharon, even if my dragon pal did not reveal himself to grandfather when he was alive. But just before he passed, he saw Pharon and asked him to look after me. Pharon promised he will connect with David in the afterlife. My fantastical friend had been with me throughout these trying times. I would be lost without him. He told me he had reconnected with grandpa in the other realm and they got on splendidly.

David made me promise to stay in touch with the both of you. He said you guys will guide and counsel me on problems I might encounter. Grandpa also assured that if I need his help; to call his name, and he will steer me through difficulties I may face.

Before I sign off, I want to thank the both of you for your advice. I will be in touch again.

Love,
Jacob

Splintered Emotions (Chapter Seventy)

"We must let go of the life we have planned, to accept the one that is waiting for us."

Joseph Campbell

March 1969
Ritz Paris, France

Many say that love is an unfathomable mystery that no mortal can fully understand. But they're wrong. Love is like a leech. It's invasive, it sucks the blood out of you and leaves you exhausted. Instead of healing, it gives you a fever and causes you to spend a lot of time crying.

Of course, there is also much to be said in favor of love. As many of us know, Shakespeare said most of it. Who can forget The Bard's inspiring words in his Sonnet 18:

"Shall I compare thee to a summer's day?
Thou art more lovely and more temperate:
Rough winds do shake the darling buds of May,
And summer's lease hath all too short a date:
Sometime too hot the eye of heaven shines,
And often is his gold complexion dimm'd;
And every fair from fair sometime declines,
By chance or nature's changing course untrimm'd;
But thy eternal summer shall not fade
Nor lose possession of that fair thou owest;
Nor shall Death brag thou wander'st in his shade,
When in eternal lines to time thou growest:
So long as men can breathe or eyes can see,

So long lives this and this gives life to thee."

But that was Shakespeare the genius. We, the ordinary folks must struggle along as best as we can, and this was precisely what transpired on that fateful evening at the glamorous Swarovski Fashion Extravaganza.

Our entourage entered the ballroom with sparkling exuberance. Dressed to the nines, our youthful party rubbed elbows with the international elite. Never in my wildest dreams did I ever imagine I would be in such a ritzy occasion. But then I was in the Ritz and what better place than the Ritz, to put on the ritz.

Like my charges, I was enthralled by the exoticism that floated by. I did not notice Prince P and Sheik Fahrib's approach until I was spun around and were greeted with sincere affections. A couple of Middle Eastern gentlemen were next to them.

The prince announced. *"These are my cousins from Ajman; Rash and Amm. They saw your party from a distance. When I told them, I know Andy and you, they requested introductions."*

Andy and I shook the men's hands.

The sheik commented, *"Rush and Amm were my ex-schoolmates and neighbors and my country borders theirs."*

Before my Valet and I had a chance to introduce Samuel and Helius to the men, a loud crash rendered us senseless. A large ceiling chandelier had smashed onto Table 5. Broken and splintered glass laid shattered atop and around the nearby tables and floors. For a split second, the room went quiet before anguish screams came from all directions. A judicious gentleman shouted for exigency to be summoned and to assist a couple of blood-soaked guests who lay unconscious on the carpeted floor.

Dr. Fahrib, Curt, and Andy rushed to the victims' aid. The ambulances arrived post haste to careen the wounded to the nearest hospital. The once festive atmosphere had transformed into an ambiance of distress, and the fashion presentation was postponed until further notice. Most of the invitees left in harrowed agitation while others remained to assist those with minor abrasions.

Rush and Amm disappeared with the prince and the sheik while Professor Eberhardt escorted Samuel and Helius back to their room. I waited for Andy's return before we proceeded to the hotel lounge for an aftermath repose. I did not anticipate that this unprecedented catastrophe would provide me the opportunity to come clean to my beloved.

My Valet gulped a glass full of cognac before he voiced, *"What a horrible accident! Luckily, no one died. The hotel will be held accountable for this dreadful dilemma."*

My lover sighed before he resumed, *"I'm glad we weren't in the disaster zone. If anything happens to you, I'll be devastated."*

He looked at me before he remarked, *"You know I love you more than you can fathom."*

"I am well aware of that," I replied.

He took another swig. As if he was drunk in love, he began to quote one of Shakespeare's love sonnet

"Shall I compare thee to a summer's day? Thou art lovelier and more temperate: Rough winds do shake the darling buds of May," he recited frivolously.

Before he could continue, I interrupted, *"Andy, I have something important to tell you."*

"What do you have to tell me, my love? That you love me?" he sallied giddily.

"I love you," I ensured before I blurted, *"but…, but I've decided not to follow you to New Zealand."*

He glanced at me as if I was silly.

Without paying attention to my declaration, Andy picked up where he left off.

"And summer's lease hath all too short a date: Sometime too hot the eye of heaven shines, and often is his gold complexion dimm'd; and every fair from fair sometime declines..."

I jumped in before he could resume, *"Andy, did you hear what I said?"*

Suspicious that my lover had one too many, I repeated, *"Andy, I'm not going with you Down Under."*

He did not answer. Instead, he recommenced his recitation, *"By chance or nature's changing course untrimm'd, but thy eternal summer shall not fade nor lose possession of that fair thou owest...,"*

This time around, I vociferated, *"Andy, listen to me. I'm not going to Christchurch with you. I'm staying in London for my fashion education."*

As if to defy my proclamation, he cited loudly, *"Nor shall Death brag thou wander'st in his shade, when in eternal lines to time thou growest...."*

Andy could no longer continue his citation and broke into tears. My heart reached out to him. I could not bear to see my lover in such a volatile state and wished I could retract my declaration. It was too late. I'd spoken, and I've to live with the ramifications.

I reached to clasp Andy's hands to lessen the verbal blow I had inflicted, but he coiled into self-deprivation. Not only had I had shattered his optimism for a rosy future he had planned for us, but I had also injured his pride. I wanted to renounce my decision, but I knew that would be perfidious if I did.

I assured myself that Andy would come to the realization that my honesty would set us free and we would weather this storm. Little did I realize that it was a separation that would last for forty-five years and we would not reconnect again until 2012.

"So long as men can breathe, or eyes can see, so long lives this and this gives life to thee...," **were my**

lover's final words of desolation before he left me to ponder the misery I had imbued on my gallant beau.

Last Week of March 2015
My Condolence Message to Jacob

Hi Jacob

I am deeply sorry for your loss. Although David and I were friends for a short time, I feel akin to him. We shared similar experiences during our young years. If he were alive, he would have told you more.

Do not hesitate to contact Andy and me if you require assistance. We will do our best to advise and guide you.

I am delighted that David met Pharon before he passed, and they had already reconnected in the other realm. Mythical creatures are known to transmogrify from one sphere to another with ease as they vibrate at a higher frequency than humans. They can be visible and/or invisible to the naked eyes. The Latin word for dragon is drak. It means to "watch closely" or "see clearly."

Dragons are incredibly alert, and I am confident he'll keep you safe. Dragon wisdom is well known, and those who communicate with humans will deliver shrewd counsel and prophesies. I won't be surprised if you receive messages from David through your dragon friend.

Jacob, my advice to you, is to hearken Pharon's words of wisdom. Your trusted friend will help you through these trying times.

Do feel free to contact me anytime.
Stay healthy and safe.

Love,
Young

There Are No Gay People In The Arab World (chapter seventy-one)

"I've never talked about my sexual orientation because it is my concern. I'm not brought up to talk about my sex life with others."

Amman bin Ahmad Al Nuaimi

March 1969
Ritz Paris, France

Four beautiful floral bouquets with gifts were delivered by the Ritz Hotel bellboys to our chambers **the morning after the** Swarovski Fashion fiasco. These princely presents were from the Ajman gentlemen we met at the Swarovski soiree. When they opened our packages, Samuel and Helius were beyond themselves.

The Junior exclaimed, *"Gosh! What a stunning watch."*

He flaunted his lavish timepiece for us to inspect.

"How magnificent! It's a Vacheron Constantin," Andy marveled aloud.

Helius asked, *"What's Vacheron Constantin?"*

"It's a famous Swiss watch company, and their watches are of the most exceptional quality," my Valet remarked.

Before my chaperone and I had a chance to open our largesse, the Freshman cried in astonishment, *"Oh My God, I got a watch too."*

Like his boyfriend, Helius paraded his wristwatch for us to inspect.

"And what brand is my timepiece?" the adolescent questioned.

Andy pronounced excitedly, *"It's a Blancpain. Another prestigious Swiss watchmaker."*

I couldn't wait to see what was in my box. An elegant silver pocket watch revealed itself when I opened my container.

"Wow! Mine is a Jaeger-LeCoultre," I blurted excitedly.

Andy gave me an envious glance before he announced, *"Young, your pocket watch isn't cheap. Jaeger-LeCoultre creates the world's smallest and most exquisite timepieces of near-perpetual movement."*

I chirped, *"All our presents don't come cheap. What's in your box, Mr. Timepiece expert?"*

When my lover opened his gift, he couldn't believe what he saw.

"It's a spectacular Girard-Perregaux!" my lover shrieked animatedly.

We leaped with joy when a knock on the door brought us to our senses. It was Professor **Eberhardt**.

He waved his hand jubilantly and trumpeted, *"What's the excitement?"*

Andy announced, *"We've been bestowed lavish gifts."*

The sports trainer gave an exhilarated nod and joined in the celebration. We bounced around like a gang of juveniles before we collapsed onto the settee.

Curt declared, *"I'm sure you guys know the reasons behind these expensive gifts."*

"Because, Rash and Amm like us," Helius blazoned.

"No," Andy contradicted.

"Why?" Samuel questioned.

"They want to get into our pants. That's why," I posed.

"Young's correct. They want to bed all of us. The more, the merrier," Curt stated unabashedly.

Samuel remarked, *"I thought there are no gay people in the Arab world."*

Curt, Andy and I laughed at the Junior's naiveté before Eberhardt proposed, *"Let's go to Stohrer and have something sweet to celebrate. We can have a 'no gay people in the Arab world' discussion there."*

He waved his hand spiritedly to usher us off the couch and to show off his prestigious Piaget Polo. A gift from Rash and Amm.

At *Stohrer*

Driss and Kaalib met us at the oldest pastry shop in Paris - *Stohrer*, located at No 51 Rue Montorgueil. This scrumptious temple of sweets was founded by the pastry chef of King Louis XV, Nicolas Stohrer in 1730 and later certified by Monsieur Paul Baudry, the interior decorator of the infamous Opera Garnier.

Driss recommended the moment we entered this delectable establishment. *"This patisserie serves the best Baba au rhum."*

"What's Baba au rhum?" I queried.

Eberhardt chimed, *"It is a yeast pastry soaked in a helluva lot of rum and brushed with apricot jam before being garnished with candied cherries and angelica."*

"Sounds decadent," **Andy commented.**

The model remarked, *"All the goodies here are freshly made, especially their tarte du citron. I love it, it's my favorite."*

It was challenging to make my choice since the pastries were mouthwateringly enticing. These delicacies seduced me to consume more than a piece. It is of little wonder that the phrase *"Qu'ils mangent de la brioche (Let them eat cake)"* was attributed to the French Queen Marie Antoinette; even though there is no official record of her having muttered the sentence.

As soon as we were comfortably seated, we chomped at our puffs, pies, and cakes.

Curt said to Samuel, *"Let me give you some insights to the comment you made - 'there are no gay people in the Arab world.'"*

Samuel stared at the professor with cream dripping off the corners of his mouth.

Eberhardt continued, *"Apparently, you are unaware of the homosexuality issues in the Middle East. You see, Muslim society is strongly patriarchal, and patriarchy by nature extols masculinity."*

He paused to observe the Junior who continued to gulp at his éclair.

The professor resumed, *"In the Quranic version of Paradise, there are not only seventy-two female virgins in attendance, but there is also an abundance of handsome young men who serve an endless supply of non-alcoholic drinks. Although it is not a sin to appreciate male beauty; same-sex admirations and relationships don't always stop at the platonic level.*

"Muslim societies have acknowledged and tolerated same-sex relationships in the past. In the 19th and early 20th centuries, European men who had been persecuted for their homosexuality often sought refuge in Morocco and in the remote Egyptian oasis of Siwa where male-on-male unions were recognized and marked with a 'life partnership' ceremony."

Curt looked to Driss for confirmation.

The French-Moroccan expressed, *"Many of my Caucasian friends who visited Morocco were struck by the sight of men holding hands in the street, especially soldiers in uniform. Even though several of my Moroccan male friends spend hours preening themselves, they are not* homosexuals. Very often it is a cross-cultural misunderstanding."

"That said, it is true that conservative Muslim countries encourage homosocial behavior, where men are often more comfortable in the presence of other men. For me when I place my hand on another man's knee, it is a sign of friendship and not necessarily an invitation to sex."

Eberhardt resumed, *"According to the muṭawwiʿūn, Arab men hug and kiss a lot. They ascertained that there is nothing wrong with same-sex kissing as long as there is 'no chance for any temptation.'"*

Helius questioned, *"Who or what are muṭawwiʿūn?"*

Andy informed, *"They are the Islamic religious police and official vice squad of the Islamic states who enforce Sharia law in respect to ethical and moral behaviors on behalf of their country. They are also referred to as mutaṭawwiʿa, and muṭṭawwiʿa."*

Curt recommenced, *"To promote virtue and prevent vice, the establishment of a religious police force is considered legitimate with the Quran doctrine. Even when opinions differ, and controversy exists on the function and purpose of this religious police bureau."*

Kaalib opined, *"I see the muṭawwiʿūn as an outdated over-conservative annoyance and a hindrance to my country's secularization."*

"Where are you from?" Eberhardt inquired.

"I live in Barcelona, but I was born in Saudi Arabia," the danseur replied before he voiced, *"I left Jeddah because of the restrictions. It includes sodomy and is punishable by death. And I am not gay."*

"You're not gay!" we chorused.

Our exclamation surprised the Eurasian.

He clarified, *"Just because I enjoy sex with men doesn't mean I am gay. The fact that a man has sex with another man has little to do with 'gayness.' For me, sex is a desirable fulfillment of a need. It does not constitute my identity, nor does it strip away my masculinity. Gays are 'bottoms,' and I am a 'top.' Therefore, I am not gay."*

"What kind of reasoning is that?" I countered.

The professor inculcated, *"When the sexes are strictly segregated, and Islamic laws forbid men to have little contact with women outside their families; it is not surprising that men turn to other men for sexual gratifications. This homo sexual behavior remains just that - an act, and not an orientation. That is not to say that Middle Eastern men who have sex with other men are freely tolerated, even though they are not automatically labeled deviant. The taxonomy revolved around the roles of 'top' and 'bottom,' with little stigma attached to the 'top.' Sexuality is distinguished not between homosexual and heterosexual but between taking pleasure and being used for gratification."*

Kaalib expounded, *"I play the role of a man by being a 'top,' and I'm in control. I set the tone. Hence, I'm not ashamed of having sex with a 'bottom.'"*

"I didn't feel threatened by my sexual orientation when I was stationed at the various Arabian households," I blurted.

Andy interjected before I could put my foot in my mouth. *"During our student exchange programme, we were stationed in royal and aristocratic households. Unlike plebeians, our aristocratic paterfamilias operates under a vastly different set of rules."*

Curt stepped in to verify, *"That is indeed correct. The Middle Eastern culture thrives in double standards and contradictions, especially for the haves and have-nots. Young, your educational experiences would differ immensely if you were stationed in median households."*

Driss adduced, *"When I was growing up in Marrakesh, I grew my hair long and wore glitzy costume jewelry; like the band members I saw in western rock and* roll magazines. My parents were horrified and warned that I would have a run-in with the authorities. True to their words, I was carted to the police station by a muṭṭawwiʿa.

"He took me to a back room and threatened me prison if I didn't give him a blowjob and let him plow me. I lied and insisted that I'm not a homosexual. He said he didn't give a damn what I did privately, as long as I do what he wants of me."

"And did you do what he demanded?" Samuel pressed.

The model nodded and turned away shamefully.

Eberhardt vociferated, "This demeaning view of sexual behavior, together with the strict segregation of the sexes, serves to foster unwarranted homosexual acts. It shifts the stigma onto 'bottoms' and permits older men to excuse their offensive behavior.

"A beardless adolescent is considered an object of beauty and desired by men. The youth would eventually grow into an older bearded man and in turn, desires adolescent males for gratification. Sexual practices in the Islamic world are not fixed into lifelong patterns of sexual orientation."

Samuel expressed, "In other words, I am correct; there are no gay people in the Arab world."

"Well, that's debatable. It is safe to say that homo sexuals are aplenty in Arab societies but to assert that there are no gay Arabians in that part of the world is spurious," the professor avowed.

"Family and society attitudes toward those who identify themselves as gay, lesbian and transgender are a much bigger issue. How families respond to a coming-out depends on several factors. It is mostly based on the person's social class and his/her family's level of education. In extreme cases, coming-out results in the person being ostracised or worse, being physically attacked.

"A lesser reaction is to seek a 'cure' through religion or in well-to-do families; through expensive but futile psychiatric treatments," the erudite professor dispensed.

"I can attest to that," Driss affirmed before he declared, *"When I told my brother I'm into men, he thought I prefer the company of males as friends and thought nothing of it. But when I confided that I am sexually attracted to men, he freaked out and threatened to tell my parents. I retracted my confession out of fear and professed that I've outgrown that inclination and am now a heterosexual."*

Helius questioned, *"How bizarre! Is that why you relocated to Paris?"*

"That's one of the reasons, but it is not the sole purpose for my relocation. There are a lot more modeling and acting jobs in Paris than Marrakech. Besides, I couldn't wait to leave my family. Otherwise, they'll pester me to marry," the French Moroccan explained.

Helius added, *"Why is same-sex love such a taboo in the Islamic world when it was once tolerated?"*

My Valet stated before Eberhardt could counsel. *"Like the Old Testament in Christianity, Muslim condemnations of homosexuality, are based on the story of God's punishment of Sodom and Gomorrah.*

"The difference is that over the last decade many Christians have taken a fresh look at this story and concluded that it's about attempted male rape and the ill-treatment of strangers, rather than consensual sex between males."

Curt injected, *"A few Muslim clerics are willing to reappraise this story. The point is, while the written words are fixed and unchangeable they are subject to human interpretation, and interpretations vary according to time, place and social conditions. This is what Muslim and Christian fundamentalists want to deny.*

"*It is a mistake to view homophobia as a self-contained problem even when Muslim societies are generally homophobic. It is a syndrome in which the individual rights are colligated in the perceived interests of the Islamic community and ethos. Muslim society places a high value on conformity and individuality are frowned upon. The Arabian patriarchal system plays a significant part in this issue when it comes to uphold social norms and to keep up appearances; at least in public but not necessarily in private. Gay men, especially those who show feminine traits are regarded as challenging the social order.*"

Kaalib inferred, "*Masculine men, like me who have sex with other men are viewed differently. Although state and traditional Islamic law consider the anal sex penetrator and the penetrated as equally culpable; popular opinions of the 'top' tend to be less hostile. He is a man, and he does what men naturally do, even if it is not with a woman. However, the 'bottom' is viewed with disgust. He behaves like a woman. Therefore, it is assumed that he is a prostitute because he is not doing it for pleasure.*"

"What an antithetical world we live in," I declared.

By now we had our fill. It was time to return to the Ritz for another fancy schmancy night out with our evening's hosts; the Ajman gentlemen - Rash and Amm.

Double Standards (Chapter Seventy-Two)

"I love Paris, and Paris loves us. We can be ourselves no matter what our sexual inclination."

Bernard Tristan Foong

March 1969
At *Le Train Bleu*, Paris, France

At the turn of the twentieth century, Paris received a significant new Universal Exhibition. After the grand Saint-Lazare train station, built in 1889, it was the Gare de Lyon's turn to take the appearance of a palace to showcase the new PLM Company (Paris Lyon Marseille) terminal; that operated lines of France Southeast network. This monumental task was entrusted to the architect Marius Toudoire, who had built the 64 meters belfry (the Clock-Tower) and the impressive façade of the station a few years prior. The PLM also wanted a prestigious restaurant to showcase the station's state-of-the-art technical innovation in luxury travel. In 1901, the buffet was unveiled by Emile Loubet, the then President of the French Republic.

Fast forward to 1963, Albert Chazal renamed the buffet as *Le Train Bleu (the Blue Train)* to honor the legendary Calais-Mediterranée Express; a luxury French night express train that operated from 1886 to 2003. Before the onset of World War II, the Calais-Mediterranée Express gained international recognition as the preferred transportation for the rich and famous between Calais and the French Riviera. The locomotive's dark blue sleeping compartments color became the designated hue for this top-of-the-line restaurant.

It was in *Le Train Bleu (The Blue Train)* that we were treated to a sumptuous dinner by the two Ajman gentlemen, Rash and Amm.

As soon as we entered the premise, Samuel, Helius, Andy and I gawked at the impressive artworks that lined its gilded walls by famous artists like François Flameng, Henri Gervex, Gaston Casimir Saint-Pierre, and René Billotte who painted views of Paris, and the Cote d'Azur. These paintings were priceless.

The maître d'hôtel greeted Prince P and Sheik Fahrib with gusto before he escorted our party to a private section of this opulent establishment.

The prince introduced his Emirati cousins to the maître d', Monsieur Gaétan Hector Giroux.

"*C'est son éminence, Rashid bin Abdullah Al Nuaimi et son frère Amman bin Ahmad al Nuaimi. Ils sont mes cousins royale de la famille régnante d'Ajman. Ils sont à Paris pour quelques semaines. Prendre bien soin d'eux* (This is His Eminence, Rashid bin Abdullah Al Nuaimi, and his brother Amman bin Ahmad Al Nuaimi. They are my royal cousins from the ruling family of Ajman. They are in Paris for a couple of weeks. Take good care of them)."

Up until then, neither Curt, Andy, or I had any knowledge that the Arabian brothers were Ajman royalties.

Monsieur Giroux pronounced excitedly, "*Bienvenue, bienvenue dans notre humble établissement cheiks.* (Welcome, welcome sheiks to our humble establishment)."

He added, "*Merci, merci, votre Altesse, d'introduction de ces illustres invités à notre restaurant* (Thank you, thank you, your Highness, for introducing these illustrious guests to our restaurant)."

As soon as we were seated, we thanked the Ajman royals for their opulent gifts before I enquired, *"Sirs, are you enjoying Paris?"*

"Very much!" Amm replied. *"It is nice to be away from Ajman. It's a small city, and tongues wag when our backs are turned."*

"What do they wag about?" I queried.

"About me and my brother."

Before my Valet could interrupt. I blurted, *"What about your brother and you?"*

The Arab answered troublingly, *"They muse over our closeness. We go everywhere together."*

Andy posed before I could continue, *"Of course, the both of you are close. You are brothers."*

Amm sniggered before he responded without constraint, *"They think we are more than that."*

Eberhardt remarked, *"I'm sure your denizens propagate the magnanimity you, your brother and your family are doing for your country."*

Prince P declared unreservedly, *"We can be candid since we are of like-minded proclivities."*

Rash championed, *"It is such a relief to be me in Paris. I don't have to pretend to be a heterosexual. Ajman is too conservative. Like you, P; Rash and I should buy an apartment in Paris, so we can escape our family's travails."*

Amm seconded his brother's proposition.

"If you don't already know, Rash and Amm are a couple; like P and me," Fahrib promulgated.

Eberhardt indicated, *"There are four couples around this table; except for the Count, Tad and me."*

"In that case, we can speak our minds," the sheik declared.

The professor questioned, *"What happened to that liberal society of yesteryears where Arab literature, poetry, and prose are filled with explicit homoerotic poems and romantic stories of homosexual encounters."*

"Eberhardt, there are no clear-cut answers to your question. My response would be to blame the exegetes (interpreters of scripture), and jurists (creators of law) for condemning homosexual acts," the sheik opined.

Rash commented, *"Fahrib, although your assessment is partially correct, there is no reason to think that exegetes and jurists alone define what is 'Islamic.' What people think and do are vastly different from what the laws say they can or cannot perform."*

Amm injected, *"To my knowledge, there are no philosophical studies to give us a definitive idea on the percentage of homosexuals, bisexuals, lesbians, and transsexuals in the Arab population. Since the majority of us are hiding behind a veil of secrecy. Personally, I think our kind is on the rise."*

"What makes you think that?" P expressed.

"As our erudite professor pointed out, homosexual practices have been around since the beginning of man. Even though we are driven underground or hidden from view, people like us don't disappear." Amm answered.

He re-commenced, *"As you are aware, one of the greatest Arab poets of all time, Abu Nuwas, was famous for his homoerotic poems. He praised and rued the charms of boys and described his homosexual encounters unambiguously."*

Tad remarked, *"Didn't Abu Nuwas live during the period when the Islamic world was ruled by an openly gay ruler, Caliph Al-Amin? Stories of his male harem abound."*

"That's correct," **Curt** confirmed.

The prince stated, *"For centuries, Islamic societies from Morocco to China had sexual landscapes as diverse as the lands they were built on. Multiple sexual behaviors have existed as long as Islam itself."*

Count Mario who had remained a silent listener, commented, *"The idea that sex should only occur between two married heterosexuals is a relatively recent norm and one that came about during the Westernization process in the late nineteenth century."*

"When 'homosexuality' first appeared as a medical term in the late eighteen hundred, it was appropriate to speak of homoeroticism in Islamic societies. This topic was not considered taboo. Homoeroticism and homoerotic behavior were found everywhere from the ostentatious caliph's court to the humblest Sufi lodge," the doctor affirmed.

"Why is it prohibited and banned in Islamic societies now?" I questioned.

Rash explicated, *"Generally, Muslims and non-Muslims who claim that the Quran condemns homosexuality have relied on the story of 'Lot's folk' as their foundation for homophobia. However, the Quranic narrative can be interpreted in different ways. Even though many exegetes claim that the 'deed of Lot's folk' was homosexual behavior, there are no verses in the Quran that give a legal punishment for either homoerotic inclinations or behaviors. Some Muslims have argued that the condemned action is rape rather than homosexuality. Yet, there are those of our faith who ascertain verses of the Quran as carrying homoerotic allusions, such as those describing Allah's Paradise."*

Amm irradiated, *"There are non-Quranic Islamic scriptures that speak of a group of men in the Prophet Muhammad's city, Medina, known as the mukhannaths. These men have been labeled differently; from homosexuals, transgender women, intersex individuals, bisexuals, and hermaphrodites. But the actual identities of the mukhannaths remain unclear. What is evident is that mukhannaths have no sexual desires for women. In Medinan society, they were allowed access to women's private spaces. This gave them the social power to act as matchmakers."*

"The mukhannaths are said to have lived in the Prophet's city during his lifetime and after. As far as I know, they remained a staple of Islamic society well into the Abbasid period; two hundred years after the Prophet's death. It was during this era when the creators of Islamic scripture began to document polemical and condemnatory commentaries against the mukhannaths as an attempt to regulate public sexuality. The fact that the exegetes and jurists made an effort to do this implies the vast diversity of sexual life in medieval Islamic societies," Tad averred.

My Valet, curious of the Ajman brothers consanguinity, probed, *"Is incestuous relationship permitted in Islam?"*

Amm detected my chaperone's cognition. He explained, *"Andy, you'll be surprised by what I'm to tell you. In Islam, there is a religious rule that is taught and upheld by prominent Islamic scholars that incest is approved within its theology."*

The Ajman's proclamation came as an eye-opener for the non-Arabs in our party.

Fahrib divulged, *"In accordance to the authentic teaching of Islam, a Muslim man is permitted to marry and consummate the marriage with his biological daughter if she was conceived illegitimately.*

"Surah 25:54 states: It is He Who has created man from water: then has He established relationships of lineage and marriage: for thy Lord has power over all things."

"Wait, let me analyze this Islamic rule carefully. You are saying that in accordance to the authentic teachings of Islamic scholars and the teachings of Islam, a daughter born under wedlock is not considered the daughter of the man? Consequently, it is permissible for him to marry her? As a result, the daughter is regarded as

an unrelated woman, and Islam permits the marriage between the father and his biological daughter conceived through fornication and/or adultery? What type of reasoning and justification is that?" Eberhardt questioned.

Tad blazoned, "I'd long ago realized that the religion I'm born into is absurd. Islam's logic is like saying - it is a crime to drive recklessly and injure someone if you possess a valid driving license. But if you do not own a valid driving license and drive dangerously and hurt someone, then it becomes a crime. Likewise, not having a legal marital status (marriage license) justifies the father to have sex with his illegitimate daughter. To me, these religious dogmas are a bunch of baloney. They are created by fanatical zealots to free men from their crimes and to have their way with women."

He continues to vociferate vexedly, "How can an illegal act, adultery, make another unlawful act, incest, lawful? How can the sin of adultery nullify the crime of incest and make it an acceptable action? I'm afraid two wrongs do not make a right. How does having a daughter from an adulterous relationship make her sexually permissible for the father when she is his flesh and blood? In my books, she is his biological child and should be sexually off-limits to her old man. This violation of the divine standard of morality is beyond my comprehension."

Amm declared, "But there are no rules for brothers, sisters, mothers and sons, mothers and daughters to have intimate relationships. This is mind-boggling to me."

The Ajman turned to Andy and said mischievously, "Since there are no religious rules for or against two brothers being intimate; Rash and I are free to be lovers."

Rash remarked roguishly. "Even if the secular world considers our love sacrilegious, we keep our intimacy confidential. Present company excluded."

I chimed, *"No wonder you find Paris liberating. We love Paris and Paris loves us. We can be ourselves no matter what our sexual inclination."*

As if it was our last supper, we dipped into our cuisine with one of Amm's hand resting on my thigh and Andy's palm on my other.

The Anatomy of Unconditional Love
(Chapter Seventy-Three)

"The most powerful weapon on earth is the human soul on fire."

Ferdinand Foch

Early April 2015
Andy's Private Message to Me

Young,

Sorry to hear of David's passing. I sent Jacob an email and condolence card. If he requires guidance and help, I'll be there for him too.

Today, I received unanticipated news from my physician. Do you recall that some time ago, I mentioned to you about my bladder problems? After several Cat-Scans, blood and urine tests; Doctor Phillip told me I have CKD (Chronic Kidney Disease). Although there are treatments to slow the progression of this infection, it is an incurable disease. Eventually, I will require dialysis or a kidney transplant to survive.

After my regular rowing and workout exercises, I often feel dizzy, dyspnea and tired. I thought I was overworking my body. With the onslaught of this malice, I have to be more assiduous with my diet. I have to control the amount of protein, sodium, potassium, and phosphorus intake. If my kidney worsens, I'll need to limit some other nutrients as well. I am determined to overcome this virulence even though this piece of information has cast a shadow over me.

I like to know what you've been up to lately rather than dwell on this scathing issue? It is always a pleasure to read your sanguine stories of lust, love and more. ☺ It diverts my attention to those halcyon days we shared oh-so-long-ago.

I look forward to your correspondence.

Love,
Andy
XOXOXO

June 1969
At Daltonbury Hall, England

The months flew by after our return from The City of Romance. Paris had given the Junior and the Freshman a taste of Eudaimonia they envisaged my Valet, and I lived. Although there was a lot to be said for the world we inhabited, it was a demanding world where the survival of the fittest maneuvered through as if with ease and grace. Little were the uninitiated aware of the astuteness, dexterity, and sagacity that went on behind the scenes. As Shakespeare wrote so eloquently:

All the world's a stage,
And all the men and women merely players;
They have their exits and their entrances,
And one man in his time plays many parts....

That was precisely what transpired that evening at *Le Train Bleu*. Besides being a guardian and chaperone to Samuel and Helius, I had to disport the flirtatious Ajman gentlemen without appearing standoffish. Atop that, Andy's tacit covetousness of *moi* kept me on my toes. Not just for that evening but for the final months before our separation.

By and large, the Count and our Arabian patriarchs took heed of my Valet's counsel and kept their hands off the adolescents. Helius, the natural flirt had the men in sexual teeters; especially Rash, who lusted after both the Freshman and his doting boyfriend.

On the one hand, Andy and I had to tread with caution not to ruffle the libertines. We had to protect our charges' dignities; at least until they are ripe for the picking – i.e., after the boys' acceptance into the Enlightened Royal Oracle Society and the completion of their three months Bahriji erotic training. Only then were they ready for harem services. Until that time, they were off limits to the Arabian courtiers. Except for the Italian playboy, Mario, who did not fall under the E.R.O.S. jurisdiction. While in the City of love, this philanderer took the opportunity to solicit a photoshoot with the adolescents.

The Junior and Freshman were flattered by the photographer's proposition and agreed to pose for Mario's *Sacred Sex in Sacred Places* erotic project. Andy and I shepherded the adolescents to the shoot since we were featured in this endeavor. Although the boys had no idea that my Valet and I were scrutinizing their conduct to add to their E.R.O.S. acceptance prospects, their artful eroticism won us over.

Needless to say, in the Fall of 1969, the clandestine organization warranted both boys acceptance into the Enlightened Royal Oracle Society. They were overjoyed by the fraternity's proclamation and were eager to start their new term at the elite Bahriji (Oasis) Academy.

Since my Valet and I had steered the once rascally Samuel back on track, I was officially entrusted Big Brothership duties to assist both Helius and Samuel through their Bahriji training. Although Dean Dawson Higgins (Daltonbury Hall's headmaster) and several E.R.O.S. professors implored Andy to stay and be Samuel's Valet, they were well aware that he was to leave for New Zealand to pursue his graduate studies. Hence, Marcus, an able E.R.O.S. Big-Brother was assigned the task as Sam's chaperone.

The few months before Andy and my separation, our relationship fluctuated from conflagrations to pacifications. Our lovemaking was fiercely impassioned when ardencies took flight, but discordance abounded when ambivalence seized the day. Like untamed forest fires, our sanguinities would scorch and charred our sanity beyond recognition. During those trying times, promises that we would visit each other during semester breaks kept us lucid. Although these pledges were made in good faith, they did not materialize. Breaking up was indeed hard to do even if done amicably.

Aboard the *Ship*

Andy and I had numerous conversations during those final months, but I recall this particular dialogue that transpired on the first day of our 1969 Daltonbury Hall summer holidays. We were aboard the *Ship* (Sheik Fahrib's private jet) that flew both my ex-tutors, Monsieur Alain Dubois, Senor Victor Angel Triqueros, and my ex-Valet Zac, together with Andy and me to Amsterdam to Jabril Zev Saliba (Sheik Fahrib's private secretary) and Kifah bint Mustapha Khan's (Sheik Fahrib's second wife, Roya's lady-in-waiting) lavish wedding.

Lust and Love

"*I* wonder if Jabril is genuinely in love with Kifah or is he marrying her to fulfill his filial duties to his parents?" Zac inquired.

Dubois remarked, *"I think he is marrying her out of lust. After all, he got her pregnant, and to legitimize their illegal union he has to be a gentleman and marry the girl."*

"The way I view it; the man is killing two birds with one stone. On the one hand, he is fulfilling his family duty, but he is also using the marriage as a facade for his secret tryst. If you ask me, there is more fire than stability," Victor surmised.

"You might be right, Angel. Genuine love is about communication and commitment. Both are crucial components of a secure relationship. Although passion is very much a part of the equation, when there are lots of drama, chaos and emotional gut blows than butterflies; it is a lustful situation," Andy expressed vehemently.

When I paused to assess my lover and my situation of late, there were indeed a lot of dramas, chaos and emotional gut blows than butterflies.

I directed my question to Andy. *"Does that mean our relationship is built on lust instead of love since we have an abundance of drama, chaos and emotional gut blows than butterflies, lately?"*

"What makes you think that?" Andy responded shockingly.

The men looked at us bewildered and wondered what had transpired between my lover and me.

I resumed, *"At times you will stare at me and tell me how gorgeous, fabulous and flawless I am; but later you'll turn on me as if you're facing a hideous monster."*

My lover did not respond to my unexpected proclamation. Dubois jumped to his aid.

"Young, anyone who's been in love can attest that love is unconditional and Andy's love for you is definitely unconditional," Alain soothed.

Triqueros who sensed Andy and my unease, counseled, *"Young when you're in love, you want to share your dreams, fears, goals, past, and your future with your* beloved. You'll confide secrets you've never told anyone before. Not only are you sharing minor and significant decisions together, but the issues the both of you are facing also become more profound and personal in nature."

Andy reclaimed his equipoise and stated, "As my departure draws closer by the day, my emotions are frazzled. It is difficult to accept the fact that you are not coming with me to New Zealand. It is easy to say that true love has no expectations, but when push comes to shove, parting is extremely hard to do."

My pragmatic lover broke down in tears. The compassionate Dubois put his arms around my guardian to comfort his dis-ease. I was also close to tears.

My guardian uttered through sobs. "It's not that I don't have empathy for Young to follow his dreams and make a success of his aspiration in the fashion capitals of the world. I want the best for him. Yet, the thought of life without him propels me into a state of discombobulation. I am mad at myself when I turn unreasonable and lose control of my rationale. I lash out at the person I cherish the most and hurt my beloved when the sense of abandonment hits me. As soon as this negativity subsides, I regret my actions. This emotional roller coaster is taking a toll on me."

My heart reached out to my gallant lover. Tears rolled down my cheeks.

Victor consoled, "Andy, you are too hard on yourself. Don't forget that love is joy, contentment, and satisfaction and the absence of fear and insecurities. Cherish the beautiful times you have with one another and will share again when you reunite."

Alain palliated, "Love doesn't play the role of a victim or blame others for their decisions. More significantly, love doesn't think their loved ones are wrong. Love works together for the lovers' common good. It *forgives and allows your beloved's actions to be his journey."*

"*Andy if you love Young, you must set him free to pursue his life's path. If he chooses to return to you, the love that the both of you share will be stronger and more resilient. True love does not possess. On the contrary, set the boy free and when the time is ripe, the universe will bring him back to you.*

"*Needing someone is fear based but wanting that person in your life gives him the freedom to leave, and it demonstrates your unconditional love for him,*" Zac appeased.

"*Well put, Zac. Love is the highest emotional vibration and science has proven that love and fear have profoundly different vibrational frequencies. Love pulsates extremely fast, whereas fear-based emotions, such as jealousy, possessiveness, hatred, so on and so forth oscillate slowly. Fearlessness happens when you love completely and unconditionally. If you channel and remain focused on love's heartfelt sentiment, its reverberations will lighten your dis-ease,*" Triqueros enjoined.

"*I know these are trying times for you and Young. When pangs of uncertainties seep into both your minds, remember that love is unconditional. And there are no set expectations and limitations to unconditional love.*

"*We are all dissimilar. Each person has different experiences and outlooks to what he/she wish to accomplish during his/her lifetime. Andy, if you genuinely love Young, understand and accept his desire to stay in London and Paris to enter the fashion world. Support his aspirations and in turn, Young; you must champion Andy's engineering goal to be internationally successful wherever he chooses to relocate,*" Alain adjured.

Our discussion was cut short when the air steward announced for us to buckle up for landing at *Schiphol*.

The Wedding (Chapter Seventy-Four)

"Marriage is neither heaven nor hell, it is simply purgatory."

Abraham Lincoln

June 1969
Kasteel de Haar (De Haar Castel), Utrecht, Netherlands

In the enchanting month of June 1969, the nuptials of Kifah bint Mustapha Khan, and Jabril Zev Saliba took shape in and out of *Kasteel de Haar,* the largest castle in the Netherlands. Back then, it was the private residence of the Van Zuylen family. Behind this medieval fortress with its imposing towers, ramparts, moats, gates, drawbridges, colorful gardens, and winsome deer parks were captivating tales of forbidden love, gripping romances, and clandestine affaires de coeur. Coco Chanel, Brigitte Bardot, Maria Callas, Gregory Peck, Yves Saint Laurent, Joan Collins, Roger Moore together with a host of other celebrities had left their marks in its magnificent halls.

In 1887, when Baron Etienne van Zuylen van Nijevelt, married Hélène de Rothschild, of the Rothschild family; the interior of this once opulent castle was in ruins. With Hélène's inheritance, the couple set to rebuild and restore the castle with the help of Pierre Cuypers, the famous Dutch architect who had designed and built the Amsterdam Central Station, and the Rijksmuseum. By the time *Kasteel de Haar* was refurbished to its former glory, the 200 rooms and 30 bathrooms were the most resplendent in the Netherlands.

It was at this fairy-tale property that the gnostic, Jabril and the Muslim, Kifah signed a legal marriage contract which they would later regret. But on that sunny morning, beneath a host of ancient statuettes and amidst an abundance of blossoming blooms; the ethos of romance had encircled the bridal couple to surmise that their match was indeed made in heaven.

Little did the callow Kifah realize that Islamic marriages are not adjudged to be made in heaven or soul-mates destined for each other; but social contracts that provided rights and obligations to the involved parties. And these moral imperatives can only be successful if they were mutually respected and cherished. Unfortunate for this girlish lady-in-waiting, her marriage expectations were made within the mind and lacked intimacy. She saw the handsome Jabril as a fairytale prince charming who would dote over her every wish without reciprocations. She also envisioned a life of endless romance, passion, and affinity that automatically came with marriage.

On the contrary, the strapping Muslim-Jew regarded his nuptial as an obligation. After all, he had gotten the girl pregnant, and the right thing a gentleman would do was to marry her so the forthcoming child would not be deemed a bastard. Nor would the woman be considered an outcast if he had abandoned his responsibility. For Jabril, love did not enter the nuptial equation but obligations to his soon-to-be wife and parents; to provide an heir to continue his family's genealogy. As far as he was concerned, this union was also a legal façade to camouflage his bisexuality. He saw no reason to discontinue his philandering after the completion of his filial duties.

The Ceremony

When Andy and I arrived at the grand hall, hundreds of guests were already ensconced in their assigned seats. Andy's departure to Christchurch after the wedding had cast a foreboding shadow over us. Like Siamese twins, we were inseparable. Our fiery intimacy had grown intense during the weeks that led up to Jabril and Kifah's nuptials. Unlike the bridal couple whose relationship was based on private reveries; Andy and my union were of collective hearts, minds, and souls. Over the years, our camaraderie had amalgamated into oneness. The more impassioned our amorousness, the more grueling it was to say our final farewell.

When the wedding couple uttered their "I Dos," within the walls of this primordial hall; my lover and I broke into sorrowful sobs. We held each other's quivering hands as anguished tears trickled down our cheeks. We wept in silence. Little were we cognizant that we were about to sacrifice the potent enamoredness we had shared so resplendently. The love that many seek but granted to few. Even these utopian halls of romanticism could not mend our shattered dreams of living happily ever after.

Back then, my lover and I were too ambitious, and career-driven to settle for anything less but to succeed in our chosen métiers. We thought true love would find us if we sauntered by but this unique flowering waits for no one, and certainly not for those who decide to forgo this once-in-a-lifetime opportunity. Yet my lover and I charged full steam ahead on our resolutions. Decisions that would eventually crash us like a ton of bricks as I documented in *A Harem Boy's Saga – book II – Unbridled; a memoir by Young*.

The Reception

Under a majestic outdoor tent, resplendent guests sipped the finest champagne, alcoholic beverages and savored gourmet cuisine served on silver platters prepared by a three-star Michelin chef. The groom who was born and raised in the Netherlands wanted a westernized nuptial, and the bride who had dreamed of a Disneyesque fairytale wedding was more than happy to oblige. Hence, an occidental celebration was appropriated to the Amsterdamian. To appease the bride and her esteemed Saudi family, an elaborate Islamic jamboree would be held after the Amsterdam bash. Not only would the Riyadh ceremony showcase Kifah's family's social standing, but it also provided the bride with another opportunity to don her many haute couture ensembles that were specifically designed for her special day.

That late afternoon, *Kasteel de Haar* was ablaze with an idyllic glow. The evening sun had cast a gleaming radiance over this palatial estate. **When the party was in full swing, Andy and I slipped away. We wanted to relive our time in Holland's picturesque parks mainly in the Keukenhof Gardens where we had attained** Sahasrāra ("thousand-petaled" – White Lotus). My lover held my hand as we ventured away from the madding crowd. As soon as we disappeared into the serene gardenscape, our heavy hearts grew lighter.

Like carefree children, we discarded our formal attires and bounced around joyously. We soared like blithe fletching through this glorious field of dreams before we collapsed atop one another in a loving embrace. My lover gazed at me as if he desired this enchantment never to end. Unwilling to relinquish the affection we had fostered over the years I held onto his sinewy physique. Once again, woeful tears welled in our eyes before our playfulness gave way to a lingering kiss. Our lips brushed tenderly against one another as if it was our first osculation. The rhythmic silent of our oral dance soon gave way to Andy's dominance. His hypnotic greenish blues never left my gaze as I gave in to his supremacy. I was at once bewitched and bewildered by his sanguine amorousness. My Valet, chaperone, guardian, and mentor would soon be oceans away. I wanted to ravish my handsome beau and to cherish this dazzling moment as if our intimacy would never end. Time stood still as we traverse to rediscover love's transient beauty.

Neither of us desired our closeness to cease as our palpitating hardness drummed in synchronicity. We wanted our souls to envelop us in an inextricable cocoon of devotion. Unable to defy our urgencies Andy eased into my unbridled sanctity. To sanction nature's potency to govern his quivering bulbousness, we remained unmoved. Not only did our nonaction ignite my yearning pruriency, but his pulsations had also aroused my debaucherous concupiscence to pleasure his intemperance. We merged into the Oneness of Being as our imperceptible gyrations catapulted us to precipices of ineffable moksha. As we journeyed through love's expansive mindscape, a nonspatial continuum of events occurred in constant succession. The past, present, and future flashed through our minds eyes. Within this Aleph of timelessness, our intimacy magnified a thousand-fold. Neither of us desired to renounce our fruits of verboten pleasures in this heavenly garden of earthly delights. Yet all good things must end no matter how disinclined we were to conserve those treasured moments. Even though we knew this was the final residuum of our consecrated union, Andy's forceful potencies claimed my sacredness as our heightened eroticism impelled us across the Rubicon.

I spilled my venerated blest into his oral fissure when I straddled my lover's muscular chest. As if my seeds were Eucharist divinity, he savored my sacrosanctity with reverence. We remained buried in the confines of each other's bosom until the first light of dawn reminded us that we would soon be separated permanently. Only then did we return to the castle in the hope that time would stand still for us to relive that nirvanic state of Sahasrāra.

Emptiness (The Final Chapter)

"The inner emptiness is the door to God."

Swami Dhyan Giten

Early April 2015
My Response to Andy's Private Message

Dearest Andy,

I am saddened by your news. I hope you are coping well with your CKD treatment. You are a resilient man, and I am sure you will overcome this virulence.

After your departure to Christchurch, I was devastated by your absence. I made it through those difficult times. Like me, you are an irrepressible survivor, and you will trump this complication.

That June 1969 afternoon, after Monsieur Alain Dubois, Señor Victor Angel Triqueros and I saw you off at Amsterdam airport, emptiness overshadowed my person. I could not stop crying. I would have drowned my sorrows with alcohol and drugs, if not for Alain and Victor. That sense of inner emptiness left me emotionally numb, anxious, despondent, and isolated. I was at a loss. Self-doubt and a lack of purpose seeped in like the world had crashed on me. That heaviness drained my energy. Thoughts of catching the next flight to New Zealand did enter my mind. It was Dubois and Triqueros who stopped me.

Before Alain and I boarded our respective flights to Paris and London, my ex-tutors counseled me at the *Schiphol* first-class lounge.

"Young, I know you are lost without Andy, and you feel like a stranger to yourself." Alain commented before he resumed, *"It is okay to cry because our emotions are an essential aspect of our experience. If we refuse to acknowledge these sentiments, they will lurk in the shadows of our minds and obstruct our emotions. It will eventually cut us off from ourselves."*

Victor added, *"That would be devastating. We have a pulse, but we are not really 'alive.' We'll experience feelings of emptiness."*

Even though I nodded in acknowledgment, I was absorbed in my desolation and continued to weep.

Triqueros consoled, *"I'll give you some suggestions. Hopefully, these tips will help you out of your miserable state."*

I stared at the professor blankly.

He spoke, *"Young, you're an extraordinary individual. Your purpose springs from that uniqueness and your E.R.O.S. education provided you with a solid sense of who you are. I understand that during this challenging time, it is hard to be in touch with your purpose but remember...."* He paused before he recommenced, *"You have a unique narrative, and you are the star of that story. Do not look outside the self for your sense of purpose but search within for the answer."*

Alain added, *"Your authentic self is the person who cries when you're sad and laughs when you're tickled. At this very instant, it is your authenticity who wish to inhabit the void you are experiencing. The self wants to fill you with purpose, meaning, and connection. I propose you ask yourself how you'll feel if you weren't feeling empty? Do a checklist on your past, present, and future. Emptiness, disappointment, and despair are temporary numbing blankets to protect you from sliding into depression.*

"Embrace your current emotions. Although feelings aren't exactly a part of you, they are a genuine reflection of

you at this point. How you feel in any given moment is the map that connects you with your authentic self. By all means, wallow in your emotions. But remember that curiosity and compassion is the recovery from emptiness. Not judgment."

Victor championed, *"Share your feelings with others like you are doing with us. A grief support group will help you fill the void, but do not regret or shame yourself with the decisions you've made. Remember, there are no right or wrong choices. A choice does not judge. It is the person who made the determination that judges. My advice to you is to hold up an allegorical mirror to help you appreciate the authentic you, the person you really are. You deserve a great relationship and a purposeful life with yourself. This emptiness is a griefing phase and will pass in due course."*

Śūnyatā (Emptiness)

Unable to contain myself, I continued to bawl.

My teacher put his arms around me and said, *"My dear boy, look at it this way. In my Zentology awareness, emptiness is a mode of perception, a method of looking at experience. It adds nothing to or takes away anything from the raw data of physical and mental events. Without judgment, you discern the facts and senses within the mind. This 'emptiness' approach is void of assumptions to explain the stories and worldviews we fashion to define who you are and the world you live in."*

The Zentologist paused to see if I understood his exegesis.

He resumed, *"Although our stories and views have their uses; the questions raised, and your perceived reality distracts you from the experience of the present. Therefore,* the adjudged fact gets in the way when you try to understand and solve your dis-ease."

Since I had no idea to Dubois' explication, I stared at the professor puzzlingly.

Alain, conscious of my obfuscation, explicated, "Let me give you an example: you are meditating, and an angry resentment towards your father appears. The mind's immediate reaction identifies the vexation as 'my' indignation, and say, 'I'm' outraged. It then amplifies on the feeling by working it into the story of your relationship with your father and to your overviews about when and where your displeasures towards your dad are justified.

"The problem is that these stories and views entail a lot of anguish. The more you get involved in your mind's stories, the more distracted you are from seeing the actual cause of your agony. Labels such as 'I,' 'me' and 'mine' set the entire process in motion. As a result, you have difficulty unraveling the cause that brought on the pain and to terminate the anger once and for all."

I questioned, *"How can I stop this unpleasantness permanently?"*

"Simple!" Alain exclaimed.

I looked at the erudite professor for clarification.

"By adopting the emptiness mode and not acting on or reacting to the agony. By observing it as a series of events - in and of themselves. You will realize that the dis-ease is empty of any identification or possession. When you master the emptiness mode, you'll automatically register that this truth holds not just for emotions like indignations, but also for subtle events in the realm of our experience," Dubois advised.

Victor injected, *"Śūnyatā is the sense in which all things are empty. Once you comprehend Śūnyatā, you will realize that labels like 'I,' 'me,' and 'mine' are inconsequential and unnecessary. These ego-driven tags do nothing but create stress and pain. Discard them completely, and you'll discover an experience that will wholly free you from pain."*

"How do I master Śūnyatā?" I pressed.

"To master this emptiness approach of perception requires training in virtue, concentration, and discernment. Without these practices, the mind will continue to stay in the manner that keeps creating stories and worldviews. From the Śūnyatā perspective, the teaching of emptiness merely sounds like another story or worldview with new ground rules," Triqueros stated.

Victor paused before he continued, *"Though stories and worldviews do serve a purpose; dis-ease comes from the perceptions of a person's actions, and the freedom from pain comes from being more insightful.*

"Focus on the quality of the consciousness and intentions within the mind in the present. In other words, get the self into Śūnyatā. Once you are in that realm, apply the Śūnyatā teachings for your intended purpose - to detach all attachments to views, stories, assumptions, and leave the mind empty of disillusionment. Only then can you nullify dis-ease, anger, and stress. The emptiness that holds your current unhappiness is also the key to your enlightenment."

I perked up and chirped, *"You are telling me that the flip side of emptiness is contentment?"*

Both sages nodded in unison before they concluded.

"Young, when you see a plum blossom or hear the sound of a small stone hitting bamboo, that is a letter from the world of emptiness," Victor declared equitably before Alain finalized, *"To empty is not the same as to deny. When we reject something, we want to replace it with something else. The effort is to be rid of self-centeredness. This is the secret to cleanse our experience from dis-ease."*

The Monsieur, the Señor and I held each other's hands before the announcements to board our respective flights came over the intercom. That was the last I saw of my two erudite teachers.

My dearest Andy, here we are, forty-nine years to date. Again, I find myself in a state of discombobulation by the news of your life-threatening health issues. Walter and I pray for your rapid recovery and be in excellent health for a long time to come. My dear friend, keep us posted on your progress.

      Love and hugs,
      Young
      XOXOXO

Epilogue

"Keep love in your heart. A life without it is like a sunless garden when the flowers are dead."

Oscar Wilde

Moi

The months following Andy's departure, I plunged myself into work. Not only did I graduate with a magnum cum laude from Daltonbury Hall School for Boys, but I also drove full steam ahead as Samuel and Helius' prudent Big-Brother. I mentored and groomed the new E.R.O.S. recruits to the best of my ability. When the boys were assigned to their first Arabian Household – *Alqalea (The Castle)*, the official residence of the two Ajman aristocrats, Rash and Amm; I handed the reins to their respective Valets, Marcus and Anthony.

With my responsibilities behind me, I applied to several Art and Design colleges in the United Kingdom. I was accepted into The Belfast College of Art & Technology, Northern Ireland for a two-year Foundation course. Although in the early days of Andy and my separation, we corresponded regularly; that nagging emptiness never left my person. The harder I worked on my allotted tasks, the more depressed I became. There were many nights I cried myself to sleep. When morning broke, I had joined the ranks of the walking dead.

The nights I suffered from insomnia, I visited egregious places I shouldn't have; in the hope of finding that which was amiss in my heart, Not only did I not find love, but I also descended into the underbelly of the gay BDSM world. The months following my departure from the nurturing bosom of the Enlightened Royal Oracle Society, I was confronted with the harsh reality of life. Although I stayed in the posh side of town at Uncle James' residence; I would venture to sleazy sex clubs for a night of debaucherous exploits before I headed back to respectable Mayfair for another day of mainstream activities. As much as I kept my sordid sexcapades a secret, prying eyes were hard to avoid; especially when Charles (James R. Pinkerton's butler) and I lived under the same roof. It was a matter of time before he disclosed my nightly comings and goings to my judicious surrogate father.

My English guardian sat me down for a heart-to-heart talk. Thanks to divine intervention, my Belfast College of Art & Technology acceptance letter arrived a day after our critical discussion. Not only was Mr. Pinkerton elated for my future college undertaking, but he also realized that time away from London would be beneficial for my sexual addiction recovery; especially in war-torn Belfast where little to no nightlife existed, due to the Northern Ireland conflict. My time in Northern Ireland was indeed a blessing in disguise. I plunged into my fashion design studies with newfound enthusiasm. I had a strong fashion portfolio on hand by the end of my first year at Belfast College of Art & Technology. Ms. Emily Keens, the fashion counselor at my school supported my application to one of London's renowned fashion schools - The Harrow College of Art & Technology.

Thanks to Ms. Keens and Uncle James' recommendation letters; Professor Lipman, the then head of Harrow College fashion department and the eccentric fashion lecturer, Ms. Gay Yates whom I had met several years prior at Le Gavroche, accepted *moi* into the fashion programme without delay. No longer inundated with melancholic hypersexuality, I returned to London, a changed man. I careered head-on into my fashion education with a renewed passion.

Under the skillful guidance of Harrow's fashion professors, I graduated with honors in 1974 before being accepted into the prestigious London Royal College of Art to further my Master of Design. In 1976, I graduated as a full-fledged fashion designer with ten job offers under my belt. To put it mildly, the rest is history. A history that I will document in my next autobiographical series – *Life After A Harem Boy's Saga; a memoir by Young.*

Andy

After our separation, Andy's life was not altogether comfortable. Like me, he drove into his passion like a fish to water. He came up trumps in his selected career and excelled in many engineering successes. But the both of us failed miserably when it came to love. Neither my ex-lover nor I recovered from our severance. Although we had other loves, none came close to the erotic transcendence we experienced during our four years together. We were soulmates destined for each other, but our determinations to make a mark at our chosen métiers tore us apart. By the time we realized that true love held not just the key to our aspirations, but it also succors the bond to a meaningful relationship; that opportunity had passed us by. Life had moved on. By then we had pressing responsibilities and obligations that were too preposterous for us to omit.

In a person's lifetime, true love is known to strike once, and cupid seldom knocks twice. Since I reconnected with my ex-lover six years ago, our newfound friendship had brought us closer than we ever imagine. Although love continues to shackle us, our affection had morphed to faithful comradeship than romantic intimacy.

Although Andy recovered from his CKD (Chronic Kidney Disease) setback in 2015, he also fell in love with Jumiro, the Japanese nurse who nursed him back to health at St Vincent's Hospital, Sydney. In the summer of 2017, they married and planned for a second home in Sapporo, Japan.

Before their intentions could be realized, Andy suffered another health crisis. His CKD had deteriorated, and a kidney replacement was urgently required for him to survive. Ari came to the rescue. He generously proffered one of his kidneys to his younger brother. My ex is in surgery as I write this epilogue. Without a doubt, the outcome will be brought to light when I document *Life After A Harem Boy's Saga; a memoir by Young*. The follow-up series to *A Harem Boy's Saga; a memoir by Young*. At this juncture, neither I nor anyone knows the result of Andy's well-being except the man himself.

As a fitting conclusion to my autobiographical series, I apposite the dialogue below between Mufasa and Simba in *The Lion King*.

Mufasa: *Everything you see exists together in a delicate balance. As a king, you need to understand that the balance and respect all the creatures; from the crawling ant to the leaping antelope.*

Simba: *But, Dad, don't we eat the antelope?*

Mufasa: *Yes, Simba, but let me explain. When we die, our bodies become the grass, and the antelope eat the grass. And so, we are all connected in the great Circle of Life.*

As songwriters, Elton John and Tim Rice so rightly wrote in the lyrics to *Circle of Life*. Nominated for the 1994 Academy Awards for Best Song:

> *From the day we arrive on the planet*
> *And blinking, step into the sun*
> *There's more to see than can ever be seen*

More to do than can ever be done
There's far too much to take in here
More to find than can ever be found
But the sun rolling high
Through the sapphire sky
Keeps great and small on the endless round
It's the circle of life
And it moves us all
Through despair and hope
Through faith and love
Till we find our place
On the path unwinding
In the circle
The circle of life.

Young.
young@aharemboysaga.com
www.aharemboysaga.com

Author's Bio

Young alias Bernard Foong is, first and foremost, a sensitivist. He finds nuance in everything. To experience the world, he inhabits is an adventure which is mystical, childlike and refreshing. He has a rare ability to create beauty in a unique fashion. His palettes have been material, paint, words and human experiences.

By Christine Maynard (screenwriter and novelist).

Bernard Foong (designer) – A brief history

Born in Kuala Lumpur, Malaysia. At the age of 8, he was assisting his aunt and cousin, learning the art of sewing and fabrics/colors matching. He attended an exclusive private boarding school in the United Kingdom before obtaining his Diploma in Fashion Design at the Harrow College of Art & Technology in London, England. He went on to complete his Master of Design at the Royal College of Art & Design, London, England. During his college years, he won several international fashion awards and was already retailing bridal and evening dresses to several well-known department stores in England. Liberty of London, Selfridges, Harrods, and Harvey Nichols to name a few that carried his designs. His Royal College of Art graduation wedding/evening wear collection was sold to Liberty of London and displayed in their store windows for the entire month of June that year.

For four years, he worked for Liberty's bridal department as their in-house designer until a trip to Hong Kong, while working on a freelance project for 'Bird's'(casual wear) company, he was recruited by the Hong Kong Polytechnic

University as their Fashion professor for the next 6 years. During his stay in Hong Kong, he freelanced for numerous fashion companies. From designing casual wear, swimwear, lingerie, and fur garments, men's wear, bridal and evening fashions to accessories (bags, shoes, and headwear). He also participated and organized numerous fashion shows, events, functions, and presentations in the Asia Pacific region.

Working for Keys Far East Hong Kong as chief lingerie designer - traveling extensively to the United States, he was soon recruited as an Associate Fashion Design/Illustration Professor to the University of Wisconsin, Madison and also lectured at the Minneapolis College of Art & Design for a couple of years.

Foong was then appointed as the Fashion Development Manager by an established department store – Parkson Grand (22 stores in Malaysia and one in Shanghai, China). Producing under the label, Natural Life by Bernard Foong, he designed casual-wear collections for the Parkson Grand's flagship store in Kuala Lumpur. After a couple of years later, he was invited by the Temasek Polytechnic, Singapore to join their design school to establish a Fashion Design department. For two years, he assisted several founding members of the design school - working on the fashion department's teaching curriculum.

The Fitzgerald Theatre Department, University of Hawaii, Manoa, Oahu, Hawaii awarded a full scholarship for Foong to complete his second Master of Art in Theatre Costuming. Now a resident on the Island of Maui, he has assisted many charity organizations in their fundraising events with his extravagant fashion and performance shows/presentations. In 2005, he and his partner, Mr. Walter Jay Bissett opened Fire Dragon Bistro Orient &

Design Shop. He also designs costumes/fashions for numerous theatrical productions in Hawaii and abroad.

Appointed as Chief lingerie designer for Cerie International Limited – Hong Kong, his lingerie designs can be found in major department stores in Canada, Europe, and the United Kingdom.

He showcased the BERNARD FOONG R-T-W collections and BERNARD FOONG @ Modern Classic Ltd. (an established – Hong Kong bridal & evening wear company) collections in Hong Kong. His 2008 & 2009 bridal/evening/bridal lingerie fashion show, "Grace" & "Coming Up Roses" were premiered at Hong Kong Fashion Week in July 2007 and January 2008 respectively at the Hong Kong Convention & Exhibition Center, garnering positive interest in many Asian press reviews, including a China nationwide television broadcast of his latest collection. Aika (International Opera Singer) wore several Bernard Foong special occasion dresses at her Japan & European tour in September & October 2009.

Foong was the Chief Creative Director for Official (Special Occasion fashion manufacturing company) Guangzhou, China producing – BERNARD FOONG Couture (specialty one-of-a-kind creations), White (RTW - Wedding/Special Occasion wear), Foxy Cute (Smart Casual/Cocktail wear), SexZ (decorative bustier) & Diva Bitch (sexual lingerie inner/outer-wear) collections.

Besides working on his regular haute couture, R-T-W and lingerie collections he is a visiting consultant/advisor for • Pivot Point fashion college, Chengdu, China. • Hong Kong Design Institute (fashion department), Hong Kong, SAR.

- Hong Kong Poly/U, Hong Kong (School of Apparel Design & Merchandising), SAR. • Hong Kong Fashion Designers Association, Hong Kong. • Singapore Temasek Polytechnic – School of Apparel Design & Merchandising (ADM), Singapore.

Bernard just completed his autobiographical five-book series of Mr. Foong's young life: A Harem Boy's Saga: A Memoir by Young. A Harem Boy's Saga series is published by Solstice Publishing and is available in print, audio, and E-books internationally.

A Harem Boy's Saga series Film Contract has been secured with an independent UK Producer, operating in Hollywood.

Acknowledgments

A beautiful lady I would like to thank is Ms. Emerantia Antonia Parnell-Gilbert, my Literary Agent from Gilbert Literary Agency. Besides providing me with valuable advice and securing Solstice Publishing to publish A Harem Boy's Saga series, Ms. Parnell-Gilbert has also procured a Film Option Agreement for A Harem Boy's Saga with a UK Film production company. I am excited to see this memoir series adapted for the screen in the form of feature films and/or a TV miniseries. Emerantia's unfaltering support and faith in my writing gave me the incentive to continue on this long and winding road to complete my series.

I also thank Ms. Melissa Miller of Solstice Publishing for her credence in my memoirs and to Ms. Kathi Sprayberry (my Solstice Publishing Editor-in-Chief) for devoting time to format and upload A Harem Boy's Saga for international distribution. I am also indebted to Solstice Publishing for providing me an editor, Wendy Tyndall to edit this lengthy volume of A Harem Boy's Saga – V – Metanoia; a memoir by Young.

I am deeply grateful to Ms. Fiona Jayde of Fiona Jayde Media for her exquisite and mesmerizing book cover designs. Working with this talented designer was a breeze. Her instinctive mind captured my ideas with ease and grace, and she created cover images for A Harem Boy's Saga that readers and I fell in love with instantly.

I cannot forget my dear friend Mr. Robert DeNigris, who took time from his busy schedule to proofread Metanoia's manuscript. Mahalo, Bob! You are a gem.

At this juncture, I would like to say a big "Thank You" to all my friends and supporters who have continued to champion my revelations from the beginning, before Initiation, Unbridled, Debauchery, Turpitude and Metanoia came to fruition.

Last but not least, I am deeply appreciative of both my life partner, Mr. Walter Jay Bissett, and my ex-Valet, mentor, guardian, and lover, Mr. Andrew A. Finckenstein, for their resolute support, contribution and encouragement to tell my story truthfully.

In Walter Jay Bissett words: "The truth will set you free."

And in Andrew A. Finckenstein's: *"Dwell not in the past, dream not of the future, but concentrate on the present."*

Young.
young@aharemboysaga.com
www.aharemboysaga.com

If you enjoyed this story, check out the other Solstice Publishing books by Young:

A Harem Boy's Saga Book 1: Initiation

This provocative story is about an adolescent who was initiated into a clandestine sexual society. He was spirited to the Middle East, from his UK boarding school. He attended the Bahriji School (Oasis,) in The United Arab Emirates in preparation for serving in Harems for the wealthy and elite.

It is also a love story between the young man and his 'Valet' who served as his chaperone and mentor during the boy's Harem service.

http://bookgoodies.com/a/B00KOEXWQQ

A Harem Boy's Saga Book 2: Unbridled

Unbridled is the sequel to Initiation - A provocative story about a boy who was initiated into a clandestine sexual society. He was spirited to the Middle East, from his UK boarding school. He attended the Bahriji School (Oasis,) in The United Arab Emirates in preparation for serving in Harems for the wealthy and elite.

It is also a love story between the young man, his 'Big Brother' and his 'Valet' who served as his chaperones and mentors during the boy's Harem services.

This book follows the boy's erotic and exotic adventures and experiences at his 2nd Arab Household Harem, the Sekham. He was an apprentice and model, for the household patriarch's controversial photography project, "Sacred Sex in Sacred Places".

The author's experiences present facts that are truthful. Through these truths, which are often demonized by contemporary societies that deem such behaviors inappropriate, the author hopes to dispel condemnations and negativity which relate to his experiences.

There are 5 volumes in A Harem Boy's Saga series.

http://bookgoodies.com/a/B00L8F1RYO

A Harem Boy's Saga Book 3: Debauchery

"Being deeply loved by someone gives you strength, while loving someone deeply gives you courage."

Lao Tzu

Debauchery is the triquel to A Harem Boy's Saga, a provocative story about a young man who was initiated into a clandestine sexual society through his UK boarding school. From there, he was spirited to the Middle East to attend the Bahriji (Oasis) School in The United Arab Emirates in preparation for Harem services for the wealthy elite.

It is also a love story between the young man, his 'Big Brother,' and his 'Valet,' who served as his chaperones and mentors.

This book follows the teenagers' erotic and exotic adventures and experiences at their third Arabian Household Harem, the Quwah. There, they became confidants to a prince, assistants in an international dance club venture, "Carousel," and apprentices and models in a controversial photography project, "Sacred Sex in Sacred Places."

This story is an account of the author's experiences. Through these truths, often demonized by contemporary societies that deem such behaviors inappropriate, the author hopes to dispel condemnation and negativity related to sexuality, love, and personal freedom.

A Harem Boy's Saga is a series of five volumes.

http://bookgoodies.com/a/B00N2FRQMA

No Distance Between Us

This provocative story is about a young man who was initiated into a clandestine sexual society. He was spirited to the Middle East, from his UK boarding school. He attended the Bahriji School (Oasis,) in The United Arab Emirates in preparation for serving in Harems for the wealthy and elite.

It is also a love story between the young man and his 'Valet' who served as his chaperone and mentor during the boy's Harem service.

Author's note:

I had a privileged and unique upbringing in Malaysia. Following in my brothers' footsteps, I was sent to an exclusive boarding school in England. It is there that I was inducted into a clandestine organization, E.R.O.S. The Enlightened Royal Oracle Society. For four years, unbeknownst to my family, I was willingly and happily part of a Harem.

My story has been kept under wraps for close to 45 years. The correct moment has arrived for me to make known my unique education.

There are 5 books to this series.

> http://bookgoodies.com/a/B00P9UOJSU

The Truth Will Set You Free

> "Being deeply loved by someone gives you strength, while loving someone deeply gives you courage."
>
> Lao Tzu

The Truth Will Set You Free is section from Debauchery - the triquel to A Harem Boy's Saga, a provocative story about a young man who was initiated into a clandestine sexual society through his UK boarding school. From there, he was spirited to the Middle East to attend the Bahriji (Oasis) School in The United Arab Emirates in preparation for Harem services for the wealthy elite.

It is also a love story between the young man, his 'Big Brother,' and his 'Valet,' who served as his chaperones and mentors.

This book follows the teenagers' erotic and exotic adventures and experiences at their third Arabian Household Harem, the Quwah. There, they became confidants to a prince, assistants in an international dance club venture, "Carousel," and apprentices and models in a controversial photography project, *"Sacred Sex in Sacred Places."*

This story is an account of the author's experiences. Through these truths, often demonized by contemporary societies that deem such behaviors inappropriate, the author hopes to dispel condemnation and negativity related to sexuality, love, and personal freedom.

A Harem Boy's Saga is a series of five volumes.

http://bookgoodies.com/a/B01COB1MPY

www.ingramcontent.com/pod-product-compliance
Lightning Source LLC
Chambersburg PA
CBHW071933220426
43662CB00009B/899